Narrative And Miscellaneous Papers

by

Thomas De Quincey

Narrative And Miscellaneous Papers
by Thomas De Quincey

ISBN: 978-93-63053-85-4

Published by

DOUBLE 9 BOOKS

2/13-B, Ansari Road
Daryaganj, New Delhi – 110002
info@double9books.com
www.double9books.com
Tel. 011-40042856

This book is under public domain

ABOUT THE AUTHOR

Thomas De Quincey (1785-1859) was an English essayist, literary critic, and memoirist, best known for his work "Confessions of an English Opium-Eater." Born in Manchester, England, De Quincey was educated at Oxford University, but he left without earning a degree. In 1821, De Quincey published his most famous work, "Confessions of an English Opium-Eater," a memoir that described his experiences with opium addiction. The book was well-received and helped to establish De Quincey as a leading literary figure. De Quincey continued to write prolifically throughout his life, producing numerous essays and articles on a wide range of topics, including literature, philosophy, and politics. Despite his literary success, De Quincey struggled with financial problems throughout his life. He was often in debt and frequently moved from place to place, including spending several years living in Edinburgh. De Quincey died in 1859, at the age of 74. His work has had a lasting influence on English literature and has been praised for its imaginative power, its wit and intelligence, and its deep understanding of human psychology.

CONTENTS

VOLUME I

THE HOUSEHOLD WRECK

'To be weak,' we need not the great archangel's voice to tell us, '*is to be miserable*.' All weakness is suffering and humiliation, no matter for its mode or its subject. Beyond all other weakness, therefore, and by a sad prerogative, as more miserable than what is most miserable in all, that capital weakness of man which regards the *tenure* of his enjoyments and his power to protect, even for a moment, the crown of flowers—flowers, at the best, how frail and few!—which sometimes settles upon his haughty brow. There is no end, there never will be an end, of the lamentations which ascend from earth and the rebellious heart of her children, upon this huge opprobrium of human pride—the everlasting mutabilities of all which man can grasp by his power or by his aspirations, the fragility of all which he inherits, and the hollowness visible amid the very raptures of enjoyment to every eye which looks for a moment underneath the draperies of the shadowy *present*, the hollowness, the blank treachery of hollowness, upon which all the pomps and vanities of life ultimately repose. This trite but unwearying theme, this impassioned common-place of humanity, is the subject in every age of variation without end, from the poet, the rhetorician, the fabulist, the moralist, the divine, and the philosopher. All, amidst the sad vanity of their sighs and groans, labor to put on record and to establish this monotonous complaint, which needs not other record or evidence than those very sighs and groans. What is life? Darkness and formless vacancy for a beginning, or something beyond all beginning—then next a dim lotos of human consciousness, finding itself afloat upon the bosom of waters without a shore—then a few sunny smiles and many tears—a little love and infinite strife—whisperings from paradise and fierce mockeries from the anarchy of chaos—dust and ashes—and once more darkness circling round, as if from the beginning, and in this way rounding or making an island of our fantastic existence,—*that* is human life; *that* the inevitable amount of man's laughter and his tears—of what he suffers and he does—of his motions this way and that way—to the right or to the left—backwards or forwards—of all his seeming realities and all his absolute negations—his shadowy pomps and his pompous shadows—of whatsoever he thinks, finds, makes or mars, creates or animates, loves, hates, or in dread hope anticipates;—so it is, so it has been, so it will be, for ever and ever.

Yet in the lowest deep there still yawns a lower deep; and in the vast halls of man's frailty, there are separate and more gloomy chambers of a frailty more exquisite and consummate. We account it frailty that threescore years and ten make the upshot of man's pleasurable existence, and that, far before that time is reached, his beauty and his power have fallen among weeds and forgetfulness. But there is a frailty, by comparison with which this ordinary flux of the human race seems to have a vast duration. Cases there are, and those not rare, in which a single week, a day, an hour sweeps away all vestiges and landmarks of a memorable felicity; in which the ruin travels faster than the flying showers upon the mountain-side, faster 'than a musician scatters sounds;' in which 'it was' and 'it is not' are words of the self-same tongue, in the self-same minute; in which the sun that at noon beheld all sound and prosperous, long before its setting hour looks out upon a total wreck, and sometimes upon the total abolition of any fugitive memorial that there ever had been a vessel to be wrecked, or a wreck to be obliterated.

These cases, though here spoken of rhetorically, are of daily occurrence; and, though they may seem few by comparison with the infinite millions of the species, they are many indeed, if they be reckoned absolutely for themselves; and throughout the limits of a whole nation, not a day passes over us but many families are robbed of their heads, or even swallowed up in ruin themselves, or their course turned out of the sunny beams into a dark wilderness. Shipwrecks and nightly conflagrations are sometimes, and especially among some nations, wholesale calamities; battles yet more so; earthquakes, the famine, the pestilence, though rarer, are visitations yet wider in their desolation. Sickness and commercial ill-luck, if narrower, are more frequent scourges. And most of all, or with most darkness in its train, comes the sickness of the brain—lunacy—which, visiting nearly one thousand in every million, must, in every populous nation, make many ruins in each particular day. 'Babylon in ruins,' says a great author, 'is not so sad a sight as a human soul overthrown by lunacy.' But there is a sadder even than *that*,—the sight of a family-ruin wrought by crime is even more appalling. Forgery, breaches of trust, embezzlement, of private or public funds—(a crime sadly on the increase since the example of Fauntleroy, and the suggestion of its great feasibility first made by him)—these enormities, followed too often, and countersigned for their final result to the future happiness of families, by the appalling catastrophe of suicide, must naturally, in every wealthy nation, or wherever property and the modes of property are much developed, constitute the vast majority of all that come under the review of public justice. Any of these is sufficient to make shipwreck of all peace and comfort for a family; and often, indeed, it happens that the desolation is accomplished within the course of one revolving sun; often the whole dire catastrophe, together with its total consequences, is both accomplished and made known to those whom it chiefly concerns within one and the same hour. The mighty Juggernaut of social life, moving onwards with its everlasting thunders, pauses not for a moment to spare — to pity — to look aside, but rushes forward for ever, impassive as the marble in the quarry — caring not for whom it destroys, for the how many, or for the results, direct and indirect, whether many or few. The increasing grandeur and magnitude of the social system, the more it multiplies and extends its victims, the more it conceals them; and for the very same reason: just as in the Roman amphitheatres, when they grew to the magnitude of mighty cities, (in some instances accommodating four hundred thousand spectators, in many a fifth part of that amount,) births and deaths became ordinary events, which, in a small modern theatre, are rare and memorable; and exactly as these prodigious accidents multiplied, *pari passu*, they were disregarded and easily concealed: for curiosity was no longer excited; the sensation attached to them was little or none.

From these terrific tragedies, which, like monsoons or tornadoes, accomplish the work of years in an hour, not merely an impressive lesson is derived, sometimes, perhaps, a warning, but also (and this is of universal application) some consolation. Whatever may have been the misfortunes or the sorrows of a man's life, he is still privileged to regard himself and his friends as amongst the fortunate by comparison, in so far as he has escaped these wholesale storms, either as an actor in producing them, or a contributor to their violence — or even more innocently, (though oftentimes not less miserably) — as a participator in the instant ruin, or in the long arrears of suffering which they entail.

The following story falls within the class of hasty tragedies, and sudden desolations here described. The reader is assured that every incident is strictly true: nothing, in that respect, has been altered; nor, indeed, anywhere except in the conversations, of which, though the results and general outline are known, the separate details have necessarily been lost under the agitating circumstances which produced them. It has been judged right and delicate to conceal the name of the great city, and therefore of the nation in which these events occurred, chiefly out of consideration for the descendants of one person concerned in the narrative: otherwise, it might not have been requisite: for it is proper to mention, that every person directly a party to the case has been long laid in the grave: all of them, with one solitary exception, upwards of fifty years.

It was early spring in the year 17—; the day was the 6th of April; and the weather, which had been of a wintry fierceness for the preceding six or seven weeks—cold indeed beyond anything known for many years, gloomy for ever, and broken by continual storms—was now by a Swedish transformation all at once bright, genial, heavenly. So sudden and so early a prelusion of summer, it was generally feared, could not last. But that only made every body the more eager to lose no hour of an enjoyment that might prove so fleeting. It seemed as if the whole population of the place, a population among the most numerous in Christendom, had been composed of hybernating animals suddenly awakened by the balmy sunshine from their long winter's torpor. Through every hour of the golden morning the streets were resonant with female parties of young and old, the timid and the bold, nay, even of the most delicate valetudinarians, now first tempted to lay aside their wintry clothing together with their fireside habits, whilst the whole rural environs of our vast city, the woodlands, and the interminable meadows began daily to re-echo the glad voices of the young and jovial awaking once again, like the birds and the flowers, and universal nature, to the luxurious happiness of this most delightful season.

Happiness do I say? Yes, happiness; happiness to me above all others. For I also in those days was among the young and the gay; I was healthy; I was strong; I was prosperous in a worldly sense! I owed no man a shilling; feared no man's face; shunned no man's presence. I held a respectable station in society; I was myself, let me venture to say it, respected generally for my personal qualities, apart from any advantages I might draw from fortune or inheritance; I had reason to think myself popular amongst the very slender circle of my acquaintance; and finally, which perhaps was the crowning grace to all these elements of happiness, I suffered not from the presence of *ennui*, nor ever feared to suffer: for my temperament was constitutionally ardent; I had a powerful animal sensibility; and I knew the one great secret for maintaining its equipoise, viz., by powerful daily exercise; and thus I lived in the light and presence, or, (if I should not be suspected of seeking rhetorical expressions, I would say,) in one eternal solstice of unclouded hope.

These, you will say, were blessings; these were golden elements of felicity. They were so; and yet, with the single exception of my healthy frame and firm animal organization, I feel that I have mentioned hitherto nothing but what by comparison might be thought of a vulgar quality. All the other advantages that I have enumerated, had they been yet wanting, might have been acquired; had they been forfeited, might have been reconquered; had they been even irretrievably lost, might, by a philosophic effort, have been dispensed with; compensations might have been found for any of them, many equivalents, or if not, consolations at least, for their absence. But now it remains to speak of other blessings too mighty to be valued, not merely as transcending in rank and dignity all other constituents of happiness, but for a reason far sadder than that—because, once lost, they were incapable of restoration, and because not to be dispensed with; blessings in which 'either we must live or have no life:' lights to the darkness of our paths and to the infirmity of our steps—which, once extinguished, never more on this side the gates of Paradise can any man hope to see re-illumined for himself. Amongst these I may mention an intellect, whether powerful or not in itself, at any rate most elaborately cultivated; and, to say the truth, I had little other business before me in this life than to pursue this lofty and delightful task. I may add, as a blessing, not in the same *positive* sense as that which I have just mentioned, because not of a nature to contribute so hourly to the employment of the thoughts, but yet in this sense equal, that the absence of either would have been an equal affliction,—namely, a conscience void of all offence. It was little indeed that I, drawn by no necessities of situation into temptations of that nature, had done no injury to any man. That was fortunate; but I could not much value myself upon what was so much an accident of my situation. Something, however, I might pretend to beyond this *negative* merit; for I had originally a benign nature; and, as I advanced in years and thoughtfulness, the gratitude which possessed me for my own exceeding happiness led me to do that by principle and system which I had already done upon blind impulse; and thus upon a double argument I was incapable of turning away from the prayer of the afflicted, whatever had been the sacrifice to myself. Hardly, perhaps, could it have been said in a sufficient sense at that time that I was a religious man: yet, undoubtedly, I had all the foundations within me upon which religion might hereafter have grown. My heart overflowed with thankfulness to Providence: I had a natural tone of unaffected piety; and thus far, at least, I might have been called a religious man, that in the simplicity of truth I could have exclaimed,

> 'O, Abner, I fear God, and I fear none beside.'

But wherefore seek to delay ascending by a natural climax to that final consummation and perfect crown of my felicity—that almighty blessing which ratified their value to all the rest? Wherefore, oh! wherefore do I shrink in miserable weakness from—what? Is it from reviving, from calling up again into fierce and insufferable light the images and features of a long-buried happiness? That would be a natural shrinking and a reasonable weakness. But how escape from reviving, whether I give it utterance or not, that which is for ever vividly before me? What need to call into artificial light that which, whether sleeping or waking, by night or by day, for eight-and-thirty years has seemed by its miserable splendor to scorch my brain? Wherefore shrink from giving language, simple vocal utterance, to that burden of anguish which by so long an endurance has lost no atom of its weight, nor can gain any most surely by the loudest publication? Need there can be none, after this, to say that the priceless blessing, which I have left to the final place in this ascending review, was the companion of my life—my darling and youthful wife. Oh! dovelike woman! fated in an hour the most defenceless to meet with the ravening vulture,—lamb fallen amongst wolves,—trembling—fluttering fawn, whose path was inevitably to be crossed by the bloody tiger;—angel, whose most innocent heart fitted thee for too early a flight from this impure planet; if indeed it were a necessity that thou shouldst find no rest for thy footing except amidst thy native heavens, if indeed to leave what was not worthy of thee were a destiny not to be evaded—a summons not to be put by,—yet why, why, again and again I demand—why was it also necessary that this, thy departure, so full of wo to me, should also to thyself be heralded by the pangs of martyrdom? Sainted love, if, like the ancient children of the Hebrews, like Meshech and Abednego, thou wert called by divine command, whilst yet almost a child, to walk, and to walk alone, through the fiery furnace,—wherefore then couldst not thou, like that Meshech and that Abednego, walk unsinged by the dreadful torment, and come forth unharmed? Why, if the sacrifice were to be total, was it necessary to reach it by so dire a struggle? and if the cup, the bitter cup, of final separation from those that were the light of thy eyes and the pulse of thy heart might not be put aside,—yet wherefore was it that thou mightest not drink it up in the natural peace which belongs to a sinless heart?

But these are murmurings, you will say, rebellious murmurings against the proclamations of God. Not so: I have long since submitted myself, resigned myself, nay, even reconciled myself, perhaps, to the great wreck of my life, in so far as it was the will of God, and according to the weakness of my imperfect nature. But my wrath still rises, like a towering flame, against all the earthly instruments of this ruin; I am still at times as unresigned as ever to this tragedy, in so far as it was the work of human malice. Vengeance, as a mission for *me*, as a task for *my* hands in particular, is no longer possible; the thunderbolts of retribution have been long since launched by other hands; and yet still it happens that at times I do—I must—I shall perhaps to the hour of death, rise in maniac fury, and seek, in the very impotence of vindictive madness, groping as it were in blindness of heart, for that tiger from hell-gates that tore away my darling from my heart. Let me pause, and interrupt this painful strain, to say a word or two upon what she was—and how far worthy of a love more honorable to her (that was possible) and deeper (but that was not possible) than mine. When first I saw her, she—my Agnes—was merely a child, not much (if anything) above sixteen. But, as in perfect womanhood she retained a most childlike expression of countenance, so even then in absolute childhood she put forward the blossoms and the dignity of a woman. Never yet did my eye light upon creature that was born of woman, nor could it enter my heart to conceive one, possessing a figure more matchless in its proportions, more statuesque, and more deliberately and advisedly to be characterized by no adequate word but the word *magnificent*, (a word too often and lightly abused.) In reality, speaking of women, I have seen many beautiful figures, but hardly one except Agnes that could, without hyperbole, be styled truly and memorably magnificent. Though in the first order of tall women, yet, being full in person, and with a symmetry that was absolutely faultless, she seemed to the random sight as little above the ordinary height. Possibly from the dignity of her person, assisted by the dignity of her movements, a stranger would have been disposed to call her at a distance a woman of *commanding* presence; but never, after he had approached near enough to behold her face. Every thought of artifice, of practised effect, or of haughty pretension, fled before the childlike innocence, the sweet feminine timidity, and the more than cherub loveliness of that countenance, which yet in its lineaments was noble, whilst its expression was purely gentle and confiding. A shade of pensiveness there was about her; but *that* was in her manners, scarcely ever in her features; and the exquisite fairness of her complexion, enriched by the very sweetest and most delicate bloom that ever I have beheld, should rather have allied it to a tone of cheerfulness. Looking at this noble creature, as I first looked at her, when yet upon the early threshold of womanhood

> 'With household motions light and free,
> And steps of virgin liberty'

you might have supposed her some Hebe or young Aurora of the dawn. When you saw only her superb figure, and its promise of womanly development, with the measured dignity of her step, you might for a moment have fancied her some imperial Medea of the Athenian stage— some Volumnia from Rome,

> 'Or ruling bandit's wife amidst the Grecian isles.'
> But catch one glance from her angelic countenance—and then
> combining the face and the person, you would have dismissed
> all such fancies, and have pronounced her a Pandora or an Eve,

expressly accomplished and held forth by nature as an exemplary model or ideal pattern for the future female sex:—

'A perfect woman, nobly plann'd,
To warm, to comfort, to command:
And yet a spirit too, and bright
With something of an angel light.'

To this superb young woman, such as I have here sketched her, I surrendered my heart for ever, almost from my first opportunity of seeing her: for so natural and without disguise was her character, and so winning the simplicity of her manners, due in part to her own native dignity of mind, and in part to the deep solitude in which she had been reared, that little penetration was required to put me in possession of all her thoughts; and to win her love, not very much more than to let her see, as see she could not avoid, in connection with that chivalrous homage which at any rate was due to her sex and her sexual perfections, a love for herself on my part, which was in its nature as exalted a passion and as profoundly rooted as any merely human affection can ever yet have been.

On the seventeenth birthday of Agnes we were married. Oh! calendar of everlasting months—months that, like the mighty rivers, shall flow on for ever, immortal as thou, Nile, or Danube, Euphrates, or St. Lawrence! and ye, summer and winter, day and night, wherefore do you bring round continually your signs, and seasons, and revolving hours, that still point and barb the anguish of local recollections, telling me of this and that celestial morning that never shall return, and of too blessed expectations, travelling like yourselves through a heavenly zodiac of changes, till at once and for ever they sank into the grave! Often do I think of seeking for some quiet cell either in the Tropics or in Arctic latitudes, where the changes of the year, and the external signs corresponding to them, express themselves by no features like those in which the same seasons are invested under our temperate climes: so that, if knowing, we cannot at least feel the identity of their revolutions. We were married, I have said, on the birthday—the seventeenth birthday—of Agnes; and pretty nearly on her eighteenth it was that she placed me at the summit of my happiness, whilst for herself she thus completed the circle of her relations to this life's duties, by presenting me with a son. Of this child, knowing how wearisome to strangers is the fond exultation of parents, I shall simply say, that he inherited his mother's beauty; the same touching loveliness and innocence of expression, the same chiselled nose, mouth, and chin, the same exquisite auburn hair. In many other features, not of person merely, but also of mind and manners, as they gradually began to open before me, this child deepened my love to him by recalling the image of his mother; and what other image was there that I so much wished to keep before me, whether waking or asleep? At the time to which I am now coming but too rapidly, this child, still our only one, and unusually premature, was within four months of completing his third year; consequently Agnes was at that time in her twenty-first year; and I may here add, with respect to myself, that I was in my twenty-sixth.

But, before I come to that period of wo, let me say one word on the temper of mind which so fluent and serene a current of prosperity may be thought to have generated. Too common a course I know it is, when the stream of life flows with absolute tranquillity, and ruffled by no menace of a breeze—the azure overhead never dimmed by a passing cloud, that in such circumstances the blood stagnates: life, from excess and plethora of sweets, becomes insipid: the spirit of action droops: and it is oftentimes found at such seasons that slight annoyances and molestations, or even misfortunes in a lower key, are not wholly undesirable, as means of stimulating the lazy energies, and disturbing a slumber which is, or soon will be, morbid in its character. I have known myself cases not a few, where, by the very nicest gradations, and by steps too silent and insensible for daily notice, the utmost harmony and reciprocal love had shaded down into fretfulness and petulance, purely from too easy a life, and because all nobler agitations that might have ruffled the sensations occasionally, and all distresses even on the narrowest scale that might have re-awakened the solicitudes of love, by opening necessities for sympathy, for counsel, or for mutual aid, had been shut out by foresight too elaborate, or by prosperity too cloying. But all this, had it otherwise been possible with my particular mind, and at my early age, was utterly precluded by one remarkable peculiarity in my temper. Whether it were that I derived from nature some jealousy and suspicion of all happiness which seems too perfect and unalloyed—[a spirit of restless distrust, which in ancient times often led men to throw valuable gems into the sea, in the hope of thus propitiating the dire deity of misfortune, by voluntarily breaking the fearful chain of prosperity, and led some of them to weep and groan when the gems thus sacrificed were afterwards brought back to their hand by simple fishermen, who had recovered them in the intestines of fishes—a portentous omen, which was interpreted into a sorrowful indication that the deity thus answered the propitiatory appeal, and made solemn proclamation that he had rejected it]—whether, I say, it were this spirit of jealousy awaked in me by too steady and too profound a felicity—or whether it were that great overthrows and calamities have some mysterious power to send forward a dim misgiving of their advancing footsteps, and really and indeed, or whether it were partly, as I have already put the case in my first supposition, a natural instinct of distrust, but irritated and enlivened by a particular shock of superstitious alarm; which, or whether any of these causes it were that kept me apprehensive, and on the watch for disastrous change, I will not here undertake to determine. Too certain it is that I was so. I never ridded myself of an over-mastering and brooding sense, shadowy and vague, a dim abiding feeling (that sometimes was and sometimes was not exalted into a conscious presentiment) of some great calamity travelling towards me; not perhaps immediately impending—perhaps even at a great distance; but already—dating from some secret hour—already in motion upon some remote line of approach. This feeling I could not assuage by sharing it with Agnes. No motive could be strong enough for persuading me to communicate so gloomy a thought with one who, considering her extreme healthiness, was but too remarkably prone to pensive, if not to sorrowful, contemplations. And thus the obligation which I felt to silence and reserve, strengthened the morbid impression I had received; whilst the remarkable incident I have adverted to served powerfully to rivet the superstitious chain which was continually gathering round me. The incident was this—and before I repeat it, let me pledge my word of honor, that I report to you the bare facts of the case, without exaggeration, and in the simplicity of truth:—There was at that time resident in the great city, which is the scene of my narrative, a woman, from some part of Hungary, who pretended to the gift of looking into futurity. She had made herself known advantageously in several of the greatest cities of Europe, under the designation of the Hungarian Prophetess; and very extraordinary instances were cited amongst the highest circles of her success in the art which she professed. So ample were the pecuniary tributes which she levied upon the hopes and the fears, or the simple curiosity of the aristocracy, that she was thus able to display not unfrequently a disinterestedness and a generosity, which seemed native to her disposition, amongst the humbler classes of her applicants; for she rejected no addresses that were made to her, provided only they were not expressed in levity or scorn, but with sincerity, and in a spirit of confiding respect. It happened, on one occasion, when a nursery-servant of ours was waiting in her anteroom for the purpose of taking her turn in consulting the prophetess professionally, that she had witnessed a scene of consternation and unaffected maternal grief in this Hungarian lady upon the sudden seizure of her son, a child of four or five years old, by a spasmodic inflammation of the throat (since called croup) peculiar to children, and in those days not very well understood by medical men.

The poor Hungarian, who had lived chiefly in warm, or at least not damp, climates, and had never so much as heard of this complaint, was almost wild with alarm at the rapid increase of the symptoms which attend the paroxysms, and especially of that loud and distressing sound which marks the impeded respiration. Great, therefore, was her joy and gratitude on finding from our servant that she had herself been in attendance more than once upon cases of the same nature, but very much more violent,—and that, consequently, she was well qualified to suggest and to superintend all the measures of instant necessity, such as the hot-bath, the peculiar medicines, &c., which are almost sure of success when applied in an early stage. Staying to give her assistance until a considerable improvement had taken place in the child, our servant then hurried home to her mistress. Agnes, it may be imagined, dispatched her back with such further and more precise directions as in a very short time availed to re-establish the child in convalescence. These practical services, and the messages of maternal sympathy repeatedly conveyed from Agnes, had completely won the heart of the grateful Hungarian, and she announced her intention of calling with her little boy, to make her personal acknowledgments for the kindness which had been shown to her. She did so, and we were as much impressed by the sultana-like style of her Oriental beauty, as she, on her part, was touched and captivated by the youthful loveliness of my angelic wife. After sitting for above an hour, during which time she talked with a simplicity and good feeling that struck us as remarkable in a person professing an art usually connected with so much of conscious fraud, she rose to take her leave. I must mention that she had previously had our little boy sitting on her knee, and had at intervals thrown a hasty glance upon the palms of his hands. On parting, Agnes, with her usual frankness, held out her hand. The Hungarian took it with an air of sad solemnity, pressed it fervently, and said:—'Lady, it is my part in this life to look behind the curtain of fate; and oftentimes I see such sights in futurity—some near, some far off— as willingly I would *not* see. For you, young and charming lady, looking like that angel which you are, no destiny can be equal to your deserts. Yet sometimes, true it is, God sees not as man sees; and he ordains, after his unfathomable counsels, to the heavenly-minded a portion in heaven, and to the children whom he loves a rest and a haven not built with hands. Something that I have seen dimly warns me to look no farther. Yet, if you desire it, I will do my office, and I will read for you with truth the lines of fate as they are written upon your hands.' Agnes was a little startled, or even shocked, by this solemn address; but, in a minute or so, a mixed feeling—one half of which was curiosity, and the other half a light-hearted mockery of her own mysterious awe in the presence of what she had been taught to view as either fraud or insanity—prompted her playfully to insist upon the fullest application of the Hungarian's art to her own case; nay, she would have the hands of our little Francis read and interpreted as well as her own, and she desired to hear the full professional judgment delivered without suppression or softening of its harshest awards. She laughed whilst she said all this; but she also trembled a little. The Hungarian first took the hand of our young child, and perused it with a long and steady scrutiny. She said nothing, but sighed heavily as she resigned it. She then took the hand of Agnes—looked bewildered and aghast—then gazed piteously from Agnes to her child—and at last, bursting into tears, began to move steadily out of the room. I followed her hastily, and remonstrated upon this conduct, by pointing her attention to the obvious truth—that these mysterious suppressions and insinuations, which left all shadowy and indistinct, were far more alarming than the most definite denunciations. Her answer yet rings in my ear:—'Why should I make myself odious to you and to your innocent wife? Messenger of evil I am, and have been to many; but evil I will not prophecy to her. Watch and pray! Much may be done by effectual prayer. Human means, fleshly arms, are vain. There is an enemy in the house of life,' [here she quitted her palmistry for the language of astrology;] 'there is a frightful danger at hand, both for your wife and your child. Already on that dark ocean, over which we are all sailing, I can see dimly the point at which the enemy's course shall cross your wife's. There is but little interval remaining—not many hours. All is finished; all is accomplished; and already he is almost up with the darlings of your heart. Be vigilant, be vigilant, and yet look not to yourself, but to Heaven, for deliverance.'

This woman was not an impostor: she spoke and uttered her oracles under a wild sense of possession by some superior being, and of mystic compulsion to say what she would have willingly left unsaid; and never yet, before or since, have I seen the light of sadness settle with so solemn an expression into human eyes as when she dropped my wife's hand, and refused to deliver that burden of prophetic wo with which she believed herself to be inspired.

The prophetess departed; and what mood of mind did she leave behind her in Agnes and myself? Naturally there was a little drooping of spirits at first; the solemnity and the heart-felt sincerity of fear and grief which marked her demeanor, made it impossible, at the moment when we were just fresh from their natural influences, that we should recoil into our ordinary spirits. But with the inevitable elasticity of youth and youthful gaiety we soon did so; we could not attempt to persuade ourselves that there had been any conscious fraud or any attempt at scenical effect in the Hungarian's conduct. She had no motive for deceiving us; she had refused all offerings of money, and her whole visit had evidently been made under an overflow of the most grateful feelings for the attentions shown to her child. We acquitted her, therefore, of sinister intentions; and with our feelings of jealousy, feelings in which we had been educated, towards everything that tended to superstition, we soon agreed to think her some gentle maniac or sad enthusiast, suffering under some form of morbid melancholy. Forty-eight hours, with two nights' sleep, sufficed to restore the wonted equilibrium of our spirits; and that interval brought us onwards to the 6th of April—the day on which, as I have already said, my story properly commences.

On that day, on that lovely 6th of April, such as I have described it, that 6th of April, about nine o'clock in the morning, we were seated at breakfast near the open window—we, that is, Agnes, myself, and little Francis; the freshness of morning spirits rested upon us; the golden light of the morning sun illuminated the room; incense was floating through the air from the gorgeous flowers within and without the house; there in youthful happiness we sat gathered together, a family of love, and there we never sat again. Never again were we three gathered together, nor ever shall be, so long as the sun and its golden light—the morning and the evening—the earth and its flowers endure.

Often have I occupied myself in recalling every circumstance the most trivial of this the final morning of what merits to be called my life. Eleven o'clock, I remember, was striking when Agnes came into my study, and said that she would go into the city, (for we lived in a quite rural suburb,) that she would execute some trifling commissions which she had received from a friend in the country, and would be at home again between one and two for a stroll which we had agreed to take in the neighboring meadows. About twenty minutes after this she again came into my study dressed for going abroad; for such was my admiration of her, that I had a fancy—fancy it must have been, and yet still I felt it to be real—that under every change she looked best; if she put on a shawl, then a shawl became the most feminine of ornaments; if she laid aside her shawl and her bonnet, then how nymph-like she seemed in her undisguised and unadorned beauty! Full-dress seemed for the time to be best, as bringing forward into relief the splendor of her person, and allowing the exposure of her arms; a simple morning-dress, again, seemed better still, as fitted to call out the childlike innocence of her face, by confining the attention to that. But all these are feelings of fond and blind affection, hanging with rapture over the object of something too like idolatry. God knows, if that be a sin, I was but too profound a sinner; yet sin it never was, sin it could not be, to adore a beauty such as thine, my Agnes. Neither was it her beauty by itself, and that only, which I sought at such times to admire; there was a peculiar sort of double relation in which she stood at moments of pleasurable expectation and excitement, since our little Francis had become of an age to join our party, which made some aspects of her character trebly interesting. She was a wife—and wife to one whom she looked up to as her superior in understanding and in knowledge of the world, whom, therefore, she leaned to for protection. On the other hand, she was also a mother. Whilst, therefore, to her child she supported the matronly part of guide, and the air of an experienced person; to me she wore, ingenuously and without disguise, the part of a child herself, with all the giddy hopes and unchastised imaginings of that buoyant age. This double character, one aspect of which looks towards her husband and one to her children, sits most gracefully upon many a young wife whose heart is pure and innocent; and the collision between the two separate parts imposed by duty on the one hand, by extreme youth on the other, the one telling her that she is a responsible head of a family and the depository of her husband's honor in its tenderest and most vital interests, the other telling her, through the liveliest language of animal sensibility, and through the very pulses of her blood, that she is herself a child; this collision gives an inexpressible charm to the whole demeanor of many a young married woman, making her other fascinations more touching to her husband, and deepening the admiration she excites; and the more so, as it is a collision which cannot exist except among the very innocent. Years, at any rate, will irresistibly remove this peculiar charm, and gradually replace it by the graces of the matronly character. But in Agnes this change had not yet been effected, partly from nature, and partly from the extreme seclusion of her life. Hitherto she still retained the unaffected expression of her childlike nature; and so lovely in my eyes was this perfect exhibition of natural feminine character, that she rarely or never went out alone upon any little errand to town which might require her to rely upon her own good sense and courage, that she did not previously come to exhibit herself before me. Partly this was desired by me in that lover-like feeling of admiration already explained, which leads one to court the sight of a beloved object under every change of dress, and under all effects of novelty. Partly it was the interest I took in that exhibition of sweet timidity, and almost childish apprehensiveness, half disguised or imperfectly acknowledged by herself, which (in the way I have just explained) so touchingly contrasted with (and for that very reason so touchingly drew forth) her matronly character. But I hear some objector say at this point, ought not this very timidity, founded (as in part at least it was) upon inexperience and conscious inability to face the dangers of the world, to have suggested reasons for not leaving her to her own protection? And does it not argue, on my part, an arrogant or too blind a confidence in the durability of my happiness, as though charmed against assaults, and liable to no shocks of sudden revolution? I reply that, from the very constitution of society, and the tone of manners in the city which we inhabited, there seemed to be a moral impossibility that any dangers of consequence should meet her in the course of those brief absences from my protection, which only were possible; that even to herself any dangers, of a nature to be anticipated under the known circumstances of the case, seemed almost imaginary; that even *she* acknowledged a propriety in being trained, by slight and brief separations from my guardianship, to face more boldly those cases of longer separation and of more absolute consignment to her own resources which circumstances might arise to create necessarily, and perhaps abruptly. And it is evident that, had she been the wife of any man engaged in the duties of a profession, she might have been summoned from the very first, and without the possibility of any such gradual training, to the necessity of relying almost singly upon her own courage and discretion. For the other question, whether I did not depend too blindly and presumptuously upon my good luck in not at least affording her my protection so long as nothing occurred to make it impossible? I may reply, most truly, that all my feelings ran naturally in the very opposite channel. So far from confiding too much in my luck, in the present instance I was engaged in a task of writing upon some points of business which could not admit of further delay; but now, and at all times, I had a secret aversion to seeing so gentle a creature thrown even for an hour upon her own resources, though in situations which scarcely seemed to admit of any occasion for taxing those resources; and often I have felt anger towards myself for what appeared to be an irrational or effeminate timidity, and have struggled with my own mind upon occasions like the present, when I knew that I could not have acknowledged my tremors to a friend without something like shame, and a fear to excite his ridicule. No; if in anything I ran into excess, it was in this very point of anxiety as to all that regarded my wife's security. Her good sense, her prudence, her courage, (for courage she had in the midst of her timidity,) her dignity of manner, the more impressive from the childlike character of her countenance, all should have combined to reassure me, and yet they did not. I was still anxious for her safety to an irrational extent; and to sum up the whole in a most weighty line of Shakspeare, I lived under the constant presence of a feeling which only that great observer of human nature (so far as I am aware) has ever noticed, viz., that merely the excess of my happiness made me jealous of its ability to last, and in that extent less capable of enjoying it; that in fact the prelibation of my tears, as a homage to its fragility, was drawn forth by my very sense that my felicity was too exquisite; or, in the words of the great master

'*I wept to have'* [*absolutely, by anticipation, shed tears in possessing*] '*what I so feared to lose.*'

Thus end my explanations, and I now pursue my narrative: Agnes, as I have said, came into my room again before leaving the house—we conversed for five minutes—we parted—she went out—her last words being that she would return at half-past one o'clock; and not long after that time, if ever mimic bells—bells of rejoicing, or bells of mourning, are heard in desert spaces of the air, and (as some have said) in unreal worlds, that mock our own, and repeat, for ridicule, the vain and unprofitable motions of man, then too surely, about this hour, began to toll the funeral knell of my earthly happiness—its final hour had sounded.

One o'clock had arrived; fifteen minutes after, I strolled into the garden, and began to look over the little garden-gate in expectation of every moment descrying Agnes in the distance. Half an hour passed, and for ten minutes more I was tolerably quiet. From this time till half-past two I became constantly more agitated—*agitated*, perhaps, is too strong a word—but I was restless and anxious beyond what I should have chosen to acknowledge. Still I kept arguing, What is half an hour? what is an hour? A thousand things might have occurred to cause that delay, without needing to suppose any accident; or, if an accident, why not a very trifling one? She may have slightly hurt her foot—she may have slightly sprained her ankle. 'Oh, doubtless,' I exclaimed to myself, 'it will be a mere trifle, or perhaps nothing at all.' But I remember that, even whilst I was saying this, I took my hat and walked with nervous haste into the little quiet lane upon which our garden-gate opened. The lane led by a few turnings, and after a course of about five hundred yards, into a broad high-road, which even at that day had begun to assume the character of a street, and allowed an unobstructed range of view in the direction of the city for at least a mile. Here I stationed myself, for the air was so clear that I could distinguish dress and figure to a much greater distance than usual. Even on such a day, however, the remote distance was hazy and indistinct, and at any other season I should have been diverted with the various mistakes I made. From occasional combinations of color, modified by light and shade, and of course powerfully assisted by the creative state of the eye under this nervous apprehensiveness, I continued to shape into images of Agnes forms without end, that upon nearer approach presented the most grotesque contrasts to her impressive appearance. But I had ceased even to comprehend the ludicrous; my agitation was now so overruling and engrossing that I lost even my intellectual sense of it; and now first I understood practically and feelingly the anguish of hope alternating with disappointment, as it may be supposed to act upon the poor shipwrecked seaman, alone and upon a desolate coast, straining his sight for ever to the fickle element which has betrayed him, but which only can deliver him, and with his eyes still tracing in the far distance,

'Ships, dim-discover'd, dropping from the clouds,' —

which a brief interval of suspense still for ever disperses into hollow pageants of air or vapor. One deception melted away only to be succeeded by another; still I fancied that at last to a certainty I could descry the tall figure of Agnes, her gipsy hat, and even the peculiar elegance of her walk. Often I went so far as to laugh at myself, and even to tax my recent fears with unmanliness and effeminacy, on recollecting the audible throbbings of my heart, and the nervous palpitations which had besieged me; but these symptoms, whether effeminate or not, began to come back tumultuously under the gloomy doubts that succeeded almost before I had uttered this self-reproach. Still I found myself mocked and deluded with false hopes; yet still I renewed my quick walk, and the intensity of my watch for that radiant form that was fated never more to be seen returning from the cruel city.

It was nearly half-past three, and therefore close upon two hours beyond the time fixed by Agnes for her return, when I became absolutely incapable of supporting the further torture of suspense, and I suddenly took the resolution of returning home and concerting with my female servants some energetic measures, though *what* I could hardly say, on behalf of their mistress. On entering the garden-gate I met our little child Francis, who unconsciously inflicted a pang upon me which he neither could have meditated nor have understood. I passed him at his play, perhaps even unaware of his presence, but he recalled me to that perception by crying aloud that he had just seen his mamma.

'When—where?' I asked convulsively.

'Up stairs in her bedroom,' was his instantaneous answer.

His manner was such as forbade me to suppose that he could be joking; and, as it was barely possible (though, for reasons well known to me, in the highest degree improbable) that Agnes might have returned by a by-path, which, leading through a dangerous and disreputable suburb, would not have coincided at any one point with the public road where I had been keeping my station. I sprang forward into the house, up stairs, and in rapid succession into every room where it was likely that she might be found; but everywhere there was a dead silence, disturbed only by myself, for, in my growing confusion of thought, I believe that I rang the bell violently in every room I entered. No such summons, however, was needed, for the servants, two of whom at the least were most faithful creatures, and devotedly attached to their young mistress, stood ready of themselves to come and make inquiries of me as soon as they became aware of the alarming fact, that I had returned without her.

Until this moment, though having some private reasons for surprise that she should have failed to come into the house for a minute or two at the hour prefixed, in order to make some promised domestic arrangements for the day, they had taken it for granted that she must have met with me at some distance from home—and that either the extreme beauty of the day had beguiled her of all petty household recollections, or (as a conjecture more in harmony with past experiences) that my impatience and solicitations had persuaded her to lay aside her own plans for the moment at the risk of some little domestic inconvenience. Now, however, in a single instant vanished *every* mode of accounting for their mistress's absence; and the consternation of our looks communicated contagiously, by the most unerring of all languages, from each to the other what thoughts were uppermost in our panic-stricken hearts. If to any person it should seem that our alarm was disproportioned to the occasion, and not justified at least by anything as yet made known to us, let that person consider the weight due to the two following facts: First, that from the recency of our settlement in this neighborhood, and from the extreme seclusion of my wife's previous life at a vast distance from the metropolis, she had positively no friends on her list of visitors who resided in this great capital; secondly, and far above all beside, let him remember the awful denunciations, so unexpectedly tallying with this alarming and mysterious absence, of the Hungarian prophetess; these had been slighted—almost dismissed from our thoughts; but now in sudden reaction they came back upon us with a frightful power to lacerate and to sting—the shadowy outline of a spiritual agency, such as that which could at all predict the events, combining in one mysterious effect, with the shadowy outline of those very predictions. The power, that could have predicted, was as dim and as hard to grasp as was the precise nature of the evil that had been predicted.

An icy terror froze my blood at this moment when I looked at the significant glances, too easily understood by me, that were exchanged between the servants. My mouth had been for the last two hours growing more and more parched, so that at present, from mere want of moisture, I could not separate my lips to speak. One of the women saw the vain efforts I was making, and hastily brought me a glass of water. With the first recovery of speech, I asked them what little Francis had meant by saying that he had seen his mother in her bedroom. Their reply was, that they were as much at a loss to discover his meaning as I was; that he had made the same assertion to them, and with so much earnestness, that they had, all in succession, gone up stairs to look for her, and with the fullest expectation of finding her. This was a mystery which remained such to the very last; there was no doubt whatsoever that the child believed himself to have seen his mother; that he could not have seen her in her human bodily presence, there is as little doubt as there is, alas! that in this world he never *did* see her again. The poor child constantly adhered to his story, and with a circumstantiality far beyond all power of invention that could be presumed in an artless infant. Every attempt at puzzling him or entangling him in contradictions by means of cross-examination was but labor thrown away; though indeed, it is true enough that for those attempts, as will soon be seen, there was but a brief interval allowed.

Not dwelling upon this subject at present, I turned to Hannah—a woman who held the nominal office of cook in our little establishment, but whose real duties had been much more about her mistress's person— and with a searching look of appeal I asked her whether, in this moment of trial, when (as she might see) I was not so perfectly master of myself as perhaps always to depend upon seeing what was best to be done, she would consent to accompany me into the city, and take upon herself those obvious considerations of policy or prudence which might but too easily escape my mind, darkened, and likely to be darkened, as to its power of discernment by the hurricane of affliction now too probably at hand. She answered my appeal with the fervor I expected from what I had already known of her character. She was a woman of a strong, fiery, perhaps I might say of heroic mind, supported by a courage that was absolutely indomitable, and by a strength of bodily frame very unusual in a woman, and beyond the promise even of her person. She had suffered as deep a wrench in her own affections as a human being can suffer; she had lost her one sole child, a fair-haired boy of most striking beauty and interesting disposition, at the age of seventeen, and by the worst of all possible fates; he lived (as we did at that time) in a large commercial city overflowing with profligacy, and with temptations of every order; he had been led astray; culpable he had been, but by very much the least culpable of the set into which accident had thrown him, as regarded acts and probable intentions; and as regarded palliations from childish years, from total inexperience, or any other alleviating circumstances that could be urged, having everything to plead— and of all his accomplices the only one who had anything to plead. Interest, however, he had little or none; and whilst some hoary villains of the party, who happened to be more powerfully befriended, were finally allowed to escape with a punishment little more than nominal, he and two others were selected as sacrifices to the offended laws. They suffered capitally. All three behaved well; but the poor boy in particular, with a courage, a resignation, and a meekness, so distinguished and beyond his years as to attract the admiration and the liveliest sympathy of the public universally. If strangers could feel in that way, if the mere hardened executioner could be melted at the final scene,—it may be judged to what a fierce and terrific height would ascend the affliction of a doating mother, constitutionally too fervid in her affections. I have heard an official person declare, that the spectacle of her desolation and frantic anguish was the most frightful thing he had ever witnessed, and so harrowing to the feelings, that all who could by their rank venture upon such an irregularity, absented themselves during the critical period from the office which corresponded with the government; for, as I have said, the affair took place in a large provincial city, at a great distance from the capital. All who knew this woman, or who were witnesses to the alteration which one fortnight had wrought in her person as well as her demeanor, fancied it impossible that she could continue to live; or that, if she did, it must be through the giving way of her reason. They proved, however, to be mistaken; or, at least, if (as some thought) her reason did suffer in some degree, this result showed itself in the inequality of her temper, in moody fits of abstraction, and the morbid energy of her manner at times under the absence of all adequate external excitement, rather than in any positive and apparent hallucinations of thought. The charm which had mainly carried off the instant danger to her faculties, was doubtless the intense sympathy which she met with. And in these offices of consolation my wife stood foremost. For, and that was fortunate, she had found herself able, without violence to her own sincerest opinions in the case, to offer precisely that form of sympathy which was most soothing to the angry irritation of the poor mother; not only had she shown a *direct* interest in the boy, and not a mere interest of *reflection* from that which she took in the mother, and had expressed it by visits to his dungeon, and by every sort of attention to his comforts which his case called for, or the prison regulations allowed; not only had she wept with the distracted woman as if for a brother of her own; but, which went farther than all the rest in softening the mother's heart, she had loudly and indignantly proclaimed her belief in the boy's innocence, and in the same tone her sense of the crying injustice committed as to the selection of the victims, and the proportion of the punishment awarded. Others, in the language of a great poet,

'Had pitied her, and not her grief;'

they had either not been able to see, or, from carelessness, had neglected to see, any peculiar wrong done to her in the matter which occasioned her grief,—but had simply felt compassion for her as for one summoned, in a regular course of providential and human dispensation, to face an affliction, heavy in itself, but not heavy from any special defect of equity. Consequently their very sympathy, being so much built upon the assumption that an only child had offended to the extent implied in his sentence, oftentimes clothed itself in expressions which she felt to be not consolations but insults, and, in fact, so many justifications of those whom it relieved her overcharged heart to regard as the very worst of enemies. Agnes, on the other hand, took the very same view of the case as herself; and, though otherwise the gentlest of all gentle creatures, yet here, from the generous fervor of her reverence for justice, and her abhorrence of oppression, she gave herself no trouble to moderate the energy of her language: nor did I, on my part, feeling that substantially she was in the right, think it of importance to dispute about the exact degrees of the wrong done or the indignation due to it. In this way it happened naturally enough that at one and the same time, though little contemplating either of these results, Agnes had done a prodigious service to the poor desolate mother by breaking the force of her misery, as well as by arming the active agencies of indignation against the depressing ones of solitary grief, and for herself had won a most grateful and devoted friend, who would have gone through fire and water to serve her, and was thenceforwards most anxious for some opportunity to testify how deep had been her sense of the goodness shown to her by her benign young mistress, and how incapable of suffering abatement by time. It remains to add, which I have slightly noticed before, that this woman was of unusual personal strength: her bodily frame matched with her intellectual: and I notice this *now* with the more emphasis, because I am coming rapidly upon ground where it will be seen that this one qualification was of more summary importance to us—did us more 'yeoman's service' at a crisis the most awful—than other qualities of greater name and pretension. *Hannah* was this woman's Christian name; and her name and her memory are to me amongst the most hallowed of my earthly recollections.

One of her two fellow-servants, known technically amongst us as the 'parlor maid,' was also, but not equally, attached to her mistress; and merely because her nature, less powerfully formed and endowed, did not allow her to entertain or to comprehend any service equally fervid of passion or of impassioned action. She, however, was good, affectionate, and worthy to be trusted. But a third there was, a nursery maid, and therefore more naturally and more immediately standing within the confidence of her mistress—her I could not trust: her I suspected. But of that hereafter. Meantime, Hannah, she upon whom I leaned as upon a staff in all which respected her mistress, ran up stairs, after I had spoken and received her answer, in order hastily to dress and prepare herself for going out along with me to the city. I did not ask her to be quick in her movements: I knew there was no need: and, whilst she was absent, I took up, in one of my fretful movements of nervousness, a book which was lying upon a side-table: the book fell open of itself at a particular page; and in that, perhaps, there was nothing extraordinary, for it was a little portable edition of *Paradise Lost*; and the page was one which I must naturally have turned to many a time: for to Agnes I had read all the great masters of literature, especially those of modern times; so that few people knew the high classics more familiarly: and as to the passage in question, from its divine beauty I had read it aloud to her, perhaps, on fifty separate occasions. All this I mention to take away any appearance of a vulgar attempt to create omens; but still, in the very act of confessing the simple truth, and thus weakening the marvellous character of the anecdote, I must notice it as a strange instance of the '*Sortes Miltonianæ*,'—that precisely at such a moment as this I should find thrown in my way, should feel tempted to take up, and should open, a volume containing such a passage as the following: and observe, moreover, that although the volume, *once being taken up*, would naturally open where it had been most frequently read, there were, however, many passages which had been read *as* frequently—or more so. The particular passage upon which I opened at this moment was that most beautiful one in which the fatal morning separation is described between Adam and his bride—that separation so pregnant with wo, which eventually proved the occasion of the mortal transgression—the last scene between our first parents at which both were innocent and both were happy—although the superior intellect already felt, and, in the slight altercation preceding this separation, had already expressed a dim misgiving of some coming change: these are the words, and in depth of pathos they have rarely been approached:—

'Oft he to her his charge of quick return
Repeated; she to him as oft engag'd
To be returned by noon amid the bow'r,
And all things in best order to invite
Noon-tide repast, or afternoon's repose.
Oh much deceived, much failing, hapless Eve!
Of thy presumed return, event perverse!
Thou never from that hour in Paradise
Found'st either sweet repast, or sound repose.'

'*My* Eve!' I exclaimed, 'partner in *my* paradise, where art thou? *Much failing* thou wilt not be found, nor *much deceived*; innocent in any case thou art; but, alas! too surely by this time *hapless*, and the victim of some diabolic wickedness.' Thus I murmured to myself; thus I ejaculated; thus I apostrophized my Agnes; then again came a stormier mood. I could not sit still; I could not stand in quiet; I threw the book from me with violence against the wall; I began to hurry backwards and forwards in a short uneasy walk, when suddenly a sound, a step; it was the sound of the garden-gate opening, followed by a hasty tread. Whose tread? Not for a moment could it be fancied the oread step which belonged to that daughter of the hills—my wife, my Agnes; no, it was the dull massy tread of a man: and immediately there came a loud blow upon the door, and in the next moment, the bell having been found, a furious peal of ringing. Oh coward heart! not for a lease of immortality could I have gone forwards myself. My breath failed me; an interval came in which respiration seemed to be stifled—the blood to halt in its current; and then and there I recognised in myself the force and living truth of that Scriptural description of a heart consciously beset by evil without escape: 'Susannah *sighed*.' Yes, a long, long sigh—a deep, deep sigh—that is, the natural language by which the over-charged heart utters forth the wo that else would break it. I sighed—oh how profoundly! But that did not give me power to move. Who will go to the door? I whispered audibly. Who is at the door? was the inaudible whisper of my heart. Then might be seen the characteristic differences of the three women. That one, whom I suspected, I heard raising an upper window to look out and reconnoitre. The affectionate Rachael, on the other hand, ran eagerly down stairs; but Hannah, half dressed, even her bosom exposed, passed her like a storm; and before I heard any sound of opening a door, I saw from the spot where I stood the door already wide open, and a man in the costume of a policeman. All that he said I could not hear; but this I heard—that I was wanted at the police office, and had better come off without delay. He seemed then to get a glimpse of me, and to make an effort towards coming nearer; but I slunk away, and left to Hannah the task of drawing from him any circumstances which he might know. But apparently there was not much to tell, or rather, said I, there is too much, the *much* absorbs the *many*; some one mighty evil transcends and quells all particulars. At length the door was closed, and the man was gone. Hannah crept slowly along the passage, and looked in hesitatingly. Her very movements and stealthy pace testified that she had heard nothing which, even by comparison, she could think good news. 'Tell me not now, Hannah,' I said; 'wait till we are in the open air.' She went up stairs again. How short seemed the time till she descended! how I longed for further respite! 'Hannah!' I said at length when we were fairly moving upon the road, 'Hannah! I am too sure you have nothing good to tell. But now tell me the worst, and let that be in the fewest words possible.'

'Sir,' she said, 'we had better wait until we reach the office; for really I could not understand the man. He says that my mistress is detained upon some charge; but *what*, I could not at all make out. He was a man that knew something of you, Sir, I believe, and he wished to be civil, and kept saying, "Oh! I dare say it will turn out nothing at all, many such charges are made idly and carelessly, and some maliciously." "But what charges?" I cried, and then he wanted to speak privately to you. But I told him that of all persons he must not speak to you, if he had anything painful to tell; for that you were too much disturbed already, and had been for some hours, out of anxiety and terror about my mistress, to bear much more. So, when he heard that, he was less willing to speak freely than before. He might prove wrong, he said; he might give offence; things might turn out far otherwise than according to first appearances; for his part, he could not believe anything amiss of so sweet a lady. And after all, it would be better to wait till we reached the office.'

Thus much then was clear—Agnes was under some accusation. This was already worse than the worst I had anticipated. 'And then,' said I, thinking aloud to Hannah, 'one of two things is apparent to me; either the accusation is one of pure hellish malice, without a color of probability or the shadow of a foundation, and that way, alas! I am driven in my fears by that Hungarian woman's prophecy; or, which but for my desponding heart I should be more inclined to think, the charge has grown out of my poor wife's rustic ignorance as to the usages then recently established by law with regard to the kind of money that could be legally tendered. This, however, was a suggestion that did not tend to alleviate my anxiety; and my nervousness had mounted to a painful, almost to a disabling degree, by the time we reached the office. Already on our road thither some parties had passed us who were conversing with eagerness upon the case: so much we collected from the many and ardent expressions about 'the lady's beauty,' though the rest of such words as we could catch were ill calculated to relieve my suspense. This, then, at least, was certain—that my poor timid Agnes had already been exhibited before a tumultuous crowd; that her name and reputation had gone forth as a subject of discussion for the public; and that the domestic seclusion and privacy within which it was her matronly privilege to move had already undergone a rude violation.

The office, and all the purlieus of the office, were occupied by a dense crowd. That, perhaps, was always the case, more or less, at this time of day; but at present the crowd was manifestly possessed by a more than ordinary interest; and there was a unity in this possessing interest; all were talking on the same subject, the case in which Agnes had so recently appeared in some character or other; and by this time it became but too certain in the character of an accused person. Pity was the prevailing sentiment amongst the mob; but the opinions varied much as to the probable criminality of the prisoner. I made my way into the office. The presiding magistrates had all retired for the afternoon, and would not reassemble until eight o'clock in the evening. Some clerks only or officers of the court remained, who were too much harassed by applications for various forms and papers connected with the routine of public business, and by other official duties which required signatures or attestations, to find much leisure for answering individual questions. Some, however, listened with a marked air of attention to my earnest request for the circumstantial details of the case, but finally referred me to a vast folio volume, in which were entered all the charges, of whatever nature, involving any serious tendency—in fact, all that exceeded a misdemeanor—in the regular chronological succession according to which they came before the magistrate. Here, in this vast calendar of guilt and misery, amidst the *aliases* or cant designations of ruffians, prostitutes, felons, stood the description, at full length, Christian and surnames all properly registered, of my Agnes—of her whose very name had always sounded to my ears like the very echo of mountain innocence, purity, and pastoral simplicity. Here in another column stood the name and residence of her accuser. I shall call him *Barratt*, for that was amongst his names, and a name by which he had at one period of his infamous life been known to the public, though not his principal name, or the one which he had thought fit to assume at this era. James Barratt, then, as I shall here call him, was a haberdasher—keeping a large and conspicuous shop in a very crowded and what was then considered a fashionable part of the city. The charge was plain and short. Did I live to read it? It accused Agnes M— — of having on that morning secreted in her muff, and feloniously carried away, a valuable piece of Mechlin lace, the property of James Barratt. And the result of the first examination was thus communicated in a separate column, written in red ink—'Remanded to the second day after to-morrow for final examination.' Everything in this sin-polluted register was in manuscript; but at night the records of each day were regularly transferred to a printed journal, enlarged by comments and explanatory descriptions from some one of the clerks, whose province it was to furnish this intelligence to the public journals. On that same night, therefore, would go forth to the world such an account of the case, and such a description of my wife's person, as would inevitably summon to the next exhibition of her misery, as by special invitation and advertisement, the whole world of this vast metropolis—the idle, the curious, the brutal, the hardened amateur in spectacles of wo, and the benign philanthropist who frequents such scenes with the purpose of carrying alleviation to their afflictions. All alike, whatever might be their motives or the spirit of their actions, would rush (as to some grand festival of curiosity and sentimental luxury) to this public martyrdom of my innocent wife.

Meantime, what was the first thing to be done? Manifestly, to see Agnes: her account of the affair might suggest the steps to be taken. Prudence, therefore, at any rate, prescribed this course; and my heart would not have tolerated any other. I applied, therefore, at once, for information as to the proper mode of effecting this purpose without delay. What was my horror at learning that, by a recent regulation of all the police-offices, under the direction of the public minister who presided over that department of the national administration, no person could be admitted to an interview with any accused party during the progress of the official examinations; or, in fact, until the final committal of the prisoner for trial. This rule was supposed to be attended by great public advantages, and had rarely been relaxed—never, indeed, without a special interposition of the police minister authorizing its suspension. But was the exclusion absolute and universal? Might not, at least, a female servant, simply as the bearer of such articles as were indispensable to female delicacy and comfort, have access to her mistress? No; the exclusion was total and unconditional. To argue the point was manifestly idle; the subordinate officers had no discretion in the matter; nor, in fact, had any other official person, whatever were his rank, except the supreme one; and to him I neither had any obvious means of introduction, nor (in case of obtaining such an introduction) any chance of success; for the spirit of the rule, I foresaw it would be answered, applied with especial force to cases like the present.

Mere human feelings of pity, sympathy with my too visible agitation, superadded to something of perhaps reverence for the blighting misery that was now opening its artillery upon me—for misery has a privilege, and everywhere is felt to be a holy thing—had combined to procure for me some attention and some indulgence hitherto. Answers had been given with precision, explanations made at length, and anxiety shown to satisfy my inquiries. But this could not last; the inexorable necessities of public business coming back in a torrent upon the official people after this momentary interruption, forbade them to indulge any further consideration for an individual case, and I saw that I must not stay any longer. I was rapidly coming to be regarded as a hinderance to the movement of public affairs; and the recollection that I might again have occasion for some appeal to these men in their official characters, admonished me not to abuse my privilege of the moment. After returning thanks, therefore, for the disposition shown to oblige me, I retired.

Slowly did I and Hannah retrace our steps. Hannah sustained, in the tone of her spirits, by the extremity of her anger, a mood of feeling which I did not share. Indignation was to her in the stead of consolation and hope. I, for my part, could not seek even a momentary shelter from my tempestuous affliction in that temper of mind. The man who could accuse my Agnes, and accuse her of such a crime, I felt to be a monster; and in my thoughts he was already doomed to a bloody atonement (atonement! alas! what atonement!) whenever the time arrived that *her* cause would not be prejudiced, or the current of public feeling made to turn in his favor by investing him with the semblance of an injured or suffering person. So much was settled in my thoughts with the stern serenity of a decree issuing from a judgment-seat. But that gave no relief, no shadow of relief, to the misery which was now consuming me. Here was an end, in one hour, to the happiness of a life. In one hour it had given way, root and branch—had melted like so much frost-work, or a pageant of vapory exhalations. In a moment, in the twinkling of an eye, and yet for ever and ever, I comprehended the total ruin of my situation. The case, as others might think, was yet in suspense; and there was room enough for very rational hopes, especially where there was an absolute certainty of innocence. Total freedom from all doubt on that point seemed to justify almost more than hopes. This might be said, and most people would have been more or less consoled by it. I was not. I felt as certain, as irredeemably, as hopelessly certain of the final results as though I had seen the record in the books of Heaven. 'Hope nothing,' I said to myself; 'think not of hope in this world, but think only how best to walk steadily, and not to reel like a creature wanting discourse of reason, or incapable of religious hopes under the burden which it has pleased God to impose, and which in this life cannot be shaken off. The countenance of man is made to look upward and to the skies. Thither also point henceforwards your heart and your thoughts. Never again let your thoughts travel earthwards. Settle them on the heavens, to which your Agnes is already summoned. The call is clear, and not to be mistaken. Little in *her* fate now depends upon you, or upon anything that man can do. Look, therefore, to yourself; see that you make not shipwreck of your heavenly freight because your earthly freight is lost; and miss not, by any acts of wild and presumptuous despair, that final reunion with your Agnes, which can only be descried through vistas that open through the heavens.'

Such were the thoughts, thoughts often made audible, which came spontaneously like oracles from afar, as I strode homewards with Hannah by my side. Her, meantime, I seemed to hear; for at times I seemed and I intended to answer her. But answer her I did not; for not ten words of all that she said did I really and consciously hear. How I went through that night is more entirely a blank in my memory, more entirely a chapter of chaos and the confusion of chaos, than any other passage the most impressive in my life. If I even slumbered for a moment, as at intervals I did sometimes, though never sitting down, but standing or pacing about throughout the night, and if in this way I attained a momentary respite from self-consciousness, no sooner had I reached this enviable state of oblivion, than some internal sting of irritation *as* rapidly dispersed the whole fickle fabric of sleep; and as if the momentary trance—this fugitive beguilement of my wo—had been conceded by a demon's subtle malice only with the purpose of barbing the pang, by thus forcing it into a stronger relief through the insidious peace preceding it. It is a well known and most familiar experience to all the sons and daughters of affliction, that under no circumstances is the piercing, lancinating torment of a recent calamity felt so keenly as in the first moments of awaking in the morning from the night's slumbers. Just at the very instant when the clouds of sleep, and the whole fantastic illusions of dreaminess are dispersing, just as the realities of life are re-assuming their steadfast forms—re-shaping themselves—and settling anew into those fixed relations which they are to preserve throughout the waking hours; in that particular crisis of transition from the unreal to the real, the wo which besieges the brain and the life-springs at the heart rushes in afresh amongst the other crowd of realities, and has at the moment of restoration literally the force and liveliness of a new birth—the very same pang, and no whit feebler, as that which belonged to it when it was first made known. From the total hush of oblivion which had buried it and sealed it up, as it were, during the sleeping hours, it starts into sudden life on our first awaking, and is to all intents and purposes a new and not an old affliction—one which brings with it the old original shock which attended its first annunciation.

That night—that first night of separation from my wife—*how* it passed, I know not; I know only *that* it passed, I being in our common bed-chamber, that holiest of all temples that are consecrated to human attachments, whenever the heart is pure of man and woman, and the love is strong—I being in that bedchamber, once the temple now the sepulchre of our happiness,—I there, and my wife—my innocent wife—in a dungeon. As the morning light began to break, somebody knocked at the door; it was Hannah: she took my hand—misery levels all feeble distinctions of station, sex, age—she noticed my excessive feverishness, and gravely remonstrated with me upon the necessity there was that I should maintain as much health as possible for the sake of 'others,' if not for myself. She then brought me some tea, which refreshed me greatly; for I had tasted nothing at all beyond a little water since the preceding morning's breakfast. This refreshment seemed to relax and thaw the stiff frozen state of cheerless, rayless despair in which I had passed the night; I became susceptible of consolation—that consolation which lies involved in kindness and gentleness of manner—if not susceptible more than before of any positive hope. I sat down; and, having no witnesses to my weakness but this kind and faithful woman, I wept, and I found a relief in tears; and she, with the ready sympathy of woman, wept along with me. All at once she ventured upon the circumstances (so far as she had been able to collect them from the reports of those who had been present at the examination) of our calamity. There was little indeed either to excite or to gratify any interest or curiosity separate from the *personal* interest inevitably connected with a case to which there were two such parties as a brutal, sensual, degraded ruffian, on one side in character of accuser, and on the other as defendant, a meek angel of a woman, timid and fainting from the horrors of her situation, and under the licentious gaze of the crowd—yet, at the same time, bold in conscious innocence, and in the very teeth of the suspicions which beset her, winning the good opinion, as well as the good wishes of all who saw her. There had been at this first examination little for her to say beyond the assigning her name, age, and place of abode; and here it was fortunate that her own excellent good sense concurred with her perfect integrity and intuitive hatred of all indirect or crooked courses in prompting her to an undisguised statement of the simple truth, without a momentary hesitation or attempt either at evasion or suppression. With equally good intentions in similar situations many a woman has seriously injured her cause by slight evasions of the entire truth, where nevertheless her only purpose has been the natural and ingenuous one of seeking to save the reputation untainted of a name which she felt to have been confided to her keeping. The purpose was an honorable one, but erroneously pursued. Agnes fell into no such error. She answered calmly, simply, and truly, to every question put by the magistrates; and beyond *that* there was little opportunity for her to speak; the whole business of this preliminary examination being confined to the deposition of the accuser as to the circumstances under which he alleged the act of felonious appropriation to have taken place. These circumstances were perfectly uninteresting, considered in themselves; but amongst them was one which to us had the most shocking interest, from the absolute proof thus furnished of a deep-laid plot against Agnes. But for this one circumstance there would have been a possibility that the whole had originated in error—error growing out of and acting upon a nature originally suspicious, and confirmed perhaps by an unfortunate experience. And in proportion as that was possible, the chances increased that the accuser might, as the examinations advanced, and the winning character of the accused party began to develop itself, begin to see his error, and to retract his own over-hasty suspicions. But now we saw at a glance that for this hope there was no countenance whatever, since one solitary circumstance sufficed to establish a conspiracy. The deposition bore—that the lace had been secreted and afterwards detected in a muff; now it was a fact as well known to both of us as the fact of Agnes having gone out at all—that she had laid aside her winter's dress for the first time on this genial sunny day. Muff she had not at the time, nor could have had appropriately from the style of her costume in other respects. What was the effect upon us of this remarkable discovery! Of course there died at once the hope of any abandonment by the prosecutor of his purpose; because here was proof of a predetermined plot. This hope died at once; but then, as it was one which never had presented itself to my mind, I lost nothing by which I had ever been solaced. On the other hand, it will be obvious that a new hope at the same time arose to take its place, viz., the reasonable one that by this single detection, if once established, we might raise a strong presumption of conspiracy, and moreover that, as a leading fact or clue, it might serve to guide us in detecting others. Hannah was sanguine in this expectation; and for a moment her hopes were contagiously exciting to mine. But the hideous despondency which in my mind had settled upon the whole affair from the very first, the superstitious presentiment I had of a total blight brooding over the entire harvest of my life and its promises, (tracing itself originally, I am almost ashamed to own, up to that prediction of the Hungarian woman)—denied me steady light, anything—all in short but a wandering ray of hope. It was right, of course, nay, indispensable, that the circumstance of the muff should be strongly insisted upon at the next examination, pressed against the prosecutor, and sifted to the uttermost. An able lawyer would turn this to a triumphant account; and it would be admirable as a means of pre-engaging the good opinion as well as the sympathies of the public in behalf of the prisoner. But, for its final effect— my conviction remained, not to be shaken, that all would be useless; that our doom had gone forth, and was irrevocable.

Let me not linger too much over those sad times. Morning came on as usual; for it is strange, but true, that to the very wretched it seems wonderful that times and seasons should keep their appointed courses in the midst of such mighty overthrows, and such interruption to the courses of their own wonted happiness and their habitual expectations. Why should morning and night, why should all movements in the natural world be so regular, whilst in the moral world all is so irregular and anomalous? Yet the sun and the moon rise and set as usual upon the mightiest revolutions of empire and of worldly fortune that this planet ever beholds; and it is sometimes even a comfort to know that this will be the case. A great criminal, sentenced to an agonizing punishment, has derived a fortitude and a consolation from recollecting that the day would run its inevitable course—that a day after all was *but* a day—that the mighty wheel of alternate light and darkness must and would revolve—and that the evening star would rise as usual, and shine with its untroubled lustre upon the dust and ashes of what *had* indeed suffered, and so recently, the most bitter pangs, but would then have ceased to suffer. 'La Journée,' said Damien,

'*La journée sera dure, mais elle se passera.*'

'——*Se passera:*' yes, that is true, I whispered to myself; my day also, my season of trial will be hard to bear; but that also will have an end; that also '*se passera.*' Thus I talked or thought so long as I thought at all; for the hour was now rapidly approaching, when thinking in any shape would for some time be at an end for me.

That day, as the morning advanced, I went again, accompanied by Hannah, to the police court and to the prison—a vast, ancient, in parts ruinous, and most gloomy pile of building. In those days the administration of justice was, if not more corrupt, certainly in its inferior departments by far more careless than it is at present; and liable to thousands of interruptions and mal-practices, supporting themselves upon old traditionary usages which required at least half a century, and the shattering everywhere given to old systems by the French Revolution, together with the universal energy of mind applied to those subjects over the whole length and breadth of Christendom, to approach with any effectual reforms. Knowing this, and having myself had direct personal cognisance of various cases in which bribery had been applied with success, I was not without considerable hope that perhaps Hannah and myself might avail ourselves of this irregular passport through the gates of the prison. And, had the new regulation been of somewhat longer standing, there is little doubt that I should have been found right; unfortunately, as yet it had all the freshness of newborn vigor, and kept itself in remembrance by the singular irritation it excited. Besides this, it was a pet novelty of one particular minister, new to the possession of power, anxious to distinguish himself, proud of his creative functions within the range of his office, and very sensitively jealous on the point of opposition to his mandates. Vain, therefore, on this day were all my efforts to corrupt the jailers; and, in fact, anticipating a time when I might have occasion to corrupt some of them for a more important purpose and on a larger scale, I did not think it prudent to proclaim my character beforehand as one who tampered with such means, and thus to arm against myself those jealousies in official people, which it was so peculiarly important that I should keep asleep.

All that day, however, I lingered about the avenues and vast courts in the precincts of the prison, and near one particular wing of the building, which had been pointed out to me by a jailer as the section allotted to those who were in the situation of Agnes; that is, waiting their final commitment for trial. The building generally he could indicate with certainty, but he professed himself unable to indicate the particular part of it which 'the young woman brought in on the day previous' would be likely to occupy; consequently he could not point out the window from which her cell (her 'cell!' what a word!) would be lighted. 'But, master,' he went on to say, 'I would advise nobody to try that game.' He looked with an air so significant, and at the same time used a gesture so indicative of private understanding, that I at once apprehended his meaning, and assured him that he had altogether misconstrued my drift; that, as to attempts at escape, or at any mode of communicating with the prisoner from the outside, I trusted all *that* was perfectly needless; and that at any rate in my eyes it was perfectly hopeless. 'Well, master,' he replied, 'that's neither here nor there. You've come down handsomely, that I *will* say; and where a gentleman acts like a gentleman, and behaves himself as such, I'm not the man to go and split upon him for a word. To be sure it's quite nat'ral that a gentleman— put case that a young woman is his fancy woman—it's nothing but nat'ral that he should want to get her out of such an old rat-hole as this, where many's the fine-timbered creature, both he and she, that has lain to rot, and has never got out of the old trap at all, first or last'— —'How so?' I interrupted him; 'surely they don't detain the corpses of prisoners?' 'Ay, but mind you—put case that he or that she should die in this rat-trap before sentence is past, why then the prison counts them as its own children, and buries them in its own chapel—that old stack of pigeon-holes that you see up yonder to the right hand.' So then, after all, thought I, if my poor Agnes should, in her desolation and solitary confinement to these wretched walls, find her frail strength give way—should the moral horrors of her situation work their natural effect upon her health, and she should chance to die within this dungeon, here within this same dungeon will she lie to the resurrection, and in that case her prison-doors have already closed upon her for ever. The man, who perhaps had some rough kindness in his nature, though tainted by the mercenary feelings too inevitably belonging to his situation, seemed to guess at the character of my ruminations by the change of my countenance, for he expressed some pity for my being 'in so much trouble;' and it seemed to increase his respect for me that this trouble should be directed to the case of a woman, for he appeared to have a manly sense of the peculiar appeal made to the honor and gallantry of man, by the mere general fact of the feebleness and the dependence of woman. I looked at him more attentively in consequence of the feeling tone in which he now spoke, and was surprised that I had not more particularly noticed him before; he was a fine looking, youngish man, with a bold Robin-hood style of figure and appearance; and, morally speaking, he was absolutely transfigured to my eyes by the effect worked upon him for the moment, through the simple calling up of his better nature. However, he recurred to his cautions about the peril in a legal sense of tampering with the windows, bolts, and bars of the old decaying prison; which, in fact, precisely according to the degree in which its absolute power over its prisoners was annually growing less and less, grew more and more jealous of its own reputation, and punished the attempts to break loose with the more severity, in exact proportion as they were the more tempting by the chances of success. I persisted in disowning any schemes of the sort, and especially upon the ground of their hopelessness. But this, on the other hand, was a ground that in his inner thoughts he treated with scorn; and I could easily see that, with a little skilful management of opportunity, I might, upon occasion, draw from him all the secrets he knew as to the special points of infirmity in this old ruinous building. For the present, and until it should certainly appear that there was some use to be derived from this species of knowledge, I forbore to raise superfluous suspicions by availing myself further of his communicative disposition. Taking, however, the precaution of securing his name, together with his particular office and designation in the prison, I parted from him as if to go home, but in fact to resume my sad roamings up and down the precincts of the jail.

What made these precincts much larger than otherwise they would have been, was the circumstance that, by a usage derived from older days, both criminal prisoners and those who were prisoners for debt, equally fell under the custody of this huge caravanserai for the indifferent reception of crime, of misdemeanor, and of misfortune. And those who came under the two first titles, were lodged here through all stages of their connection with public justice; alike when mere objects of vague suspicion to the police, when under examination upon a specific charge, when fully committed for trial, when convicted and under sentence, awaiting the execution of that sentence, and, in a large proportion of cases, even through their final stage of punishment, when it happened to be of any nature compatible with in-door confinement. Hence it arose that the number of those who haunted the prison gates, with or without a title to admission, was enormous; all the relatives, or more properly the acquaintances and connections of the criminal population within the prison, being swelled by all the families of needy debtors who came daily, either to offer the consolation of their society, or to diminish their common expenditure by uniting their slender establishments. One of the rules applied to the management of this vast multitude that were every day candidates for admission was, that to save the endless trouble as well as risk, perhaps, of opening and shutting the main gates to every successive arrival, periodic intervals were fixed for the admission by wholesale; and as these periods came round every two hours, it would happen at many parts of the day that vast crowds accumulated waiting for the next opening of the gate. These crowds were assembled in two or three large outer courts, in which also were many stalls and booths, kept there upon some local privilege of ancient inheritance, or upon some other plea made good by gifts or bribes—some by Jews and others by Christians, perhaps equally Jewish. Superadded to these stationary elements of this miscellaneous population, were others drawn thither by pure motives of curiosity, so that altogether an almost permanent mob was gathered together in these courts; and amid this mob it was,—from I know not what definite motive, partly because I thought it probable that amongst these people I should hear the cause of Agnes peculiarly the subject of conversation; and so, in fact, it did really happen,—but partly, and even more, I believe, because I now awfully began to shrink from solitude. Tumult I must have, and distraction of thought. Amid this mob, I say, it was that I passed two days. Feverish I had been from the first—and from bad to worse, in such a case, was, at any rate, a natural progress; but, perhaps, also amongst this crowd of the poor, the abjectly wretched, the ill-fed, the desponding, and the dissolute, there might be very naturally a larger body of contagion lurking than according to their mere numerical expectations. There was at that season a very extensive depopulation going on in some quarters of this great metropolis, and in other cities of the same empire, by means of a very malignant typhus. This fever is supposed to be the peculiar product of jails; and though it had not as yet been felt as a scourge and devastator of this particular jail, or at least the consequent mortality had been hitherto kept down to a moderate amount, yet it was highly probable that a certain quantity of contagion, much beyond the proportion of other popular assemblages less uniformly wretched in their composition, was here to be found all day long; and doubtless my excited state, and irritable habit of body, had offered a peculiar predisposition that favored the rapid development of this contagion. However this might be, the result was, that on the evening of the second day which I spent in haunting the purlieus of the prison, (consequently the night preceding the second public examination of Agnes,) I was attacked by ardent fever in such unmitigated fury, that before morning I had lost all command of my intellectual faculties. For some weeks

I became a pitiable maniac, and in every sense the wreck of my former self; and seven entire weeks, together with the better half of an eighth week, had passed over my head whilst I lay unconscious of time and its dreadful freight of events, excepting in so far as my disordered brain, by its fantastic coinages, created endless mimicries and mockeries of these events—less substantial, but oftentimes less afflicting, or less agitating. It would have been well for me had my destiny decided that I was not to be recalled to this world of wo. But I had no such happiness in store. I recovered, and through twenty and eight years my groans have recorded the sorrow I feel that I did.

I shall not rehearse circumstantially, and point by point, the sad unfolding, as it proceeded through successive revelations to me, of all which had happened during my state of physical incapacity. When I first became aware that my wandering senses had returned to me, and knew, by the cessation of all throbbings, and the unutterable pains that had so long possessed my brain, that I was now returning from the gates of death, a sad confusion assailed me as to some indefinite cloud of evil that had been hovering over me at the time when I first fell into a state of insensibility. For a time I struggled vainly to recover the lost connection of my thoughts, and I endeavored ineffectually to address myself to sleep. I opened my eyes, but found the glare of light painful beyond measure. Strength, however, it seemed to me that I had, and more than enough, to raise myself out of bed. I made the attempt, but fell back, almost giddy with the effort. At the sound of the disturbance which I had thus made, a woman whom I did not know came from behind a curtain, and spoke to me. Shrinking from any communication with a stranger, especially one whose discretion I could not estimate in making discoveries to me with the requisite caution, I asked her simply what o'clock it was.

'Eleven in the forenoon,' she replied.

'And what day of the month?'

'The second,' was her brief answer.

I felt almost a sense of shame in adding—; 'The second! but of what month?'

'Of June,' was the startling rejoinder.

On the 8th of April I had fallen ill, and it was now actually the 2d of June. Oh! sickening calculation! revolting register of hours! for in that same moment which brought back this one recollection, perhaps by steadying my brain, rushed back in a torrent all the other dreadful remembrances of the period, and now the more so, because, though the event was still uncertain as regarded my knowledge, it must have become dreadfully certain as regarded the facts of the case, and the happiness of all who were concerned. Alas! one little circumstance too painfully assured me that this event had not been a happy one. Had Agnes been restored to her liberty and her home, where would she have been found but watching at my bed-side? That too certainly I knew, and the inference was too bitter to support.

On this same day, some hours afterwards, upon Hannah's return from the city, I received from her, and heard with perfect calmness, the whole sum of evil which awaited me. Little Francis—she took up her tale at that point—'was with God:' so she expressed herself. He had died of the same fever which had attacked me—had died and been buried nearly five weeks before. Too probably he had caught the infection from me. Almost—such are the caprices of human feeling—almost I could have rejoiced that this young memorial of my vanished happiness had vanished also. It gave me a pang, nevertheless, that the grave should thus have closed upon him before I had seen his fair little face again. But I steeled my heart to hear worse things than this. Next she went on to inform me that already, on the first or second day of our calamity, she had taken upon herself, without waiting for authority, on observing the rapid approaches of illness in me, and arguing the state of helplessness which would follow, to write off at once a summons in the most urgent terms to the brother of my wife. This gentleman, whom I shall call Pierpoint, was a high-spirited, generous young man as I have ever known. When I say that he was a sportsman, that at one season of the year he did little else than pursue his darling amusement of fox-hunting, for which indeed he had almost a maniacal passion—saying this, I shall already have prejudged him in the opinions of many, who fancy all such persons the slaves of corporeal enjoyments. But, with submission, the truth lies the other way. According to my experience, people of these habits have their bodies more than usually under their command, as being subdued by severe exercise; and their minds, neither better nor worse on an average than those of their neighbors, are more available from being so much more rarely clogged by morbid habits in that uneasy yoke-fellow of the intellectual part—the body. He at all events was a man to justify in his own person this way of thinking; for he was a man not only of sound, but even of bold and energetic intellect, and in all moral respects one whom any man might feel proud to call his friend. This young man, Pierpoint, without delay obeyed the summons; and on being made acquainted with what had already passed, the first step he took was to call upon Barratt, and without further question than what might ascertain his identity, he proceeded to inflict upon him a severe horsewhipping. A worse step on his sister's account he could not have taken. Previously to this the popular feeling had run strongly against Barratt, but now its unity was broken. A new element was introduced into the question: Democratic feelings were armed against this outrage; gentlemen and nobles, it was said, thought themselves not amenable to justice; and again, the majesty of the law was offended at this intrusion upon an affair already under solemn course of adjudication. Everything, however, passes away under the healing hand of time, and this also faded from the public mind. People remembered also that he was a brother, and in that character, at any rate, had a right to some allowances for his intemperance; and what quickened the oblivion of the affair was, which in itself was sufficiently strange, that Barratt did not revive the case in the public mind by seeking legal reparation for his injuries. It was, however, still matter of regret that Pierpoint should have indulged himself in this movement of passion, since undoubtedly it broke and disturbed the else uniform stream of public indignation, by investing the original aggressor with something like the character of an injured person; and therefore with some set-off to plead against his own wantonness of malice;—his malice might now assume the nobler aspect of revenge.

Thus far, in reporting the circumstances, Hannah had dallied—thus far I had rejoiced that she dallied, with the main burden of the wo; but now there remained nothing to dally with any longer—and she rushed along in her narrative, hurrying to tell—I hurrying to hear. A second, a third examination had ensued, then a final committal—all this within a week. By that time all the world was agitated with the case; literally not the city only, vast as that city was, but the nation was convulsed and divided into parties upon the question, Whether the prosecution were one of mere malice or not? The very government of the land was reported to be equally interested, and almost equally divided in opinion. In this state of public feeling came the trial. Image to yourself, oh reader, whosoever you are, the intensity of the excitement which by that time had arisen in all people to be spectators of the scene—then image to yourself the effect of all this, a perfect consciousness that in herself as a centre was settled the whole mighty interest of the exhibition—that interest again of so dubious and mixed a character—sympathy in some with mere misfortune—sympathy in others with female frailty and guilt, not perhaps founded upon an absolute unwavering belief in her innocence, even amongst those who were most loud and positive as partisans in affirming it,—and then remember that all this hideous scenical display and notoriety settled upon one whose very nature, constitutionally timid, recoiled with the triple agony of womanly shame—of matronly dignity—of insulted innocence, from every mode and shape of public display. Combine all these circumstances and elements of the case, and you may faintly enter into the situation of my poor Agnes. Perhaps the best way to express it at once is by recurring to the case of a young female Christian martyr, in the early ages of Christianity, exposed in the bloody amphitheatre of Rome or Verona, to 'fight with wild beasts,' as it was expressed in mockery—she to fight the lamb to fight with lions! But in reality the young martyr *had* a fight to maintain, and a fight (in contempt of that cruel mockery) fiercer than the fiercest of her persecutors could have faced perhaps—the combat with the instincts of her own shrinking, trembling, fainting nature. Such a fight had my Agnes to maintain; and at that time there was a large party of gentlemen in whom the gentlemanly instinct was predominant, and who felt so powerfully the cruel indignities of her situation, that they made a public appeal in her behalf. One thing, and a strong one, which they said, was this:—'We all talk and move in this case as if, because the question appears doubtful to some people, and the accused party to some people wears a doubtful character, it would follow that she therefore had in reality a mixed character composed in joint proportions of the best and the worst that is imputed to her. But let us not forget that this mixed character belongs not to her, but to the infirmity of our human judgments—*they* are mixed—*they* are dubious—but she is not—she is, or she is not, guilty—there is no middle case—and let us consider for a single moment, that if this young lady (as many among us heartily believe) *is* innocent, then and upon that supposition let us consider how cruel we should all think the public exposure which aggravates the other injuries (as in that case they must be thought) to which her situation exposes her.' They went on to make some suggestions for the officers of the court in preparing the arrangements for the trial, and some also for the guidance of the audience, which showed the same generous anxiety for sparing the feelings of the prisoner. If these did not wholly succeed in repressing the open avowal of coarse and brutal curiosity amongst the intensely vulgar, at least they availed to diffuse amongst the neutral and indifferent part of the public a sentiment of respect and forbearance which, emanating from high quarters, had a very extensive influence upon most of what met the eye or the ear of my poor wife. She, on the day of trial, was supported by her brother; and by that time she needed support indeed. I was reported to be dying; her little son was dead; neither had she been allowed to see him. Perhaps these things, by weaning her from all further care about life, might have found their natural effect in making her indifferent to the course of the trial, or even to its issue. And so, perhaps, in the main, they did. But at times some lingering sense of outraged dignity, some fitful gleams of old sympathies, 'the hectic of a moment,' came back upon her, and prevailed over the deadening stupor of her grief. Then she shone for a moment into a starry light—sweet and woful to remember. Then——but why linger? I hurry to the close: she was pronounced guilty; whether by a jury or a bench of judges, I do not say—having determined, from the beginning, to give no hint of the land in which all these events happened; neither is that of the slightest consequence. Guilty she was pronounced: but sentence at that time was deferred. Ask me not, I beseech you, about the muff or other circumstances inconsistent with the hostile evidence. These circumstances had the testimony, you will observe, of my own servants only; nay, as it turned out, of one servant exclusively: *that* naturally diminished their value. And, on the other side, evidence was arrayed, perjury was suborned, that would have wrecked a wilderness of simple truth trusting to its own unaided forces. What followed? Did this judgment of the court settle the opinion of the public? Opinion of the public! Did it settle the winds? Did it settle the motion of the Atlantic? Wilder, fiercer, and louder grew the cry against the wretched accuser: mighty had been the power over the vast audience of the dignity, the affliction, the perfect simplicity, and the Madonna beauty of the prisoner. That beauty so childlike, and at the same time so saintly, made, besides, so touching in its pathos by means of the abandonment—the careless abandonment and the infinite desolation of her air and manner—would of itself, and without further aid, have made many converts. Much more was done by the simplicity of her statements, and the indifference with which she neglected to improve any strong points in her own favor—the indifference, as every heart perceived, of despairing grief. Then came the manners on the hostile side—the haggard consciousness of guilt, the drooping tone, the bravado and fierce strut which sought to dissemble all this. Not one amongst all the witnesses, assembled on that side, had (by all agreement) the bold natural tone of conscious uprightness. Hence it could not be surprising that the storm of popular opinion made itself heard with a louder and a louder sound. The government itself began to be disturbed; the ministers of the sovereign were agitated; and, had no menaces been thrown out, it was generally understood that they would have given way to the popular voice, now continually more distinct and clamorous. In the midst of all this tumult, obscure murmurs began to arise that Barratt had practised the same or similar villanies in former instances. One case in particular was beginning to be whispered about, which at once threw a light upon the whole affair: it was the case of a young and very beautiful married woman, who had been on the very brink of a catastrophe such as had befallen my own wife, when some seasonable interference, of what nature was not known, had critically delivered her. This case arose 'like a little cloud no bigger than a man's hand,' then spread and threatened to burst in tempest upon the public mind, when all at once, more suddenly even than it had arisen, it was hushed up, or in some way disappeared. But a trifling circumstance made it possible to trace this case:—in after times, when means offered, but unfortunately no particular purpose of good, nor any purpose, in fact, beyond that of curiosity, it *was* traced; and enough was soon ascertained to have blown to fragments any possible conspiracy emanating from this Barratt, had that been of any further importance. However, in spite of all that money or art could effect, a sullen growl continued to be heard amongst the populace of villanies many and profound that had been effected or attempted by this Barratt; and accordingly, much in the same way as was many years afterwards practised in London, when a hosier had caused several young people to be prosecuted to death for passing forged bank-notes, the wrath of the people showed itself in marking the shop for vengeance upon any favorable occasion offering through fire or riots, and in the mean time in deserting it. These things had been going on for some time when I awoke from my long delirium; but the effect they had produced upon a weak and obstinate and haughty government, or at least upon the weak and obstinate and haughty member of the government who presided in the police administration, was, to confirm and rivet the line of conduct which had been made the object of popular denunciation. More energetically, more scornfully, to express that determination of flying in the face of public opinion and censure, four days before my awakening, Agnes had been brought up to receive her sentence. On that same day (nay, it was said in that same hour,) petitions, very numerously signed, and various petitions from different ranks, different ages, different sexes, were carried up to the throne, praying, upon manifold grounds, but all noticing the extreme doubtfulness of the case, for an unconditional pardon. By whose advice or influence, it was guessed easily, though never exactly ascertained, these petitions were unanimously, almost contemptuously rejected. And to express the contempt of public opinion as powerfully as possible, Agnes was sentenced by the court, reassembled in full pomp, order, and ceremonial costume, to a punishment the severest that the laws allowed—viz. hard labor for ten years. The people raged more than ever; threats public and private were conveyed to the ears of the minister chiefly concerned in the responsibility, and who had indeed, by empty and ostentatious talking, assumed that responsibility to himself in a way that was perfectly needless.

Thus stood matters when I awoke to consciousness: and this was the fatal journal of the interval—interval so long as measured by my fierce calendar of delirium—so brief measured by the huge circuit of events which it embraced, and their mightiness for evil. Wrath, wrath immeasurable, unimaginable, unmitigable, burned at my heart like a cancer. The worst had come. And the thing which kills a man for action—the living in two climates at once—a torrid and a frigid zone—of hope and fear—that was past. Weak—suppose I were for the moment: I felt that a day or two might bring back my strength. No miserable tremors of hope *now* shook my nerves: if they shook from that inevitable rocking of the waters that follows a storm, so much might be pardoned to the infirmity of a nature that could not lay aside its fleshly necessities, nor altogether forego its homage to 'these frail elements,' but which by inspiration already lived within a region where no voices were heard but the spiritual voices of transcendent passions—of

'Wrongs unrevenged, and insults unredress'd.'

Six days from that time I was well—well and strong. I rose from bed; I bathed; I dressed; dressed as if I were a bridegroom. And that *was* in fact a great day in my life. I was to see Agnes. Oh! yes: permission had been obtained from the lordly minister that I should see my wife. Is it possible? Can such condescensions exist? Yes: solicitations from ladies, eloquent notes wet with ducal tears, these had won from the thrice-radiant secretary, redolent of roseate attar, a countersign to some order or other, by which I— yes I—under license of a fop, and supervision of a jailer—was to see and for a time to converse with my own wife.

The hour appointed for the first day's interview was eight o'clock in the evening. On the outside of the jail all was summer light and animation. The sports of children in the streets of mighty cities are but sad, and too painfully recall the circumstances of freedom and breezy nature that are not there. But still the pomp of glorious summer, and the presence, 'not to be put by,' of the everlasting light, that is either always present, or always dawning—these potent elements impregnate the very city life, and the dim reflex of nature which is found at the bottom of well-like streets, with more solemn powers to move and to soothe in summer. I struck upon the prison gates, the first among multitudes waiting to strike. Not because we struck, but because the hour had sounded, suddenly the gate opened; and in we streamed. I, as a visitor for the first time, was immediately distinguished by the jailers, whose glance of the eye is fatally unerring. 'Who was it that I wanted?' At the name a stir of emotion was manifest, even there: the dry bones stirred and moved: the passions outside had long ago passed to the interior of this gloomy prison: and not a man but had his hypothesis on the case; not a man but had almost fought with some comrade (many had literally fought) about the merits of their several opinions.

If any man had expected a scene at this reunion, he would have been disappointed. Exhaustion, and the ravages of sorrow, had left to dear Agnes so little power of animation or of action, that her emotions were rather to be guessed at, both for kind and for degree, than directly to have been perceived. She was in fact a sick patient, far gone in an illness that should properly have confined her to bed; and was as much past the power of replying to my frenzied exclamations, as a dying victim of fever of entering upon a strife of argument. In bed, however, she was not. When the door opened she was discovered sitting at a table placed against the opposite wall, her head pillowed upon her arms, and these resting upon the table. Her beautiful long auburn hair had escaped from its confinement, and was floating over the table and her own person. She took no notice of the disturbance made by our entrance, did not turn, did not raise her head, nor make an effort to do so, nor by any sign whatever intimate that she was conscious of our presence, until the turnkey in a respectful tone announced me. Upon that a low groan, or rather a feeble moan, showed that she had become aware of my presence, and relieved me from all apprehension of causing too sudden a shock by taking her in my arms. The turnkey had now retired; we were alone. I knelt by her side, threw my arms about her, and pressed her to my heart. She drooped her head upon my shoulder, and lay for some time like one who slumbered; but, alas! not as she had used to slumber. Her breathing, which had been like that of sinless infancy, was now frightfully short and quick; she seemed not properly to breathe, but to gasp. This, thought I, may be sudden agitation, and in that case she will gradually recover; half an hour will restore her. Wo is me! she did *not* recover; and internally I said—she never *will* recover. The arrows have gone too deep for a frame so exquisite in its sensibility, and already her hours are numbered.

At this first visit I said nothing to her about the past; *that*, and the whole extent to which our communications should go, I left rather to her own choice. At the second visit, however, upon some word or other arising which furnished an occasion for touching on this hateful topic, I pressed her, contrary to my own previous intention, for as full an account of the fatal event as she could without a distressing effort communicate. To my surprise she was silent—gloomily—almost it might have seemed obstinately silent. A horrid thought came into my mind; could it, might it have been possible that my noble-minded wife, such she had ever seemed to me, was open to temptations of this nature? Could it have been that in some moment of infirmity, when her better angel was away from her side, she had yielded to a sudden impulse of frailty, such as a second moment for consideration would have resisted, but which unhappily had been followed by no such opportunity of retrieval? I had heard of such things. Cases there were in our own times (and not confined to one nation), when irregular impulses of this sort were known to have haunted and besieged natures not otherwise ignoble and base. I ran over some of the names amongst those which were taxed with this propensity. More than one were the names of people in a technical sense held noble. That, nor any other consideration abated my horror. Better, I said, better, (because more compatible with elevation of mind,) better to have committed some bloody act—some murderous act. Dreadful was the panic I underwent. God pardon the wrong I did; and even now I pray to him—as though the past thing were a future thing and capable of change—that he would forbid her for ever to know what was the derogatory thought I had admitted. I sometimes think, by recollecting a momentary blush that suffused her marble countenance,—I think—I fear that she might have read what was fighting in my mind. Yet that would admit of another explanation. If she did read the very worst, meek saint! she suffered no complaint or sense of that injury to escape her. It might, however, be that perception, or it might be that fear which roused her to an effort that otherwise had seemed too revolting to undertake. She now rehearsed the whole steps of the affair from first to last; but the only material addition, which her narrative made to that which the trial itself had involved, was the following:—On two separate occasions previous to the last and fatal one, when she had happened to walk unaccompanied by me in the city, the monster Barratt had met her in the street. He had probably—and this was, indeed, subsequently ascertained—at first, and for some time afterwards, mistaken her rank, and had addressed some proposals to her, which, from the suppressed tone of his speaking, or from her own terror and surprise, she had not clearly understood; but enough had reached her alarmed ear to satisfy her that they were of a nature in the last degree licentious and insulting. Terrified and shocked rather than indignant, for she too easily presumed the man to be a maniac, she hurried homewards; and was rejoiced, on first venturing to look round when close to her own gate, to perceive that the man was not following. There, however, she was mistaken; for either on this occasion, or on some other, he had traced her homewards. The last of these rencontres had occurred just three months before the fatal 6th of April; and if, in any one instance, Agnes had departed from the strict line of her duty as a wife, or had shown a defect of judgment, it was at this point—in not having frankly and fully reported the circumstances to me. On the last of these occasions I had met her at the garden-gate, and had particularly remarked that she seemed agitated; and now, at recalling these incidents, Agnes reminded me that I had noticed that circumstance to herself, and that she had answered me faithfully as to the main fact. It was true she had done so; for she had said that she had just met a lunatic who had alarmed her by fixing his attention upon herself, and speaking to her in a ruffian manner; and it was also true that she did sincerely regard him in that light. This led me at the time to construe the whole affair into a casual collision with some poor maniac escaping from his keepers, and of no future moment, having passed by without present consequences. But had she, instead of thus reporting her own erroneous impression, reported the entire circumstances of the case, I should have given them a very different interpretation. Affection for me, and fear to throw me needlessly into a quarrel with a man of apparently brutal and violent nature—these considerations, as too often they do with the most upright wives, had operated to check Agnes in the perfect sincerity of her communications. She had told nothing *but* the truth—only, and fatally it turned out for us both, she had not told the *whole* truth. The very suppression, to which she had reconciled herself, under the belief that thus she was providing for my safety and her own consequent happiness, had been the indirect occasion of ruin to both. It was impossible to show displeasure under such circumstances, or under any circumstances, to one whose self-reproaches were at any rate too bitter; but certainly, as a general rule, every conscientious woman should resolve to consider her husband's honor in the first case, and far before all other regards whatsoever; to make this the first, the second, the third law of her conduct, and his personal safety but the fourth or fifth. Yet women, and especially when the interests of children are at stake upon their husbands' safety, rarely indeed are able to take this Roman view of their duties.

To return to the narrative. Agnes had not, nor could have, the most remote suspicion of this Barratt's connection with the shop which he had not accidentally entered; and the sudden appearance of this wretch it was, at the very moment of finding herself charged with so vile and degrading an offence, that contributed most of all to rob her of her natural firmness, by suddenly revealing to her terrified heart the depth of the conspiracy which thus yawned like a gulf below her. And not only had this sudden horror, upon discovering a guilty design in what before had seemed accident, and links uniting remote incidents which else seemed casual and disconnected, greatly disturbed and confused her manner, which confusion again had become more intense upon her own consciousness that she *was* confused, and that her manner was greatly to her disadvantage; but—which was the worst effect of all, because the rest could not operate against her, except upon those who were present to witness it, whereas this was noted down and recorded—so utterly did her confusion strip her of all presence of mind, that she did not consciously notice (and consequently could not protest against at the moment when it was most important to do so, and most natural) the important circumstance of the muff. This capital objection, therefore, though dwelt upon and improved to the utmost at the trial, was looked upon by the judges as an after-thought; and merely because it had not been seized upon by herself, and urged in the first moments of her almost incapacitating terror on finding this amongst the circumstances of the charge against her— as if an ingenuous nature, in the very act of recoiling with horror from a criminal charge the most degrading, and in the very instant of discovering, with a perfect rapture of alarm, the too plausible appearance of probability amongst the circumstances, would be likely to pause, and with attorney-like dexterity, to pick out the particular circumstance that might admit of being *proved* to be false, when the conscience proclaimed, though in despondence for the result, that all the circumstances were, as to the use made of them, one tissue of falsehoods. Agnes, who had made a powerful effort in speaking of the case at all, found her calmness increase as she advanced; and she now told me, that in reality there were two discoveries which she made in the same instant, and not one only, which had disarmed her firmness and ordinary presence of mind. One I have mentioned—the fact of Barratt, the proprietor of the shop, being the same person who had in former instances persecuted her in the street; but the other was even more alarming—it has been said already that it was *not* a pure matter of accident that she had visited this particular shop. In reality, that nursery-maid, of whom some mention has been made above, and in terms expressing the suspicion with which even then I regarded her, had persuaded her into going thither by some representations which Agnes had already ascertained to be altogether unwarranted. Other presumptions against this girl's fidelity crowded dimly upon my wife's mind at the very moment of finding her eyes thus suddenly opened. And it was not five minutes after her first examination, and in fact five minutes after it had ceased to be of use to her, that she remembered another circumstance which now, when combined with the sequel, told its own tale,—the muff had been missed some little time before the 6th of April. Search had been made for it; but, the particular occasion which required it having passed off, this search was laid aside for the present, in the expectation that it would soon reappear in some corner of the house before it was wanted: then came the sunny day, which made it no longer useful, and would perhaps have dismissed it entirely from the recollection of all parties, until it was now brought back in this memorable way. The name of my wife was embroidered within, upon the lining, and it thus became a serviceable link to the hellish cabal against her. Upon reviewing the circumstances from first to last, upon recalling the manner of the girl at the time, when the muff was missed, and upon combining the whole with her recent deception, by which she had misled her poor mistress into visiting this shop, Agnes began to see the entire truth as to this servant's wicked collusion with Barratt, though, perhaps, it might be too much to suppose her aware of the unhappy result to which her collusion tended. All this she saw at a glance when it was too late, for her first examination was over. This girl, I must add, had left our house during my illness, and she had afterwards a melancholy end.

One thing surprised me in all this. Barratt's purpose must manifestly have been to create merely a terror in my poor wife's mind, and to stop short of any legal consequences, in order to profit of that panic and confusion for extorting compliances with his hideous pretensions. It perplexed me, therefore, that he did not appear to have pursued this manifestly his primary purpose, the other being merely a mask to conceal his true ends, and also (as he fancied) a means for effecting them. In this, however, I had soon occasion to find that I was deceived. He had, but without the knowledge of Agnes, taken such steps as were then open to him, for making overtures to her with regard to the terms upon which he would agree to defeat the charge against her by failing to appear. But the law had travelled too fast for him, and too determinately; so that, by the time he supposed terror to have operated sufficiently in favor of his views, it had already become unsafe to venture upon such explicit proposals as he would otherwise have tried. His own safety was now at stake, and would have been compromised by any open or written avowal of the motives on which he had been all along acting. In fact, at this time he was foiled by the agent in whom he confided; but much more he had been confounded upon another point—the prodigious interest manifested by the public. Thus it seems—that, whilst he meditated only a snare for my poor Agnes, he had prepared one for himself; and finally, to evade the suspicions which began to arise powerfully as to his true motives, and thus to stave off his own ruin, had found himself in a manner obliged to go forward and consummate the ruin of another.

The state of Agnes, as to health and bodily strength, was now becoming such that I was forcibly warned—whatsoever I meditated doing, to do quickly. There was this urgent reason for alarm: once conveyed into that region of the prison in which sentences like hers were executed, it became hopeless that I could communicate with her again. All intercourse whatsoever, and with whomsoever, was then placed under the most rigorous interdict; and the alarming circumstance was, that this transfer was governed by no settled rules, but might take place at any hour, and would certainly be precipitated by the slightest violence on my part, the slightest indiscretion, or the slightest argument for suspicion. Hard indeed was the part I had to play, for it was indispensable that I should appear calm and tranquil, in order to disarm suspicions around me, whilst continually contemplating the possibility that I myself might be summoned to extremities which I could not so much as trust myself to name or distinctly to conceive. But thus stood the case: the Government, it was understood, angered by the public opposition, resolute for the triumph of what they called 'principle,' had settled finally that the sentence should be carried into execution. Now that she, that my Agnes, being the frail wreck that she had become, could have stood one week of this sentence practically and literally enforced—was a mere chimera. A few hours probably of the experiment would have settled that question by dismissing her to the death she longed for; but because the suffering would be short, was I to stand by and to witness the degradation—the pollution—attempted to be fastened upon her. What! to know that her beautiful tresses would be shorn ignominiously—a felon's dress forced upon her—a vile taskmaster with authority to——; blistered be the tongue that could go on to utter, in connection with her innocent name, the vile dishonors which were to settle upon her person! I, however, and her brother had taken such resolutions that this result was one barely possible; and yet I sickened (yes, literally I many times experienced the effect of physical sickness) at contemplating our own utter childish helplessness, and recollecting that every night during our seclusion from the prison the last irreversible step might be taken—and in the morning we might find a solitary cell, and the angel form that had illuminated it gone where we could not follow, and leaving behind her the certainty that we should see her no more. Every night, at the hour of locking up, *she*, at least, manifestly had a fear that she saw us for the last time; she put her arms feebly about my neck, sobbed convulsively, and, I believe, guessed—but, if really so, did not much reprove or quarrel with the desperate purposes which I struggled with in regard to her own life. One thing was quite evident— that to the peace of her latter days, now hurrying to their close, it was indispensable that she should pass them undivided from me; and possibly, as was afterwards alleged, when it became easy to allege any thing, some relenting did take place in high quarters at this time; for upon some medical reports made just now, a most seasonable indulgence was granted, viz. that Hannah was permitted to attend her mistress constantly; and it was also felt as a great alleviation of the horrors belonging to this prison, that candles were now allowed throughout the nights. But I was warned privately that these indulgences were with no consent from the police minister; and that circumstances might soon withdraw the momentary intercession by which we profited. With this knowledge, we could not linger in our preparations; we had resolved upon accomplishing an escape for Agnes, at whatever risk or price; the main difficulty was her own extreme feebleness, which might forbid her to co-operate with us in any degree at the critical moment; and the main danger was—delay. We pushed forward, therefore, in our attempts with prodigious energy, and I for my part with an energy like that of insanity.

The first attempt we made was upon the fidelity to his trust of the chief jailer. He was a coarse, vulgar man, brutal in his manners, but with vestiges of generosity in his character—though damaged a good deal by his daily associates. Him we invited to a meeting at a tavern in the neighborhood of the prison, disguising our names as too certain to betray our objects, and baiting our invitation with some hints which we had ascertained were likely to prove temptations under his immediate circumstances. He had a graceless young son whom he was most anxious to wean from his dissolute connections, and to steady, by placing him in some office of no great responsibility. Upon this knowledge we framed the terms of our invitation.

These proved to be effectual, as regarded our immediate object of obtaining an interview of persuasion. The night was wet; and at seven o'clock, the hour fixed for the interview, we were seated in readiness, much perplexed to know whether he would take any notice of our invitation. We had waited three quarters of an hour, when we heard a heavy lumbering step ascending the stair. The door was thrown open to its widest extent, and in the centre of the door-way stood a short stout-built man, and the very broadest I ever beheld—staring at us with bold inquiring eyes. His salutation was something to this effect.

'What the hell do you gay fellows want with me? What the blazes is this humbugging letter about? My son, and be hanged! What do you know of my son?'

Upon this overture we ventured to request that he would come in and suffer us to shut the door, which we also locked. Next we produced the official paper nominating his son to a small place in the customs,—not yielding much, it was true, in the way of salary, but fortunately, and in accordance with the known wishes of the father, unburdened with any dangerous trust.

'Well, I suppose I must say thank ye: but what comes next? What am I to do to pay the damages?' We informed him that for this particular little service we asked no return.

'No, no,' said he, 'that'll not go down: that cat'll not jump. I'm not green enough for that. So, say away—what's the damage?' We then explained that we had certainly a favor and a great one to ask: ['Ay, I'll be bound you have,' was his parenthesis:] but that for this we were prepared to offer a separate remuneration; repeating that with respect to the little place procured for his son, it had not cost us anything, and therefore we did really and sincerely decline to receive anything in return; satisfied that, by this little offering, we had procured the opportunity of this present interview. At this point we withdrew a covering from the table upon which we had previously arranged a heap of gold coins, amounting in value to twelve hundred English guineas: this being the entire sum which circumstances allowed us to raise on so sudden a warning: for some landed property that we both had was so settled and limited, that we could not convert it into money either by way of sale, loan, or mortgage. This sum, stating to him its exact amount, we offered to his acceptance, upon the single condition that he would look aside, or wink hard, or (in whatever way he chose to express it) would make, or suffer to be made, such facilities for our liberating a female prisoner as we would point out. He mused: full five minutes he sat deliberating without opening his lips. At length he shocked us by saying, in a firm, decisive tone, that left us little hope of altering his resolution,—'No: gentlemen, it's a very fair offer, and a good deal of money for a single prisoner. I think I can guess at the person. It's a fair offer—fair enough. But, bless your heart! if I were to do the thing you want—why perhaps another case might be overlooked: but this prisoner, no: there's too much depending. No, they would turn me out of my place. Now the place is worth more to me in the long run than what you offer: though you bid fair enough, if it were only for my time in it. But look here: in case I can get my son to come into harness, I'm expecting to get the office for him after I've retired. So I can't do it. But I'll tell you what: you've been kind to my son: and therefore I'll not say a word about it. You're safe for me. And so good-night to you.' Saying which, and standing no further question, he walked resolutely out of the room and down stairs.

Two days we mourned over this failure, and scarcely knew which way to turn for another ray of hope;—on the third morning we received intelligence that this very jailer had been attacked by the fever, which, after long desolating the city, had at length made its way into the prison. In a very few days the jailer was lying without hope of recovery: and of necessity another person was appointed to fill his station for the present. This person I had seen, and I liked him less by much than the one he succeeded: he had an Italian appearance, and he wore an air of Italian subtlety and dissimulation. I was surprised to find, on proposing the same service to him, and on the same terms, that he made no objection whatever, but closed instantly with my offers. In prudence, however, I had made this change in the articles: a sum equal to two hundred English guineas, or one-sixth part of the whole money, he was to receive beforehand as a retaining fee; but the remainder was to be paid only to himself, or to anybody of his appointing, at the very moment of our finding the prison gates thrown open to us. He spoke fairly enough, and seemed to meditate no treachery; nor was there any obvious or known interest to serve by treachery; and yet I doubted him grievously.

The night came: it was chosen as a gala night, one of two nights throughout the year in which the prisoners were allowed to celebrate a great national event: and in those days of relaxed prison management the utmost license was allowed to the rejoicing. This indulgence was extended to prisoners of all classes, though, of course, under more restrictions with regard to the criminal class. Ten o'clock came—the hour at which we had been instructed to hold ourselves in readiness. We had been long prepared. Agnes had been dressed by Hannah in such a costume externally (a man's hat and cloak, &c.) that, from her height, she might easily have passed amongst a mob of masquerading figures in the debtors' halls and galleries for a young stripling. Pierpoint and myself were also to a certain degree disguised; so far, at least, that we should not have been recognized at any hurried glance by those of the prison officers who had become acquainted with our persons. We were all more or less disguised about the face; and in that age when masks were commonly used at all hours by people of a certain rank, there would have been nothing suspicious in any possible costume of the kind in a night like this, if we could succeed in passing for friends of debtors.

I am impatient of these details, and I hasten over the ground. One entire hour passed away, and no jailer appeared. We began to despond heavily; and Agnes, poor thing! was now the most agitated of us all. At length eleven struck in the harsh tones of the prison-clock. A few minutes after, we heard the sound of bolts drawing, and bars unfastening. The jailer entered—drunk, and much disposed to be insolent. I thought it advisable to give him another bribe, and he resumed the fawning insinuation of his manner. He now directed us, by passages which he pointed out, to gain the other side of the prison. There we were to mix with the debtors and their mob of friends, and to await his joining us, which in that crowd he could do without much suspicion. He wished us to traverse the passages separately; but this was impossible, for it was necessary that one of us should support Agnes on each side. I previously persuaded her to take a small quantity of brandy, which we rejoiced to see had given her, at this moment of starting, a most seasonable strength and animation. The gloomy passages were more than usually empty, for all the turnkeys were employed in a vigilant custody of the gates, and examination of the parties going out. So the jailer had told us, and the news alarmed us. We came at length to a turning which brought us in sight of a strong iron gate, that divided the two main quarters of the prison. For this we had not been prepared. The man, however, opened the gate without a word spoken, only putting out his hand for a fee; and in my joy, perhaps, I gave him one imprudently large. After passing this gate, the distant uproar of the debtors guided us to the scene of their merriment; and when there, such was the tumult and the vast multitude assembled, that we now hoped in good earnest to accomplish our purpose without accident. Just at this moment the jailer appeared in the distance; he seemed looking towards us, and at length one of our party could distinguish that he was beckoning to us. We went forward, and found him in some agitation, real or counterfeit. He muttered a word or two quite unintelligible about the man at the wicket, told us we must wait a while, and he would then see what could be done for us. We were beginning to demur, and to express the suspicions which now too seriously arose, when he, seeing, or affecting to see some object of alarm, pushed us with a hurried movement into a cell opening upon the part of the gallery at which we were now standing. Not knowing whether we really might not be retreating from some danger, we could do no otherwise than comply with his signals; but we were troubled at finding ourselves immediately locked in from the outside, and thus apparently all our motions had only sufficed to exchange one prison for another.

We were now completely in the dark, and found, by a hard breathing from one corner of the little dormitory, that it was not unoccupied. Having taken care to provide ourselves separately with means for striking a light, we soon had more than one torch burning. The brilliant light falling upon the eyes of a man who lay stretched on the iron bedstead, woke him. It proved to be my friend the under-jailer, Ratcliffe, but no longer holding any office in the prison. He sprang up, and a rapid explanation took place. He had become a prisoner for debt; and on this evening, after having caroused through the day with some friends from the country, had retired at an early hour to sleep away his intoxication. I on my part thought it prudent to intrust him unreservedly with our situation and purposes, not omitting our gloomy suspicions. Ratcliffe looked, with a pity that won my love, upon the poor wasted Agnes. He had seen her on her first entrance into the prison, had spoken to her, and therefore knew *from* what she had fallen, *to* what. Even then he had felt for her; how much more at this time, when he beheld, by the fierce light of the torches, her wo-worn features!

'Who was it,' he asked eagerly, 'you made the bargain with? Manasseh?'

'The same.'

'Then I can tell you this—not a greater villain walks the earth. He is a Jew from Portugal; he has betrayed many a man, and will many another, unless he gets his own neck stretched, which might happen, if I told all I know.'

'But what was it probable that this man meditated? Or how could it profit him to betray us?'

'That's more than I can tell. He wants to get your money, and that he doesn't know how to bring about without doing his part. But that's what he never *will* do, take my word for it. That would cut him out of all chance for the head-jailer's place.' He mused a little, and then told us that he could himself put us outside the prison walls, and *would* do it without fee or reward. 'But we must be quiet, or that devil will bethink him of me. I'll wager something he thought that I was out merry-making like the rest; and if he should chance to light upon the truth, he'll be back in no time.' Ratcliffe then removed an old fire-grate, at the back of which was an iron plate, that swung round into a similar fire-place in the contiguous cell. From that, by a removal of a few slight obstacles, we passed, by a long avenue, into the chapel. Then he left us, whilst he went out alone to reconnoitre his ground. Agnes was now in so pitiable a condition of weakness, as we stood on the very brink of our final effort, that we placed her in a pew, where she could rest as upon a sofa. Previously we had stood upon graves, and with monuments more or less conspicuous all around us: some raised by friends to the memory of friends—some by subscriptions in the prison—some by children, who had risen into prosperity, to the memory of a father, brother, or other relative, who had died in captivity. I was grieved that these sad memorials should meet the eye of my wife at this moment of awe and terrific anxiety. Pierpoint and I were well armed, and all of us determined not to suffer a recapture, now that we were free of the crowds that made resistance hopeless. This Agnes easily perceived; and *that*, by suggesting a bloody arbitration, did not lessen her agitation. I hoped therefore, that, by placing her in the pew, I might at least liberate her for the moment from the besetting memorials of sorrow and calamity. But, as if in the very teeth of my purpose, one of the large columns which supported the roof of the chapel, had its basis and lower part of the shaft in this very pew. On the side of it, and just facing her as she lay reclining on the cushions, appeared a mural tablet, with a bas-relief in white marble, to the memory of two children, twins, who had lived and died at the same time, and in this prison—children who had never breathed another air than that of captivity, their parents having passed many years within these walls, under confinement for debt. The sculptures were not remarkable, being a trite, but not the less affecting, representation of angels descending to receive the infants; but the hallowed words of the inscription, distinct and legible—'Suffer little children to come unto me, and forbid them not, for of such is the kingdom of God'—met her eye, and, by the thoughts they awakened, made me fear that she would become unequal to the exertions which yet awaited her. At this moment Ratcliffe returned, and informed us that all was right; and that, from the ruinous state of all the buildings which surrounded the chapel, no difficulty remained for us, who were, in fact, beyond the strong part of the prison, excepting at a single door, which we should be obliged to break down. But had we any means arranged for pursuing our flight, and turning this escape to account when out of confinement? All that, I assured him, was provided for long ago. We proceeded, and soon reached the door. We had one crow-bar amongst us, but beyond that had no better weapons than the loose stones found about some new-made graves in the chapel. Ratcliffe and Pierpoint, both powerful men, applied themselves by turns to the door, whilst Hannah and I supported Agnes. The door did not yield, being of enormous strength; but the wall did, and a large mass of stone-work fell outwards, twisting the door aside; so that, by afterwards working with our hands, we removed stones many enough to admit of our egress. Unfortunately this aperture was high above the ground, and it was necessary to climb over a huge heap of loose rubbish in order to profit by it. My brother-in-law passed first in order to receive my wife, quite helpless at surmounting the obstacle by her own efforts, out of my arms. He had gone through the opening, and, turning round so as to face me, he naturally could see something that I did *not* see. 'Look behind!' he called out rapidly. I did so, and saw the murderous villain Manasseh with his arm uplifted, and in the act of cutting at my wife, nearly insensible as she was, with a cutlass. The blow was not for me, but for her, as the fugitive prisoner; and the law would have borne him out in the act. I saw, I comprehended the whole. I groped, as far as I could without letting my wife drop, for my pistols; but all that I could do would have been unavailing, and too late—she would have been murdered in my arms. But—and that was what none of us saw—neither I, nor Pierpoint, nor the hound Manasseh—one person stood back in the shade; one person had seen, but had not uttered a word on seeing Manasseh advancing through the shades; one person only had forecast the exact succession of all that was coming; me she saw embarrassed and my hands preoccupied—Pierpoint and Ratcliffe useless by position—and the gleam of the dog's eye directed her to his aim. The crow-bar was leaning against the shattered wall. This she had silently seized. One blow knocked up the sword; a second laid the villain prostrate. At this moment appeared another of the turnkeys advancing from the rear, for the noise of our assault upon the door had drawn attention in the interior of the prison, from which, however, no great number of assistants could on this dangerous night venture to absent themselves. What followed for the next few minutes hurried onwards, incident crowding upon incident, like the motions of a dream:—Manasseh, lying on the ground, yelled out, 'The bell! the bell!' to him who followed. The man understood, and made for the belfry-door attached to the chapel; upon which Pierpoint drew a pistol, and sent the bullet whizzing past his ear so truly, that fear made the man obedient to the counter-orders of Pierpoint for the moment. He paused and awaited the issue. In a moment had all cleared the wall, traversed the waste ground beyond it, lifted Agnes over the low railing, shaken hands with our benefactor Ratcliffe, and pushed onwards as rapidly as we were able to the little dark lane, a quarter of a mile distant, where had stood waiting for the last two hours a chaise-and-four.

[Ratcliffe, before my story closes, I will pursue to the last of my acquaintance with him, according to the just claims of his services. He had privately whispered to me, as we went along, that he could speak to the innocence of that lady, pointing to my wife, better than anybody. He was the person whom (as then holding an office in the prison) Barratt had attempted to employ as agent in conveying any messages that he found it safe to send—obscurely hinting the terms on which he would desist from prosecution. Ratcliffe had at first undertaken the negotiation from mere levity of character. But when the story and the public interest spread, and after himself becoming deeply struck by the prisoner's affliction, beauty, and reputed innocence, he had pursued it only as a means of entrapping Barratt into such written communications and such private confessions of the truth as might have served Agnes effectually. He wanted the art, however, to disguise his purposes: Barratt came to suspect him violently, and feared his evidence so far, even for those imperfect and merely oral overtures which he had really sent through Ratcliffe—that on the very day of the trial, he, as was believed, though by another nominally, contrived that Ratcliffe should be arrested for debt; and, after harassing him with intricate forms of business, had finally caused him to be conveyed to prison. Ratcliffe was thus involved in his own troubles at the time; and afterwards supposed that, without written documents to support his evidence, he could not be of much service to the re-establisment of my wife's reputation. Six months after his services in the night-escape from the prison, I saw him, and pressed him to take the money so justly forfeited to him by Manasseh's perfidy. He would, however, be persuaded to take no more than paid his debts. A second and a third time his debts were paid by myself and Pierpoint. But the same habits of intemperance and dissolute pleasure which led him into these debts, finally ruined his constitution; and he died, though otherwise of a fine generous manly nature, a martyr to dissipation at the early age of twenty-nine. With respect to his prison confinement, it was so frequently recurring in his life, and was alleviated by so many indulgences, that he scarcely viewed it as a hardship: having once been an officer of the prison, and having thus formed connections with the whole official establishment, and done services to many of them, and being of so convivial a turn, he was, even as a prisoner, treated with distinction, and considered as a privileged son of the house.]

It was just striking twelve o'clock as we entered the lane where the carriage was drawn up. Rain, about the profoundest I had ever witnessed, was falling. Though near to midsummer, the night had been unusually dark to begin with, and from the increasing rain had become much more so. We could see nothing; and at first we feared that some mistake had occurred as to the station of the carriage—in which case we might have sought for it vainly through the intricate labyrinth of the streets in that quarter. I first descried it by the light of a torch, reflected powerfully from the large eyes of the leaders. All was ready. Horse-keepers were at the horses' heads. The postilions were mounted; each door had the steps let down: Agnes was lifted in: Hannah and I followed: Pierpoint mounted his horse; and at the word—Oh! how strange a word!—'*All's right*,' the horses sprang off like leopards, a manner ill-suited to the slippery pavement of a narrow street. At that moment, but we valued it little indeed, we heard the prison-bell ringing out loud and clear. Thrice within the first three minutes we had to pull up suddenly, on the brink of formidable accidents, from the dangerous speed we maintained, and which, nevertheless, the driver had orders to maintain, as essential to our plan. All the stoppages and hinderances of every kind along the road had been anticipated previously, and met by contrivance, of one kind or other; and Pierpoint was constantly a little ahead of us to attend to anything that had been neglected. The consequence of these arrangements was—that no person along the road could possibly have assisted to trace us by any thing in our appearance: for we passed all objects at too flying a pace, and through darkness too profound, to allow of any one feature in our equipage being distinctly noticed. Ten miles out of town, a space which we traversed in forty-four minutes, a second relay of horses was ready; but we carried on the same postilions throughout. Six miles ahead of this distance we had a second relay; and with this set of horses, after pushing two miles further along the road, we crossed by a miserable lane five miles long, scarcely even a bridge road, into another of the great roads from the capital; and by thus crossing the country, we came back upon the city at a point far distant from that at which we left it. We had performed a distance of forty-two miles in three hours, and lost a fourth hour upon the wretched five miles of cross-road. It was, therefore, four o'clock, and broad daylight, when we drew near the suburbs of the city; but a most happy accident now favored us; a fog the most intense now prevailed; nobody could see an object six feet distant; we alighted in an uninhabited new-built street, plunged into the fog, thus confounding our traces to any observer. We then stepped into a hackney-coach which had been stationed at a little distance. Thence, according to our plan, we drove to a miserable quarter of the town, whither the poor only and the wretched resorted; mounted a gloomy dirty staircase, and, befriended by the fog, still growing thicker and thicker, and by the early hour of the morning, reached a house previously hired, which, if shocking to the eye and the imagination from its squalid appearance and its gloom, still was a home—a sanctuary—an asylum from treachery, from captivity, from persecution. Here Pierpoint for the present quitted us: and once more Agnes, Hannah, and I, the shattered members of a shattered family, were thus gathered together in a house of our own.

Yes: once again, daughter of the hills, thou sleptst as heretofore in my encircling arms; but not again in that peace which crowned thy innocence in those days, and should have crowned it now. Through the whole of our flying journey, in some circumstances at its outset strikingly recalling to me that blessed one which followed our marriage, Agnes slept away unconscious of our movements. She slept through all that day and the following night; and I watched over her with as much jealousy of all that might disturb her, as a mother watches over her new-born baby; for I hoped, I fancied, that a long—long rest, a rest, a halcyon calm, a deep, deep Sabbath of security, might prove healing and medicinal. I thought wrong; her breathing became more disturbed, and sleep was now haunted by dreams; all of us, indeed, were agitated by dreams; the past pursued me, and the present, for high rewards had been advertised by Government to those who traced us; and though for the moment we were secure, because we never went abroad, and could not have been naturally sought in such a neighborhood, still that very circumstance would eventually operate against us. At length, every night I dreamed of our insecurity under a thousand forms; but more often by far my dreams turned upon our wrongs; wrath moved me rather than fear. Every night, for the greater part, I lay painfully and elaborately involved, by deep sense of wrong,

> '—in long orations, which I pleaded
> Before unjust tribunals.'
> [Footnote: From a MS. poem of a great living Poet.]

And for poor Agnes, her also did the remembrance of mighty wrongs occupy through vast worlds of sleep in the same way—though colored by that tenderness which belonged to her gentler nature. One dream in particular—a dream of sublime circumstances—she repeated to me so movingly, with a pathos so thrilling, that by some profound sympathy it transplanted itself to my own sleep, settled itself there, and is to this hour a part of the fixed dream scenery which revolves at intervals through my sleeping life. This it was:—She would hear a trumpet sound—though perhaps as having been the prelude to the solemn entry of the judges at a town which she had once visited in her childhood; other preparations would follow, and at last all the solemnities of a great trial would shape themselves and fall into settled images. The audience was assembled, the judges were arrayed, the court was set. The prisoner was cited. Inquest was made, witnesses were called; and false witnesses came tumultuously to the bar. Then again a trumpet was heard, but the trumpet of a mighty archangel; and then would roll away thick clouds and vapors. Again the audience, but another audience, was assembled; again the tribunal was established; again the court was set; but a tribunal and a court—how different to her! *That* had been composed of men seeking indeed for truth, but themselves erring and fallible creatures; the witnesses had been full of lies, the judges of darkness. But here was a court composed of heavenly witnesses—here was a righteous tribunal—and then at last a judge that could not be deceived. The judge smote with his eye a person who sought to hide himself in the crowd; the guilty man stepped forward; the poor prisoner was called up to the presence of the mighty judge; suddenly the voice of a little child was heard ascending before her. Then the trumpet sounded once again; and then there were new heavens and a new earth; and her tears and her agitation (for she had seen her little Francis) awoke the poor palpitating dreamer.

Two months passed on: nothing could possibly be done materially to raise the standard of those wretched accommodations which the house offered. The dilapidated walls, the mouldering plaster, the blackened mantel-pieces, the stained and polluted wainscots—what could be attempted to hide or to repair all this by those who durst not venture abroad? Yet whatever could be done, Hannah did; and, in the mean time, very soon indeed my Agnes ceased to see or to be offended by these objects. First of all her sight went from her; and nothing which appealed to that sense could ever more offend her. It is to me the one only consolation I have, that my presence and that of Hannah, with such innocent frauds as we concerted together, made her latter days pass in a heavenly calm, by persuading her that our security was absolute, and that all search after us had ceased, under a belief on the part of Government that we had gained the shelter of a foreign land. All this was a delusion; but it was a delusion—blessed be Heaven! which lasted exactly as long as her life, and was just commensurate with its necessity. I hurry over the final circumstances.

There was fortunately now, even for me, no fear that the hand of any policeman or emissary of justice could effectually disturb the latter days of my wife; for, besides pistols always lying loaded in an inner room, there happened to be a long narrow passage on entering the house, which, by means of a blunderbuss, I could have swept effectually, and cleared many times over; and I know what to do in a last extremity. Just two months it was, to a day, since we had entered the house; and it happened that the medical attendant upon Agnes, who awakened no suspicion by his visits, had prescribed some opiate or anodyne which had not come; being dark early, for it was now September, I had ventured out to fetch it. In this I conceived there could be no danger. On my return I saw a man examining the fastenings of the door. He made no opposition to my entrance, nor seemed much to observe it—but I was disturbed. Two hours after, both

Hannah and I heard a noise about the door, and voices in low conversation. It is remarkable that Agnes heard this also—so quick had grown her hearing. She was agitated, but was easily calmed; and at ten o'clock we were all in bed. The hand of Agnes was in mine; so only she felt herself in security. She had been restless for an hour, and talking at intervals in sleep. Once she certainly wakened, for she pressed her lips to mine. Two minutes after, I heard something in her breathing which did not please me. I rose hastily—brought a light—raised her head—two long, long gentle sighs, that scarcely moved the lips, were all that could be perceived. At that moment, at that very moment, Hannah called out to me that the door was surrounded. 'Open it!' I said; six men entered; Agnes it was they sought; I pointed to the bed; they advanced, gazed, and walked away in silence.

After this I wandered about, caring little for life or its affairs, and roused only at times to think of vengeance upon all who had contributed to lay waste my happiness. In this pursuit, however, I was confounded as much by my own thoughts as by the difficulties of accomplishing my purpose. To assault and murder either of the two principal agents in this tragedy, what would it be, what other effect could it have, than to invest them with the character of injured and suffering people, and thus to attract a pity or a forgiveness at least to their persons which never otherwise could have illustrated their deaths? I remembered, indeed, the words of a sea-captain who had taken such vengeance as had offered at the moment upon his bitter enemy and persecutor (a young passenger on board his ship), who had informed against him at the Custom-house on his arrival in port, and had thus effected the confiscation of his ship, and the ruin of the captain's family. The vengeance, and it was all that circumstances allowed, consisted in coming behind the young man clandestinely and pushing him into the deep waters of the dock, when, being unable to swim, he perished by drowning. 'And the like,' said the captain, when musing on his trivial vengeance, 'and the like happens to many an honest sailor.' Yes, thought I, the captain was right. The momentary shock of a pistol-bullet—what is it? Perhaps it may save the wretch after all from the pangs of some lingering disease; and then again I shall have the character of a murderer, if known to have shot him; he will with many people have no such character, but at worst the character of a man too harsh (they will say), and possibly mistaken in protecting his property. And then, if not known as the man who shot him, where is the shadow even of vengeance? Strange it seemed to me, and passing strange, that I should be the person to urge arguments in behalf of letting this man escape. For at one time I had as certainly, as inexorably, doomed him as ever I took any resolution in my life. But the fact is, and I began to see it upon closer view, it is not easy by any means to take an adequate vengeance for any injury beyond a very trivial standard; and that with common magnanimity one does not care to avenge. Whilst I was in this mood of mind, still debating with myself whether I should or should not contaminate my hands with the blood of this monster, and still unable to shut my eyes upon one fact, viz. that my buried Agnes could above all things have urged me to abstain from such acts of violence, too evidently useless, listlessly and scarcely knowing what I was in quest of, I strayed by accident into a church where a venerable old man was preaching at the very moment I entered; he was either delivering as a text, or repeating in the course of his sermon, these words—'Vengeance is mine, I will repay, saith the Lord.' By some accident also he fixed his eyes upon me at the moment; and this concurrence with the subject then occupying my thoughts so much impressed me, that I determined very seriously to review my half-formed purposes of revenge; and well it was that I did so: for in that same week an explosion of popular fury brought the life of this wretched Barratt to a shocking termination, pretty much resembling the fate of the De Witts in Holland. And the consequences to me were such, and so full of all the consolation and indemnification which this world could give me, that I have often shuddered since then at the narrow escape I had had from myself intercepting this remarkable retribution. The villain had again been attempting to play off the same hellish scheme with a beautiful young rustic which had succeeded in the case of my ill-fated Agnes. But the young woman in this instance had a high, and, in fact, termagant spirit. Rustic as she was, she had been warned of the character of the man; everybody, in fact, was familiar with the recent tragedy. Either her lover or her brother happened to be waiting for her outside the window. He saw in part the very tricks in the act of perpetration by which some article or other, meant to be claimed as stolen property, was conveyed into a parcel she had incautiously laid down. He heard the charge against her made by Barratt, and seconded by his creatures—heard her appeal—sprang to her aid—dragged the ruffian into the street, when in less time than the tale could be told, and before the police (though tolerably alert) could effectually interpose for his rescue, the mob had so used or so abused the opportunity they had long wished for, that he remained the mere disfigured wreck of what had once been a man, rather than a creature with any resemblance to humanity. I myself heard the uproar at a distance, and the shouts and yells of savage exultation; they were sounds I shall never forget, though I did not at that time know them for what they were, or understood their meaning. The result, however, to me was something beyond this, and worthy to have been purchased with my heart's blood. Barratt still breathed; spite of his mutilations he could speak; he was rational. One only thing he demanded—it was that his dying confession might be taken. Two magistrates and a clergyman attended. He gave a list of those whom he had trepanned, and had failed to trepan, by his artifices and threats, into the sacrifice of their honor. He expired before the record was closed, but not before he had placed my wife's name in the latter list as the one whose injuries in his dying moments most appalled him. This confession on the following day went into the hands of the hostile minister, and my revenge was perfect.

THE SPANISH NUN

Why is it that *Adventures* are so generally repulsive to people of meditative minds? It is for the same reason that any other want of law, that any other anarchy is repulsive. Floating passively from action to action, as helplessly as a withered leaf surrendered to the breath of winds, the human spirit (out of which comes all grandeur of human motions) is exhibited in mere *Adventures*, as either entirely laid asleep, or as acting only by lower organs that regulate the *means*, whilst the *ends* are derived from alien sources, and are imperiously predetermined. It is a case of exception, however, when even amongst such adventures the agent reacts upon his own difficulties and necessities by a temper of extraordinary courage, and a mind of premature decision. Further strength arises to such an exception, if the very moulding accidents of the life, if the very external coercions are themselves unusually romantic. They may thus gain a separate interest of their own. And, lastly, the whole is locked into validity of interest, even for the psychological philosopher, by complete authentication of its truth. In the case now brought before him, the reader must not doubt; for no memoir exists, or personal biography, that is so trebly authenticated by proofs and attestations direct and collateral. From the archives of the Royal Marine at Seville, from the autobiography or the heroine, from contemporary chronicles, and from several official sources scattered in and out of Spain, some of them ecclesiastical, the amplest proofs have been drawn, and may yet be greatly extended, of the extraordinary events here recorded. M. de Ferrer, a Spaniard of much research, and originally incredulous as to the facts, published about seventeen years ago a selection from the leading documents, accompanied by his *palinode* as to their accuracy. His materials have been since used for the basis of more than one narrative, not inaccurate, in French, German and Spanish journals of high authority. It is seldom the case that French writers err by prolixity. They *have* done so in this case. The present narrative, which contains no sentence derived from any foreign one, has the great advantage of close compression; my own pages, after equating the size, being as 1 to 3 of the shortest continental form. In the mode of narration, I am vain enough to flatter myself that the reader will find little reason to hesitate between us. Mine at least, weary nobody; which is more than can be always said for the continental versions.

On a night in the year 1592, (but which night is a secret liable to 365 answers,) a Spanish 'son of somebody,' [Footnote: i.e. 'Hidalgo'] in the fortified town of St. Sebastian, received the disagreeable intelligence from a nurse, that his wife had just presented him with a daughter. No present that the poor misjudging lady could possibly have made him was so entirely useless for any purpose of his. He had three daughters already, which happened to be more by 2 1 than *his* reckoning assumed as a reasonable allowance of daughters. A supernumerary son might have been stowed away; but daughters in excess were the very nuisance of Spain. He did, therefore, what in such cases every proud and lazy Spanish gentleman was apt to do—he wrapped the new little daughter, odious to his paternal eyes, in a pocket handkerchief; and then, wrapping up his own throat with a good deal more care, off he bolted to the neighboring convent of St. Sebastian, not merely of that city, but also (amongst several convents) the one dedicated to that saint. It is well that in this quarrelsome world we quarrel furiously about tastes; since agreeing too closely about the objects to be liked and appropriated would breed much more fighting than is bred by disagreeing. That little human tadpole, which the old toad of a father would not suffer to stay ten minutes in his house, proved as welcome at the nunnery of St. Sebastian as she was odious elsewhere. The superior of the convent was aunt, by the mother's side, to the new-born stranger. She, therefore, kissed and blessed the little lady. The poor nuns, who were never to have any babies of their own, and were languishing for some amusement, perfectly doated on this prospect of a wee pet. The superior thanked the hidalgo for his very splendid present. The nuns thanked him each and all; until the old crocodile actually began to cry and whimper sentimentally at what he now perceived to be excess of munificence in himself. Munificence, indeed, he remarked, was his foible next after parental tenderness.

What a luxury it is sometimes to a cynic that there go two words to a bargain. In the convent of St. Sebastian all was gratitude; gratitude (as aforesaid) to the hidalgo from all the convent for his present, until at last the hidalgo began to express gratitude to *them* for their gratitude to *him*. Then came a rolling fire of thanks to St. Sebastian; from the superior, for sending a future saint; from the nuns, for sending such a love of a plaything; and, finally, from papa, for sending such substantial board and well-bolted lodgings, 'from which,' said the malicious old fellow, 'my pussy will never find her way out to a thorny and dangerous world.' Won't she? I suspect, son of somebody, that the next time you see 'pussy,' which may happen to be also the last, will not be in a convent of any kind. At present, whilst this general rendering of thanks was going on, one person only took no part in them. That person was 'pussy,' whose little figure lay quietly stretched out in the arms of a smiling young nun, with eyes nearly shut, yet peering a little at the candles. Pussy said nothing. It's of no great use to say much, when all the world is against you. But if St. Sebastian had enabled her to speak out the whole truth, pussy *would* have said: 'So, Mr. Hidalgo, you have been engaging lodgings for me; lodgings for life. Wait a little. We'll try that question, when my claws are grown a little longer.'

Disappointment, therefore, was gathering ahead. But for the present there was nothing of the kind. That noble old crocodile, papa, was not in the least disappointed as regarded *his* expectation of having no anxiety to waste, and no money to pay, on account of his youngest daughter. He insisted on his right to forget her; and in a week *had* forgotten her, never to think of her again but once. The lady superior, as regarded *her* demands, was equally content, and through a course of several years; for, as often as she asked pussy if she would be a saint, pussy replied that she would, if saints were allowed plenty of sweetmeats. But least of all were the nuns disappointed. Everything that they had fancied possible in a human plaything fell short of what pussy realized in racketing, racing, and eternal plots against the peace of the elder nuns. No fox ever kept a hen-roost in such alarm as pussy kept the dormitory of the senior sisters; whilst the younger ladies were run off their legs by the eternal wiles, and had their chapel gravity discomposed, even in chapel, by the eternal antics of this privileged little kitten.

. The kitten had long ago received a baptismal name, which was Kitty; this is Catharine, or Kate, or *Hispanice* Catalina. It was a good name, as it recalled her original name of pussy. And, by the way, she had also an ancient and honorable surname, viz., *De Erauso*, which is to this day a name rooted in Biscay. Her father, the *hidalgo*, was a military officer in the Spanish service, and had little care whether his kitten should turn out a wolf or a lamb, having made over the fee simple of his own interest in the little Kate to St. Sebastian, 'to have and to hold,' so long as Kate should keep her hold of this present life. Kate had no apparent intention to let slip that hold, for she was blooming as a rose-bush in June, tall and strong as a young cedar. Yet, notwithstanding this robust health and the strength of the convent walls, the time was drawing near when St. Sebastian's lease in Kate must, in legal phrase, 'determine;' and any *chateaux en Espagne*, that the Saint might have built on the cloisteral fidelity of his pet Catalina, must suddenly give way in one hour, like many other vanities in our own days of Spanish bonds and promises. After reaching her tenth year, Catalina became thoughtful, and not very docile. At times she was even headstrong and turbulent, so that the gentle sisterhood of St. Sebastian, who had no other pet or plaything in the world, began to weep in secret—fearing that they might have been rearing by mistake some future tigress—for as to infancy, *that*, you know, is playful and innocent even in the cubs of a tigress. But *there* the ladies were going too far. Catalina was impetuous and aspiring, but not cruel. She was gentle, if people would let her be so. But woe to those that took liberties with *her!* A female servant of the convent, in some authority, one day, in passing up the aisle to matins, *wilfully* gave Kate a push; and in return, Kate, who never left her debts in arrear, gave the servant for a keepsake a look which that servant carried with her in fearful remembrance to her grave. It seemed, as if Kate had tropic blood in her veins, that continually called her away to the tropics. It was all the fault of that 'blue rejoicing sky,' of those purple Biscayan mountains, of that tumultuous ocean, which she beheld daily from the nunnery gardens. Or, if only half of it was *their* fault, the other half lay in those golden tales, streaming upwards even into the sanctuaries of convents, like morning mists touched by earliest sunlight, of kingdoms overshadowing a new world which had been founded by her kinsmen with the simple aid of a horse and a lance. The reader is to remember that this is no romance, or at least no fiction, that he is reading; and it is proper to remind the reader of real romances in Ariosto or our own Spenser, that such martial ladies as the *Marfisa*, or *Bradamant* of the first, and *Britomart* of the other, were really not the improbabilities that modern society imagines. Many a stout man, as you will soon see, found that Kate, with a sabre in hand, and well mounted, was but too serious a fact.

The day is come—the evening is come—when our poor Kate, that had for fifteen years been so tenderly rocked in the arms of St. Sebastian and his daughters, and that henceforth shall hardly find a breathing space between eternal storms, must see her peaceful cell, must see the holy chapel, for the last time. It was at vespers, it was during the chanting of the vesper service, that she finally read the secret signal for her departure, which long she had been looking for. It happened that her aunt, the Lady Principal, had forgotten her breviary. As this was in a private 'scrutoire, she did not choose to send a servant for it, but gave the key to her niece. The niece, on opening the 'scrutoire, saw, with that rapidity of eye-glance for the one thing needed in any great emergency, which ever attended her through life, that *now* was the moment for an attempt which, if neglected, might never return. There lay the total keys, in one massive *trousseau*, of that fortress impregnable even to armies from without. Saint Sebastian! do you see what your pet is going to do? And do it she will, as sure as your name is St. Sebastian. Kate went back to her aunt with the breviary and the key; but taking good care to leave that awful door, on whose hinge revolved her whole life, unlocked. Delivering the two articles to the Superior, she complained of a headache—[Ah, Kate! what did you know of headaches, except now and then afterwards from a stray bullet, or so?]—upon which her aunt, kissing her forehead, dismissed her to bed. Now, then, through three-fourths of an hour Kate will have free elbow-room for unanchoring her boat, for unshipping her oars, and for pulling ahead right out of St. Sebastian's cove into the main ocean of life.

Catalina, the reader is to understand, does not belong to the class of persons in whom chiefly I pretend to an interest. But everywhere one loves energy and indomitable courage. I, for my part, admire not, by preference, anything that points to this world. It is the child of reverie and profounder sensibility who turns *away* from the world as hateful and insufficient, that engages *my* interest: whereas Catalina was the very model of the class fitted for facing this world, and who express their love to it by fighting with it and kicking it from year to year. But, always, what is best in its kind one admires, even though the kind be disagreeable. Kate's advantages for her *role* in this life lay in four things, viz., in a well-built person, and a particularly strong wrist; 2d, in a heart that nothing could appal; 3d, in a sagacious head, never drawn aside from the *hoc age* [from the instant question of life] by any weakness of imagination; 4th, in a tolerably thick skin—not literally, for she was fair and blooming, and decidedly handsome, having such a skin as became a young woman of family in northernmost Spain. But her sensibilities were obtuse as regarded *some* modes of delicacy, *some* modes of equity, *some* modes of the world's opinion, and *all* modes whatever of personal hardship. Lay a stress on that word *some*—for, as to delicacy, she never lost sight of the kind which peculiarly concerns her sex. Long afterwards she told the Pope himself, when confessing without disguise her sad and infinite wanderings to the paternal old man (and I feel convinced of her veracity), that in this respect, even then, at middle age, she was as pure as is a child. And, as to equity, it was only that she substituted the equity of camps for the polished (but often more iniquitous) equity of courts and towns. As to the third item—the world's opinion—I don't know that you need lay a stress on *some*; for, generally speaking, *all* that the world did, said, or thought, was alike contemptible in her eyes, in which, perhaps, she was not so *very* far wrong. I must add, though at the cost of interrupting the story by two or three more sentences, that Catalina had also a fifth advantage, which sounds humbly, but is really of use in a world, where even to fold and seal a letter adroitly is not the least of accomplishments. She was a *handy* girl. She could turn her hand to anything, of which I will give you two memorable instances. Was there ever a girl in this world but herself that cheated and snapped her fingers at that awful Inquisition, which brooded over the convents of Spain, that did this without collusion from outside, trusting to nobody, but to herself, and what? to one needle, two hanks of thread, and a very inferior pair of scissors? For, that the scissors were bad, though Kate does not say so in her memoirs, I knew by an *a priori* argument, viz., because *all* scissors were bad in the year 1607. Now, say all decent logicians, from a universal to a particular *valet consequentia*, *all* scissors were bad: *ergo, some* scissors were bad. The second instance of her handiness will surprise you even more:—She once stood upon a scaffold, under sentence of death—[but, understand, on the evidence of false witnesses]. Jack Ketch was absolutely tying the knot under her ear, and the shameful man of ropes fumbled so deplorably, that Kate (who by much nautical experience had learned from another sort of 'Jack' how a knot *should* be tied in this world,) lost all patience with the contemptible artist, told him she was ashamed of him, took the rope out of his hand, and tied the knot irreproachably herself. The crowd saluted her with a festal roll, long and loud, of *vivas*; and this word *viva* of good augury—but stop; let me not anticipate.

From this sketch of Catalina's character, the reader is prepared to understand the decision of her present proceeding. She had no time to lose: the twilight favored her; but she must get under hiding before pursuit commenced. Consequently she lost not one of her forty-five minutes in picking and choosing. No *shilly-shally* in Kate. She saw with the eyeball of an eagle what was indispensable. Some little money perhaps to pay the first toll-bar of life: so, out of four shillings in Aunty's purse, she took one. You can't say *that* was exorbitant. Which of us wouldn't subscribe a shilling for poor Katy to put into the first trouser pockets that ever she will wear? I remember even yet, as a personal experience, that when first arrayed, at four years old, in nankeen trousers, though still so far retaining hermaphrodite relations of dress as to wear a petticoat above my trousers, all my female friends (because they pitied me, as one that had suffered from years of ague) filled my pockets with half-crowns, of which I can render no account at this day. But what were my poor pretensions by the side of Kate's? Kate was a fine blooming girl of fifteen, with no touch of ague, and, before the next sun rises, Kate shall draw on her first trousers, and made by her own hand; and, that she may do so, of all the valuables in Aunty's repository she takes nothing beside the shilling, *quantum sufficit* of thread, one stout needle, and (as I told you before, if you would please to remember things) one bad pair of scissors. Now she was ready; ready to cast off St. Sebastian's towing-rope; ready to cut and run for port anywhere. The finishing touch of her preparations was to pick out the proper keys: even there she showed the same discretion. She did do no gratuitous mischief. She did not take the wine-cellar key, which would have irritated the good father confessor; she took those keys only that belonged to *her*, if ever keys did; for they were the keys that locked her out from her natural birthright of liberty. 'Show me,' says the Romish Casuist, 'her right in law to let herself out of that nunnery.' 'Show us,' we reply, '*your* right to lock her in.'

Right or wrong, however, in strict casuistry, Kate was resolved to let herself out; and did so; and, for fear any man should creep in whilst vespers lasted, and steal the kitchen grate, she locked her old friends *in*. Then she sought a shelter. The air was not cold. She hurried into a chestnut wood, and upon withered leaves slept till dawn. Spanish diet and youth leaves the digestion undisordered, and the slumbers light. When the lark rose, up rose Catalina. No time to lose, for she was still in the dress of a nun, and liable to be arrested by any man in Spain. With her *armed* finger, [aye, by the way, I forgot the thimble; but Kate did *not*]—she set to work upon her amply-embroidered petticoat. She turned it wrong side out; and with the magic that only female hands possess, she had soon sketched and finished a dashing pair of Wellington trousers. All other changes were made according to the materials she possessed, and quite sufficiently to disguise the two main perils—her sex, and her monastic dedication. What was she to do next. Speaking of Wellington trousers would remind *us*, but could hardly remind *her*, of Vittoria, where she dimly had heard of some maternal relative. To Vittoria, therefore, she bent her course; and, like the Duke of Wellington, but arriving more than two centuries earlier, [though *he* too is an early riser,] she gained a great victory at that place. She had made a two days' march, baggage far in the rear, and no provisions but wild berries; she depended for anything better, as light-heartedly as the Duke, upon attacking, sword in hand, storming her dear friend's entrenchments, and effecting a lodgment in his breakfast-room, should he happen to have one. This amiable relative, an elderly man, had but one foible, or perhaps one virtue in this world; but *that* he had in perfection,—it was pedantry. On that hint Catalina spoke: she knew by heart, from the services of the convent, a few Latin phrases. Latin!—Oh, but *that* was charming; and in one so young! The grave Don owned the soft impeachment; relented at once, and clasped the hopeful young gentleman in the Wellington trousers to his *uncular* and rather angular breast. In this house the yarn of life was of a mingled quality. The table was good, but that was exactly what Kate cared little about. The amusement was of the worst kind. It consisted chiefly in conjugating Latin verbs, especially such as were obstinately irregular. To show him a withered frost-bitten verb, that wanted its preterite, wanted its supines, wanted, in fact, everything in this world, fruits or blossoms, that make a verb desirable, was to earn the Don's gratitude for life. All day long he was marching and countermarching his favorite brigades of verbs—verbs frequentative, verbs inceptive, verbs desiderative—horse, foot, and artillery; changing front, advancing from the rear, throwing out skirmishing parties, until Kate, not given to faint, must have thought of such a resource, as once in her life she had thought so seasonably of a vesper headache. This was really worse than St. Sebastian's. It reminds one of a French gayety in Thiebault or some such author, who describes a rustic party, under equal despair, as employing themselves in conjugating the verb *s'ennuyer, —Je m'ennuie, tu t'ennuies, il s'ennuit; nous nous ennuyons,* &c.; thence to the imperfect—*Je m'ennuyois, tu t'ennuyois,* &c.; thence to the imperative—*Qu'il s'ennuye,* &c.; and so on through the whole melancholy conjugation. Now, you know, when the time comes that, *nous nous ennuyons,* the best course is, to part. Kate saw *that;* and she walked off from the Don's [of whose amorous passion for defective verbs one would have wished to know the catastrophe], and took from his mantel-piece rather move silver than she had levied on her aunt. But the Don also was a relative; and really he owed her a small cheque on his banker for turning out on his field-days. A man, if he *is* a kinsman, has no right to bore one *gratis.*

From Vittoria, Kate was guided by a carrier to Valladolid. Luckily, as it seemed at first, but it made little difference in the end, here, at Valladolid, were the King and his Court. Consequently, there was plenty of regiments and plenty of regimental bands. Attracted by one of these, Catalina was quietly listening to the music, when some street ruffians, in derision of the gay colors and the form of her forest-made costume—[rascals! one would like to have seen what sort of trousers *they* would have made with no better scissors!]—began to pelt her with stones. Ah, my friends, of the genus *blackguard,* you little know who it is that you are selecting for experiments. This is the one creature of fifteen in all Spain, be the other male or female, whom nature, and temper, and provocation have qualified for taking the conceit out of you. This she very soon did, laying open a head or two with a sharp stone, and letting out rather too little than too much of bad Valladolid blood. But mark the constant villany of this world. Certain Alguazils—very like some other Alguazils that I know nearer home—having stood by quietly to see the friendless stranger insulted and assaulted, now felt it their duty to apprehend the poor nun for murderous violence: and had there been such a thing as a treadmill in Valladolid, Kate was booked for a place on it without further inquiry. Luckily, injustice does not *always* prosper. A gallant young cavalier, who had witnessed from his windows the whole affair, had seen the provocation, and admired Catalina's behavior—equally patient at first and bold at last—hastened into the street, pursued the officers, forced them to release their prisoner, upon stating the circumstances of the case, and instantly offered Catalina a situation amongst his retinue. He was a man of birth and fortune; and the place offered, that of an honorary page, not being at all degrading even to a 'daughter of somebody,' was cheerfully accepted. Here Catalina spent a happy month. She was now splendidly dressed in dark blue velvet, by a tailor that did not work within the gloom of a chestnut forest. She and the young cavalier,

Don Francisco de Cardenas, were mutually pleased, and had mutual confidence. All went well—when one evening, but, luckily, not until the sun had been set so long as to make all things indistinct, who should march into the ante-chamber of the cavalier but that sublime of crocodiles, *Papa*, that we lost sight of fifteen years ago, and shall never see again after this night. He had his crocodile tears all ready for use, in working order, like a good industrious fire-engine. It was absolutely to Catalina herself that he advanced; whom, for many reasons, he could not be supposed to recognise—lapse of years, male attire, twilight, were all against him. Still, she might have the family countenance; and Kate thought he looked with a suspicious scrutiny into her face, as he inquired for the young Don. To avert her own face, to announce him to Don Francisco, to wish him on the shores of that ancient river for crocodiles, the Nile, furnished but one moment's work to the active Catalina. She lingered, however, as her place entitled her to do, at the door of the audience chamber. She guessed already, but in a moment she *heard* from papa's lips what was the nature of his errand. His daughter Catharine, he informed the Don, had eloped from the convent of St. Sebastian, a place rich in delight. Then he laid open the unparalleled ingratitude of such a step. Oh, the unseen treasure that had been spent upon that girl! Oh, the untold sums of money that he had sunk in that unhappy speculation! The nights of sleeplessness suffered during her infancy! The fifteen years of solicitude thrown away in schemes for her improvement! It would have moved the heart of a stone. The *hidalgo* wept copiously at his own pathos. And to such a height of grandeur had he carried his Spanish sense of the sublime, that he disdained to mention the pocket-handkerchief which he had left at St. Sebastian's fifteen years ago, by way of envelope for 'pussy,' and which, to the best of pussy's knowledge, was the one sole memorandum of papa ever heard of at St. Sebastian's. Pussy, however, saw no use in revising and correcting the text of papa's remembrances. She showed her usual prudence, and her usual incomparable decision. It did not appear, as yet, that she would be reclaimed, or was at all suspected for the fugitive by her father. For it is an instance of that singular fatality which pursued Catalina through life, that, to her own astonishment, (as she now collected from her father's conference,) nobody had traced her to Valladolid, nor had her father's visit any connection with suspicious travelling in that direction. The case was quite different. Strangely enough, her street row had thrown her into the one sole household in all Spain that had an official connection with St. Sebastian's. That convent had been founded by the young cavalier's family; and, according to the usage of Spain, the young man (as present representative of his house) was the responsible protector of the establishment. It was not to the Don, as harborer of his daughter, but to the Don, as *ex officio* visitor of the convent, that the hidalgo was appealing.

Probably Kate might have staid safely some time longer. Yet, again, this would but have multiplied the clues for tracing her; and, finally, she would too probably have been discovered; after which, with all his youthful generosity, the poor Don could not have protected her. Too terrific was the vengeance that awaited an abettor of any fugitive nun; but, above all, if such a crime were perpetrated by an official mandatory of the church. Yet, again, so far it was the more hazardous course to abscond, that it almost revealed her to the young Don as the missing daughter. Still, if it really *had* that effect, nothing at present obliged him to pursue her, as might have been the case a few weeks later. Kate argued (I dare say) rightly, as she always did. Her prudence whispered eternally, that safety there was none for her, until she had laid the Atlantic between herself and St. Sebastian's. Life was to be for *her* a Bay of Biscay; and it was odds but she had first embarked upon this billowy life from the literal Bay of Biscay. Chance ordered otherwise. Or, as a Frenchman says with eloquent ingenuity, in connection with this story, 'Chance is but the *pseudonyme* of God for those particular cases which he does not subscribe openly with his own sign manual.' She crept up stairs to her bed-room. Simple are the travelling preparations of those that, possessing nothing, have no imperials to pack. She had Juvenal's qualification for carolling gaily through a forest full of robbers; for she had nothing to lose but a change of linen, that rode easily enough under her left arm, leaving the right free for answering any questions of impertinent customers. As she crept down stairs, she heard the Crocodile still weeping forth his sorrows to the pensive ear of twilight, and to the sympathetic Don Francisco. Now, it would not have been filial or lady-like for Kate to do what I am going to suggest; but what a pity that some gay brother page had not been there to turn aside into the room, armed with a roasted potato, and, taking a sportsman's aim, to have lodged it in the Crocodile's abominable mouth. Yet, what an anachronism! There *were* no roasted potatoes in Spain at that date, and very few in England. But anger drives a man to say anything.

Catalina had seen her last of friends and enemies in Valladolid. Short was her time there; but she had improved it so far as to make a few of both. There was an eye or two in Valladolid that would have glared with malice upon her, had she been seen by *all* eyes in that city, as she tripped through the streets in the dusk; and eyes there were that would have softened into tears, had they seen the desolate condition of the child, or in vision had seen the struggles that were before her. But what's the use of wasting tears upon our Kate? Wait till to-morrow morning at sunrise, and see if she is particularly in need of pity. What now should a young lady do—I propose it as a subject for a prize essay—that finds herself in Valladolid at nighfall, having no letters of introduction, not aware of any reason great or small for preferring any street in general, except so far as she knows of some reason for avoiding one or two streets in particular? The great problem I have stated, Kate investigated as she went along; and she solved it with the accuracy with which she ever applied to *practical* exigencies. Her conclusion was—that the best door to knock at in such a case was the door where there was no need to knock at all, as being unfastened, and open to all comers. For she argued that within such a door there would be nothing to steal, so that, at least, you could not be mistaken in the ark for a thief. Then, as to stealing from *her*, they might do that if they could.

Upon these principles, which hostile critics will in vain endeavor to undermine, she laid her hand upon what seemed a rude stable door. Such it proved. There was an empty cart inside, certainly there was, but you couldn't take *that* away in your pocket; and there were five loads of straw, but then of those a lady could take no more than her *reticule* would carry, which perhaps was allowed by the courtesy of Spain. So Kate was right as to the difficulty of being challenged for a thief. Closing the door as gently as she had opened it, she dropped her person, dressed as she was, upon the nearest heap of straw. Some ten feet further were lying two muleteers, honest and happy enough, as compared with the lords of the bed-chamber then in Valladolid: but still gross men, carnally deaf from eating garlic and onions, and other horrible substances. Accordingly, they never heard her, nor were aware, until dawn, that such a blooming person existed. But she was aware of *them*, and of their conversation. They were talking of an expedition for America, on the point of sailing under Don Ferdinand de Cordova. It was to sail from some Andalusian port. That was the very thing for *her*. At daylight she woke, and jumped up, needing no more toilet than the birds that already were singing in the gardens, or than the two muleteers, who, good, honest fellows, saluted the handsome boy kindly—thinking no ill at his making free with *their* straw, though no leave had been asked.

With these philo-garlic men Kate took her departure. The morning was divine: and leaving Valladolid with the transports that befitted such a golden dawn, feeling also already, in the very obscurity of her exit, the pledge of her escape; she cared no longer for the Crocodile, or for St. Sebastian, or (in the way of fear) for the protector of St. Sebastian, though of *him* she thought with some tenderness; so deep is the remembrance of kindness mixed with justice. Andalusia she reached rather slowly; but many months before she was sixteen years old, and quite in time for the expedition. St. Lucar being the port of rendezvous for the Peruvian expedition, thither she went. All comers were welcome on board the fleet; much more a fine young fellow like Kate. She was at once engaged as a mate; and *her* ship, in particular, after doubling Cape Horn without loss, made the coast of Peru. Paita was the port of her destination. Very near to this port they were, when a storm threw them upon a coral reef. There was little hope of the ship from the first, for she was unmanageable, and was not expected to hold together for twenty-four hours. In this condition, with death before their faces, mark what Kate did; and please to remember it for her benefit, when she does any other little thing that angers you. The crew lowered the long-boat. Vainly the captain protested against this disloyal desertion of a king's ship, which might yet perhaps be run on shore, so as to save the stores. All the crew, to a man, deserted the captain. You may say *that* literally; for the single exception was *not* a man, being our bold-hearted Kate. She was the only sailor that refused to leave her captain, or the king of Spain's ship. The rest pulled away for the shore, and with fair hopes of reaching it. But one half-hour told another tale: just about that time came a broad sheet of lightning, which, through the darkness of evening, revealed the boat in the very act of mounting like a horse upon an inner reef, instantly filling, and throwing out the crew, every man of whom disappeared amongst the breakers. The night which succeeded was gloomy for both the representatives of his Catholic Majesty. It cannot be denied by the greatest of philosophers, that the muleteer's stable at Valladolid was worth twenty such ships, though the stable was *not* insured against fire, and the ship *was* insured against the sea and the wind by some fellow that thought very little of his engagements. But what's the use of sitting down to cry? That was never any trick of Catalina's. By daybreak, she was at work with an axe in her hand. I knew it, before ever I came to this place, in her memoirs. I felt, as sure as if I had read it, that when day broke, we should find Kate hard at work. Thimble or axe, trousers or raft, all one to *her*.

The Captain, though true to his duty, seems to have desponded. He gave no help towards the raft. Signs were speaking, however, pretty loudly that he must do something; for notice to quit was now served pretty liberally. Kate's raft was ready; and she encouraged the captain to think that it would give both of them something to hold by in swimming, if not even carry double. At this moment, when all was waiting for a start, and the ship herself was waiting for a final lurch, to say *Good-bye* to the King of Spain, Kate went and did a thing which some misjudging people will object to. She knew of a box laden with gold coins, reputed to be the King of Spain's, and meant for contingencies in the voyage out. This she smashed open with her axe, and took a sum equal to one hundred guineas English; which, having well secured in a pillow-case, she then lashed firmly to the raft. Now this, you know, though not *flotsam*, because it would not float, was certainly, by maritime law, '*jetsom*.' It would be the idlest of scruples to fancy that the sea or a shark had a better right to it than a philosopher, or a splendid girl who showed herself capable of writing a very fair 8vo, to say nothing of her decapitating in battle several of the king's enemies, and recovering the king's banner. No sane moralist would hesitate to do the same thing under the same circumstances, on board an English vessel, though the First Lord of the Admiralty should be looking on. The raft was now thrown into the sea. Kate jumped after it, and then entreated the captain to follow her. He attempted it; but, wanting her youthful agility, he struck his head against a spar, and sank like lead, giving notice below that his ship was coming. Kate mounted the raft, and was gradually washed ashore, but so exhausted, as to have lost all recollection. She lay for hours until the warmth of the sun revived her. On sitting up, she saw a desolate shore stretching both ways—nothing to eat, nothing to drink, but fortunately the raft and the money had been thrown near her; none of the lashings having given way— only what is the use of a guinea amongst tangle and sea-gulls? The money she distributed amongst her pockets, and soon found strength to rise and march forward. But which *was* forward? and which backward? She knew by the conversation of the sailors that Paita must be in the neighborhood; and Paita, being a port, could not be in the inside of Peru, but, of course, somewhere on its outside—and the outside of a maritime land must be the shore; so that, if she kept the shore, and went far enough, she could not fail of hitting her foot against Paita at last, in the very darkest night, provided only she could first find out which was *up* and which was *down*; else she might walk her shoes off, and find herself six thousand miles in the wrong. Here was an awkward case, all for want of a guide-post. Still, when one thinks of Kate's prosperous horoscope, that after so long a voyage, *she* only, out of the total crew, was thrown on the American shore, with one hundred and five pounds in her purse of clear gain on the voyage, a conviction arises that she *could* not guess wrongly. She might have tossed up, having coins in her pocket, *heads or tails*? but this kind of sortilege was then coming to be thought irreligious in Christendom, as a Jewish and a Heathen mode of questioning the dark future. She simply guessed, therefore; and very soon a thing happened which, though adding nothing to strengthen her guess as a true one, did much to sweeten it if it should prove a false one. On turning a point of the shore, she came upon a barrel of biscuit washed ashore from the ship. Biscuit is about the best thing I know, but it is the soonest spoiled; and one would like to hear counsel on one puzzling point, why it is that a touch of water utterly ruins it, taking its life, and leaving a *caput mortuum* corpse! Upon this *caput* Kate breakfasted, though *her* case was worse than mine; for any water that ever plagued *me* was always fresh; now *hers* was a present from the Pacific ocean. She, that was always prudent, packed up some of the Catholic king's biscuit, as she had previously packed up far too little of his gold. But in such cases a most delicate question occurs, pressing equally on medicine and algebra. It is this: if you pack up too much, then, by this extra burthen of salt provisions, you may retard for days your arrival at fresh provisions; on the other hand, if you pack up too little, you may never arrive at all. Catalina hit the *juste milieu;* and about twilight on the second day, she found herself entering Paita, without having had to swim any river in her walk.

The first thing, in such a case of distress, which a young lady does, even if she happens to be a young gentleman, is to beautify her dress. Kate always attended to *that,* as we know, having overlooked her in the chestnut wood. The man she sent for was not properly a tailor, but one who employed tailors, he himself furnishing the materials. His name was Urquiza, a fact of very little importance to us in 1847, if it had stood only at the head and foot of Kate's little account. But unhappily for Kate's *début* on this vast American stage, the case was otherwise. Mr. Urquiza had the misfortune (equally common in the old world and the new) of being a knave; and also a showy specious knave. Kate, who had prospered under sea allowances of biscuit and hardship, was now expanding in proportions. With very little vanity or consciousness on that head, she now displayed a really fine person; and, when drest anew in the way that became a young officer in the Spanish service, she looked [Footnote: *'She looked,'* etc. If ever the reader should visit Aix-la-Chapelle, he will probably feel interest enough in the poor, wild impassioned girl, to look out for a picture of her in that city, and the only one known *certainly* to be authentic. It is in the collection of Mr. Sempeller. For some time it was supposed that the best (if not the only) portrait of her lurked somewhere in Italy. Since the discovery of the picture at Aix-la-Chapelle, that notion has been abandoned. But there is great reason to believe that, both in Madrid and Rome, many portraits of her must have been painted to meet the intense interest which arose in her history subsequently amongst all the men of rank, military or ecclesiastical, whether in Italy or Spain. The date of these would range between sixteen and twenty-two years from, the period which we have now reached (1608.)] the representative picture of a Spanish *caballador*. It is strange that such an appearance, and such a rank, should have suggested to Urquiza the presumptuous idea of wishing that Kate might become his clerk. He *did*, however wish it; for Kate wrote a beautiful hand; and a stranger thing is, that Kate accepted his proposal. This might arise from the difficulty of moving in those days to any distance in Peru. The ship had been merely bringing stores to the station of Paita; and no corps of the royal armies was readily to be reached, whilst something must be done at once for a livelihood. Urquiza had two mercantile establishments, one at Trujillo, to which he repaired in person, on Kate's agreeing to undertake the management of the other in Paita. Like the sensible girl, that we have always found her, she demanded specific instructions for her guidance in duties so new. Certainly she was in a fair way for seeing life. Telling her beads at St. Sebastian's, manoeuvreing irregular verbs at Vittoria, acting as gentleman-usher at Valladolid, serving his Spanish Majesty round Cape Horn, fighting with storms and sharks off the coast of Peru, and now commencing as book-keeper or *commis* to a draper at Paita, does she not justify the character that I myself gave her, just before dismissing her from St. Sebastian's, of being a 'handy' girl? Mr. Urquiza's instructions were short, easy to be understood, but rather comic; and yet, which is odd, they led to tragic results. There were two debtors of the shop, (*many*, it is to be hoped, but two meriting his affectionate notice,) with respect to whom he left the most opposite directions. The one was a very handsome lady; and the rule as to *her* was, that she was to have credit unlimited, strictly unlimited. That was plain. The other customer, favored by Mr. Urquiza's valedictory thoughts, was a young man, cousin to the handsome lady, and bearing the name of Reyes. This youth occupied in Mr. Urquiza's estimate the same hyperbolical rank as the handsome lady, but on the opposite side of the equation. The rule as to *him* was—that he was to have *no* credit; strictly none. In this case, also, Kate saw no difficulty; and when she came to know Mr. Reyes a little, she found the path of pleasure coinciding with the path of duty. Mr. Urquiza could not be more precise in laying down the rule than Kate was in enforcing it. But in the other case a scruple arose. *Unlimited* might be a word, not of Spanish law, but of Spanish rhetoric; such as 'Live a thousand years,' which even annuity offices hear, and perhaps utter, without a pang. Kate, therefore, wrote to Trujillo, expressing her honest fears, and desiring to have more definite instructions. These were positive. If the lady chose to send for the entire shop, her account was to be debited instantly with *that*. She had, however, as yet, not sent for the shop, but she began to manifest strong signs of sending for the shop *man*. Upon the blooming young Biscayan had her roving eye settled; and she was in a course of making up her mind to take Kate for a sweetheart. Poor Kate saw this with a heavy heart. And, at the same time that she had a prospect of a tender friend more than she wanted, she had become certain of an extra enemy that she wanted quite as little. What she had done to offend Mr. Reyes, Kate could not guess, except as to the matter of the credit; but then, in that, she only executed her instructions. Still Mr. Reyes was of opinion that there were two ways of executing orders: but the main offence was unintentional on Kate's part. Reyes, though as yet she did not know it, had himself been a candidate for the situation of clerk; and intended probably to keep the equation precisely as it was with respect to the allowance of credit, only to change places with the handsome lady—keeping *her* on the negative side, himself on the affirmative—an arrangement that you know could have made no sort of pecuniary difference to Urquiza.

Thus stood matters, when a party of strolling players strolled into Paita. Kate, as a Spaniard, being one held of the Paita aristocracy, was expected to attend. She did so; and there also was the malignant Reyes. He came and seated himself purposely so as to shut out Kate from all view of the stage. She, who had nothing of the bully in her nature, and was a gentle creature when her wild Biscayan blood had not been kindled by insult, courteously requested him to move a little; upon which Reyes remarked that it was not in his power to oblige the clerk as to that, but that he *could* oblige him by cutting his throat. The tiger that slept in Catalina wakened at once. She seized him, and would have executed vengeance on the spot, but that a party of young men interposed to part them. The next day, when Kate (always ready to forget and forgive) was thinking no more of the row, Reyes passed; by spitting at the window, and other gestures insulting to Kate, again he roused her Spanish blood. Out she rushed, sword in hand—a duel began in the street, and very soon Kate's sword had passed into the heart of Reyes. Now that the mischief was done, the police were, as usual, all alive for the pleasure of avenging it. Kate found herself suddenly in a strong prison, and with small hopes of leaving it, except for execution. The relations of the dead man were potent in Paita, and clamorous for justice, so that the *corregidor*, in a case where he saw a very poor chance of being corrupted by bribes, felt it his duty to be sublimely incorruptible. The reader knows, however, that, amongst the relatives of the deceased bully, was that handsome lady, who differed as much from her cousin in her sentiments as to Kate, as she did in the extent of her credit with Mr. Urquiza. To *her* Kate wrote a note; and, using one of the Spanish King's gold coins for bribing the jailor, got it safely delivered. That, perhaps, was unnecessary; for the lady had been already on the alert, and had summoned Urquiza from Trujillo. By some means, not very luminously stated, and by paying proper fees in proper quarters, Kate was smuggled out of the prison at nightfall, and smuggled into a pretty house in the suburbs. Had she known exactly the footing she stood on as to the law, she would have been decided. As it was, she was uneasy, and jealous of mischief abroad; and, before supper, she understood it all. Urquiza briefly informed his clerk, that it would be requisite for him to marry the handsome lady. But why? Because, said Urquiza, after talking for hours with the *corregidor*, who was infamous for obstinacy, he had found it impossible to make him 'hear reason,' and release the prisoner, until this compromise of marriage was suggested. But how could public justice be pacified for the clerk's unfortunate homicide of Reyes, by a female cousin of the deceased man engaging to love, honor, and obey the clerk for life?

Kate could not see her way through this logic. 'Nonsense, my friend,' said Urquiza, 'you don't comprehend. As it stands, the affair is a murder, and hanging the penalty. But, if you marry into the murdered man's house, then it becomes a little family murder, all quiet and comfortable amongst ourselves. What has the *corregidor* to do with that? or the public either? Now, let me introduce the bride.' Supper entered at that moment, and the bride immediately after. The thoughtfulness of Kate was narrowly observed, and even alluded to, but politely ascribed to the natural anxieties of a prisoner, and the very imperfect state of liberation even yet from prison *surveillance*. Kate had, indeed, never been in so trying a situation before. The anxieties of the farewell night at St. Sebastian were nothing to this; because, even if she had failed *then*, a failure might not have been always irreparable. It was but to watch and wait. But now, at this supper table, she was not more alive to the nature of the peril than she was to the fact, that if, before the night closed, she did not by some means escape from it, she never *would* escape with life. The deception as to her sex, though resting on no motive that pointed to these people, or at all concerned them, would be resented as if it had. The lady would resent the case as a mockery; and Urquiza would lose his opportunity of delivering himself from an imperious mistress. According to the usages of the times and country, Kate knew that in twelve hours she would be assassinated.

People of infirmer resolution would have lingered at the supper table, for the sake of putting off the evil moment of final crisis. Not so Kate. She had revolved the case on all its sides in a few minutes, and had formed her resolution. This done, she was as ready for the trial at one moment as another; and, when the lady suggested that the hardships of a prison must have made repose desirable, Kate assented, and instantly rose. A sort of procession formed, for the purpose of doing honor to the interesting guest, and escorting him in pomp to his bedroom. Kate viewed it much in the same light as the procession to which for some days she had been expecting an invitation from the *corregidor*. Far ahead ran the servant-woman as a sort of outrider. Then came Urquiza, like a Pasha of two tails, who granted two sorts of credit, viz. unlimited and none at all, bearing two wax-lights, one in each hand, and wanting only cymbals and kettle-drums to express emphatically the pathos of his Castilian strut. Next came the bride, a little in advance of the clerk, but still turning obliquely towards him, and smiling graciously into his face. Lastly, bringing up the rear, came the prisoner—our Kate—the nun, the page, the mate, the clerk, the homicide, the convict; and, for this day only, by particular desire, the bridegroom elect.

It was Kate's fixed opinion, that, if for a moment she entered any bedroom having obviously no outlet, her fate would be that of an ox once driven within the shambles. Outside, the bullock might make some defence with his horns; but once in, with no space for turning, he is muffled and gagged. She carried her eye, therefore, like a hawk's, steady, though restless, for vigilant examination of every angle she turned. Before she entered any bedroom, she was resolved to reconnoiter it from the doorway, and, in case of necessity, show fight at once, before entering—as the best chance, after all, where all chances were bad. Everything ends; and at last the procession reached the bedroom door, the outrider having filed off to the rear. One glance sufficed to satisfy Kate that windows there were none, and, therefore, no outlet for escape. Treachery appeared even in *that*; and Kate, though unfortunately without arms, was now fixed for resistance. Mr. Urquiza entered first—'Sound the trumpets! Beat the drums!' There were, as we know already, no windows; but a slight interruption to Mr. Urquiza's pompous tread showed that there were steps downwards into the room. Those, thought Kate, will suit me even better. She had watched the unlocking of the bedroom door—she had lost nothing—she had marked that the key was left in the lock. At this moment, the beautiful lady, as one acquainted with the details of the house, turning with the air of a gracious monitress, held out her fair hand to guide Kate in careful descent of the steps. This had the air of taking out Kate to dance; and Kate, at that same moment, answering to it by the gesture of a modern waltzer, threw her arm behind the lady's waist, hurled her headlong down the steps right against Mr. Urquiza, draper and haberdasher; and then, with the speed of lightning, throwing the door *home* within its architrave, doubly locked the creditor and debtor into the rat-trap which they had prepared for herself.

The affrighted out-rider fled with horror: she already knew that the clerk had committed one homicide; a second would cost him still less thought; and thus it happened that egress was left easy. But, when out and free once more in the bright starry night, which way should Kate turn? The whole city would prove but a rat-trap for her, as bad as Mr. Urquiza's, if she was not off before morning. At a glance she comprehended that the sea was her only chance. To the port she fled. All was silent. Watchmen there were none. She jumped into a boat. To use the oars was dangerous, for she had no means of muffling them. But she contrived to hoist a sail, pushed off with a boat-hook, and was soon stretching across the water for the mouth of the harbor before a breeze light but favorable. Having cleared the difficulties of exit she lay down, and unintentionally fell asleep. When she awoke the sun had been up three or four hours; all was right otherwise; but had she not served as a sailor, Kate would have trembled upon finding that, during her long sleep of perhaps seven or eight hours, she had lost sight of land; by what distance she could only guess; and in what direction, was to some degree doubtful. All this, however, seemed a great advantage to the bold girl, throwing her thoughts back on the enemies she had left behind. The disadvantage was—having no breakfast, not even damaged biscuit; and some anxiety naturally arose as to ulterior prospects a little beyond the horizon of breakfast. But who's afraid? As sailors whistle for a wind, Catalina really had but to whistle for anything with energy, and it was sure to come. Like Caesar to the pilot of Dyrrhachium, she might have said, for the comfort of her poor timorous boat, (though destined soon to perish,) '*Catalinam vehis, et fortunas ejus.*' Meantime, being very doubtful as to the best course for sailing, and content if her course did but lie offshore, she 'carried on,' as sailors say, under easy sail, going, in fact, just whither and just how the Pacific breezes suggested in the gentlest of whispers. *All right behind,* was Kate's opinion; and, what was better, very soon she might say, *all right ahead:* for some hour or two before sunset, when dinner was for once becoming, even to Kate, the most interesting of subjects for meditation, suddenly a large ship began to swell upon the brilliant atmosphere. In those latitudes, and in those years, any ship was pretty sure to be Spanish: sixty years later the odds were in favor of its being an English buccaneer; which would have given a new direction to Kate's energy. Kate continued to make signals with a handkerchief whiter than the crocodile's of Ann. Dom. 1592, else it would hardly have been noticed. Perhaps, after all, it would not, but that the ship's course carried her very nearly across Kate's. The stranger lay-to for her. It was dark by the time Kate steered herself under the ship's quarter; and *then* was seen an instance of this girl's eternal wakefulness. Something was painted on the stern of her boat, she could not see *what*; but she judged that it would express some connection with the port that she had just quitted. Now it was her wish to break the chain of traces connecting her with such a scamp as Urquiza; since else, through his commercial correspondence, he might disperse over Peru a portrait of herself by no means flattering. How should she accomplish this? It was dark; and she stood, as you may see an Etonian do at times, rocking her little boat from side to side, until it had taken in water as much as might be agreeable. Too much it proved for the boat's constitution, and the boat perished of dropsy— Kate declining to tap it. She got a ducking herself; but what cared she? Up the ship's side she went, as gaily as ever, in those years when she was called pussy, she had raced after the nuns of St. Sebastian; jumped upon deck, and told the first lieutenant, when he questioned her about her adventures, quite as much truth as any man, under the rank of admiral, had a right to expect.

This ship was full of recruits for the Spanish army, and bound to Concepcion. Even in that destiny was an iteration, or repeating memorial of the significance that ran through Catalina's most casual adventures. She had enlisted amongst the soldiers; and, on reaching port, the very first person who came off from shore was a dashing young military officer, whom at once by his name and rank, (though she had never consciously seen him,) she identified as her own brother. He was splendidly situated in the service, being the Governor-General's secretary, besides his rank as a cavalry officer; and, his errand on board being to inspect the recruits, naturally, on reading in the roll one of them described as a Biscayan, the ardent young man came up with high-bred courtesy to Catalina, took the young recruit's hand with kindness, feeling that to be a compatriot at so great a distance was to be a sort of relative, and asked with emotion after old boyish remembrances. There was a scriptural pathos in what followed, as if it were some scene of domestic re-union, opening itself from patriarchal ages. The young officer was the eldest son of the house, and had left Spain when Catalina was only three years old. But, singularly enough, Catalina it was, the little wild cat that he yet remembered seeing at St. Sebastian's, upon whom his earliest inquiries settled. 'Did the recruit know his family, the De Erausos?' O yes, every body knew *them*. 'Did the recruit know little Catalina?' Catalina smiled, as she replied that she did; and gave such an animated description of the little fiery wretch, as made the officer's eye flash with gratified tenderness, and with certainty that the recruit was no counterfeit Biscayan. Indeed, you know, if Kate couldn't give a good description of 'Pussy,' who could? The issue of the interview was—that the officer insisted on Kate's making a home of his quarters. He did other services for his unknown sister. He placed her as a trooper in his own regiment, and favored her in many a way that is open to one having authority. But the person, after all, that did most to serve our Kate, was Kate. War was then raging with Indians, both from Chili and Peru. Kate had always done her duty in action; but at length, in the decisive battle of Puren, there was an opening for doing something more. Havoc had been made of her own squadron: most of the officers were killed, and the standard was carried off. Kate gathered around her a small party—galloped after the Indian column that was carrying away the trophy—charged—saw all her own party killed—but (in spite of wounds on her face and shoulder) succeeded in bearing away the recovered standard. She rode up to the general and his staff; she dismounted; she rendered up her prize; and fainted away, much less from the blinding blood, than from the tears of joy which dimmed her eyes, as the general, waving his sword in admiration over her head, pronounced our Kate on the spot an *Alferez*, [Footnote: *Alferez*. This rank in the Spanish army is, or was, on a level with the modern *sous-lieutenant* of France.] or standard-bearer, with a commission from the King of Spain and the Indies. Bonny Kate! Noble Kate! I would there were not two centuries laid between us, so that I might have the pleasure of kissing thy fair hand.

Kate had the good sense to see the danger of revealing her sex, or her relationship, even to her own brother. The grasp of the Church never relaxed, never 'prescribed,' unless freely and by choice. The nun, if discovered, would have been taken out of the horse-barracks, or the dragoon-saddle. She had the firmness, therefore, for many years, to resist the sisterly impulses that sometimes suggested such a confidence. For years, and those years the most important of her life—the years that developed her character—she lived undetected as a brilliant cavalry officer under her brother's patronage. And the bitterest grief in poor Kate's whole life, was the tragical (and, were it not fully attested, one might say the ultra-scenical,) event that dissolved their long connection. Let me spend a word of apology on poor Kate's errors. We all commit many; both you and I, reader. No, stop; that's not civil. You, reader, I know, are a saint; I am *not*, though very near it. I *do* err at long intervals; and then I think with indulgence of the many circumstances that plead for this poor girl. The Spanish armies of that day inherited, from the days of Cortez and Pizarro, shining remembrances of martial prowess, and the very worst of ethics. To think little of bloodshed, to quarrel, to fight, to gamble, to plunder, belonged to the very atmosphere of a camp, to its indolence, to its ancient traditions. In your own defence, you were obliged to do such things. Besides all these grounds of evil, the Spanish army had just there an extra demoralization from a war with savages—faithless and bloody. Do not think, I beseech you, too much, reader, of killing a man. That word '*kill*' is sprinkled over every page of Kate's own autobiography. It ought not to be read by the light of these days. Yet, how if a man that she killed were——? Hush! It was sad; but is better hurried over in a few words. Years after this period, a young officer one day dining with Kate, entreated her to become his second in a duel. Such things were every-day affairs. However, Kate had reasons for declining the service, and did so. But the officer, as he was sullenly departing, said—that, if he were killed, (as he thought he *should* be,) his death would lie at Kate's door. I do not take *his* view of the case, and am not moved by his rhetoric or his logic. Kate *was*, and relented. The duel was fixed for eleven at night, under the walls of a monastery. Unhappily the night proved unusually dark, so that the two principals had to tie white handkerchiefs round their elbows, in order to descry each other. In the confusion they wounded each other mortally. Upon that, according to a usage not peculiar to Spaniards, but extending (as doubtless the reader knows) for a century longer to our own countrymen, the two seconds were obliged in honor to do something towards avenging their principals. Kate had her usual fatal luck. Her sword passed sheer through the body of her opponent: this unknown opponent falling dead, had just breath left to cry out, 'Ah, villain, you have killed me,' in a voice of horrific reproach; and the voice was the voice of her brother!

The monks of the monastery, under whose silent shadows this murderous duel had taken place, roused by the clashing of swords and the angry shouts of combatants, issued out with torches to find one only of the four officers surviving. Every convent and altar had a right of asylum for a short period. According to the custom, the monks carried Kate, insensible with anguish of mind, to the sanctuary of their chapel. There for some days they detained her; but then, having furnished her with a horse and some provisions, they turned her adrift. Which way should the unhappy fugitive turn? In blindness of heart she turned towards the sea. It was the sea that had brought her to Peru; it was the sea that would perhaps carry her away. It was the sea that had first showed her this land and its golden hopes; it was the sea that ought to hide from her its fearful remembrances. The sea it was that had twice spared her life in extremities; the sea it was that might now if it chose, take back the bauble that it had spared in vain.

KATE'S PASSAGE OVER THE ANDES

Three days our poor heroine followed the coast. Her horse was then almost unable to move; and on *his* account, she turned inland to a thicket for grass and shelter. As she drew near to it, a voice challenged—'*Who goes there?*' Kate answered, '*Spain.*' '*What people?*' '*A friend.*' It was two soldiers, deserters, and almost starving. Kate shared her provisions with these men: and, on hearing their plan, which was to go over the Cordilleras, she agreed to join the party. *Their* object was the wild one of seeking the river *Dorado*, whose waters rolled along golden sands, and whose pebbles were emeralds. *Hers* was to throw herself upon a line the least liable to pursuit, and the readiest for a new chapter of life in which oblivion might be found for the past. After a few days of incessant climbing and fatigue, they found themselves in the regions of perpetual snow. Summer would come as vainly to this kingdom of frost as to the grave of her brother. No fire, but the fire of human blood in youthful veins, could ever be kept burning in these aerial solitudes. Fuel was rarely to be found, and kindling a secret hardly known except to Indians. However, our Kate can do everything, and she's the girl, if ever girl *did* such a thing, or ever girl did *not* such a thing, that I back at any odds for crossing the Cordilleras. I would bet you something now, reader, if I thought you would deposit your stakes by return of post, (as they play at chess through the post-office,) that Kate does the trick, that she gets down to the other side; that the soldiers do *not*: and that the horse, if preserved at all, is preserved in a way that will leave him very little to boast of.

The party had gathered wild berries and esculent roots at the foot of the mountains, and the horse was of very great use in carrying them. But this larder was soon emptied. There was nothing then to carry; so that the horse's value, as a beast of burthen, fell cent per cent. In fact, very soon he could not carry himself, and it became easy to calculate when he would reach the bottom on the wrong side the Cordilleras. He took three steps back for one upwards. A council of war being held, the small army resolved to slaughter their horse. He, though a member of the expedition, had no vote, and if he had the votes would have stood three to one—majority, two against him. He was cut into quarters; which surprises me; for, unless *one* quarter was considered his own share, it reminds one too much of this amongst the many *facetiæ* of English midshipmen, who ask (on any one of their number looking sulky) 'if it is his intention to marry and retire from the service upon a superannuation of £4 4s. 4 1/2d. a year, paid quarterly by way of bothering the purser.' The purser can't do it with the help of farthings. And as respects aliquot parts, four shares among three persons are as incommensurable as a guinea is against any attempt at giving change in half-crowns. However, this was all the preservation that the horse found. No saltpetre or sugar could be had: but the frost was antiseptic. And the horse was preserved in as useful a sense as ever apricots were preserved or strawberries.

On a fire, painfully devised out of broom and withered leaves, a horse-steak was dressed, for drink, snow as allowed *a discretion*. This ought to have revived the party, and Kate, perhaps, it *did*. But the poor deserters were thinly clad, and they had not the boiling heart of Catalina. More and more they drooped. Kate did her best to cheer them. But the march was nearly at an end for *them*, and they were going in one half hour to receive their last billet. Yet, before this consummation, they have a strange spectacle to see; such as few places could show, but the upper chambers of the Cordilleras. They had reached a billowy scene of rocky masses, large and small, looking shockingly black on their perpendicular sides as they rose out of the vast snowy expanse. Upon the highest of these, that was accessible, Kate mounted to look around her, and she saw—oh, rapture at such an hour!—a man sitting on a shelf of rock with a gun by his side. She shouted with joy to her comrades, and ran down to communicate the joyful news. Here was a sportsman, watching, perhaps, for an eagle; and now they would have relief. One man's cheek kindled with the hectic of sudden joy, and he rose eagerly to march. The other was fast sinking under the fatal sleep that frost sends before herself as her merciful minister of death; but hearing in his dream the tidings of relief, and assisted by his friends, he also staggeringly arose. It could not be three minutes' walk, Kate thought, to the station of the sportsman. That thought supported them all. Under Kate's guidance, who had taken a sailor's glance at the bearings, they soon unthreaded the labyrinth of rocks so far as to bring the man within view. He had not left his resting-place; their steps on the soundless snow, naturally, he could not hear; and, as their road brought them upon him from the rear, still less could he see them. Kate hailed him; but so keenly was he absorbed in some speculation, or in the object of his watching, that he took no notice of them, not even moving his head. Kate began to think there would be another man to rouse from sleep. Coming close behind him, she touched his shoulder, and said, 'My friend, are you sleeping?' Yes, he *was* sleeping; sleeping the sleep from which there is no awaking; and the slight touch of Kate having disturbed the equilibrium of the corpse, down it rolled on the snow: the frozen body rang like a hollow iron cylinder; the face uppermost and blue with mould, mouth open, teeth ghastly and bleaching in the frost, and a frightful grin upon the lips. This dreadful spectacle finished the struggles of the weaker man, who sank and died at once. The other made an effort with so much spirit, that, in Kate's opinion, horror had acted upon him beneficially as a stimulant. But it was not really so. It was a spasm of morbid strength; a collapse succeeded; his blood began to freeze; he sat down in spite of Kate, and *he* also died without further struggle. Gone are the poor suffering deserters; stretched and bleaching upon the snow; and insulted discipline is avenged. Great kings have long arms; and sycophants are ever at hand for the errand of the potent. What had frost and snow to do with the quarrel? Yet *they* made themselves sycophantic servants of the King of Spain; and *they* dogged his deserters up to the summit of the Cordilleras, more surely than any Spanish bloodhound, or any Spanish tirailleur's bullet.

Now is our Kate standing alone on the summits of the Andes, in solitude that is shocking, for she is alone with her own afflicted conscience. Twice before she had stood in solitude as deep upon the wild — wild waters of the Pacific; but her conscience had been then untroubled. Now, is there nobody left that can help; her horse is dead — the soldiers are dead. There is nobody that she can speak to except God; and very soon you will find that she *does* speak to him; for already on these vast aerial deserts He has been whispering to *her*. The condition of Kate is exactly that of Coleridge's 'Ancient Mariner.' But possibly, reader, you may be amongst the many careless readers that have never fully understood what that condition was. Suffer me to enlighten you, else you ruin the story of the mariner; and by losing all its pathos, lose half the jewels of its beauty.

There are three readers of the 'Ancient Mariner.' The first is gross enough to fancy all the imagery of the mariner's visions delivered by the poet for actual facts of experience; which being impossible, the whole pulverizes, for that reader, into a baseless fairy tale. The second reader is wiser than *that*; he knows that the imagery is *not* baseless; it is the imagery of febrile delirium; really seen, but not seen as an external reality. The mariner had caught the pestilential fever, which carried off all his mates; he only had survived—the delirium had vanished; but the visions that had haunted the delirium remained. 'Yes,' says the third reader, 'they remained; naturally they did, being scorched by fever into his brain; but how did they happen to remain on his belief as gospel truths? The delirium had vanished: why had not the painted scenery of the delirium vanished, except as visionary memorials of a sorrow that was cancelled? Why was it that craziness settled upon this mariner's brain, driving him, as if he were a Cain, or another Wandering Jew, to 'pass like night—from land to land;' and, at uncertain intervals, wrenching him until he made rehearsal of his errors, even at the hard price of 'holding children from their play, and old men from the chimney corner?' [Footnote: The beautiful words of Sir Philip Sidney, in his '*Defense of Poesie.*'] That craziness, as the *third reader* deciphers, rose out of a deeper soil than any bodily affection. It had its root in penitential sorrow. Oh, bitter is the sorrow to a conscientious heart, when, too late, it discovers the depth of a love that has been trampled under foot! This mariner had slain the creature that, on all the earth, loved him best. In the darkness of his cruel superstition he had done it, to save his human brothers from a fancied inconvenience; and yet, by that very act of cruelty, he had himself called destruction upon their heads. The Nemesis that followed punished *him* through *them*—him, that wronged, through those that wrongfully he sought to benefit. That spirit who watches over the sanctities of love is a strong angel—is a jealous angel; and this angel it was

'That lov'd the bird, that lov'd the man,
That shot him with his bow.'

He it was that followed the cruel archer into silent and slumbering seas;

'Nine fathom deep he had follow'd him
Through the realms of mist and snow.'

This jealous angel it was that pursued the man into noon-day darkness, and the vision of dying oceans, into delirium, and finally, (when recovered from disease) into an unsettled mind.

Such, also, had been the offence of Kate; such, also was the punishment that now is dogging her steps. She, like the mariner, had slain the one sole creature that loved her upon the whole wide earth; she, like the mariner, for this offence, had been hunted into frost and snow—very soon will be hunted into delirium; and from *that* (if she escapes with life) will be hunted into the trouble of a heart that cannot rest. There was the excuse of one darkness for *her*; there was the excuse of another darkness for the mariner. But, with all the excuses that earth, and the darkness of earth, can furnish, bitter it would be for you or me, reader, through every hour of life, waking or dreaming, to look back upon one fatal moment when we had pierced the heart that would have died for us. In this only the darkness had been merciful to Kate—that it had hidden for ever from her victim the hand that slew him. But now in such utter solitude, her thoughts ran back to their earliest interview. She remembered with anguish, how, on first touching the shores of America, almost the very first word that met her ear had been from *him*, the brother whom she had killed, about the 'Pussy' of times long past; how the gallant young man had hung upon her words, as in her native Basque she described her own mischievous little self, of twelve years back; how his color went and came, whilst his loving memory of the little sister was revived by her own descriptive traits, giving back, as in a mirror, the fawn-like grace, the squirrel-like restlessness, that once had kindled his own delighted laughter; how he would take no denial, but showed on the spot, that, simply to have touched—to have kissed—to have played with the little wild thing, that glorified, by her innocence, the gloom of St. Sebastian's cloisters, gave a *right* to his hospitality; how, through *him* only, she had found a welcome in camps; how, through *him*, she had found the avenue to honor and distinction. And yet this brother, so loving and generous, it was that she had dismissed from life. She paused; she turned round, as if looking back for his grave; she saw the dreadful wildernesses of snow which already she had traversed.

Silent they were at this season, even as in the panting heats of noon, the Zaarrahs of the torrid zone are oftentimes silent. Dreadful was the silence; it was the nearest thing to the silence of the grave. Graves were at the foot of the Andes, *that* she knew too well; graves were at the summit of the Andes, *that* she saw too well. And, as she gazed, a sudden thought flashed upon her, when her eyes settled upon the corpses of the poor deserters—could she, like *them*, have been all this while unconsciously executing judgment upon herself? Running from a wrath that was doubtful, into the very jaws of a wrath that was inexorable? Flying in panic—and behold! there was no man that pursued? For the first time in her life, Kate trembled. *Not* for the first time, Kate wept. Far less for the first time was it, that Kate bent her knee—that Kate clasped her hands—that Kate prayed. But it *was* the first time that she prayed as *they* pray, for whom no more hope is left but in prayer.

Here let me pause a moment for the sake of making somebody angry. A Frenchman, who sadly misjudges Kate, looking at her through a Parisian opera-glass, gives it as *his* opinion—that, because Kate first *records* her prayer on this occasion, therefore, now first of all she prayed. *I* think not so. *I* love this Kate, blood-stained as she is; and I could not love a woman that never bent her knee in thankfulness or in supplication. However, we have all a right to our own little opinion; and it is not you, '*mon cher*,' you Frenchman, that I am angry with, but somebody else that stands behind you. You, Frenchman, and your compatriots, I love oftentimes for your festal gaiety of heart; and I quarrel only with your levity and that eternal worldliness that freezes too fiercely—that absolutely blisters with its frost—like the upper air of the Andes. *You* speak of Kate only as too readily you speak of all women; the instinct of a natural scepticism being to scoff at all hidden depths of truth. Else you are civil enough to Kate; and your '*homage*' (such as it may happen to be) is always at the service of a woman on the shortest notice. But behind *you*, I see a worse fellow; a gloomy fanatic; a religious sycophant that seeks to propitiate his circle by bitterness against the offences that are most unlike his own. And against him, I must say one word for Kate to the too hasty reader. This villain, whom I mark for a shot if he does not get out of the way, opens his fire on our Kate under shelter of a lie. For there is a standing lie in the very constitution of civil society, a *necessity* of error, misleading us as to the proportions of crime. Mere necessity obliges man to create many acts into felonies, and to punish them as the heaviest offences, which his better sense teaches him secretly to regard as perhaps among the lightest. Those poor deserters, for instance, were they necessarily without excuse? They might have been oppressively used; but in critical times of war, no matter for the individual palliations, the deserter from his colors *must* be shot: there is no help for it: as in extremities of general famine, we shoot the man (alas! we are *obliged* to shoot him) that is found robbing the common stores in order to feed his own perishing children, though the offence is hardly visible in the sight of God. Only blockheads adjust their scale of guilt to the scale of human punishments. Now, our wicked friend the fanatic, who calumniates Kate, abuses the advantage which, for such a purpose, he derives from the exaggerated social estimate of all violence. Personal security being so main an object of social union, we are obliged to frown upon all modes of violence as hostile to the central principle of that union. We are *obliged* to rate it, according to the universal results towards which it tends, and scarcely at all, according to the special condition of circumstances, in which it may originate. Hence a horror arises for that class of offences, which is (philosophically speaking) exaggerated; and by daily use, the ethics of a police-office translate themselves, insensibly, into the ethics even of religious people. But I tell that sycophantish fanatic—not this only, viz., that he abuses unfairly, against Kate, the advantage which he has from the inevitably distorted bias of society; but also, I tell him this second little thing, viz., that upon turning away the glass from that one obvious aspect of Kate's character, her too fiery disposition to vindicate all rights by violence, and viewing her in relation to *general* religious capacities, she was a thousand times more promisingly endowed than himself. It is impossible to be noble in many things, without having many points of contact with true religion. If you deny *that* you it is that calumniate religion. Kate *was* noble in many things. Her worst errors never took a shape of self-interest or deceit. She was brave, she was generous, she was forgiving, she bore no malice, she was full of truth—qualities that God loves either in man or woman. She hated sycophants and dissemblers. *I* hate them; and more than ever at this moment on her behalf. I wish she were but here—to give a punch on the head to that fellow who traduces her. And, coming round again to the occasion from which this short digression has started, viz., the question raised by the Frenchman—whether Kate were a person likely to *pray* under other circumstances than those of extreme danger? I offer it as *my* opinion that she was. Violent people are not always such from choice, but perhaps from situation. And, though the circumstances of Kate's position allowed her little means for realizing her own wishes, it is certain that those wishes pointed continually to peace and an unworldly happiness, if *that* were possible. The stormy clouds that enveloped her in camps, opened overhead at intervals—showing her a far distant blue serene. She yearned, at many times, for the rest which is not in camps or armies; and it is certain, that she ever combined with any plans or day-dreams of tranquillity, as their most essential ally, some aid derived from that dovelike religion which, at St. Sebastian's, as an infant and through girlhood, she had been taught so profoundly to adore.

Now, let us rise from this discussion of Kate against libellers, as Kate herself is rising from prayer, and consider, in conjunction with *her*, the character and promise of that dreadful ground which lies immediately before her. What is to be thought of it? I could wish we had a theodolite here, and a spirit-level, and other instruments, for settling some important questions. Yet no: on consideration, if one *had* a wish allowed by that kind fairy, without whose assistance it would be quite impossible to send, even for the spirit-level, nobody would throw away the wish upon things so paltry. I would not put the fairy upon any such errand: I would order the good creature to bring no spirit-level, but a stiff glass of spirits for Kate—a palanquin, and relays of fifty stout bearers—all drunk, in order that they might not feel the cold. The main interest at this moment, and the main difficulty—indeed, the 'open question' of the case—was, to ascertain whether the ascent were yet accomplished or not; and when would the descent commence? or had it, perhaps, long commenced? The character of the ground, in those immediate successions that could be connected by the eye, decided nothing; for the undulations of the level had been so continual for miles, as to perplex any eye but an engineer's, in attempting to judge whether, upon the whole, the tendency were upwards or downwards. Possibly it was yet neither way; it is, indeed, probable, that Kate had been for some time travelling along a series of terraces, that traversed the whole breadth of the topmost area at that point of crossing the Cordilleras, and which perhaps, but not certainly, compensated any casual tendencies downwards by corresponding reascents. Then came the question—how long would these terraces yet continue? and had the ascending parts *really* balanced the descending?—upon *that* seemed to rest the final chance for Kate. Because, unless she very soon reached a lower level, and a warmer atmosphere, mere weariness would oblige her to lie down, under a fierceness of cold, that would not suffer her to rise after once losing the warmth of motion; or, inversely, if she even continued in motion, mere extremity of cold would, of itself, speedily absorb the little surplus energy for moving, which yet remained unexhausted by weariness.

At this stage of her progress, and whilst the agonizing question seemed yet as indeterminate as ever, Kate's struggle with despair, which had been greatly soothed by the fervor of her prayer, revolved upon her in deadlier blackness. All turned, she saw, upon a race against time, and the arrears of the road; and she, poor thing! how little qualified could *she* be, in such a condition, for a race of any kind; and against two such obstinate brutes as time and space! This hour of the progress, this noontide of Kate's struggle, must have been the very crisis of the whole. Despair was rapidly tending to ratify itself. Hope, in any degree, would be a cordial for sustaining her efforts. But to flounder along a dreadful chaos of snow-drifts, or snow-chasms, towards a point of rock, which, being turned, should expose only another interminable succession of the same character—might *that* be endured by ebbing spirits, by stiffening limbs, by the ghastly darkness that was now beginning to gather upon the inner eye? And, if once despair became triumphant, all the little arrear of physical strength would collapse at once.

Oh! verdure of human fields, cottages of men and women, (that now suddenly seemed all brothers and sisters,) cottages with children around them at play, that are so far below—oh! summer and spring, flowers and blossoms, to which, as to *his* symbols, God has given the gorgeous privilege of rehearsing for ever upon earth his most mysterious perfection—Life, and the resurrections of Life—is it indeed true, that poor Kate must never see you more? Mutteringly she put that question to herself. But strange are the caprices of ebb and flow in the deep fountains of human sensibilities. At this very moment, when the utter incapacitation of despair was gathering fast at Kate's heart, a sudden lightening shot far into her spirit, a reflux almost supernatural, from the earliest effects of her prayer. A thought had struck her all at once, and this thought prompted her immediately to turn round. Perhaps it was in some blind yearning after the only memorials of life in this frightful region, that she fixed her eye upon a point of hilly ground by which she identified the spot near which the three corpses were lying. The silence seemed deeper than ever. Neither was there any phantom memorial of life for the eye or for the ear, nor wing of bird, nor echo, nor green leaf, nor creeping thing, that moved or stirred, upon the soundless waste. Oh, what a relief to this burthen of silence would be a human groan! Here seemed a motive for still darker despair. And yet, at that very moment, a pulse of joy began to thaw the ice at her heart. It struck her, as she reviewed the ground, that undoubtedly it had been for some time slowly descending. Her senses were much dulled by suffering; but this thought it was, suggested by a sudden apprehension of a continued descending movement, which had caused her to turn round. Sight had confirmed the suggestion first derived from her own steps. The distance attained was now sufficient to establish the tendency. Oh, yes, yes, to a certainty she had been descending for some time. Frightful was the spasm of joy which whispered that the worst was over. It was as when the shadow of midnight, that murderers had relied on, is passing away from your beleagured shelter, and dawn will soon be manifest. It was as when a flood, that all day long has raved against the walls of your house, has ceased (you suddenly think) to rise; yes! measured by a golden plummet, it *is* sinking beyond a doubt, and the darlings of your household are saved. Kate faced round in agitation to her proper direction. She saw, what previously, in her stunning confusion, she had *not* seen, that, hardly two stones' throw in advance, lay a mass of rock, split as into a gateway. Through that opening it now became probable that the road was lying. Hurrying forward, she passed within the natural gates. Gates of paradise they were. Ah, what a vista did that gateway expose before her dazzled eye? what a revelation of heavenly promise? Full two miles long, stretched a long narrow glen, everywhere descending, and in many parts rapidly. All was now placed beyond a doubt. She *was* descending—for hours, perhaps, *had* been descending insensibly, the mighty staircase. Yes, Kate is leaving behind her the kingdom of frost and the victories of death. Two miles farther there may be rest, if there is not shelter. And very soon, as the crest of her new-born happiness, she distinguished at the other end of that rocky vista, a pavilion-shaped mass of dark green foliage—a belt of trees, such as we see in the lovely parks of England, but islanded by a screen (though not everywhere occupied by the usurpations) of a thick bushy undergrowth. Oh, verdure of dark olive foliage, offered suddenly to fainting eyes, as if by some winged patriarchal herald of wrath relenting—solitary Arab's tent, rising with saintly signals of peace, in the dreadful desert, must Kate indeed die even yet, whilst she sees but cannot reach you? Outpost on the frontier of man's dominions, standing within life, but looking out upon everlasting death, wilt thou hold up the anguish of thy mocking invitation, only to betray? Never, perhaps, in this world was the line so exquisitely grazed, that parts salvation and ruin. As the dove to her dove-cot from the swooping hawk—as the Christian pinnace to Christian batteries, from the bloody Mahometan corsair, so flew—so tried to fly towards the anchoring thickets, that, alas! could not weigh their anchors and make sail to meet her—the poor exhausted Kate from the vengeance of pursuing frost.

And she reached them; staggering, fainting, reeling, she entered beneath the canopy of umbrageous trees. But, as oftentimes, the Hebrew fugitive to a city of refuge, flying for his life before the avenger of blood, was pressed so hotly that, on entering the archway of what seemed to *him* the heavenly city-gate, as he kneeled in deep thankfulness to kiss its holy merciful shadow, he could not rise again, but sank instantly with infant weakness into sleep— sometimes to wake no more; so sank, so collapsed upon the ground, without power to choose her couch, and with little prospect of ever rising again to her feet, the martial nun. She lay as luck had ordered it, with her head screened by the undergrowth of bushes, from any gales that might arise; she lay exactly as she sank, with her eyes up to heaven; and thus it was that the nun saw, before falling asleep, the two sights that upon earth are fittest for the closing eyes of a nun, whether destined to open again, or to close for ever. She saw the interlacing of boughs overhead forming a dome, that seemed like the dome of a cathedral. She saw through the fretwork of the foliage, another dome, far beyond, the dome of an evening sky, the dome of some heavenly cathedral, not built with hands. She saw upon this upper dome the vesper lights, all alive with pathetic grandeur of coloring from a sunset that had just been rolling down like a chorus. She had not, till now, consciously observed the time of day; whether it were morning, or whether it were afternoon, in her confusion she had not distinctly known. But now she whispered to herself—'*It is evening:*' and what lurked half unconsciously in these words might be—'The sun, that rejoices, has finished his daily toil; man, that labors, has finished *his*; I, that suffer, have finished mine.' That might be what she thought, but what she *said* was—'It is evening; and the hour is come when the *Angelus* is sounding through St. Sebastian.' What made her think of St. Sebastian, so far away in depths of space and time? Her brain was wandering, now that her feet were *not*; and, because her eyes had descended from the heavenly to the earthly dome, *that* made her think of earthly cathedrals, and of cathedral choirs, and of St. Sebastian's chapel, with its silvery bells that carried the *Angelus* far into mountain recesses. Perhaps, as her wanderings increased, she thought herself back in childhood; became 'pussy' once again; fancied that all since then was a frightful dream; that she was not upon the dreadful Andes, but still kneeling in the holy chapel at vespers; still innocent as then; loved as then she had been loved;

and that all men were liars, who said her hand was ever stained with blood. Little enough is mentioned of the delusions which possessed her; but that little gives a key to the impulse which her palpitating heart obeyed, and which her rambling brain for ever reproduced in multiplying mirrors. Restlessness kept her in waking dreams for a brief half hour. But then, fever and delirium would wait no longer; the killing exhaustion would no longer be refused; the fever, the delirium, and the exhaustion, swept in together with power like an army with banners; and the nun ceased through the gathering twilight any more to watch the cathedrals of earth, or the more solemn cathedrals that rose in the heavens above.

All night long she slept in her verdurous St. Bernard's hospice without awaking, and whether she would *ever* awake seemed to depend upon an accident. The slumber that towered above her brain was like that fluctuating silvery column which stands in scientific tubes sinking, rising, deepening, lightening, contracting, expanding; or like the mist that sits, through sultry afternoons, upon the river of the American St. Peter, sometimes rarefying for minutes into sunny gauze, sometimes condensing for hours into palls of funeral darkness. You fancy that, after twelve hours of *any* sleep, she must have been refreshed; better at least than she was last night. Ah! but sleep is not always sent upon missions of refreshment. Sleep is sometimes the secret chamber in which death arranges his machinery. Sleep is sometimes that deep mysterious atmosphere, in which the human spirit is slowly unsettling its wings for flight from earthly tenements. It is now eight o'clock in the morning; and, to all appearance, if Kate should receive no aid before noon, when next the sun is departing to his rest, Kate will be departing to hers; when next the sun is holding out his golden Christian signal to man, that the hour is come for letting his anger go down, Kate will be sleeping away for ever into the arms of brotherly forgiveness.

What is wanted just now for Kate, supposing Kate herself to be wanted by this world, is, that this world would be kind enough to send her a little brandy before it is too late. The simple truth was, and a truth which I have known to take place in more ladies than Kate, who died or did *not* die, accordingly, as they had or had not an adviser like myself, capable of giving so sound an opinion, that the jewelly star of life had descended too far down the arch towards setting, for any chance of re-ascending by *spontaneous* effort. The fire was still burning in secret, but needed to be rekindled by potent artificial breath. It lingered, and *might* linger, but would never culminate again without some stimulus from earthly vineyards. [Footnote: Though not exactly in the same circumstances as Kate, or sleeping, *à la belle étoile*, on a declivity of the Andes, I have known (or heard circumstantially reported) the cases of many ladies besides Kate, who were in precisely the same critical danger of perishing for want of a little brandy. A dessert spoonful or two would have saved them. Avaunt! you wicked 'Temperance' medallist! repent as fast as ever you can, or, perhaps the next time we hear of you, *anasarca* and *hydro-thorax* will be running after you to punish your shocking excesses in water. Seriously, the case is one of constant recurrence, and constantly ending fatally from *unseasonable* and pedantic rigor of temperance. The fact is, that the medical profession composes the most generous and liberal body of men amongst us; taken generally, by much the most enlightened; but professionally, the most timid. Want of boldness in the administration of opium, &c., though they can be bold enough with mercury, is their besetting infirmity. And from this infirmity females suffer most. One instance I need hardly mention, the fatal case of an august lady, mourned by nations, with respect to whom it was, and is, the belief of multitudes to this hour (well able to judge), that she would have been saved by a glass of brandy; and her attendant, who shot himself, came to think so too late—too late for *her*, and too late for himself. Amongst many cases of the same nature, which personally I have been acquainted with, twenty years ago, a man, illustrious for his intellectual accomplishments, mentioned to me that his own wife, during her first or second confinement, was suddenly reported to him, by one of her female attendants, (who slipped away unobserved by the medical people,) as undoubtedly sinking fast. He hurried to her chamber, and *saw* that it was so. The presiding medical authority, however, was inexorable. 'Oh, by no means,' shaking his ambrosial wig, 'any stimulant at this crisis would be fatal.' But no authority could overrule the concurrent testimony of all symptoms, and of all unprofessional opinions. By some pious falsehood my friend smuggled the doctor out of the room, and immediately smuggled a glass of brandy into the poor lady's lips. She recovered with magical power. The doctor is now dead, and went to his grave under the delusive persuasion—that not any vile glass of brandy, but the stern refusal of all brandy, was the thing that saved his collapsing patient. The patient herself, who might naturally know something of the matter, was of a different opinion. She sided with the factious body around her bed, (comprehending all beside the doctor,) who felt sure that death was rapidly approaching, *barring* that brandy. The same result in the same appalling crisis, I have known repeatedly produced by twenty-five drops of laudanum. An obstinate man will say—'Oh, never listen to a non-medical man like this writer. Consult in such a case your medical adviser.' You will, will you? Then let me tell you, that you are missing the very logic of all I have been saying for the improvement of blockheads, which is—that you should consult any man *but* a medical man, since no other man has any obstinate prejudice of professional timidity. N. B.—I prescribe for Kate *gratis*, because she, poor thing! has so little to give.

But from other ladies, who may have the happiness to benefit by my advice, I expect a fee—not so large a one considering the service—a flowering plant, suppose the *second* best in their collection. I know it would be of no use to ask for the *very* best, (which else I could wish to do,) because that would only be leading them into little fibs. I don't insist on a *Yucca gloriosa*, or a *Magnolia speciosissima*, (I hope there *is* such a plant)—a rose or a violet will do. I am sure there is such a plant as that. And if they settle their debts justly, I shall very soon be master of the prettiest little conservatory in England. For, treat it not as a jest, reader; no case of timid practice is so fatally frequent.]

Kate was ever lucky, though ever unfortunate; and the world, being of my opinion that Kate was worth saving, made up its mind about half-past eight o'clock in the morning to save her. Just at that time, when the night was over, and its sufferings were hidden—in one of those intermitting gleams that for a moment or two lightened the clouds of her slumber, Kate's dull ear caught a sound that for years had spoken a familiar language to *her*. What was it? It was the sound, though muffled and deadened, like the ear that heard it, of horsemen advancing. Interpreted by the tumultuous dreams of Kate, was it the cavalry of Spain, at whose head so often she had charged the bloody Indian scalpers? Was it, according to the legend of ancient days, cavalry that had been sown by her brother's blood, cavalry that rose from the ground on an inquest of retribution, and were racing up the Andes to seize her? Her dreams that had opened sullenly to the sound waited for no answer, but closed again into pompous darkness. Happily, the horsemen had caught the glimpse of some bright ornament, clasp, or aiguillette, on Kate's dress. They were hunters and foresters from below; servants in the household of a beneficent lady; and in some pursuit of flying game had wandered beyond their ordinary limits. Struck by the sudden scintillation from Kate's dress played upon by the morning sun, they rode up to the thicket. Great was their surprise, great their pity, to see a young officer in uniform stretched within the bushes upon the ground, and perhaps dying. Borderers from childhood on this dreadful frontier, sacred to winter and death, they understood the case at once. They dismounted: and with the tenderness of women, raising the poor frozen cornet in their arms, washed her temples with brandy, whilst one, at intervals, suffered a few drops to trickle within her lips. As the restoration of a warm bed was now most likely to be successful, they lifted the helpless stranger upon a horse, walking on each side with supporting arms. Once again our Kate is in the saddle; once again a Spanish Caballador. But Kate's bridle-hand is deadly cold. And her spurs, that she had never unfastened since leaving the monastic asylum, hung as idle as the flapping sail that fills unsteadily with the breeze upon a stranded ship.

This procession had some miles to go, and over difficult ground; but at length it reached the forest-like park and the chateau of the wealthy proprietress. Kate was still half-frozen and speechless, except at intervals. Heavens! can this corpse-like, languishing young woman, be the Kate that once, in her radiant girlhood, rode with a handful of comrades into a column of two thousand enemies, that saw her comrades die, that persisted when all were dead, that tore from the heart of all resistance the banner of her native Spain? Chance and change have 'written strange defeatures in her face.' Much is changed; but some things are not changed: there is still kindness that overflows with pity: there is still helplessness that asks for this pity without a voice: she is now received by a Senora, not less kind than that maternal aunt, who, on the night of her birth, first welcomed her to a loving home; and she, the heroine of Spain, is herself as helpless now as that little lady who, then at ten minutes of age, was kissed and blessed by all the household of St. Sebastian.

Let us suppose Kate placed in a warm bed. Let us suppose her in a few hours recovering steady consciousness; in a few days recovering some power of self-support; in a fortnight able to seek the gay saloon, where the Senora was sitting alone, and rendering thanks, with that deep sincerity which ever characterized our wild-hearted Kate, for the critical services received from that lady and her establishment.

This lady, a widow, was what the French call a *métisse*, the Spaniards a *mestizza*; that is, the daughter of a genuine Spaniard, and an Indian mother. I shall call her simply a *creole*, [Footnote: 'Creole.'—At that time the infusion of negro or African blood was small. Consequently none of the negro hideousness was diffused. After these intercomplexities had arisen between all complications of descent from three original strands, European, American, African, the distinctions of social consideration founded on them bred names so many, that a court calendar was necessary to keep you from blundering. As yet, the varieties were few. Meantime, the word *creole* has always been misapplied in our English colonies to a person (though of strictly European blood,) simply because *born* in the West Indies. In this English use, it expresses the same difference as the Romans indicated by *Hispanus* and *Hispanicus*. The first meant a person of Spanish blood, a native of Spain; the second, a Roman born in Spain. So of *Germanus* and *Germanicus, Italus* and *Italicus, Anglus* and *Anglicus*, &c.; an important distinction, on which see Casaubon *apud Scriptores. Hist. Augustan.*] which will indicate her want of pure Spanish blood sufficiently to explain her deference for those who had it. She was a kind, liberal woman; rich rather more than needed where there were no opera boxes to rent—a widow about fifty years old in the wicked world's account, some forty-four in her own; and happy, above all, in the possession of a most lovely daughter, whom even the wicked world did not accuse of more than sixteen years. This daughter, Juana, was—But stop—let her open the door of the saloon in which the Senora and the cornet are conversing, and speak for herself. She did so, after an hour had passed; which length of time, to *her* that never had any business whatever in her innocent life, seemed sufficient to settle the business of the old world and the new. Had Pietro Diaz (as Catalina now called herself) been really a Peter, and not a sham Peter, what a vision of loveliness would have rushed upon his sensibilities as the door opened! Do not expect me to describe her, for which, however, there are materials extant, sleeping in archives, where they have slept for two hundred and twenty years. It is enough that she is reported to have united the stately tread of Andalusian women with the innocent voluptuousness of Peruvian eyes. As to her complexion and figure, be it known that Juana's father was a gentleman from Grenada, having in his veins the grandest blood of all this earth, blood of Goths and Vandals, tainted (for which Heaven be thanked!) twice over with blood of Arabs—once through Moors, once through Jews; [Footnote: It is well known, that the very reason why the Spanish of all nations became the most gloomily jealous of a Jewish cross in the pedigree, was because, until the vigilance of the Church rose into ferocity, in no nation was such a cross so common. The hatred of fear is ever the deepest. And men hated the Jewish taint, as once in Jerusalem they hated the leprosy, because even whilst they raved against it, the secret proofs of it might be detected amongst their own kindred, even as in the Temple, whilst once a king rose in mutiny against the priesthood, (2 Chron. xxvi 16-20,) suddenly the leprosy that dethroned him, blazed out upon his forehead.] whilst from her grandmother, Juana drew the deep subtle melancholy and the beautiful contours of limb which belong to the Indian race—a race destined silently and slowly to fade from the earth. No awkwardness was or could be in this antelope, when gliding with forest grace into the room—no town-bred shame—nothing but the unaffected pleasure of one who wishes to speak a fervent welcome, but knows not if she ought—the astonishment of a Miranda, bred in utter solitude, when first beholding a princely Ferdinand— and just so much reserve as to remind you, that if Catalina thought fit to dissemble her sex, she did *not*. And consider, reader, if you look back and are a great arithmetician, that whilst the Senora had only fifty per cent of Spanish blood, Juana had seventy-five; so that her Indian melancholy after all was swallowed up for the present by her Vandal, by her Arab, by her Spanish fire.

Catalina, seared as she was by the world, has left it evident in her memoirs that she was touched more than she wished to be by this innocent child. Juana formed a brief lull for Catalina in her too stormy existence. And if for *her* in this life the sweet reality of a sister had been possible, here was the sister she would have chosen. On the other hand, what might Juana think of the cornet? To have been thrown upon the kind hospitalities of her native home, to have been rescued by her mother's servants from that fearful death which, lying but a few miles off, had filled her nursery with traditionary tragedies, — *that* was sufficient to create an interest in the stranger. But his bold martial demeanor, his yet youthful style of beauty, his frank manners, his animated conversation that reported a hundred contests with suffering and peril, wakened for the first time her admiration. Men she had never seen before, except menial servants, or a casual priest. But here was a gentleman, young like herself, that rode in the cavalry of Spain — that carried the banner of the only potentate whom Peruvians knew of — the King of the Spains and the Indies — that had doubled Cape Horn, that had crossed the Andes, that had suffered shipwreck, that had rocked upon fifty storms, and had wrestled for life through fifty battles.

The reader knows all that followed. The sisterly love which Catalina did really feel for this young mountaineer was inevitably misconstrued. Embarrassed, but not able, from sincere affection, or almost in bare propriety, to refuse such expressions of feeling as corresponded to the artless and involuntary kindnesses of the ingenuous Juana, one day the cornet was surprised by mamma in the act of encircling her daughter's waist with his martial arm, although waltzing was premature by at least two centuries in Peru. She taxed him instantly with dishonorably abusing her confidence. The cornet made but a bad defence. He muttered something about '*fraternal affection*,' about 'esteem,' and a great deal of metaphysical words that are destined to remain untranslated in their original Spanish. The good Senora, though she could boast only of forty-four years' experience, was not altogether to be '*had*' in that fashion — she was as learned as if she had been fifty, and she brought matters to a speedy crisis. 'You are a Spaniard,' she said, 'a gentleman, therefore; *remember* that you are a gentleman. This very night, if your intentions are not serious, quit my house. Go to Tucuman; you shall command my horses and servants; but stay no longer to increase the sorrow that already you will have left behind you. My daughter loves you. That is sorrow enough, if you are trifling with us. But, if not, and you also love *her*, and can be happy in our solitary mode of life, stay with us — stay for ever. Marry Juana with my free consent. I ask not for wealth. Mine is sufficient for you both.' The cornet protested that the honor was one never contemplated by *him* — that it was too great — that—. But, of course, reader, you know that 'gammon' flourishes in Peru, amongst the silver mines, as well as in some more boreal lands that produce little better than copper and tin.

'Tin,' however, has its uses. The delighted Senora overruled all objections, great and small; and she confirmed Juana's notion that the business of two worlds could be transacted in an hour, by settling her daughter's future happiness in exactly twenty minutes. The poor, weak Catalina, not acting now in any spirit of recklessness, grieving sincerely for the gulf that was opening before her, and yet shrinking effeminately from the momentary shock that would be inflicted by a firm adherence to her duty, clinging to the anodyne of a short delay, allowed herself to be installed as the lover of Juana. Considerations of convenience, however, postponed the marriage. It was requisite to make various purchases; and for this, it was requisite to visit Tucuman, where, also, the marriage ceremony could be performed with more circumstantial splendor. To Tucuman, therefore, after some weeks' interval, the whole party repaired. And at Tucuman it was that the tragical events arose, which, whilst interrupting such a mockery for ever, left the poor Juana still happily deceived, and never believing for a moment that hers was a rejected or a deluded heart.

One reporter of Mr. De Ferrer's narrative forgets his usual generosity, when he says that the Senora's gift of her daughter to the Alferez was not quite so disinterested as it seemed to be. Certainly it was not so disinterested as European ignorance might fancy it: but it was quite as much so as it ought to have been, in balancing the interests of a child. Very true it is—that, being a genuine Spaniard, who was still a rare creature in so vast a world as Peru, being a Spartan amongst Helots, an Englishman amongst Savages, an Alferez would in those days have been a natural noble. His alliance created honor for his wife and for his descendants. Something, therefore, the cornet would add to the family consideration. But, instead of selfishness, it argued just regard for her daughter's interest to build upon this, as some sort of equipoise to the wealth which her daughter would bring.

Spaniard, however, as he was, our Alferez on reaching Tucuman found no Spaniards to mix with, but instead twelve Portuguese.

Catalina remembered the Spanish proverb—'Subtract from a Spaniard all his good qualities, and the remainder makes a pretty fair Portuguese;' but, as there was nobody else to gamble with, she entered freely into their society. Very soon she suspected that there was foul play: all modes of doctoring dice had been made familiar to *her* by the experience of camps. She watched; and, by the time she had lost her final coin, she was satisfied that she had been plundered. In her first anger she would have been glad to switch the whole dozen across the eyes; but, as twelve to one were too great odds, she determined on limiting her vengeance to the immediate culprit. Him she followed into the street; and coming near enough to distinguish his profile reflected on a wall, she continued to keep him in view from a short distance. The light-hearted young cavalier whistled, as he went, an old Portuguese ballad of romance; and in a quarter of an hour came up to an house, the front door of which he began to open with a pass-key. This operation was the signal for Catalina that the hour of vengeance had struck; and, stepping hastily up, she tapped the Portuguese on the shoulder, saying—'Senor, you are a robber!' The Portuguese turned coolly round, and, seeing his gaming antagonist, replied—'Possibly, Sir; but I have no particular fancy for being told so,' at the same time drawing his sword. Catalina had not designed to take any advantage; and the touching him on the shoulder, with the interchange of speeches, and the known character of Kate, sufficiently imply it. But it is too probable in such cases, that the party whose intention has been regularly settled from the first, will, and must have an advantage unconsciously over a man so abruptly thrown on his defence. However this might be, they had not fought a minute before Catalina passed her sword through her opponent's body; and without a groan or a sigh, the Portuguese cavalier fell dead at his own door. Kate searched the street with her ears, and (as far as the indistinctness of night allowed) with her eyes. All was profoundly silent; and she was satisfied that no human figure was in motion. What should be done with the body? A glance at the door of the house settled *that*: Fernando had himself opened it at the very moment when he received the summons to turn round. She dragged the corpse in, therefore, to the foot of the staircase, put the key by the dead man's side, and then issuing softly into the street, drew the door close with as little noise as possible. Catalina again paused to listen and to watch, went home to the hospitable Senora's house, retired to bed, fell asleep, and early the next morning was awakened by the Corregidor and four alguazils.

The lawlessness of all that followed strikingly exposes the frightful state of criminal justice at that time, wherever Spanish law prevailed. No evidence appeared to connect Catalina in any way with the death of Fernando Acosta. The Portuguese gamblers, besides that perhaps they thought lightly of such an accident, might have reasons of their own for drawing off public attention from their pursuits in Tucuman: not one of these men came forward openly; else the circumstances at the gaming table, and the departure of Catalina so closely on the heels of her opponent, would have suggested reasonable grounds for detaining her until some further light should be obtained. As it was, her imprisonment rested upon no colorable ground whatever, unless the magistrate had received some anonymous information, which, however, he never alleged. One comfort there was, meantime, in Spanish injustice: it did not loiter. Full gallop it went over the ground: one week often sufficed for informations—for trial—for execution; and the only bad consequence was, that a second or a third week sometimes exposed the disagreeable fact that everything had been 'premature;' a solemn sacrifice had been made to offended justice, in which all was right except as to the victim; it was the wrong man; and *that* gave extra trouble; for then all was to do over again, another man to be executed, and, possibly, still to be caught.

Justice moved at her usual Spanish rate in the present case. Kate was obliged to rise instantly; not suffered to speak to anybody in the house, though, in going out, a door opened, and she saw the young Juana looking out with saddest Indian expression. In one day the trial was all finished. Catalina said (which was true) that she hardly knew Acosta; and that people of her rank were used to attack their enemies face to face, not by murderous surprises. The magistrates were impressed with Catalina's answers (yet answered to *what*?) Things were beginning to look well, when all was suddenly upset by two witnesses, whom the reader (who is a sort of accomplice after the fact, having been privately let into the truths of the case, and having concealed his knowledge), will know at once to be false witnesses, but whom the old Spanish buzwigs doated on as models of all that could be looked for in the best. Both were very ill-looking fellows, as it was their duty to be. And the first deposed as follows:—That through his quarter of Tucuman, the fact was notorious of Acosta's wife being the object of a criminal pursuit on the part of the Alferez (Catalina): that, *doubtless*, the injured husband had surprised the prisoner, which, of course, had led to the murder, to the staircase, to the key—to everything, in short, that could be wished; no—stop! what am I saying?—to everything that ought to be abominated. Finally—for he had now settled the main question—that he had a friend who would take up the case where he himself, from short-sightedness, was obliged to lay it down.' This friend, the Pythias of this short-sighted Damon started up in a frenzy of virtue at this summons, and, rushing to the front of the alguazils, said, 'That since his friend had proved sufficiently the fact of the Alferez having been lurking in the house, and having murdered a man, all that rested upon *him* to show was, how that murderer got out of the house; which he could do satisfactorily; for there was a balcony running along the windows on the second floor, one of which windows he himself, lurking in a corner of the street, saw the Alferez throw up, and from the said balcony take a flying leap into the said street.' Evidence like this was conclusive; no defence was listened to, nor indeed had the prisoner any to produce. The Alferez could deny neither the staircase nor the balcony: the street is there to this day, like the bricks in Jack Cade's Chimney, testifying all that may be required; and, as to our friend who saw the leap, there he was; nobody could deny *him*. The prisoner might indeed have suggested that she never heard of Acosta's wife, nor had the existence of such a wife been ripened even into a suspicion. But the bench were satisfied; chopping logic was of no use; and sentence was pronounced—that on the eighth day from the day of arrest, the Alferez should be executed in the public square.

It was not amongst the weaknesses of Catalina—who had so often inflicted death, and, by her own journal, thought so lightly of inflicting it (if not under cowardly advantages)—to shrink from facing death in her own person. Many incidents in her career show the coolness and even gaiety with which, in any case where death was apparently inevitable, she would have gone to meet it. But in this case she *had* a temptation for escaping it, which was probably in her power. She had only to reveal the secret of her sex, and the ridiculous witnesses, beyond whose testimony there was nothing at all against her, must at once be covered with derision. Catalina had some liking for fun; and a main inducement to this course was, that it would enable her to say to the judges, 'Now you see what old fools you've made of yourselves; every woman and child in Peru will soon be laughing at you.' I must acknowledge my own weakness; this last temptation I could *not* have withstood; flesh is weak, and fun is strong. But Catalina *did*. On consideration she fancied, that although the particular motive for murdering Acosta would be dismissed with laughter, still this might not clear her of the murder, which on some *other* motive she might have committed. But supposing that she were cleared altogether, what most of all she feared was, that the publication of her sex would throw a reflex light upon many past transactions in her life—would instantly find its way to Spain—and would probably soon bring her within the tender attentions of the Inquisition. She kept firm to the resolution of not saving her life by this discovery. And so far as her fate lay in her own hands, she would (as the reader will perceive from a little incident at the scaffold) have perished to a certainty. But even at this point, how strange a case! A woman *falsely* accused of an act which she really *did* commit! And falsely accused of a true offence upon a motive that was impossible!

As the sun set upon the seventh day, when the hours were numbered for the prisoner, there filed into her cell four persons in religious habits. They came on the charitable mission of preparing the poor convict for death. Catalina, however, watching all things narrowly, remarked something earnest and significant in the eye of the leader, as of one who had some secret communication to make. She contrived to clasp this man's hands, as if in the energy of internal struggles, and *he* contrived to slip into hers the very smallest of billets from poor Juana. It contained, for indeed it *could* contain, only these three words—'Do not confess. J.' This one caution, so simple and so brief, was a talisman. It did not refer to any confession of the crime; *that* would have been assuming what Juana was neither entitled nor disposed to assume, but, in the technical sense of the Church, to the act of devotional confession. Catalina found a single moment for a glance at it—understood the whole—resolutely refused to confess, as a person unsettled in her religious opinions, that needed spiritual instructions, and the four monks withdrew to make their report. The principal judge, upon hearing of the prisoner's impenitence, granted another day. At the end of *that*, no change having occurred either in the prisoner's mind, or in the circumstances, he issued his warrant for the execution. Accordingly, as the sun went down, the sad procession formed within the prison. Into the great square of Tucuman it moved, where the scaffold had been built, and the whole city had assembled for the spectacle. Catalina steadily ascended the ladder of the scaffold; even then she resolved not to benefit by revealing her sex; even then it was that she expressed her scorn for the lubberly executioner's mode of tying a knot; did it herself in a 'ship-shape,' orthodox manner; received in return the enthusiastic plaudits of the crowd, and so far ran the risk of precipitating her fate; for the timid magistrates, fearing a rescue from the impetuous mob, angrily ordered the executioner to finish the scene. The clatter of a galloping horse, however, at this instant forced them to pause. The crowd opened a road for the agitated horseman, who was the bearer of an order from the President of La Plata to suspend the execution until two prisoners could be examined. The whole was the work of the Senora and her daughter. The elder lady, having gathered informations against the witnesses, had pursued them to La Plata. There, by her influence with the Governor, they were arrested; recognised as old malefactors; and in their terror had partly confessed their perjury. Catalina was removed to La Plata; solemnly acquitted; and, by the advice of the President, for the present the connection with the Senora's family was postponed indefinitely.

Now was the last adventure approaching that ever Catalina should see in the new world. Some fine sights she may yet see in Europe, but nothing after this (*which she has recorded*) in America. Europe, if it had ever heard of her name (which very shortly it *shall*), Kings, Pope, Cardinals, if they were but aware of her existence (which in six months they *shall* be), would thirst for an introduction to our Catalina. You hardly thought now, reader, that she was such a great person, or anybody's pet but yours and mine. Bless you, Sir, she would scorn to look at *us*. I tell you, royalties are languishing to see her, or soon *will* be. But how can this come to pass, if she is to continue in her present obscurity? Certainly it cannot without some great *peripetteia* or vertiginous whirl of fortune; which, therefore, you shall now behold taking place in one turn of her next adventure. *That* shall let in a light, *that* shall throw back a Claude Lorraine gleam over all the past, able to make Kings, that would have cared not for her under Peruvian daylight, come to glorify her setting beams.

The Senora—and, observe, whatever kindness she does to Catalina speaks secretly from two hearts, her own and Juana's—had, by the advice of Mr. President Mendonia, given sufficient money for Catalina's travelling expenses. So far well. But Mr. M. chose to add a little codicil to this bequest of the Senora's, never suggested by her or by her daughter. 'Pray,' said this inquisitive President, who surely might have found business enough in La Plata, 'Pray, Senor Pietro Diaz, did you ever live at Concepcion? And were you ever acquainted there with Senor Miguel de Erauso? That man, Sir, was my friend.' What a pity that on this occasion Catalina could not venture to be candid! What a capital speech it would have made to say—'*Friend* were you? I think you could hardly be *that*, with seven hundred miles between you. But that man was *my* friend also; and, secondly, my brother. True it is I killed him. But if you happen to know that this was by pure mistake in the dark, what an old rogue you must be to throw *that* in my teeth, which is the affliction of my life!' Again, however, as so often in the same circumstances, Catalina thought that it would cause more ruin than it could heal to be candid; and, indeed, if she were really *P. Diaz, Esq.* , how came she to be brother to the late Mr. Erauso? On consideration, also, if she could not tell *all*, merely to have professed a fraternal connection which never was avowed by either whilst living together, would not have brightened the reputation of Catalina, which too surely required a scouring. Still, from my kindness for poor Kate, I feel uncharitably towards the president for advising Senor Pietro 'to travel for his health.' What had *he* to do with people's health? However, Mr. Peter, as he had pocketed the Senora's money, thought it right to pocket also the advice that accompanied its payment. That he might be in a condition to do so, he went off to buy a horse. He was in luck to-day. For beside money and advice, he obtained, at a low rate, a horse both beautiful and serviceable for a journey. To Paz it was, a city of prosperous name, that the cornet first moved. But Paz did not fulfil the promise of its name. For it laid the grounds of a feud that drove our Kate out of America.

Her first adventure was a bagatelle, and fitter for a jest-book than a history; yet it proved no jest either, since it led to the tragedy that followed. Riding into Paz, our gallant standard-bearer and her bonny black horse drew all eyes, *comme de raison*, upon their separate charms. This was inevitable amongst the indolent population of a Spanish town; and Kate was used to it. But, having recently had a little too much of the public attention, she felt nervous on remarking two soldiers eyeing the handsome horse and the handsome rider, with an attention that seemed too solemn for mere *aesthetics*. However, Kate was not the kind of person to let anything dwell on her spirits, especially if it took the shape of impudence; and, whistling gaily, she was riding forward—when, who should cross her path but the Alcalde! Ah! Alcalde, you see a person now that has a mission against you, though quite unknown to herself. He looked so sternly, that Kate asked if his worship had any commands. 'These men,' said the Alcalde, 'these two soldiers, say that this horse is stolen.' To one who had so narrowly and so lately escaped the balcony witness and his friend, it was really no laughing matter to hear of new affidavits in preparation. Kate was nervous, but never disconcerted. In a moment she had twitched off a saddle-cloth on which she sat; and throwing it over the horse's head, so as to cover up all between the ears and the mouth, she replied, 'that she had bought and paid for the horse at La Plata. But now, your worship, if this horse has really been stolen from these men, they must know well of which eye it is blind; for it *can* be only in the right eye or the left.' One of the soldiers cried out instantly, that it was the left eye; but the other said, 'No, no, you forget, it's the right.' Kate maliciously called attention to this little schism. But the men said, 'Ah, *that* was nothing—they were hurried; but now, on recollecting themselves, they were agreed that it was the left eye.' Did they stand to that? 'Oh yes, positive they were, left eye, left.'

Upon which our Kate, twitching off the horse-cloth, said gaily to the magistrate, 'Now, Sir, please to observe that this horse has nothing the matter with either eye.' And in fact it *was* so. Then his worship ordered his alguazils to apprehend the two witnesses, who posted off to bread and water, with other reversionary advantages, whilst Kate rode in quest of the best dinner that Paz could furnish.

This Alcalde's acquaintance, however, was not destined to drop here. Something had appeared in the young *caballero's* bearing, which made it painful to have addressed him with harshness, or for a moment to have entertained such a charge against such a person. He despatched his cousin, therefore, Don Antonio Calderon, to offer his apologies, and at the same time to request that the stranger, whose rank and quality he regretted not to have known, would do him the honor to come and dine with him. This explanation, and the fact that Don Antonio had already proclaimed his own position as cousin to the magistrate and nephew to the Bishop of Cuzco, obliged Catalina to say, after thanking the gentlemen for their obliging attentions, 'I myself hold the rank of Alferez in the service of his Catholic Majesty. I am a native of Biscay, and I am now repairing to Cuzco on private business.' 'To Cuzco!' exclaimed Don Antonio, 'how very fortunate! My cousin is a Basque like you; and, like you, he starts for Cuzco to-morrow morning; so that, if it is agreeable to you, Senor Alferez, we will travel together.' It was settled that they should. To travel—amongst 'balcony witnesses,' and anglers for 'blind horses'—not merely with a just man, but with the very abstract idea and riding allegory of justice, was too delightful to the storm-wearied cornet; and he cheerfully accompanied Don Antonio to the house of the magistrate, called Don Pedro de Chavarria. Distinguished was his reception; the Alcalde personally renewed his regrets for the ridiculous scene of the two scampish oculists, and presented him to his wife, a splendid Andalusian beauty, to whom he had been married about a year.

This lady there is a reason for describing; and the French reporter of Catalina's memoirs dwells upon the theme. She united, he says, the sweetness of the German lady with the energy of the Arabian, a combination hard to judge of. As to her feet, he adds, I say nothing; for she had scarcely any at all. *'Je ne parle point de ses pieds, elle n'en avait presque pas.'* 'Poor lady!' says a compassionate rustic: 'no feet! What a shocking thing that so fine a woman should have been so sadly mutilated!' Oh, my dear rustic, you're quite in the wrong box. The Frenchman means this as the very highest compliment. Beautiful, however, she must have been; and a Cinderella, I hope, not a Cinderellula, considering that she had the inimitable walk and step of the Andalusians, which cannot be accomplished without something of a proportionate basis to stand upon.

The reason which there is (as I have said) for describing this lady, arises out of her relation to the tragic events which followed. She, by her criminal levity, was the cause of all. And I must here warn the moralizing blunderer of two errors that he is too likely to make: 1st, That he is invited to read some extract from a licentious amour, as if for its own interest; 2d, Or on account of Donna Catalina's memoirs, with a view to relieve their too martial character. I have the pleasure to assure him of his being so utterly in the darkness of error, that any possible change he can make in his opinions, right or left, must be for the better: he cannot stir, but he will mend, which is a delightful thought for the moral and blundering mind. As to the first point, what little glimpse he obtains of a licentious amour is, as a court of justice will sometimes show him such a glimpse, simply to make intelligible the subsequent facts which depend upon it. Secondly, As to the conceit, that Catalina wished to embellish her memoirs, understand that no such practice then existed; certainly not in Spanish literature. Her memoirs are electrifying by their facts; else, in the manner of telling these facts, they are systematically dry.

Don Antonio Calderon was a handsome, accomplished cavalier. And in the course of dinner, Catalina was led to judge, from the behavior to each other of this gentleman and the lady, the Alcalde's beautiful wife, that they had an improper understanding. This also she inferred from the furtive language of their eyes. Her wonder was, that the Alcalde should be so blind; though upon that point she saw reason in a day or two to change her opinion. Some people see everything by affecting to see nothing. The whole affair, however, was nothing at all to *her*, and she would have dismissed it from her thoughts altogether, but for what happened on the journey.

From the miserable roads, eight hours a day of travelling was found quite enough for man and beast; the product of which eight hours was from ten to twelve leagues. On the last day but one of the journey, the travelling party, which was precisely the original dinner party, reached a little town ten leagues short of Cuzco. The Corregidor of this place was a friend of the Alcalde; and through *his* influence the party obtained better accommodations than those which they had usually had in a hovel calling itself a *venta*, or in the sheltered corner of a barn. The Alcalde was to sleep at the Corregidor's house; the two young cavaliers, Calderon and our Kate, had sleeping rooms at the public *locanda*; but for the lady was reserved a little pleasure-house in an enclosed garden. This was a plaything of a house; but the season being summer, and the house surrounded with tropical flowers, the lady preferred it (in spite of its loneliness) to the damp mansion of the official grandee, who, in her humble opinion, was quite as fusty as his mansion, and his mansion not much less so than himself.

After dining gaily together at the *locanda*, and possibly taking a 'rise' out of his worship the Corregidor, as a repeating echo of Don Quixote, (then growing popular in Spanish America,) the young man who was no young officer, and the young officer who was no young man, lounged down together to the little pavilion in the flower-garden, with the purpose of paying their respects to the presiding belle. They were graciously received, and had the honor of meeting there his Mustiness the Alcalde, and his Fustiness the Corregidor; whose conversation was surely improving, but not equally brilliant. How they got on under the weight of two such muffs, has been a mystery for two centuries. But they *did* to a certainty, for the party did not break up till eleven. *Tea and turn out* you could not call it; for there was the *turn out* in rigor, but not the *tea*. One thing, however, Catalina by mere accident had an opportunity of observing, and observed with pain. The two official gentlemen had gone down the steps into the garden. Catalina, having forgot her hat, went back into the little vestibule to look for it. There stood the lady and Don Antonio, exchanging a few final words (they *were* final) and a few final signs. Amongst the last Kate observed distinctly this, and distinctly she understood it. First drawing Calderon's attention to the gesture, as one of significant pantomime, by raising her forefinger, the lady snuffed out one of the candles. The young man answered it by a look of intelligence, and all three passed down the steps together. The lady was disposed to take the cool air, and accompanied them to the garden-gate; but, in passing down the walk, Catalina noticed a second ill-omened sign that all was not right. Two glaring eyes she distinguished amongst the shrubs for a moment, and a rustling immediately after. 'What's that?' said the lady, and Don Antonio answered carelessly, 'A bird flying out of the bushes.'

Catalina, as usual, had read everything. Not a wrinkle or a rustle was lost upon *her*. And, therefore, when she reached the *locanda*, knowing to an iota all that was coming, she did not retire to bed, but paced before the house. She had not long to wait: in fifteen minutes the door opened softly, and out stepped Calderon. Kate walked forward, and faced him immediately; telling him laughingly that it was not good for his health to go abroad on this night. The young man showed some impatience; upon which, very seriously, Kate acquainted him with her suspicions, and with the certainty that the Alcalde was not so blind as he had seemed. Calderon thanked her for the information; would be upon his guard; but, to prevent further expostulation, he wheeled round instantly into the darkness. Catalina was too well convinced, however, of the mischief on foot, to leave him thus. She followed rapidly, and passed silently into the garden, almost at the same time with Calderon. Both took their stations behind trees; Calderon watching nothing but the burning candles, Catalina watching circumstances to direct her movements. The candles burned brightly in the little pavilion. Presently one was extinguished. Upon this, Calderon pressed forward to the steps, hastily ascended them, and passed into the vestibule. Catalina followed on his traces. What succeeded was all one scene of continued, dreadful dumb show; different passions of panic, or deadly struggle, or hellish malice absolutely suffocated all articulate words.

In a moment a gurgling sound was heard, as of a wild beast attempting vainly to yell over some creature that it was strangling. Next came a tumbling out at the door of one black mass, which heaved and parted at intervals into two figures, which closed, which parted again, which at last fell down the steps together. Then appeared a figure in white. It was the unhappy Andalusian; and she seeing the outline of Catalina's person, ran up to her, unable to utter one syllable. Pitying the agony of her horror, Catalina took her within her own cloak, and carried her out at the garden gate. Calderon had by this time died; and the maniacal Alcalde had risen up to pursue his wife. But Kate, foreseeing what he would do, had stepped silently within the shadow of the garden wall. Looking down the road to the town, and seeing nobody moving, the maniac, for some purpose, went back to the house. This moment Kate used to recover the *locanda* with the lady still panting in horror. What was to be done? To think of concealment in this little place was out of the question. The Alcalde was a man of local power, and it was certain that he would kill his wife on the spot. Kate's generosity would not allow her to have any collusion with this murderous purpose. At Cuzco, the principal convent was ruled by a near relative of the Andalusian; and there she would find shelter. Kate, therefore, saddled her horse rapidly, placed the lady behind, and rode off in the darkness. About five miles out of the town their road was crossed by a torrent, over which they could not hit the bridge. 'Forward!' cried the lady; and Kate repeating the word to the horse, the docile creature leaped down into the water. They were all sinking at first; but having its head free, the horse swam clear of all obstacles through the midnight darkness, and scrambled out on the opposite bank. The two riders were dripping from the shoulders downward. But, seeing a light twinkling from a cottage window, Kate rode up; obtained a little refreshment, and the benefit of a fire, from a poor laboring man. From this man she also bought a warm mantle for the lady, who, besides her torrent bath, was dressed in a light evening robe, so that but for the horseman's cloak of Kate she would have perished. But there was no time to lose. They had already lost two hours from the consequences of their cold bath. Cuzco was still eighteen miles distant; and the Alcalde's shrewdness would at once divine this to be his wife's mark. They remounted: very soon the silent night echoed the hoofs of a pursuing rider; and now commenced the most frantic race, in which each party rode as if the whole game of life were staked upon the issue. The pace was killing: and Kate has delivered it as her opinion, in the memoirs which she wrote, that the Alcalde was the better mounted. This may be doubted. And certainly Kate had ridden too many years in the Spanish cavalry to have any fear of his worship's horsemanship; but it was a prodigious disadvantage that *her* horse had to carry double; while the horse ridden by her opponent was one of those belonging to the murdered Don Antonio, and known to Kate as a powerful animal. At length they had come within three miles at Cuzco. The road after this descended the whole way to the city, and in some places rapidly, so as to require a cool rider. Suddenly a deep trench appeared traversing the whole extent of a broad heath. It was useless to evade it. To have hesitated was to be lost. Kate saw the necessity of clearing it, but doubted much whether her poor exhausted horse, after twenty-one miles of work so severe, had strength for the effort. Kate's maxim, however, which never yet had failed, both figuratively for life, and literally for the saddle, was—to ride at everything that showed a front of resistance. She did so now. Having come upon the trench rather too suddenly, she wheeled round for the advantage of coming down upon it more determinately, rode resolutely at it, and gained the opposite bank. The hind feet of her horse were sinking back from the rottenness of the ground; but the strong supporting bridle-hand of Kate carried him forward; and in ten minutes more they would be in Cuzco. This being seen by the vicious

Alcalde, who had built great hopes on the trench, he unslung his carbine, pulled up, and fired after the bonny black horse and its bonny fair riders. But this manoeuvre would have lost his worship any bet that he might have had depending on this admirable steeple-chase. Had I been stakeholder, what a pleasure it would have been, in fifteen minutes from this very vicious shot, to pay into Kate's hands every shilling of the deposits. I would have listened to no nonsense about referees or protests. The bullets, says Kate, whistled round the poor clinging lady *en croupe*—luckily none struck her; but one wounded the horse. And that settled the odds. Kate now planted herself well in her stirrups to enter Cuzco, almost dangerously a winner; for the horse was so maddened by the wound, and the road so steep, that he went like blazes; and it really became difficult for Kate to guide him with any precision through narrow episcopal paths. Henceforwards the wounded horse required Kate's continued attention; and yet, in the mere luxury of strife, it was impossible for Kate to avoid turning a little in her saddle to see the Alcalde's performance on this tight rope of the trench. His worship's horsemanship being perhaps rather rusty, and he not perfectly acquainted with his horse, it would have been agreeable to compromise the case by riding round, or dismounting. But all *that* was impossible. The job must be done. And I am happy to report, for the reader's satisfaction, the sequel—so far as Kate could attend the performance. Gathering himself up for mischief, the Alcalde took a sweep, as if ploughing out the line of some vast encampment, or tracing the *pomærium* for some future Rome; then, like thunder and lightning, with arms flying aloft in the air, down he came upon the trembling trench.

But the horse refused the leap; and, as the only compromise that *his* unlearned brain could suggest, he threw his worship right over his ears, lodging him safely in a sand-heap that rose with clouds of dust and screams of birds into the morning air. Kate had now no time to send back her compliments in a musical halloo. The Alcalde missed breaking his neck on this occasion very narrowly; but his neck was of no use to him in twenty minutes more, as the reader will soon find. Kate rode right onwards; and, coming in with a lady behind her, horse bloody, and pace such as no hounds could have lived with, she ought to have made a great sensation in Cuzco. But, unhappily, the people were all in bed.

The steeple-chase into Cuzco had been a fine headlong thing, considering the torrent, the trench, the wounded horse, the lovely lady, with her agonizing fears, mounted behind Kate, together with the meek dove-like dawn: but the finale crowded together the quickest succession of changes that out of a melodrama can ever have been witnessed. Kate reached the convent in safety; carried into the cloisters, and delivered like a parcel the fair Andalusian. But to rouse the servants caused delay; and on returning to the street through the broad gateway of the convent, whom should she face but the Alcalde! How he escaped the trench, who can tell? He had no time to write memoirs; his horse was too illiterate. But he *had* escaped; temper not at all improved by that adventure, and now raised to a hell of malignity by seeing that he had lost his prey. In the morning light he now saw how to use his sword. He attacked Kate with fury. Both were exhausted; and Kate, besides that she had no personal quarrel with the Alcalde, having now accomplished her sole object in saving the lady, would have been glad of a truce. She could with difficulty wield her sword: and the Alcalde had so far the advantage, that he wounded Kate severely. That roused her ancient blood. She turned on him now with determination. At that moment in rode two servants of the Alcalde, who took part with their master. These odds strengthened Kate's resolution, but weakened her chances. Just then, however, rode in, and ranged himself on Kate's side, the servant of the murdered Don Calderon. In an instant, Kate had pushed her sword through the Alcalde, who died upon the spot. In an instant the servant of Calderon had fled. In an instant the Alguazils had come up. They and the servants of the Alcalde pressed furiously on Kate, who now again was fighting for life. Against such odds, she was rapidly losing ground; when, in an instant, on the opposite side of the street, the great gates of the Episcopal palace rolled open. Thither it was that Calderon's servant had fled. The bishop and his attendants hurried across. 'Senor Caballador,' said the bishop, 'in the name of the Virgin, I enjoin you to surrender your sword.' 'My lord,' said Kate, 'I dare not do it with so many enemies about me.' 'But I,' replied the bishop, 'become answerable to the law for your safe keeping.' Upon which, with filial reverence, all parties dropped their swords. Kate being severely wounded, the bishop led her into his palace. In an instant came the catastrophe; Kate's discovery could no longer be delayed; the blood flowed too rapidly; the wound was in her bosom. She requested a private interview with the bishop; all was known in a moment; for surgeons and attendants were summoned hastily, and Kate had fainted. The good bishop pitied her, and had her attended in his palace; then removed to a convent; then to a second at Lima; and, after many months had passed, his report to the Spanish Government at home of all the particulars, drew from the King of Spain and from the Pope an order that the Nun should be transferred to Spain.

Yes, at length the warrior lady, the blooming cornet, this nun that is so martial, this dragoon that is so lovely, must visit again the home of her childhood, which now for seventeen years she has not seen. All Spain, Portugal, Italy, rang with her adventures. Spain, from north to south, was frantic with desire to behold her fiery child, whose girlish romance, whose patriotic heroism electrified the national imagination. The King of Spain must kiss his *faithful* daughter, that would not suffer his banner to see dishonor. The Pope must kiss his *wandering* daughter, that henceforwards will be a lamb travelling back into the Christian fold. Potentates so great as these, when *they* speak words of love, do not speak in vain. All was forgiven; the sacrilege, the bloodshed, the flight and the scorn of St. Peter's keys; the pardons were made out, were signed, were sealed, and the chanceries of earth were satisfied.

Ah! what a day of sorrow and of joy was *that* one day, in the first week of November, 1624, when the returning Kate drew near to the shore of Andalusia—when, descending into the ship's barge, she was rowed to the piers of Cadiz by bargemen in the royal liveries—when she saw every ship, street, house, convent, church, crowded, like a day of judgment, with human faces, with men, with women, with children, all bending the lights of their flashing and their loving eyes upon herself. Forty myriads of people had gathered in Cadiz alone. All Andalusia had turned out to receive her. Ah! what joy, if she had not looked back to the Andes, to their dreadful summits, and their more dreadful feet. Ah! what sorrow, if she had not been forced by music, and endless banners, and triumphant clamors, to turn away from the Andes to the joyous shore which she approached!

Upon this shore stood, ready to receive her, in front of all this mighty crowd, the Prime Minister of Spain, the same Conde Olivarez, who but one year before had been so haughty and so defying to our haughty and defying Duke of Buckingham. But a year ago the Prince of Wales was in Spain, and he also was welcomed with triumph and great joy, but not with the hundredth part of that enthusiasm which now met the returning nun. And Olivarez, that had spoken so roughly to the English Duke, to *her* 'was sweet as summer.' [Footnote: Griffith in Shakspeare, when vindicating, in that immortal scene with Queen Catherine, Cardinal Wolsey.] Through endless crowds of festive compatriots he conducted her to the King. The King folded her in his arms, and could never be satisfied with listening to her. He sent for her continually to his presence—he delighted in her conversation, so new, so natural, so spirited—he settled a pension upon her at that time, of unprecedented amount, in the case of a subaltern officer; and by *his* desire, because the year 1625 was a year of jubilee, she departed in a few months from Madrid to Rome. She went through Barcelona; there and everywhere welcomed as the lady whom the King delighted to honor. She travelled to Rome, and all doors flew open to receive her. She was presented to his Holiness, with letters from his most Catholic majesty. But letters there needed none. The Pope admired her as much as all before had done.

He caused her to recite all her adventures; and what he loved most in her account, was the sincere and sorrowing spirit in which she described herself as neither better nor worse than she had been. Neither proud was Kate, nor sycophantishly and falsely humble. Urban VIII. it was that then filled the chair of St. Peter. He did not neglect to raise his daughter's thoughts from earthly things—he pointed her eyes to the clouds that were above the dome of St. Peter's cathedral—he told her what the cathedral had told her in the gorgeous clouds of the Andes and the vesper lights, how sweet a thing, how divine a thing it was for Christ's sake to forgive all injuries, and how he trusted that no more she would think of bloodshed. He also said two words to her in Latin, which, if I had time to repeat a Spanish bishop's remark to Kate some time afterwards upon those two mysterious words, with Kate's most natural and ingenuous answer to the Bishop upon what she supposed to be their meaning, would make the reader smile not less than they made myself. You know that Kate *did* understand a little Latin, which, probably, had not been much improved by riding in the Light Dragoons. I must find time, however, whether the press and the compositors are in a fury or not, to mention that the Pope, in his farewell audience to his dear daughter, whom he was to see no more, gave her a general license to wear henceforth in all countries—even *in partibus Infidelium*—a cavalry officer's dress— boots, spurs, sabre, and sabretache; in fact, anything that she and the Horse Guards might agree upon. Consequently, reader, remember for your life never to say one word, nor suffer any tailor to say one word, against those Wellington trousers made in the chestnut forest; for, understand that the Papal indulgence, as to this point, runs backwards as well as forwards; it is equally shocking and heretical to murmur against trousers in the forgotten rear or against trousers yet to come.

From Rome, Kate returned to Spain. She even went to St. Sebastian's— to the city, but—whether it was that her heart failed her or not—never to the convent. She roamed up and down; everywhere she was welcome— everywhere an honored guest; but everywhere restless. The poor and humble never ceased from their admiration of her; and amongst the rich and aristocratic of Spain, with the King at their head, Kate found especial love from two classes of men. The Cardinals and Bishops all doated upon her—as their daughter that was returning. The military men all doated upon her—as their sister that was retiring.

Some time or other, when I am allowed more elbow-room, I will tell you why it is that I myself love this Kate. Now, at this moment, when it is necessary for me to close, if I allow you one question before laying down my pen—if I say, 'Come now, be quick, ask anything you *have* to ask, for, in one minute, I am going to write *Finis*, after which (unless the Queen wished it)

I could not add a syllable'—twenty to one, I guess what your question will be. You will ask me, What became of Kate? What was her end?

Ah, reader! but, if I answer that question, you will say I have *not* answered it. If I tell you that secret, you will say that the secret is still hidden. Yet, because I have promised, and because you will be angry if I do not, let me do my best; and bad is the best. After ten years of restlessness in Spain, with thoughts always turning back to the Andes, Kate heard of an expedition on the point of sailing to Spanish America. All soldiers knew *her*, so that she had information of everything that stirred in camps. Men of the highest military rank were going out with the expedition; but they all loved Kate as a sister, and were delighted to hear that she would join their mess on board ship. This ship, with others, sailed, whither finally bound, I really forget. But, on reaching America, all the expedition touched at *Vera Cruz*. Thither a great crowd of the military went on shore. The leading officers made a separate party for the same purpose. Their intention was, to have a gay happy dinner, after their long confinement to a ship, at the chief hotel; and happy in perfection it could not be, unless Kate would consent to join it. She, that was ever kind to brother soldiers, agreed to do so. She descended into the boat along with them, and in twenty minutes the boat touched the shore. All the bevy of gay laughing officers, junior and senior, like schoolboys escaping from school, jumped on shore, and walked hastily, as their time was limited, up to the hotel. Arriving there, all turned round in eagerness, saying, 'Where is our dear Kate?' Ah, yes, my dear Kate, at that solemn moment, where, indeed, were *you*? She had *certainly* taken her seat in the boat: that was sure. Nobody, in the general confusion, was certain of having seen her on coming ashore. The sea was searched for her—the forests were ransacked. The sea made no answer—the forests gave up no sign. I have a conjecture of my own; but her brother soldiers were lost in sorrow and confusion, and could never arrive even at a conjecture.

That happened two hundred and fourteen years ago! Here is the brief sum of all:—This nun sailed from Spain to Peru, and she found no rest for the sole of her foot. This nun sailed back from Peru to Spain, and she found no rest for the agitations of her heart. This nun sailed again from Spain to America, and she found—the rest which all of us find. But where it was, could never be made known to the father of Spanish camps, that sat in Madrid; nor to Kate's spiritual father, that sat in Rome. Known it is to the great Father that once whispered to Kate on the Andes; but else it has been a secret for two centuries; and to man it remains a secret for ever and ever!

FLIGHT OF A TARTAR TRIBE

There is no great event in modern history, or perhaps it may be said more broadly, none in all history, from its earliest records, less generally known, or more striking to the imagination, than the flight eastwards of a principal Tartar nation across the boundless *steppes* of Asia in the latter half of the last century. The *terminus a quo* of this flight, and the *terminus ad quem*, are equally magnificent; the mightiest of Christian thrones being the one, the mightiest of Pagan the other. And the grandeur of these two terminal objects, is harmoniously supported by the romantic circumstances of the flight. In the abruptness of its commencement, and the fierce velocity of its execution, we read an expression of the wild barbaric character of the agents. In the unity of purpose connecting this myriad of wills, and in the blind but unerring aim at a mark so remote, there is something which recalls to the mind those Almighty instincts that propel the migrations of the swallow, or the life-withering marches of the locust. Then again, in the gloomy vengeance of Russia and her vast artillery, which hung upon the rear and the skirts of the fugitive vassals, we are reminded of Miltonic images—such, for instance, as that of the solitary hand pursuing through desert spaces and through ancient chaos a rebellious host, and overtaking with volleying thunders those who believed themselves already within the security of darkness and of distance.

We shall have occasion farther on to compare this event with other great national catastrophes as to the magnitude of the suffering. But it may also challenge a comparison with similar events under another relation, viz., as to its dramatic capabilities. Few cases, perhaps, in romance or history, can sustain a close collation with this as to the complexity of its separate interests. The great outline of the enterprise, taken in connection with the operative motives, hidden or avowed, and the religious sanctions under which it was pursued, give to the case a triple character: 1st, That of a conspiracy, with as close a unity in the incidents, and as much of a personal interest in the moving characters, with fine dramatic contrasts, as belongs to Venice Preserved, or to the Fiesco of Schiller. 2dly, That of a great military expedition offering the same romantic features of vast distances to be traversed, vast reverses to be sustained, untried routes, enemies obscurely ascertained, and hardships too vaguely prefigured, which mark the Egyptian expedition of Cambyses—the anabasis of the younger Cyrus, and the subsequent retreat of the ten thousand to the Black Sea—the Parthian expeditions of the Romans, especially those of Crassus and Julian—or (as more disastrous than any of them, and in point of space as well as in amount of forces, more extensive,) the Russian anabasis and katabasis of Napoleon. 3dly, That of a religious Exodus, authorized by an oracle venerated throughout many nations of Asia, an Exodus, therefore, in so far resembling the great Scriptural Exodus of the Israelites, under Moses and Joshua, as well as in the very peculiar distinction of carrying along with them their entire families, women, children, slaves, their herds of cattle and of sheep, their horses and their camels.

This triple character of the enterprise naturally invests it with a more comprehensive interest. But the dramatic interest, which we ascribed to it, or its fitness for a stage representation, depends partly upon the marked variety and the strength of the personal agencies concerned, and partly upon the succession of scenical situations. Even the *steppes*, the camels, the tents, the snowy and the sandy deserts, are not beyond the scale of our modern representative powers, as often called into action in the theatres both of Paris and London; and the series of situations unfolded, beginning with the general conflagration on the Wolga—passing thence to the disastrous scenes of the flight (as it literally was in its commencement)—to the Tartar siege of the Russian fortress Koulagina—the bloody engagement with the Cossacks in the mountain passes at Ouchim—the surprisal by the Bashkirs and the advanced posts of the Russian army at Torgau—the private conspiracy at this point against the Khan—the long succession of running fights—the parting massacres at the lake of Tengis under the eyes of the Chinese—and finally, the tragical retribution to Zebek-Dorchi at the hunting-lodge of the Chinese emperor;—all these situations communicate a *scenical* animation to the wild romance, if treated dramatically; whilst a higher and a philosophic interest belongs to it as a case of authentic history, commemorating a great revolution for good and for evil, in the fortunes of a whole people—a people semi-barbarous, but simple-hearted, and of ancient descent.

On the 21st of January, 1761, the young Prince Oubacha assumed the sceptre of the Kalmucks upon the death of his father. Some part of the power attached to this dignity he had already wielded since his fourteenth year, in quality of Vice-Khan, by the express appointment, and with the avowed support of the Russian Government. He was now about eighteen years of age, amiable in his personal character, and not without titles to respect in his public character as a sovereign prince. In times more peaceable, and amongst a people more entirely civilized, or more humanized by religion, it is even probable that he might have discharged his high duties with considerable distinction. But his lot was thrown upon stormy times, and a most difficult crisis amongst tribes, whose native ferocity was exasperated by debasing forms of superstition, and by a nationality as well as an inflated conceit of their own merit absolutely unparalleled, whilst the circumstances of their hard and trying position under the jealous *surveillance* of an irresistible lord paramount, in the person of the Russian Czar, gave a fiercer edge to the natural unamiableness of the Kalmuck disposition, and irritated its gloomier qualities into action under the restless impulses of suspicion and permanent distrust. No prince could hope for a cordial allegiance from his subjects, or a peaceful reign under the circumstances of the case; for the dilemma in which a Kalmuck ruler stood at present was of this nature; *wanting* the sanction and support of the Czar, he was inevitably too weak from without to command confidence from his subjects, or resistance to his competitors: on the other hand, *with* this kind of support, and deriving his title in any degree from the favor of the Imperial Court, he became almost in that extent an object of hatred at home, and within the whole compass of his own territory. He was at once an object of hatred for the past, being a living monument of national independence, ignominiously surrendered, and an object of jealousy for the future, as one who had already advertised himself to be a fitting tool for the ultimate purposes (whatsoever those might prove to be) of the Russian Court. Coming himself to the Kalmuck sceptre under the heaviest weight of prejudice from the unfortunate circumstances of his position, it might have been expected that Oubacha would have been pre-eminently an object of detestation; for besides his known dependence upon the Cabinet of St. Petersburg, the direct line of succession had been set aside, and the principle of inheritance violently suspended, in favor of his own father, so recently as nineteen years before the era of his own accession, consequently within the lively remembrance of the existing generation. He therefore, almost equally with his father, stood within the full current of the national prejudices, and might have anticipated the most pointed hostility. But it was not so: such are the caprices in human affairs, that he was even, in a moderate sense, popular,—a benefit which wore the more cheering aspect, and the promises of permanence, inasmuch as he owed it exclusively to his personal qualities of kindness and affability, as well as to the beneficence of his government. On the other hand, to balance this unlooked-for prosperity at the outset of his reign, he met with a rival in popular favor—almost a competitor—in the person of Zebek-Dorchi, a prince with considerable pretensions to the throne, and, perhaps it might be said, with equal pretensions. Zebek-Dorchi was a direct descendant of the same royal house as himself, through a different branch. On public grounds, his claim stood, perhaps, on a footing equally good with that of Oubacha, whilst his personal qualities, even in those aspects which seemed to a philosophical observer most odious and repulsive, promised the most effectual aid to the dark purposes of an intriguer or a conspirator, and were generally fitted to win a popular support precisely in those points where *Oubacha* was most defective. He was much superior in external appearance to his rival on the throne, and so far better qualified to win the good opinion of a semi-barbarous people; whilst his dark intellectual qualities of Machiavelian dissimulation, profound hypocrisy, and perfidy which knew no touch of remorse, were admirably calculated to sustain any ground which he might win from the simple-hearted people with whom he had to deal—and from the frank carelessness of his unconscious competitor.

At the very outset of his treacherous career, Zebek-Dorchi was sagacious enough to perceive that nothing could be gained by open declaration of hostility to the reigning prince: the choice had been a deliberate act on the part of Russia, and Elizabeth Petrowna was not the person to recall her own favors with levity or upon slight grounds. Openly, therefore, to have declared his enmity towards his relative on the throne, could have had no effect but that of arming suspicions against his own ulterior purposes in a quarter where it was most essential to his interest that, for the present, all suspicion should be hoodwinked. Accordingly, after much meditation, the course he took for opening his snares was this:—He raised a rumor that his own life was in danger from the plots of several *Saissang*, (that is, Kalmuck nobles,) who were leagued together, under an oath to assassinate him; and immediately after, assuming a well-counterfeited alarm, he fled to Tcherkask, followed by sixty-five tents. From this place he kept up a correspondence with the Imperial Court; and, by way of soliciting his cause more effectually, he soon repaired in person to St. Petersburg. Once admitted to personal conferences with the Cabinet, he found no difficulty in winning over the Russian counsels to a concurrence with some of his political views, and thus covertly introducing the point of that wedge which was finally to accomplish his purposes. In particular, he persuaded the Russian Government to make a very important alteration in the constitution of the Kalmuck State Council, which in effect reorganized the whole political condition of the state, and disturbed the balance of power as previously adjusted. Of this Council—in the Kalmuck language called *Sarga*—there were eight members, called *Sargatchi;* and hitherto it had been the custom that these eight members should be entirely subordinate to the Khan; holding, in fact, the ministerial character of secretaries and assistants, but in no respect ranking as co-ordinate authorities. That had produced some inconveniences in former reigns; and it was easy for Zebek-Dorchi to point the jealousy of the Russian Court to others more serious which might arise in future circumstances of war or other contingencies. It was resolved, therefore, to place the Sargatchi henceforward on a footing of perfect independence, and therefore (as regarded responsibility) on a footing of equality with the Khan. Their independence, however, had respect only to their own sovereign; for towards Russia they were placed in a new attitude of direct duty and accountability, by the creation in their favor of small pensions (300 roubles a year), which, however, to a Kalmuck of that day were more considerable than might be supposed, and had a further value as marks of honorary distinction emanating from a great Empress. Thus far the purposes of Zebek-Dorchi were served effectually for the moment: but, apparently, it was only for the moment; since, in the further development of his plots, this very dependency upon Russian influence would be the most serious obstacle in his way. There was, however, another point carried which outweighed all inferior considerations, as it gave him a power of setting aside discretionally whatsoever should arise to disturb his plots: he was himself appointed President and Controller of the *Sargatchi*. The Russian Court had been aware of his high pretensions by birth, and hoped by this promotion to satisfy the ambition which, in some degree, was acknowledged to be a reasonable passion for any man occupying his situation.

Having thus completely blindfolded the Cabinet of Russia, Zebek-Dorchi proceeded in his new character to fulfil his political mission with the Khan of the Kalmucks. So artfully did he prepare the road for his favorable reception at the court of this Prince, that he was at once and universally welcomed as a public benefactor. The pensions of the counsellors were so much additional wealth poured into the Tartar exchequer; as to the ties of dependency thus created, experience had not yet enlightened these simple tribes as to that result. And that he himself should be the chief of these mercenary counsellors, was so far from being charged upon Zebek as any offence or any ground of suspicion, that his relative the Khan returned him hearty thanks for his services, under the belief that he could have accepted this appointment only with a view to keep out other and more unwelcome pretenders, who would not have had the same motives of consanguinity or friendship for executing its duties in a spirit of kindness to the Kalmucks. The first use which he made of his new functions about the Khan's person was to attack the Court of Russia, by a romantic villany not easy to be credited, for those very acts of interference with the council which he himself had prompted. This was a dangerous step: but it was indispensable to his further advance upon the gloomy path which he had traced out for himself. A triple vengeance was what he meditated—1, Upon the Russian Cabinet for having undervalued his own pretensions to the throne—2, upon his amiable rival for having supplanted him—and 3, upon all those of the nobility who had manifested their sense of his weakness by their neglect, or their sense of his perfidious character by their suspicions. Here was a colossal outline of wickedness; and by one in his situation, feeble (as it might seem) for the accomplishment of its humblest parts, how was the total edifice to be reared in its comprehensive grandeur? He, a worm as he was, could he venture to assail the mighty behemoth of Muscovy, the potentate who counted three hundred languages around the footsteps of his throne, and from whose 'lion ramp' recoiled alike 'baptized and infidel'—Christendom on the one side, strong by her intellect and her organization, and the 'Barbaric East' on the other, with her unnumbered numbers? The match was a monstrous one; but in its very monstrosity there lay this germ of encouragement, that it could not be suspected. The very hopelessness of the scheme grounded his hope, and he resolved to execute a vengeance which should involve as it were, in the unity of a well-laid tragic fable, all whom he judged to be his enemies. That vengeance lay in detaching from the Russian empire the whole Kalmuck nation, and breaking up that system of intercourse which had thus far been beneficial to both. This last was a consideration which moved him but little. True it was that Russia to the Kalmucks had secured lands and extensive pasturage; true it was that the Kalmucks reciprocally to Russia had furnished a powerful cavalry. But the latter loss would be part of his triumph, and the former might be more than compensated in other climates under other sovereigns. Here was a scheme which, in its final accomplishment, would avenge him bitterly on the Czarina, and in the course of its accomplishment might furnish him with ample occasions for removing his other enemies. It may be readily supposed indeed that he, who could deliberately raise his eyes to the Russian autocrat as an antagonist in single duel with himself, was not likely to feel much anxiety about Kalmuck enemies of whatever rank. He took his resolution, therefore, sternly and irrevocably to effect this astonishing translation of an ancient people across the pathless deserts of Central Asia, intersected continually by rapid rivers, rarely furnished with bridges, and of which the fords were known only to those who might think it for their interest to conceal them, through many nations inhospitable or hostile; frost and snow around them, (from the necessity of commencing their flight in the winter,) famine in their front, and the sabre, or even the artillery of an offended and mighty empress, hanging upon their rear for thousands of miles. But what was to be their final mark, the port of shelter after so fearful a course of wandering? Two things were evident: it must be some power at a great distance from Russia, so as to make return even in that view hopeless; and it must be a power of sufficient rank to ensure them protection from any hostile efforts on the part of the Czarina for reclaiming them, or for chastising their revolt. Both conditions were united obviously in the person of Kien Long, the reigning Emperor of China, who was farther recommended to them by his respect for the head of their religion. To China, therefore, and as their first rendezvous to the shadow of the great Chinese Wall, it was settled by Zebek that they should direct their flight.

Next came the question of time; *when* should the flight commence: — and finally, the more delicate question as to the choice of accomplices. To extend the knowledge of the conspiracy too far, was to insure its betrayal to the Russian Government. Yet at some stage of the preparations it was evident that a very extensive confidence must be made, because in no other way could the mass of the Kalmuck population be persuaded to furnish their families with the requisite equipments for so long a migration. This critical step, however, it was resolved to defer up to the latest possible moment, and, at all events, to make no general communication on the subject until the time of departure should be definitely settled. In the meantime, Zebek admitted only three persons to his confidence; of whom Oubacha, the reigning prince, was almost necessarily one; but him, from his yielding and somewhat feeble character, he viewed rather in the light of a tool than as one of his active accomplices. Those whom (if anybody) he admitted to an unreserved participation in his counsels, were two only, the great *Lama* among the Kalmucks, and his own father-in-law, Erempel, a ruling prince of some tribe in the neighborhood of the Caspian sea, recommended to his favor not so much by any strength of talent corresponding to the occasion, as by his blind devotion to himself, and his passionate anxiety to promote the elevation of his daughter and his son-in-law to the throne of a sovereign prince. A titular prince Zebek already was: but this dignity, without the substantial accompaniment of a sceptre, seemed but an empty sound to both of these ambitious rivals. The other accomplice, whose name was Loosang-Dchaltzan, and whose rank was that of Lama, or Kalmuck pontiff, was a person of far more distinguished pretensions; he had something of the same gloomy and terrific pride which marked the character of Zebek himself, manifesting also the same energy, accompanied by the same unfaltering cruelty, and a natural facility of dissimulation even more profound. It was by this man that the other question was settled as to the time for giving effect to their designs. His own pontifical character had suggested to him, that in order to strengthen their influence with the vast mob of simple-minded men whom they were to lead into a howling wilderness, after persuading them to lay desolate their own ancient hearths, it was indispensable that they should be able, in cases of extremity, to plead the express sanction of God for their entire enterprise. This could only be done by addressing themselves to the great head of their religion, the Dalai-Lama of Tibet. Him they easily persuaded to countenance their schemes: and an oracle was delivered solemnly at Tibet, to the effect that no ultimate prosperity would attend this great Exodus unless it were pursued through the years of the *tiger* and the *hare*. Now, the Kalmuck custom is to distinguish their years by attaching to each a denomination taken from one of twelve animals, the exact order of succession being absolutely fixed, so that the cycle revolves of course through a period of a dozen years. Consequently, if the approaching year of the *tiger* were suffered to escape them, in that case the expedition must be delayed for twelve years more, within which period, even were no other unfavorable changes to arise, it was pretty well foreseen that the Russian Government would take the most effectual means for bridling their vagrant propensities by a ring fence of forts or military posts; to say nothing of the still readier plan for securing their fidelity (a plan already talked of in all quarters), by exacting a large body of hostages selected from the families of the most influential nobles. On these cogent considerations, it was solemnly determined that this terrific experiment should be made in the next year of the *tiger*, which happened to fall upon the Christian year 1771. With respect to the month, there was, unhappily for the Kalmucks, even less latitude allowed to their choice than with respect to the year. It was absolutely necessary, or it was thought so, that the different divisions of the nation, which pastured their flocks on both banks of the Wolga, should have the means of effecting an instantaneous junction; because the danger of being intercepted by flying columns of the Imperial armies was precisely the greatest at the outset. Now, from the want of bridges, or sufficient river craft for transporting so vast a body of men, the sole means which could be depended upon (especially where so many women, children, and camels were concerned,) was *ice*: and this, in a state of sufficient firmness, could not be absolutely counted upon before the month of January. Hence it happened that this astonishing Exodus of a whole nation, before so much as a whisper of the design had begun to circulate amongst those whom it most interested, before it was even suspected that any man's wishes pointed in that direction, had been definitively appointed for January of the year 1771. And almost up to the Christmas of 1770, the poor simple Kalmuck herdsmen and their families were going nightly to their peaceful beds without even dreaming that the *fiat* had already gone forth from their rulers which consigned those quiet abodes, together with the peace and comfort which reigned within them, to a withering desolation, now close at hand.

Meantime war raged on a great scale between Russia and the Sultan. And, until the time arrived for throwing off their vassalage, it was necessary that Oubacha should contribute his usual contingent of martial aid. Nay, it had unfortunately become prudent that he should contribute much more than his usual aid. Human experience gives ample evidence that in some mysterious and unaccountable way no great design is ever agitated, no matter how few or how faithful may be the participators, but that some presentiment—some dim misgiving—is kindled amongst those whom it is chiefly important to blind. And, however it might have happened, certain it is, that already, when as yet no syllable of the conspiracy had been breathed to any man whose very existence was not staked upon its concealment, nevertheless, some vague and uneasy jealousy had arisen in the Russian Cabinet as to the future schemes of the Kalmuck Khan: and very probable it is—that, but for the war then raging, and the consequent prudence of conciliating a very important vassal, or, at least, of abstaining from what would powerfully alienate him, even at that moment such measures would have been adopted as must for ever have intercepted the Kalmuck schemes. Slight as were the jealousies of the Imperial Court, they had not escaped the Machiavelian eyes of Zebek and the Lama. And under their guidance, Oubacha, bending to the circumstances of the moment, and meeting the jealousy of the Russian Court with a policy corresponding to their own, strove by unusual zeal to efface the Czarina's unfavorable impressions. He enlarged the scale of his contributions; and *that* so prodigiously, that he absolutely carried to head-quarters a force of 35,000 cavalry fully equipped; some go further, and rate the amount beyond 40,000: but the smaller estimate is, at all events, *within* the truth.

With this magnificent array of cavalry, heavy as well as light, the Khan went into the field under great expectations; and these he more than realized. Having the good fortune to be concerned with so ill-organized and disorderly a description of force as that which at all times composed the bulk of a Turkish army, he carried victory along with his banners; gained many partial successes; and at last, in a pitched battle, overthrew the Turkish force opposed to him with a loss of 5000 men left upon the field.

These splendid achievements seemed likely to operate in various ways against the impending revolt. Oubacha had now a strong motive, in the martial glory acquired, for continuing his connection with the empire in whose service he had won it, and by whom only it could be fully appreciated. He was now a great marshal of a great empire, one of the Paladins around the imperial throne; in China he would be nobody, or (worse than that) a mendicant-alien, prostrate at the feet, and soliciting the precarious alms of a prince with whom he had no connection. Besides, it might reasonably be expected that the Czarina, grateful for the really efficient aid given by the Tartar prince, would confer upon him such eminent rewards as might be sufficient to anchor his hopes upon Russia, and to wean him from every possible seduction. These were the obvious suggestions of prudence and good sense to every man who stood neutral in the case. But they were disappointed. The Czarina knew her obligations to the Khan, but she did not acknowledge them. Wherefore? That is a mystery, perhaps never to be explained. So it was, however. The Khan went unhonored; no *ukase* ever proclaimed his merits; and, perhaps, had he even been abundantly recompensed by Russia, there were others who would have defeated these tendencies to reconciliation. Erempel, Zebek, and Loosang the Lama, were pledged life-deep to prevent any accommodation; and their efforts were unfortunately seconded by those of their deadliest enemies. In the Russian Court there were at that time some great nobles pre-occupied with feelings of hatred and blind malice towards the Kalmucks, quite as strong as any which the Kalmucks could harbor towards Russia, and not, perhaps, so well-founded. Just as much as the Kalmucks hated the Russian yoke, their galling assumption of authority, the marked air of disdain, as towards a nation of ugly, stupid, and filthy barbarians, which too generally marked the Russian bearing and language; but above all, the insolent contempt, or even outrages which the Russian governors or great military commandants tolerated in their followers towards the barbarous religion and superstitious mummeries of the Kalmuck priesthood—precisely in that extent did the ferocity of the Russian resentment, and their wrath at seeing the trampled worm turn or attempt a feeble retaliation, re-act upon the unfortunate Kalmucks. At this crisis it is probable that envy and wounded pride, upon witnessing the splendid victories of Oubacha and Momotbacha over the Turks and Bashkirs, contributed strength to the Russian irritation. And it must have been through the intrigues of those nobles about her person, who chiefly smarted under these feelings, that the Czarina could ever have lent herself to the unwise and ungrateful policy pursued at this critical period towards the Kalmuck Khan. That Czarina was no longer Elizabeth Petrowna, it was Catharine the Second; a princess who did not often err so injuriously (injuriously for herself as much as for others) in the measures of her government. She had soon ample reason for repenting of her false policy. Meantime, how much it must have co-operated with the other motives previously acting upon Oubacha in sustaining his determination to revolt; and how powerfully it must have assisted the efforts of all the Tartar chieftains in preparing the minds of their people to feel the necessity of this difficult enterprise, by arming their pride and their suspicions against the Russian Government, through the keenness of their sympathy with the wrongs of their insulted prince, may be readily imagined. It is a fact, and it has been confessed by candid Russians themselves, when treating of this great dismemberment, that the conduct of the Russian Cabinet throughout the period of suspense, and during the crisis of hesitation in the Kalmuck Council, was exactly such as was most desirable for the purposes of the conspirators; it was such, in fact, as to set the seal to all their machinations, by supplying distinct evidences and official vouchers for what could otherwise have been at the most matters of doubtful suspicion and indirect presumption.

Nevertheless, in the face of all these arguments, and even allowing their weight so far as not at all to deny the injustice or the impolicy of the Imperial Ministers, it is contended by many persons who have reviewed the affair with a command of all the documents bearing on the case, more especially the letters or minutes of Council subsequently discovered, in the handwriting of Zebek-Dorchi, and the important evidence of the Russian captive Weseloff, who was carried off by the Kalmucks in their flight, that beyond all doubt Oubacha was powerless for any purpose of impeding, or even of delaying the revolt. He himself, indeed, was under religious obligations of the most terrific solemnity never to flinch from the enterprise, or even to slacken in his zeal; for Zebek-Dorchi, distrusting the firmness of his resolution under any unusual pressure of alarm or difficulty, had, in the very earliest stage of the conspiracy, availed himself of the Khan's well known superstition, to engage him, by means of previous concert with the priests and their head the Lama, in some dark and mysterious rites of consecration, terminating in oaths under such terrific sanctions as no Kalmuck would have courage to violate. As far, therefore, as regarded the personal share of the Khan in what was to come, Zebek was entirely at his ease: he knew him to be so deeply pledged by religious terrors to the prosecution of the conspiracy, that no honors within the Czarina's gift could have possibly shaken his adhesion: and then, as to threats from the same quarter, he knew him to be sealed against those fears by others of a gloomier character, and better adapted to his peculiar temperament. For Oubacha was a brave man, as respected all bodily enemies or the dangers of human warfare, but was as sensitive and timid as the most superstitious of old women in facing the frowns of a priest, or under the vague anticipations of ghostly retributions. But had it been otherwise, and had there been any reason to apprehend an unsteady demeanor on the part of this Prince at the approach of the critical moment, such were the changes already effected in the state of their domestic politics amongst the Tartars by the undermining arts of Zebek-Dorchi, and his ally the Lama, that very little importance would have attached to that doubt. All power was now effectually lodged in the hands of Zebek-Dorchi. He was the true and absolute wielder of the Kalmuck sceptre: all measures of importance were submitted to his discretion; and nothing was finally resolved but under his dictation. This result he had brought about in a year or two by means sufficiently simple; first of all, by availing himself of the prejudice in his favor, so largely diffused amongst the lowest of the Kalmucks, that his own title to the throne, in quality of great-grandson in a direct line from Ajouka, the most illustrious of all the Kalmuck Khans, stood upon a better basis than that of Oubacha, who derived from a collateral branch: secondly, with respect to that sole advantage which Oubacha possessed above himself in the ratification of his title, by improving this difference between their situations to the disadvantage of his competitor, as one who had not scrupled to accept that triumph from an alien power at the price of his independence, which he himself (as he would have it understood) disdained to court: thirdly, by his own talents and address, coupled with the ferocious energy of his moral character: fourthly—and perhaps in an equal degree—by the criminal facility and good-nature of Oubacha: finally, (which is remarkable enough, as illustrating the character of the man,) by that very new modelling of the Sarga or Privy Council, which he had used as a principal topic of abuse and malicious insinuation against the Russian Government, whilst in reality he first had suggested the alteration to the Empress, and he chiefly appropriated the political advantages which it was fitted to yield. For, as he was himself appointed the chief of the Sargatchi, and as the pensions of the inferior Sargatchi passed through his hands, whilst in effect they owed their appointments to his nomination, it may be easily supposed that whatever power existed in the state capable of controlling the Khan, being held by the Sarga under its new organization, and this body being completely under his influence, the final result was to throw all the functions of the state, whether nominally in the Prince or in the council, substantially into the hands of this one man: whilst, at the same time, from the strict league which he maintained with the Lama, all the thunders of the spiritual power were always ready to come in aid of the magistrate, or to supply his incapacity in cases which he could not reach.

But the time was now rapidly approaching for the mighty experiment. The day was drawing near on which the signal was to be given for raising the standard of revolt, and by a combined movement on both sides of the Wolga for spreading the smoke of one vast conflagration, that should wrap in a common blaze their own huts and the stately cities of their enemies, over the breadth and length of those great provinces in which their flocks were dispersed. The year of the *tiger* was now within one little month of its commencement; the fifth morning of that year was fixed for the fatal day, when the fortunes and happiness of a whole nation were to be put upon the hazard of a dicer's throw; and as yet that nation was in profound ignorance of the whole plan. The Khan, such was the kindness of his nature, could not bring himself to make the revelation so urgently required. It was clear, however, that this could not be delayed; and Zebek-Dorchi took the task willingly upon himself. But where or how should this notification be made, so as to exclude Russian hearers? After some deliberation, the following plan was adopted:—Couriers, it was contrived, should arrive in furious haste, one upon the heels of another, reporting a sudden inroad of the Kirghises and Bashkirs upon the Kalmuck lands, at a point distant about one hundred and twenty miles. Thither all the Kalmuck families, according to immemorial custom, were required to send a separate representative; and there, accordingly, within three days, all appeared. The distance, the solitary ground appointed for the rendezvous, the rapidity of the march, all tended to make it almost certain that no Russian could be present. Zebek-Dorchi then came forward. He did not waste many words upon rhetoric. He unfurled an immense sheet of parchment, visible from the outermost distance at which any of this vast crowd could stand; the total number amounted to eighty thousand; all saw, and many heard. They were told of the oppressions of Russia; of her pride and haughty disdain, evidenced towards them by a thousand acts; of her contempt for their religion; of her determination to reduce them to absolute slavery; of the preliminary measures she had already taken by erecting forts upon many of the great rivers of their neighborhood; of the ulterior intentions she thus announced to circumscribe their pastoral lands, until they would all be obliged to renounce their flocks, and to collect in towns like Sarepta, there to pursue mechanical and servile trades of shoemaker, tailor, and weaver, such as the freeborn Tartar had always disdained. 'Then again,' said the subtle prince, 'she increases her military levies upon our population every year; we pour out our blood as young men in her defence, or more often in support of her insolent aggressions; and as old men, we reap nothing from our sufferings, nor benefit by our survivorship where so many are sacrificed.' At this point of his harangue, Zebek produced several papers, (forged, as it is generally believed, by himself and the Lama,) containing projects of the Russian court for a general transfer of the eldest sons, taken *en masse* from the greatest Kalmuck families, to the Imperial court. 'Now let this be once accomplished,' he argued, 'and there is an end of all useful resistance from that day forwards. Petitions we might make, or even remonstrances; as men of words, we might play a bold part; but for deeds, for that sort of language by which our ancestors were used to speak; holding us by such a chain, Russia would make a jest of our wishes,—knowing full well that we should not dare to make any effectual movement.'

Having thus sufficiently roused the angry passions of his vast audience, and having alarmed their fears by this pretended scheme against their first-born, (an artifice which was indispensable to his purpose, because it met beforehand *every* form of amendment to his proposal coming from the more moderate nobles, who would not otherwise have failed to insist upon trying the effect of bold addresses to the Empress, before resorting to any desperate extremity,) Zebek-Dorchi opened his scheme of revolt, and, if so, of instant revolt; since any preparations reported at St. Petersburg would be a signal for the armies of Russia to cross into such positions from all parts of Asia, as would effectually intercept their march. It is remarkable, however, that, with all his audacity and his reliance upon the momentary excitement of the Kalmucks, the subtle prince did not venture, at this stage of his seduction, to make so startling a proposal as that of a flight to China. All that he held out for the present was a rapid march to the Temba or some other great river, which they were to cross, and to take up a strong position on the further bank, from which, as from a post of conscious security, they could hold a bolder language to the Czarina, and one which would have a better chance of winning a favorable audience.

These things, in the irritated condition of the simple Tartars, passed by acclamation; and all returned homewards, to push forward with the most furious speed the preparations for their awful undertaking. Rapid and energetic these of necessity were; and in that degree they became noticeable and manifest to the Russians who happened to be intermingled with the different hordes, either on commercial errands, or as agents officially from the Russian Government, some in a financial, others in a diplomatic character.

Amongst these last (indeed at the head of them) was a Russian of some distinction, by name Kichinskoi, a man memorable for his vanity, and memorable also as one of the many victims to the Tartar revolution. This Kichinskoi had been sent by the Empress as her envoy to overlook the conduct of the Kalmucks; he was styled the *Grand Pristaw*, or Great Commissioner, and was universally known amongst the Tartar tribes by this title. His mixed character of ambassador and of political *surveillant*, combined with the dependent state of the Kalmucks, gave him a real weight in the Tartar councils, and might have given him a far greater, had not his outrageous self-conceit, and his arrogant confidence in his own authority, as due chiefly to his personal qualities for command, led him into such harsh displays of power, and menaces so odious to the Tartar pride, as very soon made him an object of their profoundest malice. He had publicly insulted the Khan; and upon making a communication to him to the effect that some reports began to circulate, and even to reach the Empress, of a design in agitation to fly from the Imperial dominions, he had ventured to say,—'But this you dare not attempt; I laugh at such rumors; yes, Khan, I laugh at them to the Empress; for you are a chained bear, and that you know.' The Khan turned away on his heel with marked disdain; and the Pristaw, foaming at the mouth, continued to utter, amongst those of the Khan's attendants who staid behind, to catch his real sentiments in a moment of unguarded passion, all that the blindest frenzy of rage could suggest to the most presumptuous of fools. It was now ascertained that suspicions *had* arisen; but at the same time it was ascertained that the Pristaw spoke no more than the truth in representing himself to have discredited these suspicions. The fact was, that the mere infatuation of vanity made him believe that nothing could go on undetected by his all-piercing sagacity, and that no rebellion could prosper when rebuked by his commanding presence. The Tartars, therefore, pursued their preparations, confiding in the obstinate blindness of the Grand Pristaw as in their perfect safeguard; and such it proved—to his own ruin, as well as that of myriads beside.

Christmas arrived; and, a little before that time, courier upon courier came dropping in, one upon the very heels of another, to St. Petersburg, assuring the Czarina that beyond all doubt the Kalmucks were in the very crisis of departure. These despatches came from the Governor of Astrachan, and copies were instantly forwarded to Kichinskoi. Now, it happened that between this governor—a Russian named Beketoff—and the Pristaw had been an ancient feud. The very name of Beketoff inflamed his resentment; and no sooner did he see that hated name attached to the despatch, than he felt himself confirmed in his former views with tenfold bigotry, and wrote instantly, in terms of the most pointed ridicule, against the new alarmist, pledging his own head upon the visionariness of his alarms. Beketoff, however, was not to be put down by a few hard words, or by ridicule: he persisted in his statements: the Russian Ministry were confounded by the obstinacy of the disputants; and some were beginning even to treat the Governor of Astrachan as a bore, and as the dupe of his own nervous terrors, when the memorable day arrived, the fatal 5th of January, which for ever terminated the dispute, and put a seal upon the earthly hopes and fortunes of unnumbered myriads. The Governor of Astrachan was the first to hear the news. Stung by the mixed furies of jealousy, of triumphant vengeance, and of anxious ambition, he sprang into his sledge, and, at the rate of three hundred miles a day, pursued his route to St. Petersburg, rushed into the Imperial presence,—announced the total realization of his worst predictions,—and upon the confirmation of this intelligence by subsequent despatches from many different posts on the Wolga, he received an imperial commission to seize the person of his deluded enemy, and to keep him in strict captivity. These orders were eagerly fulfilled, and the unfortunate Kichinskoi soon afterwards expired of grief and mortification in the gloomy solitude of a dungeon; a victim to his own immeasurable vanity, and the blinding self-delusions of a presumption that refused all warning.

The Governor of Astrachan had been but too faithful a prophet. Perhaps even *he* was surprised at the suddenness with which the verification followed his reports. Precisely on the 5th of January, the day so solemnly appointed under religious sanctions by the Lama, the Kalmucks on the east bank of the Wolga were seen at the earliest dawn of day assembling by troops and squadrons, and in the tumultuous movement of some great morning of battle. Tens of thousands continued moving off the ground at every half-hour's interval. Women and children, to the amount of two hundred thousand and upwards, were placed upon wagons, or upon camels, and drew off by masses of twenty thousand at once—placed under suitable escorts, and continually swelled in numbers by other outlying bodies of the horde who kept falling in at various distances upon the first and second day's march. From sixty to eighty thousand of those who were the best mounted stayed behind the rest of the tribes, with purposes of devastation and plunder more violent than prudence justified, or the amiable character of the Khan could be supposed to approve. But in this, as in other instances, he was completely overruled by the malignant counsels of Zebek-Dorchi. The first tempest of the desolating fury of the Tartars discharged itself upon their own habitations. But this, as cutting off all infirm looking backward from the hardships of their march, had been thought so necessary a measure by all the chieftains, that even Oubacha himself was the first to authorize the act by his own example. He seized a torch previously prepared with materials the most durable as well as combustible, and steadily applied it to the timbers of his own palace. Nothing was saved from the general wreck except the portable part of the domestic utensils, and that part of the woodwork which could be applied to the manufacture of the long Tartar lances. This chapter in their memorable day's work being finished, and the whole of their villages throughout a district of ten thousand square miles in one simultaneous blaze, the Tartars waited for further orders.

These, it was intended, should have taken a character of valedictory vengeance, and thus have left behind to the Czarina a dreadful commentary upon the main motives of their flight. It was the purpose of Zebek-Dorchi that all the Russian towns, churches, and buildings of every description, should be given up to pillage and destruction, and such treatment applied to the defenceless inhabitants as might naturally be expected from a fierce people already infuriated by the spectacle of their own outrages, and by the bloody retaliations which they must necessarily have provoked. This part of the tragedy, however, was happily intercepted by a providential disappointment at the very crisis of departure. It has been mentioned already that the motive for selecting the depth of winter as the season of flight (which otherwise was obviously the very worst possible) had been the impossibility of effecting a junction sufficiently rapid with the tribes on the west of the Wolga, in the absence of bridges, unless by a natural bridge of ice. For this one advantage the Kalmuck leaders had consented to aggravate by a thousandfold the calamities inevitable to a rapid flight over boundless tracts of country with women, children, and herds of cattle—for this one single advantage; and yet, after all, it was lost. The reason never has been explained satisfactorily, but the fact was such. Some have said that the signals were not properly concerted for marking the moment of absolute departure; that is, for signifying whether the settled intention of the Eastern Kalmucks might not have been suddenly interrupted by adverse intelligence. Others have supposed that the ice might not be equally strong on both sides of the river, and might even be generally insecure for the treading of heavy and heavily-laden animals such as camels. But the prevailing notion is, that some accidental movements on the 3d and 4th of January of Russian troops in the neighborhood of the Western Kalmucks, though really having no reference to them or their plans, had been construed into certain signs that all was discovered; and that the prudence of the Western chieftains, who, from situation, had never been exposed to those intrigues by which Zebek-Dorchi had practised upon the pride of the Eastern tribes, now stepped in to save their people from ruin. Be the cause what it might, it is certain that the Western Kalmucks were in some way prevented from forming the intended junction with their brethren of the opposite bank; and the result was, that at least one hundred thousand of these Tartars were left behind in Russia. This accident it was which saved their Russian neighbors universally from the desolation which else awaited them. One general massacre and conflagration would assuredly have surprised them, to the utter extermination of their property, their houses, and themselves, had it not been for this disappointment. But the Eastern chieftains did not dare to put to hazard the safety of their brethren under the first impulse of the Czarina's vengeance for so dreadful a tragedy; for as they were well aware of too many circumstances by which she might discover the concurrence of the Western people in the general scheme of revolt, they justly feared that she would thence infer their concurrence also in the bloody events which marked its outset.

Little did the Western Kalmucks guess what reasons they also had for gratitude on account of an interposition so unexpected, and which at the moment they so generally deplored. Could they but have witnessed the thousandth part of the sufferings which overtook their Eastern brethren in the first month of their sad flight, they would have blessed Heaven for their own narrow escape; and yet these sufferings of the first month were but a prelude or foretaste comparatively slight of those which afterwards succeeded.

For now began to unroll the most awful series of calamities, and the most extensive, which is anywhere recorded to have visited the sons and daughters of men. It is possible that the sudden inroads of destroying nations, such as the Huns, or the Avars, or the Mongol Tartars, may have inflicted misery as extensive; but there the misery and the desolation would be sudden—like the flight of volleying lightning. Those who were spared at first would generally be spared to the end; those who perished would perish instantly. It is possible that the French retreat from Moscow may have made some nearer approach to this calamity in duration, though still a feeble and miniature approach; for the French sufferings did not commence in good earnest until about one month from the time of leaving Moscow; and though it is true that afterwards the vials of wrath were emptied upon the devoted army for six or seven weeks in succession, yet what is that to this Kalmuck tragedy, which lasted for more than as many months? But the main feature of horror, by which the Tartar march was distinguished from the French, lies in the accompaniment of women [Footnote: Singular it is, and not generally known, that Grecian women accompanied the *Anabasis* of the younger Cyrus and the subsequent Retreat of the Ten Thousand. Xenophon affirms that there were 'many' women in the Greek army—pollai aesun etairai en tosratenaeazi; and in a late stage of that trying expedition it is evident that women were amongst the survivors.] and children. There were both, it is true, with the French army, but so few as to bear no visible proportion to the total numbers concerned. The French, in short, were merely an army—a host of professional destroyers, whose regular trade was bloodshed, and whose regular element was danger and suffering. But the Tartars were a nation carrying along with them more than two hundred and fifty thousand women and children, utterly unequal, for the most part, to any contest with the calamities before them. The Children of Israel were in the same circumstances as to the accompaniment of their families; but they were released from the pursuit of their enemies in a very early stage of their flight; and their subsequent residence in the Desert was not a march, but a continued halt, and under a continued interposition of Heaven for their comfortable support. Earthquakes, again, however comprehensive in their ravages, are shocks of a moment's duration. A much nearer approach made to the wide range and the long duration of the Kalmuck tragedy may have been in a pestilence such as that which visited Athens in the Peloponnesian war, or London in the reign of Charles II. There also the martyrs were counted by myriads, and the period of the desolation was counted by months. But, after all, the total amount of destruction was on a smaller scale; and there was this feature of alleviation to the *conscious* pressure of the calamity—that the misery was withdrawn from public notice into private chambers and hospitals. The siege of Jerusalem by Vespasian and his son, taken in its entire circumstances, comes nearest of all—for breadth and depth of suffering, for duration, for the exasperation of the suffering from without by internal feuds, and, finally, for that last most appalling expression of the furnace-heat of the anguish in its power to extinguish the natural affections even of maternal love. But, after all, each case had circumstances of romantic misery peculiar to itself—circumstances without precedent, and (wherever human nature is ennobled by Christianity) it may be confidently hoped—never to be repeated.

The first point to be reached, before any hope of repose could be encouraged, was the river Jaik. This was not above three hundred miles from the main point of departure on the Wolga; and if the march thither was to be a forced one, and a severe one, it was alleged on the other hand that the suffering would be the more brief and transient; one summary exertion, not to be repeated, and all was achieved. Forced the march was, and severe beyond example: there the forewarning proved correct; but the promised rest proved a mere phantom of the wilderness—a visionary rainbow, which fled before their hope-sick eyes, across these interminable solitudes, for seven months of hardship and calamity, without a pause. These sufferings, by their very nature, and the circumstances under which they arose, were (like the scenery of the *Steppes*) somewhat monotonous in their coloring and external features: what variety, however, there was, will be most naturally exhibited by tracing historically the successive stages of the general misery, exactly as it unfolded itself under the double agency of weakness still increasing from within, and hostile pressure from without. Viewed in this manner, under the real order of development, it is remarkable that these sufferings of the Tartars, though under the moulding hands of accident, arrange themselves almost with a scenical propriety. They seem combined, as with the skill of an artist; the intensity of the misery advancing regularly with the advances of the march, and the stages of the calamity corresponding to the stages of the route; so that, upon raising the curtain which veils the great catastrophe, we behold one vast climax of anguish, towering upwards by regular gradations, as if constructed artificially for picturesque effect:—a result which might not have been surprising, had it been reasonable to anticipate the same rate of speed, and even an accelerated rate, as prevailing through the later stages of the expedition. But it seemed, on the contrary, most reasonable to calculate upon a continual decrement in the rate of motion according to the increasing distance from the head-quarters of the pursuing enemy. This calculation, however, was defeated by the extraordinary circumstance, that the Russian armies did not begin to close in very fiercely upon the Kalmucks until after they had accomplished a distance of full two thousand miles; one thousand miles further on the assaults became even more tumultuous and murderous; and already the great shadows of the Chinese Wall were dimly descried, when the frenzy and *acharnement* of the pursuers, and the bloody desperation of the miserable fugitives had reached its uttermost extremity. Let us briefly rehearse the main stages of the misery, and trace the ascending steps of the tragedy, according to the great divisions of the route marked out by the central rivers of Asia.

The first stage, we have already said, was from the Wolga to the Jaik; the distance about three hundred miles; the time allowed seven days. For the first week, therefore, the rate of marching averaged about forty-three English miles a day. The weather was cold, but bracing; and, at a more moderate pace, this part of the journey might have been accomplished without much distress by a people as hardy as the Kalmucks: as it was, the cattle suffered greatly from overdriving: milk began to fail even for the children: the sheep perished by wholesale: and the children themselves were saved only by the innumerable camels.

The Cossacks, who dwelt upon the banks of the Jaik, were the first among the subjects of Russia to come into collision with the Kalmucks. Great was their surprise at the suddenness of the irruption, and great also their consternation: for, according to their settled custom, by far the greater part of their number was absent during the winter months at the fisheries upon the Caspian. Some who were liable to surprise at the most exposed points, fled in crowds to the fortress of Koulagina, which was immediately invested, and summoned by Oubacha. He had, however, in his train only a few light pieces of artillery; and the Russian commandant at Koulagina, being aware of the hurried circumstances in which the Khan was placed, and that he stood upon the very edge, as it were, of a renewed flight, felt encouraged by these considerations to a more obstinate resistance than might else have been advisable, with an enemy so little disposed to observe the usages of civilized warfare. The period of his anxiety was not long: on the fifth day of the siege, he descried from the walls a succession of Tartar couriers, mounted upon fleet Bactrian camels, crossing the vast plains around the fortress at a furious pace, and riding into the Kalmuck encampment at various points. Great agitation appeared immediately to follow; orders were soon after despatched in all directions: and it became speedily known that upon a distant flank of the Kalmuck movement a bloody and exterminating battle had been fought the day before, in which one entire tribe of the Khan's dependents, numbering not less than nine thousand fighting men, had perished to the last man. This was the *ouloss*, or clan, called *Feka-Zechorr*, between whom and the Cossacks there was a feud of ancient standing. In selecting, therefore, the points of attack, on occasion of the present hasty inroad, the Cossack chiefs were naturally eager so to direct their efforts as to combine with the service of the Empress some gratification to their own party hatreds; more especially as the present was likely to be their final opportunity for revenge if the Kalmuck evasion should prosper. Having, therefore, concentrated as large a body of Cossack cavalry as circumstances allowed, they attacked the hostile *ouloss* with a precipitation which denied to it all means for communicating with Oubacha; for the necessity of commanding an ample range of pasturage, to meet the necessities of their vast flocks and herds, had separated this *ouloss* from the Khan's head-quarters by an interval of eighty miles: and thus it was, and not from oversight, that it came to be thrown entirely upon its own resources. These had proved insufficient; retreat, from the exhausted state of their horses and camels, no less than from the prodigious encumbrances of their live stock, was absolutely out of the question: quarter was disdained on the one side, and would not have been granted on the other; and thus it had happened that the setting sun of that one day (the 13th from the first opening of the revolt) threw his parting rays upon the final agonies of an ancient *ouloss*, stretched upon a bloody field, who on that day's dawning had held and styled themselves an independent nation.

Universal consternation was diffused through the wide borders of the Khan's encampment by this disastrous intelligence; not so much on account of the numbers slain, or the total extinction of a powerful ally, as because the position of the Cossack force was likely to put to hazard the future advances of the Kalmucks, or at least to retard, and hold them in check, until the heavier columns of the Russian army should arrive upon their flanks. The siege of Koulagina was instantly raised; and that signal, so fatal to the happiness of the women and their children, once again resounded through the tents— the signal for flight, and this time for a flight more rapid than ever. About one hundred and fifty miles ahead of their present position, there arose a tract of hilly country, forming a sort of margin to the vast, sea-like expanse of champaign savannas, steppes, and occasionally of sandy deserts, which stretched away on each side of this margin both eastwards and westwards. Pretty nearly in the centre of this hilly range, lay a narrow defile, through which passed the nearest and the most practicable route to the river Torgai (the further bank of which river offered the next great station of security for a general halt.) It was the more essential to gain this pass before the Cossacks, inasmuch as not only would the delay in forcing the pass give time to the Russian pursuing columns for combining their attacks and for bringing up their artillery, but also because (even if all enemies in pursuit were thrown out of the question) it was held by those best acquainted with the difficult and obscure geography of these pathless steppes—that the loss of this one narrow strait amongst the hills would have the effect of throwing them (as their only alternative in a case where so wide a sweep of pasturage was required) upon a circuit of at least five hundred miles extra; besides that, after all, this circuitous route would carry them to the Torgai at a point ill fitted for the passage of their heavy baggage. The defile in the hills, therefore, it was resolved to gain; and yet, unless they moved upon it with the velocity of light cavalry, there was little chance but it would be found pre-occupied by the Cossacks. They, it is true, had suffered greatly in the recent sanguinary action with their enemies; but the excitement of victory, and the intense sympathy with their unexampled triumph, had again swelled their ranks—and would probably act with the force of a vortex to draw in their simple countrymen from the Caspian. The question, therefore, of pre-occupation was reduced to a race. The Cossacks were marching upon an oblique line not above fifty miles longer than that which led to the same point from the Kalmuck head-quarters before Koulagina: and therefore without the most furious haste on the part of the Kalmucks, there was not a chance for them, burdened and 'trashed' [Footnote: 'Trashed'—This is an expressive word used by Beaumont and Fletcher in their Bonduca, etc., to describe the case of a person retarded and embarrassed in flight, or in pursuit, by some encumbrance, whether thing or person, too valuable to be left behind.] as they were, to anticipate so agile a light cavalry as the Cossacks in seizing this important pass.

Dreadful were the feelings of the poor women on hearing this exposition of the case. For they easily understood that too capital an interest (the *summa rerum*) was now at stake to allow of any regard to minor interests, or what would be considered such in their present circumstances. The dreadful week already passed,—their inauguration in misery,—was yet fresh in their remembrance. The scars of suffering were impressed not only upon their memories, but upon their very persons and the persons of their children. And they knew that where no speed had much chance of meeting the cravings of the chieftains, no test would be accepted, short of absolute exhaustion, that as much had been accomplished as could be accomplished. Weseloff, the Russian captive, has recorded the silent wretchedness with which the women and elder boys assisted in drawing the tent-ropes. On the 5th of January all had been animation, and the joyousness of indefinite expectation: now, on the contrary, a brief but bitter experience had taught them to take an amended calculation of what it was that lay before them.

One whole day and far into the succeeding night had the renewed flight continued: the sufferings had been greater than before: for the cold had been more intense: and many perished out of the living creatures through every class, except only the camels—whose powers of endurance seemed equally adapted to cold and heat. The second morning, however, brought an alleviation to the distress. Snow had begun to fall: and though not deep at present, it was easily foreseen that it soon would be so; and that, as a halt would in that case become unavoidable, no plan could be better than that of staying where they were: especially as the same cause would check the advance of the Cossacks. Here then was the last interval of comfort which gleamed upon the unhappy nation during their whole migration. For ten days the snow continued to fall with little intermission. At the end of that time keen bright frosty weather succeeded: the drifting had ceased: in three days the smooth expanse became firm enough to support the treading of the camels, and the flight was recommenced. But during the halt much domestic comfort had been enjoyed: and for the last time universal plenty. The cows and oxen had perished in such vast numbers on the previous marches, that an order was now issued to turn what remained to account by slaughtering the whole, and salting whatever part should be found to exceed the immediate consumption. This measure led to a scene of general banqueting and even of festivity amongst all who were not incapacitated for joyous emotions by distress of mind, by grief for the unhappy experience of the few last days, and by anxiety for the too gloomy future. Seventy thousand persons of all ages had already perished; exclusively of the many thousand allies who had been cut down by the Cossack sabre. And the losses in reversion were likely to be many more. For rumors began now to arrive from all quarters, by the mounted couriers whom the Khan had despatched to the rear and to each flank as well as in advance, that large masses of the Imperial troops were converging from all parts of Central Asia to the fords of the river Torgai as the most convenient point for intercepting the flying tribes: and it was already well known that a powerful division was close in their rear, and was retarded only by the numerous artillery which had been judged necessary to support their operations. New motives were thus daily arising for quickening the motions of the wretched Kalmucks, and for exhausting those who were previously but too much exhausted.

It was not until the 2d day of February that the Khan's advanced guard came in sight of Ouchim, the defile among the hills of Moulgaldchares, in which they anticipated so bloody an opposition from the Cossacks. A pretty large body of these light cavalry had, in fact, pre-occupied the pass by some hours; but the Khan having too great advantages, namely, a strong body of infantry, who had been conveyed by sections of five on about two hundred camels, and some pieces of light artillery which he had not yet been forced to abandon, soon began to make a serious impression upon this unsupported detachment; and they would probably at any rate have retired; but at the very moment when they were making some dispositions in that view, Zebek-Dorchi appeared upon their rear with a body of trained riflemen, who had distinguished themselves in the war with Turkey. These men had contrived to crawl unobserved over the cliffs which skirted the ravine, availing themselves of the dry beds of the summer torrents, and other inequalities of the ground, to conceal their movement. Disorder and trepidation ensued instantly in the Cossack files; the Khan, who had been waiting with the *elite* of his heavy cavalry, charged furiously upon them; total overthrow followed to the Cossacks, and a slaughter such as in some measure avenged the recent bloody extermination of their allies, the ancient *ouloss* of Feka-Zechorr. The slight horses of the Cossacks were unable to support the weight of heavy Polish dragoons and a body of trained *cameleers* (that is, cuirassiers mounted on camels); hardy they were, but not strong, nor a match for their antagonists in weight; and their extraordinary efforts through the last few days to gain their present position, had greatly diminished their powers for effecting an escape. Very few, in fact, *did* escape; and the bloody day of Ouchim became as memorable amongst the Cossacks as that which, about twenty days before, had signalized the complete annihilation of the Faka-Zechorr. [Footnote: There was another *ouloss* equally strong with that of *Feka-Zechorr*, viz., that of Erketunn, under the government of Assarcho and Machi, whom some obligations of treaty or other hidden motives drew into the general conspiracy of revolt. But fortunately the two chieftains found means to assure the Governor of Astrachan, on the first outbreak of the insurrection, that their real wishes were for maintaining the old connection with Russia. The Cossacks, therefore, to whom the pursuit was intrusted, had instructions to act cautiously and according to circumstances on coming up with them. The result was, through the prudent management of Assarcho, that the clan, without compromising their pride or independence, made such moderate submissions as satisfied the Cossacks; and eventually both chiefs and people received from the Czarina the rewards and honors of exemplary fidelity.]

The road was now open to the river Igritch, and as yet even far beyond it to the Torgau; but how long this state of things would continue, was every day more doubtful. Certain intelligence was now received that a large Russian army, well appointed in every arm, was advancing upon the Torgau, under the command of General Traubenberg. This officer was to be joined on his route by ten thousand Bashkirs, and pretty nearly the same amount of Kirghises—both hereditary enemies of the Kalmucks—both exasperated to a point of madness by the bloody trophies which Oubacha and Momotbacha had, in late years, won from such of their compatriots as served under the Sultan. The Czarina's yoke these wild nations bore with submissive patience, but not the hands by which it had been imposed; and, accordingly, catching with eagerness at the present occasion offered to their vengeance, they sent an assurance to the Czarina of their perfect obedience to her commands, and at the same time a message significantly declaring in what spirit they meant to execute them, viz., 'That they would not trouble her Majesty with prisoners.'

Here then arose, as before with the Cossacks, a race for the Kalmucks with the regular armies of Russia, and concurrently with nations as fierce and semi-humanized as themselves, besides that they were stung into threefold activity by the furies of mortified pride and military abasement, under the eyes of the Turkish Sultan. The forces, and more especially the artillery, of Russia, were far too overwhelming to permit the thought of a regular opposition in pitched battles, even with a less dilapidated state of their resources than they could reasonably expect at the period of their arrival on the Torgau. In their speed lay their only hope—in strength of foot, as before, and not in strength of arm. Onward, therefore, the Kalmucks pressed, marking the lines of their wide-extending march over the sad solitudes of the steppes by a never-ending chain of corpses. The old and the young, the sick man on his couch, the mother with her baby—all were left behind. Sights such as these, with the many rueful aggravations incident to the helpless condition of infancy—of disease and of female weakness abandoned to the wolves amidst a howling wilderness, continued to track their course through a space of full two thousand miles; for so much at the least, it was likely to prove, including the circuits to which they were often compelled by rivers or hostile tribes, from the point of starting on the Wolga until they could reach their destined halting-ground on the east bank of the Torgau. For the first seven weeks of this march their sufferings had been embittered by the excessive severity of the cold; and every night—so long as wood was to be had for fires, either from the lading of the camels, or from the desperate sacrifice of their baggage-wagons, or (as occasionally happened) from the forests which skirted the banks of the many rivers which crossed their path—no spectacle was more frequent than that of a circle, composed of men, women, and children, gathered by hundreds round a central fire, all dead and stiff at the return of morning light. Myriads were left behind from pure exhaustion of whom none had a chance, under the combined evils which beset them, of surviving through the next twenty-four hours. Frost, however, and snow at length ceased to persecute; the vast extent of the march at length brought them into more genial latitudes, and the unusual duration of the march was gradually bringing them into the more genial seasons of the year: Two thousand miles had at least been traversed; February, March, April were gone; the balmy month of May had opened; vernal sights and sounds came from every side to comfort the heart-weary travellers; and at last, in the latter end of May, they crossed the Torgau, and took up a position where they hoped to find liberty to repose themselves for many weeks in comfort as well as in security, and to draw such supplies from the fertile neighborhood as might restore their shattered forces to a condition for executing, with less of wreck and ruin, the large remainder of the journey.

Yes; it was true that two thousand miles of wandering had been completed, but in a period of nearly five months, and with the terrific sacrifice of at least two hundred and fifty thousand souls, to say nothing of herds and flocks past all reckoning. These had all perished: ox, cow, horse, mule, ass, sheep, or goat, not one survived—only the camels. These arid and adust creatures, looking like the mummies of some antediluvian animals, without the affections or sensibilities of flesh and blood—these only still erected their speaking eyes to the eastern heavens, and had to all appearance come out from this long tempest of trial unscathed and unharmed. The Khan, knowing how much he was individually answerable for the misery which had been sustained, must have wept tears even more bitter than those of Xerxes when he threw his eyes over the myriads whom he had assembled: for the tears of Xerxes were unmingled with compunction. Whatever amends were in his power he resolved to make by sacrifices to the general good of all personal regards; and accordingly, even at this point of their advance, he once more deliberately brought under review the whole question of the revolt. The question was formally debated before the Council, whether, even at this point, they should untread their steps, and, throwing themselves upon the Czarina's mercy, return to their old allegiance? In that case, Oubacha professed himself willing to become the scapegoat for the general transgression. This, he argued, was no fantastic scheme, but even easy of accomplishment; for the unlimited and sacred power of the Khan, so well known to the Empress, made it absolutely iniquitous to attribute any separate responsibility to the people—upon the Khan rested the guilt, upon the Khan would descend the Imperial vengeance. This proposal was applauded for its generosity, but was energetically opposed by Zebek-Dorchi. Were they to lose the whole journey of two thousand miles? Was their misery to perish without fruit; true it was that they had yet reached only the half-way house; but, in that respect, the motives were evenly balanced for retreat or for advance. Either way they would have pretty nearly the same distance to traverse, but with this difference—that, forwards, their rout lay through lands comparatively fertile—backwards, through a blasted wilderness, rich only in memorials of their sorrow, and hideous to Kalmuck eyes by the trophies of their calamity. Besides, though the Empress might accept an excuse for the past, would she the less forbear to suspect for the future? The Czarina's *pardon* they might obtain, but could they ever hope to recover her *confidence*? Doubtless there would now be a standing presumption against them, an immortal ground of jealousy; and a jealous government would be but another name for a harsh one. Finally, whatever motives there ever had been for the revolt surely remained unimpaired by anything that had occurred. In reality the revolt was, after all, no revolt, but (strictly speaking) a return to their old allegiance, since, not above one hundred and fifty years ago (viz., in the year 1616,) their ancestors had revolted from the Emperor of China. They had now tried both governments; and for them China was the land of promise, and Russia the house of bondage.

Spite, however, of all that Zebek could say or do, the yearning of the people was strongly in behalf of the Khan's proposal; the pardon of their prince, they persuaded themselves, would be readily conceded by the Empress; and there is little doubt that they would at this time have thrown themselves gladly upon the Imperial mercy; when suddenly all was defeated by the arrival of two envoys from Traubenberg. This general had reached the fortress of Orsk, after a very painful march, on the 12th of April; thence he set forwards towards Oriembourg, which he reached upon the 1st of June, having been joined on his route at various times through the month of May by the Kirghises and a corps of ten thousand Bashkirs. From Oriembourg he sent forward his official offer to the Khan, which were harsh and peremptory, holding out no specific stipulations as to pardon or impunity, and exacting unconditional submission as the preliminary price of any cessation from military operations. The personal character of Traubenberg, which was anything but energetic, and the condition of his army, disorganized in a great measure by the length and severity of the march, made it probable that, with a little time for negotiation, a more conciliatory tone would have been assumed. But, unhappily for all parties, sinister events occurred in the meantime, such as effectually put an end to every hope of the kind.

The two envoys sent forward by Traubenberg had reported to this officer that a distance of only ten days' march lay between his own head-quarters and those of the Khan. Upon this fact transpiring, the Kirghises, by their prince Nourali, and the Bashkirs, entreated the Russian general to advance without delay. Once having placed his cannon in position, so as to command the Kalmuck camp, the fate of the rebel Khan and his people would be in his own hands; and they would themselves form his advanced guard. Traubenberg, however, *why* has not been certainly explained, refused to march, grounding his refusal upon the condition of his army, and their absolute need of refreshment. Long and fierce was the altercation; but at length, seeing no chance of prevailing, and dreading above all other events the escape of their detested enemy, the ferocious Bashkirs went off in a body by forced marches. In six days they reached the Torgau, crossed by swimming their horses, and fell upon the Kalmucks, who were dispersed for many a league in search of food or provender for their camels. The first day's action was one vast succession of independent skirmishes, diffused over a field of thirty to forty miles in extent; one party often breaking up into three or four, and again (according to the accidents of ground) three or four blending into one; flight and pursuit, rescue and total overthrow, going on simultaneously, under all varieties of form, in all quarters of the plain. The Bashkirs had found themselves obliged, by the scattered state of the Kalmucks, to split up into innumerable sections; and thus, for some hours, it had been impossible for the most practised eye to collect the general tendency of the day's fortune. Both the Khan and Zebek-Dorchi were at one moment made prisoners, and more than once in imminent danger of being cut down; but at length Zebek succeeded in rallying a strong column of infantry, which, with the support of the camel-corps on each flank, compelled the Bashkirs to retreat. Clouds, however, of these wild cavalry continued to arrive through the next two days and nights, followed or accompanied by the Kirghises. These being viewed as the advanced parties of Traubenberg's army, the Kalmuck chieftains saw no hope of safety but in flight; and in this way it happened that a retreat, which had so recently been brought to a pause, was resumed at the very moment when the unhappy fugitives were anticipating a deep repose without further molestation, the whole summer through.

It seemed as though every variety of wretchedness were predestined to the Kalmucks; and as if their sufferings were incomplete unless they were rounded and matured by all that the most dreadful agencies of summer's heat could superadd to those of frost and winter. To this sequel of their story we shall immediately revert, after first noticing a little romantic episode which occurred at this point between Oubacha and his unprincipled cousin Zebek-Dorchi.

There was at the time of the Kalmuck flight from the Wolga, a Russian gentleman of some rank at the court of the Khan, whom, for political reasons, it was thought necessary to carry along with them as a captive. For some weeks his confinement had been very strict, and in one or two instances cruel. But, as the increasing distance was continually diminishing the chances of escape, and perhaps, also, as the misery of the guards gradually withdrew their attention from all minor interests to their own personal sufferings, the vigilance of the custody grew more and more relaxed; until at length, upon a petition to the Khan, Mr. Weseloff was formally restored to liberty; and it was understood that he might use his liberty in whatever way he chose, even for returning to Russia, if that should be his wish. Accordingly, he was making active preparations for his journey to St. Petersburg, when it occurred to Zebek-Dorchi that, not improbably, in some of the battles which were then anticipated with Traubenberg, it might happen to them to lose some prisoner of rank, in which case the Russian Weseloff would be a pledge in their hands for negotiating an exchange. Upon this plea, to his own severe affliction, the Russian was detained until the further pleasure of the Khan. The Khan's name, indeed, was used through the whole affair, but, as it seemed, with so little concurrence on his part, that, when Weseloff in a private audience humbly remonstrated upon the injustice done him, and the cruelty of thus sporting with his feelings by setting him at liberty, and, as it were, tempting him into dreams of home and restored happiness only for the purpose of blighting them, the good-natured prince disclaimed all participation in the affair, and went so far in proving his sincerity as even to give him permission to effect his escape; and, as a ready means of commencing it without raising suspicion, the Khan mentioned to Mr. Weseloff that he had just then received a message from the Hetman of the Bashkirs, soliciting a private interview on the banks of the Torgau at a spot pointed out; that interview was arranged for the coming night; and Mr. Weseloff might go in the Khan's *suite*, which on either side was not to exceed three persons. Weseloff was a prudent man, acquainted with the world, and he read treachery in the very outline of this scheme, as stated by the Khan—treachery against the Khan's person. He mused a little, and then communicated so much of his suspicions to the Khan as might put him on his guard; but, upon further consideration, he begged leave to decline the honor of accompanying the Khan. The fact was, that three Kalmucks, who had strong motives for returning to their countrymen on the west bank of the Wolga, guessing the intentions of Weseloff, had offered to join him in his escape. These men the Khan would probably find himself obliged to countenance in their project; so that it became a point of honor with Weseloff to conceal their intentions, and therefore to accomplish the evasion from the camp, (of which the first steps only would be hazardous,) without risking the notice of the Khan.

The district in which they were now encamped abounded, through many hundred miles, with wild horses of a docile and beautiful breed. Each of the four fugitives had caught from seven to ten of these spirited creatures in the course of the last few days; this raised no suspicion; for the rest of the Kalmucks had been making the same sort of provision against the coming toils of their remaining route to China. These horses were secured by halters, and hidden about dusk in the thickets which lined the margin of the river. To these thickets, about ten at night, the four fugitives repaired; they took a circuitous path, which drew them as little as possible within danger of challenge from any of the outposts or of the patrols which had been established on the quarters where the Bashkirs lay; and in three quarters of an hour they reached the rendezvous. The moon had now risen, the horses were unfastened, and they were in the act of mounting, when the deep silence of the woods was disturbed by a violent uproar, and the clashing of arms. Weseloff fancied that he heard the voice of the Khan shouting for assistance. He remembered the communication made by that prince in the morning; and requesting his companions to support him, he rode off in the direction of the sound. A very short distance brought him to an open glade in the wood, where he beheld four men contending with a party of at least nine or ten. Two of the four were dismounted at the very instant of Weseloff's arrival; one of these he recognized almost certainly as the Khan, who was fighting hand to hand, but at great disadvantage, with two of the adverse horsemen. Seeing that no time was to be lost, Weseloff fired, and brought down one of the two. His companions discharged their carbines at the same moment, and then all rushed simultaneously into the little open area. The thundering sound of about thirty horses, all rushing at once into a narrow space, gave the impression that a whole troop of cavalry was coming down upon the assailants; who, accordingly, wheeled about and fled with one impulse. Weseloff advanced to the dismounted cavalier, who, as he expected, proved to be the Khan. The man whom Weseloff had shot was lying dead; and both were shocked, though Weseloff at least was not surprised, on stooping down and scrutinizing his features, to recognize a well known confidential servant of Zebek-Dorchi. Nothing was said by either party. The Khan rode off, escorted by Weseloff and his companions, and for some time a dead silence prevailed. The situation of Weseloff was delicate and critical; to leave the Khan at this point was probably to cancel their recent services; for he might be again crossed on his path, and again attacked by the very party from whom he had just been delivered. Yet, on the other hand, to return to the camp was to endanger the chances of accomplishing the escape. The Khan also was apparently revolving all this in his mind, for at length he broke silence, and said — 'I comprehend your situation; and, under other circumstances, I might feel it my duty to detain your companions. But it would ill become me to do so after the important service you have just rendered me. Let us turn a little to the left. There, where you see the watchfire, is an outpost. Attend me so far. I am then safe. You may turn and pursue your enterprise; for the circumstances under which you will appear, as my escort, are sufficient to shield you from all suspicion for the present. I regret having no better means at my disposal for testifying my gratitude. But tell me, before we part, was it accident only which led you to my rescue? Or had you acquired any knowledge of the plot by which I was decoyed into this snare?' Weseloff answered very candidly that mere accident had brought him to the spot at which he heard the uproar, but that *having* heard it, and connecting it with the Khan's communication of the morning, he had then designedly gone after the sound in a way which he certainly should not have done at so critical a moment, unless in the expectation of finding the Khan assaulted by assassins. A few minutes after they reached the outpost at which it became safe to leave the Tartar chieftain; and immediately the four fugitives commenced a flight which is perhaps without a parallel in the annals of travelling. Each of them led six or seven horses besides the one he rode; and by shifting from one to the other (like the ancient *Desultors* of the Roman circus,) so as never to burden the same horse for more than half an hour at a time, they continued to advance at the rate of two hundred miles in the twenty-four hours for three days consecutively. After that time, considering themselves beyond pursuit, they proceeded less rapidly; though still with a velocity which staggered the belief of Weseloff's friends in after years. He was, however, a man of high principle, and always adhered firmly to the details of his printed report. One of the circumstances there stated is, that they continued to pursue the route by which the Kalmucks had fled, never for an instant finding any difficulty in tracing it by the skeletons and other memorials of their calamities. In particular, he mentions vast heaps of money as part of the valuable property which it had been necessary to sacrifice. These heaps were found lying still untouched in the deserts. From these, Weseloff and his companions took as much as they could conveniently carry; and this it was, with the price of their beautiful horses, which they afterwards sold at one of the Russian military settlements for about £15 a-piece, which eventually enabled them to pursue their journey in Russia. This journey, as regarded Weseloff in particular, was closed by a tragical catastrophe. He was at that time young, and the only child of a doating mother. Her affliction under the violent abduction of her son had been excessive, and probably had undermined her constitution. Still she had supported it. Weseloff, giving way to the natural impulses of his filial affection, had imprudently posted through Russia, to his mother's house without warning of his approach. He rushed precipitately into her presense; and she, who had stood the shocks of sorrow, was found unequal to the shock of joy too sudden and too acute. She died upon the spot.

We now revert to the final scenes of the Kalmuck flight. These it would be useless to pursue circumstantially through the whole two thousand miles of suffering which remained; for the character of that suffering was even more monotonous than on the former half of the flight, but also more severe. Its main elements were excessive heat, with the accompaniments of famine and thirst, but aggravated at every step by the murderous attacks of their cruel enemies, the Bashkirs and the Kirghises.

These people, 'more fell than anguish, hunger, or the sea,' stuck to the unhappy Kalmucks like a swarm of enraged hornets. And very often whilst *they* were attacking them in the rear, their advanced parties and flanks were attacked with almost equal fury by the people of the country which they were traversing; and with good reason, since the law of self-preservation had now obliged the fugitive Tartars to plunder provisions, and to forage wherever they passed. In this respect their condition was a constant oscillation of wretchedness; for, sometimes, pressed by grinding famine, they took a circuit of perhaps a hundred miles, in order to strike into a land rich in the comforts of life; but in such a land they were sure to find a crowded population, of which every arm was raised in unrelenting hostility, with all the advantages of local knowledge, and with constant preoccupation of all the defensible positions, mountain passes, or bridges. Sometimes, again, wearied out with this mode of suffering, they took a circuit of perhaps a hundred miles, in order to strike into a land with few or no inhabitants. But in such a land they were sure to meet absolute starvation. Then, again, whether with or without this plague of starvation, whether with or without this plague of hostility in front, whatever might he the 'fierce varieties' of their misery in this respect, no rest ever came to their unhappy rear; *post equitem sedet atra cura*; it was a torment like the undying worm of conscience. And, upon the whole, it presented a spectacle altogether unprecedented in the history of mankind. Private and personal malignity is not unfrequently immortal; but rare indeed is it to find the same pertinacity of malice in a nation. And what embittered the interest was, that the malice was reciprocal. Thus far the parties met upon equal terms; but that equality only sharpened the sense of their dire inequality as to other circumstances. The Bashkirs were ready to fight 'from morn to dewy eve.' The Kalmucks, on the contrary, were always obliged to run; was it *from* their enemies, as creatures whom they feared? No; but *towards* their friends—towards that final haven of China—as what was hourly implored by their wives, and the tears of their children. But though they fled unwillingly, too often they fled in vain—being unwillingly recalled. There lay the torment. Every day the Bashkirs fell upon them; every day the same unprofitable battle was renewed; as a matter of course, the Kalmucks recalled part of their advanced guard to fight them; every day the battle raged for hours, and uniformly with the same result. For, no sooner did the Bashkirs find themselves too heavily pressed, and that the Kalmuck march had been retarded by some hours, than they retired into the boundless deserts where all pursuit was hopeless. But if the Kalmucks resolved to press forward, regardless of their enemies, in that case their attacks became so fierce and overwhelming, that the general safety seemed likely to be brought into question; nor could any effectual remedy be applied to the case, even for each separate day, except by a most embarrassing halt, and by countermarches, that, to men in their circumstances, were almost worse than death. It will not be surprising, that the irritation of such a systematic persecution, superadded to a previous and hereditary hatred, and accompanied by the stinging consciousness of utter impotence as regarded all effectual vengeance, should gradually have inflamed the Kalmuck animosity into the wildest expression of downright madness and frenzy. Indeed, long before the frontiers of China were approached, the hostility of both sides had assumed the appearance much more of a warfare amongst wild beasts than amongst creatures acknowledging the restraints of reason or the claims of a common nature. The spectacle became too atrocious; it was that of a host of lunatics pursued by a host of fiends.

On a fine morning in early autumn of the year 1771, Kien Long, the Emperor of China, was pursuing his amusements in a wild frontier district lying on the outside of the Great Wall. For many hundred square leagues the country was desolate of inhabitants, but rich in woods of ancient growth, and overrun with game of every description. In a central spot of this solitary region, the Emperor had built a gorgeous hunting-lodge, to which he resorted annually for recreation and relief from the cares of government. Led onwards in pursuit of game, he had rambled to a distance of two hundred miles or more from this lodge, followed at a little distance by a sufficient military escort, and every night pitching his tent in a different situation, until at length he had arrived on the very margin of the vast central deserts of Asia. [Footnote: All the circumstances are learned from a long state paper upon the subject of this Kalmuck migration, drawn up in the Chinese language by the Emperor himself. Parts of this paper have been translated by the Jesuit missionaries. The Emperor states the whole motives of his conduct and the chief incidents at great length.] Here he was standing, by accident, at an opening of his pavilion, enjoying the morning sunshine, when suddenly to the westward there arose a vast cloudy vapor, which by degrees expanded, mounted, and seemed to be slowly diffusing itself over the whole face of the heavens. By-and-by this vast sheet of mist began to thicken towards the horizon, and to roll forward in billowy volumes. The Emperor's suite assembled from all quarters. The silver trumpets were sounded in the rear, and from all the glades and forest avenues began to trot forward towards the pavilion the yagers, half cavalry, half huntsmen, who composed the Imperial escort. Conjecture was on the stretch to divine the cause of this phenomenon, and the interest continually increased, in proportion as simple curiosity gradually deepened into the anxiety of uncertain danger. At first it had been imagined that some vast troops of deer, or other wild animals of the chase, had been disturbed in their forest haunts by the Emperor's movements, or possibly by wild beasts prowling for prey, and might be fetching a compass by way of re-entering the forest grounds at some remoter points secure from molestation. But this conjecture was dissipated by the slow increase of the cloud, and the steadiness of its motion. In the course of two hours the vast phenomenon had advanced to a point which was judged to be within five miles of the spectators, though all calculations of distance were difficult, and often fallacious, when applied to the endless expanses of the Tartar deserts. Through the next hour, during which the gentle morning breeze had a little freshened, the dusty vapor had developed itself far and wide into the appearance of huge aerial draperies, hanging in mighty volumes from the sky to the earth; and at particular points, where the eddies of the breeze acted upon the pendulous skirts of these aerial curtains rents were perceived, sometimes taking the form of regular arches, portals, and windows, through which began dimly to gleam the heads of camels 'indorsed' [Footnote: *Camels 'indorsed;'* —'And elephants indorsed with towers.' MILTON in *Paradise Regained*.] with human beings — and at intervals the moving of men and horses, in tumultuous array—and then, through other openings or vistas, at far distant points, the flashing of polished arms. But sometimes, as the wind slackened or died away, all those openings, of whatever form, in the cloudy pall, would slowly close, and for a time the whole pageant was shut up from view; although the growing din, the clamors, the shrieks and groans, ascending from infuriated myriads, reported, in a language not to be misunderstood, what was going on behind the cloudy screen.

It was in fact the Kalmuck host, now in the last extremities of their exhaustion, and very fast approaching to that final stage of privation and intense misery, beyond which few or none could have lived, but also, happily for themselves, fast approaching (in a literal sense) that final stage of their long pilgrimage, at which they would meet hospitality on a scale of royal magnificence, and full protection from their enemies. These enemies, however, as yet still were hanging on their rear as fiercely as ever, though this day was destined to be the last of their hideous persecution. The Khan had, in fact, sent forward couriers with all the requisite statements and petitions, addressed to the Emperor of China. These had been duly received, and preparations made in consequence to welcome the Kalmucks with the most paternal benevolence. But as these couriers had been despatched from the Torgau at the moment of arrival thither, and before the advance of Traubenberg had made it necessary for the Khan to order a hasty renewal of the flight, the Emperor had not looked for their arrival on their frontier until full three months after the present time. The Khan had indeed expressly notified his intention to pass the summer heats on the banks of the Torgau, and to recommence his retreat about the beginning of September. The subsequent change of plan being unknown to Kien Long, left him for some time in doubt as to the true interpretation to be put upon this mighty apparition in the desert; but at length the savage clamors of hostile fury, and the clangor of weapons, unveiled to the Emperor the true nature of those unexpected calamities which had so prematurely precipitated the Kalmuck measure.

Apprehending the real state of affairs, the Emperor instantly perceived that the first act of his fatherly care for these erring children (as he esteemed them) now returning to their ancient obedience, must be—to deliver them from their pursuers. And this was less difficult than might have been supposed. Not many miles in the rear was a body of well appointed cavalry, with a strong detachment of artillery, who always attended the Emperor's motions. These were hastily summoned. Meantime it occurred to the train of courtiers that some danger might arise to the Emperor's person from the proximity of a lawless enemy; and accordingly he was induced to retire a little to the rear. It soon appeared, however, to those who watched the vapory shroud in the desert, that its motion was not such as would argue the direction of the march to be exactly upon the pavilion, but rather in a diagonal line, making an angle of full forty-five degrees with that line in which the Imperial *cortège* had been standing, and therefore with a distance continually increasing. Those who knew the country judged that the Kalmucks were making for a large fresh-water lake about seven or eight miles distant; they were right; and to that point the Imperial cavalry was ordered up; and it was precisely in that spot, and about three hours after and at noon-day on the 8th of September, that the great Exodus of the Kalmuck Tartars was brought to a final close, and with a scene of such memorable and hellish fury, as formed an appropriate winding-up to an expedition in all its parts and details so awfully disastrous. The Emperor was not personally present, or at least he saw whatever he *did* see from too great a distance to discriminate its individual features; but he records in his written memorial the report made to him of this scene by some of his own officers.

The lake of Tengis, near the frightful desert of Kobi, lay in a hollow amongst hills of a moderate height, ranging generally from two to three thousand feet high. About eleven o'clock in the forenoon, the Chinese cavalry reached the summit of a road which led through a cradle-like dip in the mountains right down upon the margin of the lake. From this pass, elevated about two thousand feet above the level of the water, they continued to descend, by a very winding and difficult road, for an hour and a half; and during the whole of this descent they were compelled to be inactive spectators of the fiendish spectacle below. The Kalmucks, reduced by this time from about six hundred thousand souls to two hundred thousand, and after enduring for two months and a half the miseries we have previously described—outrageous heat, famine, and the destroying scimitar of the Kirghises and the Bashkirs, had for the last ten days been traversing a hideous desert, where no vestiges were seen of vegetation, and no drop of water could be found. Camels and men were already so overladen, that it was a mere impossibility that they should carry a tolerable sufficiency for the passage of this frightful wilderness. On the eighth day the wretched daily allowance, which had been continually diminishing, failed entirely; and thus for two days of insupportable fatigue, the horrors of thirst had been carried to the fiercest extremity. Upon this last morning, at the sight of the hills and the forest scenery, which announced to those who acted as guides the neighborhood of the lake of Tengis, all the people rushed along with maddening eagerness to the anticipated solace. The day grew hotter and hotter, the people more and more exhausted, and gradually, in the general rush forwards to the lake, all discipline and command were lost—all attempts to preserve a rear-guard were neglected—the wild Bashkirs rode in amongst the encumbered people, and slaughtered them by wholesale, and almost without resistance. Screams and tumultuous shouts proclaimed the progress of the massacre; but none heeded—none halted; all alike, pauper or noble, continued to rush on with maniacal haste to the waters—all with faces blackened by the heat preying upon the liver, and with tongue drooping from the mouth. The cruel Bashkir was affected by the same misery, and manifested the same symptoms of his misery as the wretched Kalmuck; the murderer was oftentimes in the same frantic misery as his murdered victim—many indeed (an ordinary effect of thirst) in both nations had become lunatic—and in this state, whilst mere multitude and condensation of bodies alone opposed any check to the destroying scimitar and the trampling hoof, the lake was reached; and to that the whole vast body of enemies rushed, and together continued to rush, forgetful of all things at that moment but of one almighty instinct. This absorption of the thoughts in one maddening appetite lasted for a single minute; but in the next arose the final scene of parting vengeance. Far and wide the waters of the solitary lake were instantly dyed red with blood and gore; here rode a party of savage Bashkirs, hewing off heads as fast as the swathes fall before the mower's scythe; there stood unarmed Kalmucks in a death-grapple with their detested foes, both up to the middle in water, and oftentimes both sinking together below the surface, from weakness, or from struggles, and perishing in each other's arms. Did the Bashkirs at any point collect into a cluster for the sake of giving impetus to the assault? Thither were the camels driven in fiercely by those who rode them, generally women or boys; and even these quiet creatures were forced into a share in this carnival of murder, by trampling down as many as they could strike prostrate with the lash of their fore-legs. Every moment the water grew more polluted: and yet every moment fresh myriads came up to the lake and rushed in, not able to resist their frantic thirst, and swallowing large draughts of water, visibly contaminated with the blood of their slaughtered compatriots. Wheresoever the lake was shallow enough to allow of men raising their heads above the water, there for scores of acres were to be seen all forms of ghastly fear, of agonizing struggle, of spasm, of convulsion, of mortal conflict, death, and the fear of death—revenge, and the lunacy of revenge—hatred, and the frenzy of hatred—until the neutral spectators, of whom there were not a few, now descending the eastern side of the lake, at length averted their eyes in horror. This horror, which seemed incapable of further addition, was, however, increased by an unexpected incident. The Bashkirs, beginning to perceive here and there the approach of the Chinese cavalry, felt it prudent—wheresoever they were sufficiently at leisure from the passions of the murderous scene—to gather into bodies. This was noticed by the governor of a small Chinese fort, built upon an eminence above the lake; and immediately he threw in a broadside, which spread havoc amongst the Bashkir tribe. As often as the Bashkirs collected into 'globes' and 'turms' as their only means of meeting the long line of descending Chinese cavalry—so often did the Chinese governor of the fort pour in his exterminating broadside; until at length the lake at the lower end, became one vast seething cauldron of human bloodshed and carnage. The Chinese cavalry had reached the foot of the hills: the Bashkirs, attentive to their movements, had formed; skirmishes had been fought: and, with a quick sense that the contest was henceforwards rapidly becoming hopeless, the Bashkirs and Kirghises began to retire. The pursuit was not as vigorous as the Kalmuck hatred would have desired. But, at the same time, the very gloomiest hatred could not but find, in their own dreadful experience of the Asiatic deserts, and in the certainty that these wretched Bashkirs had to repeat that same experience a second time, for thousands of miles, as the price exacted by a retributary Providence for their vindictive cruelty—not the very gloomiest of the Kalmucks, or the least reflecting, but found in all this a retaliatory chastisement more complete and absolute than any which their swords and lances could have obtained, or human vengeance could have devised.

Here ends the tale of the Kalmuck wanderings in the Desert; for any subsequent marches which awaited them, were neither long nor painful. Every possible alleviation and refreshment for their exhausted bodies had been already provided by Kien Long with the most princely munificence; and lands of great fertility were immediately assigned to them in ample extent along the river Ily, not very far from the point at which they had first emerged from the wilderness of Kobi. But the beneficent attention of the Chinese Emperor may be best stated in his own words, as translated into French by one of the Jesuit missionaries:—"La nation des Torgotes (*savoir les Kalmuques*) arriva à Ily, toute *delabree*, n'ayant ni de quoi vivre, ni de quoi se vêtir. Je l'avais prévu; et j'avais ordonné de faire en tout genre les provisions nécessaires pour pouvoir les secourir promptement; c'est ce qui a été exécuté. On a fait la division des terres; et on a assigné à chaque famille une portion suffisante pour pouvoir servir à son entretien, soit en la cultivant, soit en y nourissant des bestiaux. On a donne a chaque particulier des étoffes pour l'habiller, des grains pour se nourrir pendant l'espace d'une année, des ustensiles pour le ménage et d'autres choses nécessaires: et outre cela plusieurs onces d'argent, pour se pourvoir de ce qu'on aurait pu oublier. On a désigné des lieux particuliers, fertiles en pâturages; et on leur a donné des boeufs, moutons, &c. pour qu'ils pussent dans la suite travailler par euxmêmes a leur entretien et à leur bienêtre."

These are the words of the Emperor himself, speaking in his own person of his own paternal cares; but another Chinese, treating the same subject, records the munificence of this prince in terms which proclaim still more forcibly the disinterested generosity which prompted, and the delicate considerateness which conducted this extensive bounty. He has been speaking of the Kalmucks, and he goes on thus:—"Lorsqu'ils arrivèrent sur nos frontières (au nombre de plusieurs centaines de mille), quoique la fatigue extrême, la faim, la soif, et toutes les autres incommodités inséparables d'une très-longue et très pénible route en eussent fait périr presque autant, ils étaient réduits a la dernière misère: ils manquaient de tout. Il" (viz. l'Empereur, Kien Long) "leur fit préparer des logemens conformes a leur manière de vivre; il leur fit distribuer des aliments et des habits; il leur fit donner des boeufs, des moutons, et des ustensiles, pour les mettre en état de former des troupeaux et de cultiver la terre, *et tout cela à ses propres frais*, qui se sont montés à des sommes immenses, sans compter l'argent qu'il a donné à chaque chef-de-famille, pour pourvoir à la subsistance de sa femme et de ses enfans."

Thus, after their memorable year of misery, the Kalmucks were replaced in territorial possessions, and in comfort equal perhaps, or even superior, to that which they had enjoyed in Russia, and with superior political advantages. But, if equal or superior, their condition was no longer the same; if not in degree, their social prosperity had altered in quality; for instead of being a purely pastoral and vagrant people, they were now in circumstances which obliged them to become essentially dependent upon agriculture; and thus far raised in social rank, that by the natural course of their habits and the necessities of life they were effectually reclaimed from roving, and from the savage customs connected with so unsettled a life. They gained also in political privileges, chiefly through the immunity from military service which their new relations enabled them to obtain. These were circumstances of advantage and gain. But one great disadvantage there was, amply to overbalance all other possible gain; the chances were lost or were removed to an incalculable distance for their conversion to Christianity, without which in these times there is no absolute advance possible on the path of true civilization.

One word remains to be said upon the *personal* interests concerned in this great drama. The catastrophe in this respect was remarkable and complete. Oubacha, with all his goodness and incapacity of suspecting, had, since the mysterious affair on the banks of the Torgau, felt his mind alienated from his cousin; he revolted from the man that would have murdered him; and he had displayed his caution so visibly as to provoke a reaction in the bearing of Zebek-Dorchi, and a displeasure which all his dissimulation could not hide. This had produced a feud, which, by keeping them aloof, had probably saved the life of Oubacha; for the friendship of Zebek-Dorchi was more fatal than his open enmity. After the settlement on the Ily this feud continued to advance, until it came under the notice of the Emperor, on occasion of a visit which all the Tartar chieftains made to his Majesty at his hunting-lodge in 1772. The Emperor informed himself accurately of all the particulars connected with the transaction—of all the rights and claims put forward—and of the way in which they would severally affect the interests of the Kalmuck people. The consequence was, that he adopted the cause of Oubacha, and repressed the pretensions of Zebek-Dorchi, who, on his part, so deeply resented this discountenance to his ambitious projects, that in conjunction with other chiefs he had the presumption even to weave nets of treason against the Emperor himself. Plots were laid—were detected—were baffled—counterplots were constructed upon the same basis, and with the benefit of the opportunities thus offered.

Finally, Zebek-Dorchi was invited to the imperial lodge, together with all his accomplices; and under the skilful management of the Chinese nobles in the Emperor's establishment, the murderous artifices of these Tartar chieftains were made to recoil upon themselves; and the whole of them perished by assassination at a great imperial banquet. For the Chinese morality is exactly of that kind which approves in everything the *lex talionis:*—

> — — '*lex nec justior ulla est (as they think)*
> *Quam necis artifices arte perire sua.*'

So perished Zebek-Dorchi, the author and originator of the great Tartar *Exodus*. Oubacha, meantime, and his people, were gradually recovering from the effects of their misery, and repairing their losses. Peace and prosperity, under the gentle rule of a fatherly lord paramount, re-dawned upon the tribes; their household *lares,* after so harsh a translation to distant climates, found again a happy reinstatement in what had in fact been their primitive abodes; they found themselves settled in quiet sylvan scenes, rich in all the luxuries of life, and endowed with the perfect loveliness of Arcadian beauty. But from the hills of this favored land and even from the level grounds as they approach its western border, they still look out upon that fearful wilderness which once beheld a nation in agony—the utter extirpation of nearly half a million from amongst its numbers, and, for the remainder, a storm of misery so fierce, that in the end (as happened also at Athens during the Peloponnesian war from a different form of misery) very many lost their memory; all records of their past life were wiped out as with a sponge—utterly erased and cancelled; and many others lost their reason; some in a gentle form of pensive melancholy, some in a more restless form of feverish delirium and nervous agitation, and others in the fixed forms of tempestuous mania, raving frenzy, or moping idiocy. Two great commemorative monuments arose in after years to mark the depth and permanence of the awe—the sacred and reverential grief with which all persons looked back upon the dread calamities attached to the year of the Tiger—all who had either personally shared in those calamities, and had themselves drunk from that cup of sorrow, or who had effectually been made witnesses to their results, and associated with their relief; two great monuments, we say; first of all, one in the religious solemnity, enjoined by the Dalai Lama, called in the Tartar language a *Romanang,* that is, a national commemoration, with music the most rich and solemn, of all the souls who departed to the rest of Paradise from the afflictions of the Desert: this took place about six years after the arrival in China. Secondly, another more durable and more commensurate to the scale of the calamity and to the grandeur of this national Exodus, in the mighty columns of granite and brass, erected by the Emperor Kien Long, near the banks of the Ily: these columns stand upon the very margin of the *steppes;* and they bear a short but emphatic inscription [Footnote: This inscription has been slightly altered in one or two phrases, and particularly in adapting to the Christian era the Emperor's expressions for the year of the original Exodus from China and the retrogressive Exodus from Russia. With respect to the designation adopted for the Russian Emperor, either it is built upon some confusion between him and the Byzantine Caesars, as though the former, being of the same religion with the latter (and occupying in part the same longitudes, though in different latitudes) might be considered as his modern successor; or else it refers simply to the Greek form of Christianity professed by the Russian Emperor and Church.] to the following effect:—

By the Will of God Here, upon the Brink of these Deserts, Which from this Point begin and stretch away Pathless, treeless, waterless, For thousands of miles—and along the margins of many mighty Nations, Rested from their labors and from great afflictions Under the shadow of the Chinese Wall, And by the favor of KIEN LONG, God's Lieutenant upon Earth, The ancient Children of the Wilderness—the Torgote Tartars Flying before the wrath of the Grecian Czar, Wandering Sheep who had strayed away from the Celestial Empire in the year 1616, But are now mercifully gathered again, after infinite sorrow, Into the fold of their forgiving Shepherd. Hallowed be the spot for ever, and Hallowed be the day—September 8, 1771! Amen.

VOLUME II

SYSTEM OF THE HEAVENS AS REVEALED BY LORD ROSSE'S TELESCOPES

[Footnote: Thoughts on Some Important Points relating to the System of the World. By J. P. Nichol, LL.D., Professor of Astronomy in the University of Glasgow. William Tait, Edinburgh. 1846.]

Some years ago, some person or other, [in fact I believe it was myself,] published a paper from the German of Kant, on a very interesting question, viz., the age of our own little Earth. Those who have never seen that paper, a class of unfortunate people whom I suspect to form *rather* the majority in our present perverse generation, will be likely to misconceive its object. Kant's purpose was, not to ascertain how many years the Earth had lived: a million of years, more or less, made very little difference to *him*. What he wished to settle was no such barren conundrum. For, had there even been any means of coercing the Earth into an honest answer, on such a delicate point, which the Sicilian canon, Recupero, fancied that there was; [Footnote: *Recupero*. See Brydone's Travels, some sixty or seventy years ago. The canon, being a beneficed clergyman in the Papal church, was naturally an infidel. He wished exceedingly to refute Moses: and he fancied that he really had done so by means of some collusive assistance from the layers of lava on Mount Etna. But there survives, at this day, very little to remind us of the canon, except an unpleasant guffaw that rises, at times, in solitary valleys of Etna.] but which, in my own opinion, there neither is, nor ought to be, — (since a man deserves to be cudgelled who could put such improper questions to a *lady* planet,) — still what would it amount to? What good would it do us to have a certificate of our dear little mother's birth and baptism? Other people — people in Jupiter, or the Uranians — may amuse themselves with her pretended foibles or infirmities: it is quite safe to do so at *their* distance; and, in a female planet like Venus, it might be natural, (though, strictly speaking, not quite correct,) to scatter abroad malicious insinuations, as though our excellent little mamma had begun to wear false hair, or had lost some of her front teeth. But all this, we men of sense know to be gammon. Our mother Tellus, beyond all doubt, is a lovely little thing. I am satisfied that she is very much admired throughout the Solar System: and, in clear seasons, when she is seen to advantage, with her bonny wee pet of a Moon tripping round her like a lamb, I should be thankful to any gentleman who will mention where he has happened to observe — either he or his telescope — will he only have the goodness to say, in what part of the heavens he has discovered a more elegant turn-out. I wish to make no personal reflections. I name no names. Only this I say, that, though some people have the gift of seeing things that other people never could see, and though some other people, or other some people are born with a silver spoon in their mouths, so that, generally, their geese count for swans, yet, after all, swans or geese, it would be a pleasure to me, and really a curiosity, to see the planet that could fancy herself entitled to sneeze at our Earth. And then, if she (viz., our Earth,) keeps but one Moon, even *that* (you know) is an advantage as regards some people that keep none. There are people, pretty well known to you and me, that can't make it convenient to keep even one Moon. And so I come to my moral; which is this, that, to all appearance, it is mere justice; but, supposing it were not, still it is *our* duty, (as children of the Earth,) right or wrong, to stand up for our bonny young mamma, if she *is* young; or for our dear old mother, if she *is* old; whether young or old, to take her part against all comers; and to argue through thick and thin, which (sober or not) I always attempt to do, that she is the most respectable member of the Copernican System.

Meantime, what Kant understood by being old, is something that still remains to be explained. If one stumbled, in the steppes of Tartary, on the grave of a Megalonyx, and, after long study, had deciphered from some pre-Adamite heiro-pothooks, the following epitaph: — '*Hic jacet* a Megalonyx, or *Hic jacet* a Mammoth, (as the case might be,) who departed this life, to the grief of his numerous acquaintance in the seventeen thousandth year of his age,' — of course, one would be sorry for him; because it must be disagreeable at *any* age to be torn away from life, and from all one's little megalonychal comforts; that's not pleasant, you know, even if one *is* seventeen thousand years old. But it would make all the difference possible in your grief, whether the record indicated a premature death, that he had been cut off, in fact, whilst just stepping into life, or had kicked the bucket when full of honors, and been followed to the grave by a train of weeping grandchildren. He had died 'in his teens,' that's past denying. But still we must know to what stage of life in a man, had corresponded seventeen thousand years in a Mammoth. Now exactly this was what Kant desired to know about our planet. Let her have lived any number of years that you suggest, (shall we say if you please, that she is in her billionth year?) still that tells us nothing about the *period* of life, the *stage*, which she may be supposed to have reached. Is she a child, in fact, or is she an adult? And, *if* an adult, and that you gave a ball to the Solar System, is she that kind of person, that you would introduce to a waltzing partner, some fiery young gentlemen like Mars, or would you rather suggest to her the sort of partnership which takes place at a whist-table? On this, as on so many other questions, Kant was perfectly sensible that people, of the finest understandings, may and do take the most opposite views. Some think that our planet is in that stage of her life, which corresponds to the playful period of twelve or thirteen in a spirited girl. Such a girl, were it not that she is checked by a sweet natural sense of feminine grace, you might call a romp; but not a hoyden, observe; no horse-play; oh, no, nothing of that sort. And these people fancy that earthquakes, volcanoes, and all such little *escapades* will be over, they will, in lawyer's phrase, 'cease and determine,' as soon as our Earth reaches the age of maidenly bashfulness. Poor thing! It's quite natural, you know, in a healthy growing girl. A little overflow of vivacity, a *pirouette* more or less, what harm should *that* do to any of us? Nobody takes more delight than I in the fawn-like sportiveness of an innocent girl, at this period of life: even a shade of *espièglerie* does not annoy me. But still my own impressions incline me rather to represent the Earth as a fine noble young woman, full of the pride which is so becoming to her sex, and well able to take her own part, in case that, at any solitary point of the heavens, she should come across one of those vulgar fussy Comets, disposed to be rude and take improper liberties. These Comets, by the way, are public nuisances, very much like the mounted messengers of butchers in great cities, who are always at full gallop, and moving upon such an infinity of angles to human shinbones, that the final purpose of such boys (one of whom lately had the audacity nearly to ride down the Duke of Wellington) seems to be—not the translation of mutton, which would certainly find its way into human mouths even if riding boys were not,—but the improved geometry of transcendental curves. They ought to be numbered, ought these boys, and to wear badges—X 10, &c. And exactly the same evil, asking therefore by implication for exactly the same remedy, affects the Comets. A respectable planet is known everywhere, and responsible for any mischief that he does. But if a cry should arise, 'Stop that wretch, who was rude to the Earth: who is he?' twenty voices will answer, perhaps, 'It's Encke's Comet; he is always doing mischief;' well, what can you say? it *may* be Encke's, it may be some other man's Comet; there are so many abroad and on so many roads, that you might as well ask upon a night of fog, such fog as may be opened with an oyster knife, whose cab that was (whose, viz., out of 27,000 in London) that floored you into the kennel.

These are constructive ideas upon the Earth's stage of evolution, which Kant was aware of, and which will always find toleration, even where they do not find patronage. But others there are, a class whom I perfectly abominate, that place our Earth in the category of decaying women, nay of decayed women, going, going, and all but gone. 'Hair like arctic snows, failure of vital heat, palsy that shakes the head as in the porcelain toys on our mantel-pieces, asthma that shakes the whole fabric—these they absolutely fancy themselves to *see*. They absolutely *hear* the tellurian lungs wheezing, panting, crying, 'Bellows to mend!' periodically as the Earth approaches her aphelion.

But suddenly at this point a demur arises upon the total question. Kant's very problem explodes, bursts, as poison in Venetian wine-glass of old shivered the glass into fragments. For is there, after all, any stationary meaning in the question? Perhaps in reality the Earth is both young and old. Young? If she is not young at present, perhaps she *will* be so in future. Old? if she is not old at this moment, perhaps she *has* been old, and has a fair chance of becoming so again. In fact, she is a Phoenix that is known to have secret processes for rebuilding herself out of her own ashes. Little doubt there is but she has seen many a birthday, many a funeral night, and many a morning of resurrection. Where now the mightiest of oceans rolls in pacific beauty, once were anchored continents and boundless forests. Where the south pole now shuts her frozen gates inhospitably against the intrusions of flesh, once were probably accumulated the ribs of empires; man's imperial forehead, woman's roseate lips, gleamed upon ten thousand hills; and there were innumerable contributions to antarctic journals almost as good (but not quite) as our own. Even within our domestic limits, even where little England, in her south-eastern quarter now devolves so quietly to the sea her sweet pastoral rivulets, once came roaring down, in pomp of waters, a regal Ganges [Footnote: *'Ganges:'*—Dr. Nichol calls it by this name for the purpose of expressing its grandeur; and certainly in breadth, in diffusion at all times, but especially in the rainy season, the Ganges is the cock of the walk in our British orient. Else, as regards the body of water discharged, the absolute payments made into the sea's exchequer, and the majesty of column riding downwards from the Himalaya, I believe that, since Sir Alexander Burnes's measurements, the Indus ranks foremost by a long chalk.], that drained some hyperbolical continent, some Quinbus Flestrin of Asiatic proportions, long since gone to the dogs. All things pass away. Generations wax old as does a garment: but eternally God says:—'Come again, ye children of men.' Wildernesses of fruit, and worlds of flowers, are annually gathered in solitary South America to ancestral graves: yet still the Pomona of Earth, yet still the Flora of Earth, does not become superannuated, but blossoms in everlasting youth. Not otherwise by secular periods, known to us geologically as facts, though obscure as durations, *Tellus* herself, the planet, as a whole, is for ever working by golden balances of change and compensation, of ruin and restoration. She recasts her glorious habitations in decomposing them; she lies down for death, which perhaps a thousand times she has suffered; she rises for a new birth, which perhaps for the thousandth time has glorified her disc. Hers is the wedding garment, hers is the shroud, that eternally is being woven in the loom. And God imposes upon her the awful necessity of working for ever at her own grave, yet of listening for ever to his far-off trumpet of *palingenesis*.

If this account of the matter be just, and were it not treasonable to insinuate the possibility of an error against so great a swell as Immanuel Kant, one would be inclined to fancy that Mr. Kant had really been dozing a little on this occasion; or, agreeably to his own illustration elsewhere, that he had realized the pleasant picture of one learned doctor trying to milk a he-goat, whilst another doctor, equally learned, holds the milk-pail below. [Footnote: Kant applied this illustration to the case where one worshipful scholar proposes some impossible problem, (as the squaring of the circle, or the perpetual motion,) which another worshipful scholar sits down to solve. The reference was of course to Virgil's line,—'Atque idem jungat vulpes, et *mulgeat hircos*.'] And there is apparently this two-edged embarrassment pressing upon the case—that, if our dear excellent mother the Earth could be persuaded to tell us her exact age in Julian years, still *that* would leave us all as much in the dark as ever: since, if the answer were, 'Why, children, at my next birth-day I shall count a matter of some million centuries,' we should still be at a loss to *value* her age: would it mean that she was a mere chicken, or that she was 'getting up in years?' On the other hand, if (declining to state any odious circumstantialities,) she were to reply,—'No matter, children, for my precise years, which are disagreeable remembrances; I confess generally to being a lady of a certain age,'—here, in the inverse order, given the *valuation* of the age, we should yet be at a loss for the *absolute* years numerically: would a 'certain age,' mean that 'mamma' was a million, be the same more or less, or perhaps not much above seventy thousand?

Every way, you see, reader, there are difficulties. But two things used to strike me, as unaccountably overlooked by Kant; who, to say the truth, was profound—yet at no time very agile—in the character of his understanding. First, what age now might we take our brother and sister planets to be? For *that* determination as to a point in *their* constitution, will do something to illustrate our own. We are as good as they, I hope, any day: perhaps in a growl, one might modestly insinuate—*better*. It's not at all likely that there can be any great disproportion of age amongst children of the same household: and therefore, since Kant always countenanced the idea that Jupiter had not quite finished the upholstery of his extensive premises, as a comfortable residence for a man, Jupiter having, in fact, a fine family of mammoths, but no family at all of 'humans,' (as brother Jonathan calls them,) Kant was bound, *ex analogo*, to hold that any little precedency in the trade of living, on the part of our own mother Earth, could not count for much in the long run. At Newmarket, or Doncaster, the start is seldom mathematically true: trifling advantages will survive all human trials after abstract equity; and the logic of this case argues, that any few thousands of years by which Tellus may have got ahead of Jupiter, such as the having finished her Roman Empire, finished her Crusades, and finished her French Revolution, virtually amounts to little or nothing; indicates no higher proportion to the total scale upon which she has to run, than the few tickings of a watch by which one horse at the start for the Leger is in advance of another. When checked in our chronology by each other, it transpires that, in effect, we are but executing the nice manoeuvre of a start; and that the small matter of six thousand years, by which we may have advanced our own position beyond some of our planetary rivals, is but the outstretched neck of an uneasy horse at Doncaster. This is *one* of the data overlooked by Kant; and the less excusably overlooked, because it was his own peculiar doctrine, — that uncle Jupiter ought to be considered a greenhorn. Jupiter may be a younger brother of our mamma; but, if he is a brother at all, he cannot be so very wide of our own chronology; and therefore the first *datum* overlooked by Kant was — the analogy of our whole planetary system. A second datum, as it always occurred to myself, might reasonably enough be derived from the intellectual vigor of us men. If our mother could, with any show of reason, be considered an old decayed lady, snoring stentorously in her arm-chair, there would naturally be some *aroma* of phthisis, or apoplexy, beginning to form about *us*, that are her children. But *is* there? If ever Dr. Johnson said a true word, it was when he replied to the Scottish judge Burnett, so well known to the world as Lord Monboddo. The judge, a learned man, but obstinate as a mule in certain prejudices, had said plaintively, querulously, piteously, — 'Ah, Doctor, we are poor creatures, we men of the eighteenth century, by comparison with our forefathers!' 'Oh, no, my Lord,' said Johnson, 'we are quite as strong as our ancestors, and a great deal wiser.' Yes; our kick is, at least, as dangerous, and our logic does three times as much execution. This would be a complex topic to treat effectively; and I wish merely to indicate the opening which it offers for a most decisive order of arguments in such a controversy. If the Earth were on her last legs, we her children could not be very strong or healthy. Whereas, if there were less pedantry amongst us, less malice, less falsehood, and less darkness of prejudice, easy it would be to show, that in almost every mode of intellectual power, we are more than a match for the most conceited of elder generations, and that in some modes we have energies or arts absolutely and exclusively our own. Amongst a thousand indications of strength and budding youth, I will mention two:— Is it likely, is it plausible, that our Earth should just begin to find out effective methods of traversing land and sea, when she had a summons to leave both? Is it not, on the contrary, a clear presumption that the great career of earthly nations is but on the point of opening, that life is but just beginning to kindle, when the great obstacles to effectual locomotion, and therefore to extensive human intercourse, are first of all beginning to give way? Secondly, I ask peremptorily,—Does it stand with good sense, is it reasonable that Earth is waning, science drooping, man looking downward, precisely in that epoch when, first of all, man's eye is arming itself for looking effectively into the mighty depths of space? A new era for the human intellect, upon a path that lies amongst its most aspiring, is promised, is inaugurated, by Lord Rosse's almost awful telescope.

What is it then that Lord Rosse has accomplished? If a man were aiming at dazzling by effects of rhetoric, he might reply: He has accomplished that which once the condition of the telescope not only refused its permission to hope for, but expressly bade man to despair of. What is it that Lord Rosse has revealed? Answer: he has revealed more by far than he found. The theatre to which he has introduced us, is *immeasurably* beyond the old one which he found. To say that he found, in the visible universe, a little wooden theatre of Thespis, a *tréteau* or shed of vagrants, and that he presented us, at a price of toil and of *anxiety* that cannot be measured, with a Roman colosseum,—*that* is to say nothing. It is to undertake the measurement of the tropics with the pocket-tape of an upholsterer. Columbus, when he introduced the Old World to the New, after all that can be said in his praise, did in fact only introduce the majority to the minority; but Lord Rosse has introduced the minority to the majority. There are two worlds, one called Ante-Rosse, and the other Post-Rosse; and, if it should come to voting, the latter would shockingly outvote the other. Augustus Cæsar made it his boast when dying, that he had found the city of Rome built of brick, and that he left it built of marble: *lateritiam invenit, marmoream reliquit.* Lord Rosse may say, even if to-day he should die, 'I found God's universe represented for human convenience, even after all the sublime discoveries of Herschel, upon a globe or spherical chart having a radius of one hundred and fifty feet; and I left it sketched upon a similar chart, keeping exactly the same scale of proportions, but now elongating its radius into one thousand feet.' The reader of course understands that this expression, founded on absolute calculations of Dr. Nichol, is simply meant to exhibit the *relative* dimensions of the *mundus Ante-Rosseanus* and the *mundus Post-Rosseanus;* for as to the *absolute* dimensions, when stated in miles, leagues or any units familiar to the human experience, they are too stunning and confounding. If, again, they are stated in larger units, as for instance diameters of the earth's orbit, the unit itself that should facilitate the grasping of the result, and which really *is* more manageable numerically, becomes itself elusive of the mental grasp: it comes in as an interpreter; and (as in some other cases) the interpreter is hardest to be understood of the two. If, finally, TIME be assumed as the exponent of the dreadful magnitudes, time combining itself with motion, as in the flight of cannon-balls or the flight of swallows, the sublimity becomes greater; but horror seizes upon the reflecting intellect, and incredulity upon the irreflective. Even a railroad generation, that *should* have faith in the miracles of velocity, lifts up its hands with an '*Incredulus odi!*' we know that Dr. Nichol speaks the truth; but he *seems* to speak falsehood. And the ignorant by-stander prays that the doctor may have grace given him and time for repentance; whilst his more liberal companion reproves his want of charity, observing that travellers into far countries have always had a license for lying, as a sort of tax or fine levied for remunerating their own risks; and that great astronomers, as necessarily far travellers into space, are entitled to a double per centage of the same Munchausen privilege.

Great is the mystery of Space, greater is the mystery of Time; either mystery grows upon man, as man himself grows; and either seems to be a function of the godlike which is in man. In reality the depths and the heights which are in man, the depths by which he searches, the heights by which he aspires, are but projected and made objective externally in the three dimensions of space which are outside of him. He trembles at the abyss into which his bodily eyes look down, or look up; not knowing that abyss to be, not always consciously suspecting it to be, but by an instinct written in his prophetic heart feeling it to be, boding it to be, fearing it to be, and sometimes hoping it to be, the mirror to a mightier abyss that will one day be expanded in himself. Even as to the sense of space, which is the lesser mystery than time, I know not whether the reader has remarked that it is one which swells upon man with the expansion of his mind, and that it is probably peculiar to the mind of man. An infant of a year old, or oftentimes even older, takes no notice of a sound, however loud, which is a quarter of a mile removed, or even in a distant chamber. And brutes, even of the most enlarged capacities, seem not to have any commerce with distance: distance is probably not revealed to them except by a *presence*, viz., by some shadow of their own animality, which, if perceived at all, is perceived as a thing *present* to their organs. An animal desire, or a deep animal hostility, may render sensible a distance which else would not be sensible; but not render it sensible *as* a distance. Hence perhaps is explained, and not out of any self-oblivion from higher enthusiasm, a fact that often has occurred, of deer, or hares, or foxes, and the pack of hounds in pursuit, chaser and chased, all going headlong over a precipice together. Depth or height does not readily manifest itself to *them*; so that any *strong* motive is sufficient to overpower the sense of it. Man only has a natural function for expanding on an illimitable sensorium, the illimitable growths of space. Man, coming to the precipice, reads his danger; the brute perishes: man is saved; and the horse is saved by his rider.

But, if this sounds in the ear of some a doubtful refinement, the doubt applies only to the lowest degrees of space. For the highest, it is certain that brutes have no perception. To man is as much reserved the prerogative of perceiving space in its higher extensions, as of geometrically constructing the relations of space. And the brute is no more capable of apprehending abysses through his eye, than he can build upwards or can analyze downwards the ærial synthesis of Geometry. Such, therefore, as is space for the grandeur of man's perceptions, such as is space for the benefit of man's towering mathematic speculations, such is the nature of our debt to Lord Rosse—as being the philosopher who has most pushed back the frontiers of our conquests upon this *exclusive* inheritance of man. We have all heard of a king that, sitting on the sea-shore, bade the waves, as they began to lave his feet, upon their allegiance to retire. *That* was said not vainly or presumptuously, but in reproof of sycophantic courtiers. Now, however, we see in good earnest another man, wielding another kind of sceptre, and sitting upon the shores of infinity, that says to the ice which had frozen up our progress,—'Melt thou before my breath!' that says to the rebellious *nebulæ*,—'Submit, and burst into blazing worlds!' that says to the gates of darkness,—'Roll back, ye barriers, and no longer hide from us the infinities of God!'

'Come, and I will show you what is beautiful.'

From the days of infancy still lingers in my ears this opening of a prose hymn by a lady, then very celebrated, viz., the late Mrs. Barbauld. The hymn began by enticing some solitary infant into some silent garden, I believe, or some forest lawn; and the opening words were, 'Come, and I will show you what is beautiful!' Well, and what beside? There is nothing beside; oh, disappointed and therefore enraged reader; positively this is the sum-total of what I can recall from the wreck of years; and certainly it is not much. Even of Sappho, though time has made mere ducks and drakes of her lyrics, we have rather more spared to us than this. And yet this trifle, simple as you think it, this shred of a fragment, if the reader will believe me, still echoes with luxurious sweetness in my ears, from some unaccountable hide-and-seek of fugitive childish memories; just as a marine shell, if applied steadily to the ear, awakens (according to the fine image of Landor [Footnote: 'Of Landor,' viz., in his 'Gebir;' but also of Wordsworth in 'The Excursion.' And I must tell the reader, that a contest raged at one time as to the *original property* in this image, not much less keen than that between Neptune and Minerva, for the chancellorship of Athens.]) the great vision of the sea; places the listener

> '*In the sun's palace-porch,*
> *And murmurs as the ocean murmurs there.'*

Now, on some moonless night, in some fitting condition of the atmosphere, if Lord Rosse would permit the reader and myself to walk into the front drawing-room of his telescope, then, in Mrs. Barbauld's words, slightly varied, I might say to him,—Come, and I will show you what is sublime! In fact, what I am going to lay before him, from Dr. Nichol's work, is, or at least *would* be, (when translated into Hebrew grandeur by the mighty telescope,) a step above even that object which some four-and-twenty years ago in the British Museum struck me as simply the sublimest sight which in this sight-seeing world I had seen. It was the Memnon's head, then recently brought from Egypt. I looked at it, as the reader must suppose, in order to understand the depth which I have here ascribed to the impression, not as a human but as a symbolic head; and what it symbolized to me were: 1. The peace which passeth all understanding. 2. The eternity which baffles and confounds all faculty of computation; the eternity which *had* been, the eternity which *was* to be. 3. The diffusive love, not such as rises and falls upon waves of life and mortality, not such as sinks and swells by undulations of time, but a procession—an emanation from some mystery of endless dawn. You durst not call it a smile that radiated from the lips; the radiation was too awful to clothe itself in adumbrations or memorials of flesh.

In *that mode* of sublimity, perhaps, I still adhere to my first opinion, that nothing so great was ever beheld. The atmosphere for *this*, for the Memnon, was the breathlessness which belongs to a saintly trance; the holy thing seemed to live by silence. But there *is* a picture, the pendant of the Memnon, there *is* a dreadful cartoon, from the gallery which has begun to open upon Lord Rosse's telescope, where the appropriate atmosphere for investing it must be drawn from another silence, from the frost and from the eternities of death. It is the famous *nebula* in the constellation of Orion; famous for the unexampled defiance with which it resisted all approaches from the most potent of former telescopes; famous for its frightful magnitude and for the frightful depth to which it is sunk in the abysses of the heavenly wilderness; famous just now for the submission with which it has begun to render up its secrets to the all-conquering telescope; and famous in all time coming for the horror of the regal phantasma which it has perfected to eyes of flesh.

Had Milton's 'incestuous mother,' with her fleshless son, and with the warrior angel, his father, that led the rebellions of heaven, been suddenly unmasked by Lord Rosse's instrument, in these dreadful distances before which, simply as expressions of resistance, the mind of man shudders and recoils, there would have been nothing more appalling in the exposure; in fact, it would have been essentially the same exposure: the same expression of power in the detestable phantom, the same rebellion in the attitude, the same pomp of malice in the features to a universe seasoned for its assaults.

The reader must look to Dr. Nichol's book, at page 51, for the picture of this abominable apparition. But then, in order to see what *I* see, the obedient reader must do what I tell him to do. Let him therefore view the wretch upside down. If he neglects that simple direction, of course I don't answer for anything that follows: without any fault of mine, my description will be unintelligible. This inversion being made, the following is the dreadful creature that will then reveal itself.

Description of the Nebula in Orion, as forced to show out by Lord Rosse.—You see a head thrown back, and raising its face, (or eyes, if eyes it had,) in the very anguish of hatred, to some unknown heavens. What *should* be its skull wears what *might* be an Assyrian tiara, only ending behind in a floating train. This head rests upon a beautifully developed neck and throat. All power being given to the awful enemy, he is beautiful where he pleases, in order to point and envenom his ghostly ugliness. The mouth, in that stage of the apocalypse which Sir John Herschel was able to arrest in his eighteen-inch mirror, is amply developed. Brutalities unspeakable sit upon the upper lip, which is confluent with a snout; for separate nostrils there are none. Were it not for this one defect of nostrils; and, even in spite of this defect, (since, in so mysterious a mixture of the angelic and the brutal, we may suppose the sense of odor to work by some compensatory organ,) one is reminded by the phantom's attitude of a passage, ever memorable, in Milton: that passage, I mean, where Death first becomes aware, soon after the original trespass, of his own future empire over man. The 'meagre shadow' even smiles (for the first time and the last) on apprehending his own abominable bliss, by apprehending from afar the savor 'of mortal change on earth.'

——'*Such a scent,*' (he says,) '*I draw*
Of carnage, prey innumerable.'

As illustrating the attitude of the phantom in Orion, let the reader allow me to quote the tremendous passage:—

'*So saying, with delight he snuff'd the smell*
Of mortal change on earth. As when a flock
Of ravenous fowl, though many a league remote,

> *Against the day of battle, to a field,*
> *Where armies lie encamp'd, come flying, lured*
> *With scent of living carcasses design'd*
> *For death, the following day, in bloody fight;*
> *So scented the grim feature,*

[Footnote: 'So scented the grim feature,' [*feature* is the old word for *form or outline that is shadowy*; and also for form (shadowy or not) which abstracts from the *matter*.] By the way, I have never seen it noticed, that Milton was indebted for the hint of this immortal passage to a superb line-and-a-half, in Lucan's Pharsalia.]

> *and upturn'd*
> *His nostril wide into the murky air,*
> *Sagacious of his quarry from so far.'*

But the lower lip, which is drawn inwards with the curve of a conch shell,—oh what a convolute of cruelty and revenge is *there*! Cruelty!—to whom? Revenge!—for what? Ask not, whisper not. Look upwards to other mysteries. In the very region of his temples, driving itself downwards into his cruel brain, and breaking the continuity of his diadem, is a horrid chasm, a ravine, a shaft, that many centuries would not traverse; and it is serrated on its posterior wall with a harrow that perhaps is partly hidden. From the anterior wall of this chasm rise, in vertical directions, two processes; one perpendicular, and rigid as a horn, the other streaming forward before some portentous breath. What these could be, seemed doubtful; but now, when further examinations by Sir John Herschel, at the Cape of Good Hope, have filled up the scattered outline with a rich umbrageous growth, one is inclined to regard them as the plumes of a sultan. Dressed he is, therefore, as well as armed. And finally comes Lord Rosse, that glorifies him with the jewellery [Footnote: *The jewellery of Stars*. And one thing is very remarkable, viz., that not only the stars justify this name of jewellery, as usual, by the life of their splendor, but also, in this case, by their arrangement. No jeweller could have set, or disposed with more art, the magnificent quadrille of stars which is placed immediately below the upright plume. There is also another, a truncated quadrille, wanting only the left hand star (or you might call it a bisected lozenge) placed on the diadem, but obliquely placed as regards the curve of that diadem. Two or three other arrangements are striking, though not equally so, both from their regularity and from their repeating each other, as the forms in a kaleidoscope.] of stars: he is now a vision 'to dream of, not to tell:' he is ready for the worship of those that are tormented in sleep: and the stages of his solemn uncovering by astronomy, first by Sir W. Herschel, secondly, by his son, and finally by Lord Rosse, is like the reversing of some heavenly doom, like the raising of the seals that had been sealed by the angel, in the Revelations. But the reader naturally asks, How does all this concern Lord Rosse's telescope on the one side, or general astronomy on the other? This *nebula*, he will say, seems a bad kind of fellow by your account; and of course it will not break my heart to hear, that he has had the conceit taken out of him. But in what way can *that* affect the pretensions of this new instrument; or, if it did, how can the character of the instrument affect the general condition of a science? Besides, is not the science a growth from very ancient times? With great respect for the Earl of Rosse, is it conceivable that he, or any man, by one hour's working the tackle of his new instrument, can have carried any stunning revolutionary effect into the heart of a section so ancient in our mathematical physics? But the reader is to consider, that the ruins made by Lord Rosse, are in *sidereal* astronomy, which is almost wholly a growth of modern times; and the particular part of it demolished by the new telescope, is almost exclusively the creation of the two Herschels, father and son. Laplace, it is true, adopted their views; and he transferred them to the particular service of our own planetary system. But he gave to them no new sanction, except what arises from showing that they would account for the appearances, as they present themselves to our experience at this day. That was a *negative* confirmation; by which I mean, that, had their views failed in the hands of Laplace, then they were proved to be false; but, *not* failing, they were not therefore proved to be true. It was like proving a gun; if the charge is insufficient, or if, in trying the strength of cast iron, timber, ropes, &c., the strain is not up to the rigor of the demand, you go away with perhaps a favorable impression as to the promises of the article; it has stood a moderate trial; it has stood all the trial that offered, which is always something; but you are still obliged to feel that, when the ultimate test is applied, smash may go the whole concern. Lord Rosse applied an ultimate test; and smash went the whole concern. Really I must have laughed, though all the world had been angry, when the shrieks and yells of expiring systems began to reverberate all the way from the belt of Orion; and positively at the very first broadside delivered from this huge four-decker of a telescope.

But what was it then that went to wreck? That is a thing more easy to ask than to answer. At least, for my own part, I complain that some vagueness hangs over all the accounts of the nebular hypothesis. However, in this place a brief sketch will suffice.

Herschel the elder, having greatly improved the telescope, began to observe with special attention a class of remarkable phenomena in the starry world hitherto unstudied, viz.: milky spots in various stages of diffusion. The nature of these appearances soon cleared itself up thus far, that generally they were found to be starry worlds, separated from ours by inconceivable distances, and in that way concealing at first their real nature. The whitish gleam was the mask conferred by the enormity of their remotion. This being so, it might have been supposed that, as was the faintness of these cloudy spots or *nebulæ*, such was the distance. But *that* did not follow: for in the treasury of nature it turned out that there were other resources for modifying the powers of distance, for muffling and unmuffling the voice of stars. Suppose a world at the distance x, which distance is so great as to make the manifestation of that world weak, milky, nebular. Now let the secret power that wields these awful orbs, push this world back to a double distance! *that* should naturally make it paler and more dilute than ever: and yet by *compression*, by deeper centralization, this effect shall be defeated; by forcing into far closer neighborhood the stars which compose this world, again it shall gleam out brighter when at $2x$ than when at x. At this point of compression, let the great moulding power a second time push it back; and a second time it will grow faint. But once more let this world be tortured into closer compression, again let the screw be put upon it, and once again it shall shake off the oppression of distance as the dew-drops are shaken from a lion's mane. And thus in fact the mysterious architect plays at hide-and-seek with his worlds. 'I will hide it,' he says, 'and it shall be found again by man; I will withdraw it into distances that shall seem fabulous, and again it shall apparel itself in glorious light; a third time I will plunge it into aboriginal darkness, and upon the vision of man a third time it shall rise with a new epiphany.'

But, says the objector, there is no such world; there is no world that has thus been driven back, and depressed from one deep to a lower deep. Granted: but the same effect, an illustration of the same law, is produced equally, whether you take four worlds, all of the same magnitude, and plunge them *simultaneously* into four different abysses, sinking by graduated distances one below another, or take one world and plunge it to the same distances *successively*. So in Geology, when men talk of substances in different stages, or of transitional states, they do not mean that they have watched the same individual *stratum* or *phenomenon*, exhibiting states removed from each other by depths of many thousand years; how could they? but they have seen one stage in the case A, another stage in the case B. They take, for instance, three objects, the same (to use the technical language of logic) generically, though numerically different, under separate circumstances, or in different stages of advance. They are one object for logic, they are three for human convenience. So again it might seem impossible to give the history of a rose tree from infancy to age: how could the same rose tree, at the same time, be young and old? Yet by taking the different developments of its flowers, even as they hang on the same tree, from the earliest bud to the full-blown rose, you may in effect pursue this vegetable growth through all its stages: you have before you the bony blushing little rose-bud, and the respectable 'mediæval' full-blown rose.

This point settled, let it now be remarked, that Herschel's resources enabled him to unmask many of these *nebulæ*: stars they were, and stars he forced them to own themselves. Why should any decent world wear an *alias*? There was nothing, you know, to be ashamed of in being an honest cluster of stars. Indeed, they seemed to be sensible of this themselves, and they now yielded to the force of Herschel's arguments so far as to show themselves in the new character of *nebulæ* spangled with stars; these are the *stellar nebulæ*; quite as much as you could expect in so short a time: Rome was not built in a day: and one must have some respect to stellar feelings. It was noticed, however, that where a bright haze, and not a weak milk-and-water haze, had revealed itself to the telescope, this, arising from a case of *compression*, (as previously explained,) required very little increase of telescopic power to force him into a fuller confession. He made a clean breast of it. But at length came a dreadful anomaly. A 'nebula' in the constellation *Andromeda* turned restive: another in *Orion*, I grieve to say it, still more so. I confine myself to the latter. A very low power sufficed to bring him to a slight confession, which in fact amounted to nothing; the very highest would not persuade him to show a star. 'Just one,' said some coaxing person; 'we'll be satisfied with only one.' But no: he would *not*. He was hardened, 'he wouldn't *split*.' And Herschel was thus led, after waiting as long as flesh and blood *could* wait, to infer two classes of *nebulæ*; one that were stars; and another that were *not* stars, nor ever were meant to be stars. Yet *that* was premature: he found at last, that, though not raised to the peerage of stars, finally they would be so: they were the matter of stars; and by gradual condensation would become suns, whose atmosphere, by a similar process of condensing, would become planets, capable of brilliant literati and philosophers, in several volumes octavo. So stood the case for a long time; it was settled to the satisfaction of Europe that there were two classes of *nebulæ*, one that *were* worlds, one that were *not*, but only the pabulum of future worlds. Silence arose. A voice was heard, 'Let there be Lord Rosse!' and immediately his telescope walked into Orion; destroyed the supposed matter of stars; but, in return, created immeasurable worlds.

As a hint for apprehending the delicacy and difficulty of the process in sidereal astronomy, let the inexperienced reader figure to himself these separate cases of perplexity: 1st, A perplexity where the dilemma arises from the collision between magnitude and distance:—is the size less, or the distance greater? 2dly, Where the dilemma arises between motions, a motion in ourselves doubtfully confounded with a motion in some external body; or, 3dly, Where it arises between possible positions of an object: is it a real proximity that we see between two stars, or simply an apparent proximity from lying in the same visual line, though in far other depths of space? As regards the first dilemma, we may suppose two laws, A and B, absolutely in contradiction, laid down at starting: A, that all fixed stars are precisely at the same *distance*; in this case every difference in the apparent magnitude will indicate a corresponding difference in the real magnitude, and will measure that difference. B, that all the fixed stars are precisely of the same *magnitude*; in which case, every variety in the size will indicate a corresponding difference in the distance, and will measure that difference. Nor could we imagine any exception to these inferences from A or from B, whichever of the two were assumed, unless through optical laws that might not equally affect objects under different circumstances; I mean, for instance, that might suffer a disturbance as applied under hypoth. B, to different depths in space, or under hypoth. A, to different arrangements of structure in the star. But thirdly, it is certain, that neither A nor B is the abiding law: and next it becomes an object by science and by instruments to distinguish more readily and more certainly between the cases where the distance has degraded the size, and the cases where the size being *really* less, has caused an exaggeration of the distance: or again, where the size being really less, yet co-operating with a distance really greater, may degrade the estimate, (though travelling in a right direction,) below the truth; or again where the size being really less, yet counteracted by a distance also less, may equally disturb the truth of human measurements, and so on.

A second large order of equivocating appearances will arise,—not as to magnitude, but as to motion. If it could be a safe assumption, that the system to which our planet is attached were absolutely fixed and motionless, except as regards its own *internal* relations of movement, then every change outside of us, every motion that the registers of astronomy had established, would be objective and not subjective. It would be safe to pronounce at once that it was a motion in the object contemplated, *not* in the subject contemplating. Or, reversely, if it were safe to assume as a universal law, that no motion was possible in the starry heavens, then every change of relations in space, between ourselves and them, would indicate and would measure a progress, or regress, on the part of our solar system, in certain known directions. But now, because it is not safe to rest in either assumption, the range of possibilities for which science has to provide, is enlarged; the immediate difficulties are multiplied; but with the result (as in the former case) of reversionally expanding the powers, and consequently the facilities, lodged both in the science and in the arts ministerial to the science. Thus, in the constellation *Cygnus*, there is a star gradually changing its relation to our system, whose distance from ourselves (as Dr. Nichol tells us) is ascertained to be about six hundred and seventy thousand times our own distance from the sun: that is, neglecting minute accuracy, about six hundred and seventy thousand stages of one hundred million miles each. This point being known, it falls within the *arts* of astronomy to translate this apparent angular motion into miles; and presuming this change of relation to be not in the star, but really in ourselves, we may deduce the velocity of our course, we may enter into our *log* daily the rate at which our whole solar system is running. Bessel, it seems, the eminent astronomer who died lately, computed this velocity to be such (viz., three times that of our own earth in its proper orbit) as would carry us to the star in forty-one thousand years. But, in the mean time, the astronomer is to hold in reserve some small share of his attention, some trifle of a side-glance, now and then, to the possibility of an error, after all, in the main assumption: he must watch the indications, if any such should arise, that not ourselves, but the star in *Cygnus*, is the real party concerned, in drifting at this shocking rate, with no prospect of coming to an anchorage. [Footnote: It is worth adding at this point, whilst the reader remembers without effort the numbers, viz., forty-one thousand years, for the time, (the space being our own distance from the sun repeated six hundred and seventy thousand times,) what would be the time required for reaching, in the *body*, that distance to which Lord Rosse's six feet mirror has so recently extended our *vision*. The time would be, as Dr. Nichol computes, about two hundred and fifty millions of years, supposing that our rate of travelling was about three times that of our earth in its orbit. Now, as the velocity is assumed to be the same in both cases, the ratio between the distance (already so tremendous) of Bessel's 61 *Cygni*, and that of Lord Rosse's farthest frontier, is as forty-one thousand to two hundred and fifty millions. This is a simple rule-of-three problem for a child. And the answer to it will, perhaps, convey the simplest expression of the superhuman power lodged in the new telescope:—as is the ratio of forty-one thousand to two hundred and fifty million, so is the ratio of our own distance from the sun multiplied by six hundred and seventy thousand, to the outermost limit of Lord Rosse's sidereal vision.]

Another class, and a frequent one, of equivocal phenomena, phenomena that are reconcilable indifferently with either of two assumptions, though less plausibly reconciled with the one than with the other, concerns the position of stars that seem connected with each other by systematic relations, and which yet *may* lie in very different depths of space, being brought into seeming connection only by the human eye. There have been, and there are, cases where two stars dissemble an interconnection which they really *have*, and other cases where they simulate an interconnection which they have not. All these cases of simulation and dissimulation torment the astronomer by multiplying his perplexities, and deepening the difficulty of escaping them. He cannot get at the truth: in many cases, magnitude and distance are in collusion with each other to deceive him: motion subjective is in collusion with motion objective; duplex systems are in collusion with fraudulent stars, having no real partnership whatever, but mimicking such a partnership by means of the limitations or errors affecting the human eye, where it can apply no other sense to aid or to correct itself. So that the business of astronomy, in these days, is no sinecure, as the reader perceives. And by another evidence, it is continually becoming less of a sinecure. Formerly, one or two men, — Tycho, suppose, or, in a later age, Cassini and Horrox, and Bradley, had observatories: one man, suppose, observed the stars for all Christendom; and the rest of Europe observed *him*. But now, up and down Europe, from the deep blue of Italian skies to the cold frosty atmospheres of St. Petersburg and Glasgow, the stars are conscious of being watched everywhere; and if all astronomers do not publish their observations, all use them in their speculations. New and brilliantly appointed observatories are rising in every latitude, or risen; and none, by the way, of these new-born observatories, is more interesting from the circumstances of its position, or more *picturesque* to a higher organ than the eye — viz., to the human heart — than the New Observatory raised by the university of Glasgow.[Footnote: It has been reported, ever since the autumn of 1845, and the report is now, (August, 1846,) gathering strength, that some railway potentate, having taken a fancy for the ancient college of Glasgow, as a bauble to hang about his wife's neck, (no accounting for tastes,) has offered, (or *will* offer,) such a price, that the good old academic lady in this her moss-grown antiquity, seriously thinks of taking him at his word, packing up her traps, and being off. When a spirit of galavanting comes across an aged lady, it is always difficult to know where it will stop: so, in fact, you know, she may choose to steam for Texas. But the present impression is, that she will settle down by the side of what you may call her married or settled daughter — the Observatory; which one would be glad to have confirmed, as indicating that no purpose of pleasure-seeking had been working in elderly minds, but the instinct of religious rest and aspiration. The Observatory would thus remind one of those early Christian anchorites, and self-exiled visionaries, that being led by almost a necessity of nature to take up their residence in deserts, sometimes drew after themselves the whole of their own neighborhood.]

The New Observatory of Glasgow is now, I believe, finished; and the only fact connected with its history that was painful, as embodying and recording that Vandal alienation from science, literature, and all their interests, which has ever marked our too haughty and Caliph-Omar-like British government, lay in the circumstance that the glasses of the apparatus, the whole mounting of the establishment, in so far as it was a scientific establishment, and even the workmen for putting up the machinery, were imported from Bavaria. We, that once bade the world stand aside when the question arose about glasses, or the graduation of instruments, were now literally obliged to stand cap in hand, bowing to Mr. Somebody, successor of Frauenhofer or Frauendevil, in Munich! Who caused *that*, we should all be glad to know, if not the wicked Treasury, that killed the hen that laid the golden eggs by taxing her until her spine broke? It is to be hoped that, at this moment, and specifically for this offence, some scores of Exchequer men, chancellors and other rubbish, are in purgatory, and perhaps working, with shirt-sleeves tucked up, in purgatorial glass-houses, with very small allowances of beer, to defray the cost of perspiration. But why trouble a festal remembrance with commemorations of crimes or criminals? What makes the Glasgow Observatory so peculiarly interesting, is its position, connected with and overlooking so vast a city, having more than three hundred thousand inhabitants, (in spite of an American sceptic,) nearly all children of toil; and a city, too, which, from the necessities of its circumstances, draws so deeply upon that fountain of misery and guilt which some ordinance, as ancient as 'our father Jacob,' with his patriarchal well for Samaria, has bequeathed to manufacturing towns,—to Ninevehs, to Babylons, to Tyres. How tarnished with eternal canopies of smoke, and of sorrow; how dark with agitations of many orders, is the mighty town below! How serene, how quiet, how lifted above the confusion and the roar, how liberated from the strifes of earth, is the solemn Observatory that crowns the grounds above! And duly, at night, just when the toil of over-wrought Glasgow is mercifully relaxing, then comes the summons to the laboring astronomer. *He* speaks not of the night, but of the day and the flaunting day-light, as the hours 'in which no man can work.' And the least reflecting of men must be impressed by the idea, that at wide intervals, but intervals scattered over Europe, whilst 'all that mighty heart' is, by sleep, resting from its labors, secret eyes are lifted up to heaven in astronomical watch-towers; eyes that keep watch and ward over spaces that make us dizzy to remember, eyes that register the promises of comets, and disentangle the labyrinths of worlds.

Another feature of interest, connected with the Glasgow Observatory, is personal, and founded on the intellectual characteristics of the present professor, Dr. Nichol; in the deep meditative style of his mind seeking for rest, yet placed in conflict for ever with the tumultuous necessity in *him* for travelling along the line of revolutionary thought, and following it loyally, wearied or not, to its natural home.

In a sonnet of Milton, one of three connected with his own blindness, he distinguishes between two classes of servants that minister to the purposes of God. 'His state,' says he, meaning God's state, the arrangement of his regular service, 'is kingly;' that is to say, it resembles the mode of service established in the courts of kings; and, in this, it resembles that service, that there are two classes of ministers attending on his pleasure. For, as in the trains of kings are some that run without resting, night or day, to carry the royal messages, and also others—great lords in waiting—that move not from the royal gates; so of the divine retinues, some are for action only, some for contemplation. 'Thousands' there are that

> — —'at his bidding speed,
> And post o'er land and ocean without rest.'

Others, on the contrary, motionless as statues, that share not in the agitations of their times, that tremble not in sympathy with the storms around them, but that listen—that watch—that wait—for secret indications to be fulfilled, or secret signs to be deciphered. And, of this latter class, he adds-that they, not less than the others, are accepted by God; or, as it is so exquisitely expressed in the closing line,

> 'They also serve, that only stand and wait.'

Something analogous to this one may see in the distributions of literature and science. Many popularize and diffuse: some reap and gather on their own account. Many translate, into languages fit for the multitude, messages which they receive from human voices: some listen, like Kubla Khan, far down in caverns or hanging over subterranean rivers, for secret whispers that mingle and confuse themselves with the general uproar of torrents, but which can be detected and kept apart by the obstinate prophetic ear, which spells into words and ominous sentences the distracted syllables of ærial voices. Dr. Nichol is one of those who pass to and fro between these classes; and has the rare function of keeping open their vital communications. As a popularizing astronomer, he has done more for the benefit of his great science than all the rest of Europe combined: and now, when he notices, without murmur, the fact that his office of popular teacher is almost taken out of his hands, (so many are they who have trained of late for the duty,) that change has, in fact, been accomplished through knowledge, through explanations, through suggestions, dispersed and prompted by himself.

For my own part, as one belonging to the laity, and not to the clerus, in the science of astronomy, I could scarcely have presumed to report minutely, or to sit in the character of dissector upon the separate details of Dr. Nichol's works, either this, or those which have preceded it, had there even been room left disposable for such a task. But in this view it is sufficient to have made the general acknowledgment which already *has* been made, that Dr. Nichol's works, and his oral lectures upon astronomy, are to be considered as the *fundus* of the knowledge on that science now working in this generation. More important it is, and more in reconciliation with the tenor of my own ordinary studies, to notice the philosophic spirit in which Dr. Nichol's works are framed; the breadth of his views, the eternal tendency of his steps in advance, or (if advance on that quarter, or at that point, happens to be absolutely walled out for the present,) the vigor of the *reconnoissances* by which he examines the hostile intrenchments. Another feature challenges notice. In reading astronomical works, there arises (from old experience of what is usually most faulty) a wish either for the naked severities of science, with a total abstinence from all display of enthusiasm; or else, if the cravings of human sensibility are to be met and gratified, that it shall be by an enthusiasm unaffected and grand as its subject. Of that kind is the enthusiasm of Dr. Nichol. The grandeurs of astronomy are such to him who has a capacity for being grandly moved. They are none at all to him who has not. To the mean they become meannesses. Space, for example, has no grandeur to him who has no space in the theatre of his own brain. I know writers who report the marvels of velocity, &c., in such a way that they become insults to yourself. It is obvious that in *their* way of insisting on our earth's speed in her annual orbit, they do not seek to exalt *her*, but to mortify *you*. And, besides, these fellows are answerable for provoking people into fibs:—for I remember one day, that reading a statement of this nature, about how many things the Earth had done that we could never hope to do, and about the number of cannon balls, harnessed as a *tandem*, which the Earth would fly past, without leaving time to say, *How are you off for soap?* in vexation of heart I could not help exclaiming—'That's nothing: I've done a great deal more myself;' though, when one turns it in one's mind, you know there must be some inaccuracy *there*. How different is Dr. Nichol's enthusiasm from this hypocritical and vulgar wonderment! It shows itself not merely in reflecting the grandeurs of his theme, and by the sure test of detecting and allying itself with all the indirect grandeurs that arrange themselves from any distance, upon or about that centre, but by the manifest promptness with which Dr. Nichol's enthusiasm awakens itself upon *every* road that leads to things elevating for man; or to things promising for knowledge; or to things which, like dubious theories or imperfect attempts at systematizing, though neutral as regards knowledge, minister to what is greater than knowledge, viz., to intellectual *power*, to the augmented power of handling your materials, though with no more materials than before. In his geological and cosmological inquiries, in his casual speculations, the same quality of intellect betrays itself; the intellect that labors in sympathy with the laboring *nisus* of these gladiatorial times;

that works (and sees the necessity of working) the apparatus of many sciences towards a composite result; the intellect that retires in one direction only to make head in another; and that already is prefiguring the route beyond the barriers, whilst yet the gates are locked.

There was a man in the last century, and an eminent man too, who used to say, that whereas people in general pretended to admire astronomy as being essentially sublime, he for *his* part looked upon all that sort of thing as a swindle; and, on the contrary, he regarded the solar system as decidedly vulgar; because the planets were all of them so infernally punctual, they kept time with such horrible precision, that they forced him, whether he would or no, to think of nothing but post-office clocks, mail-coaches, and book-keepers. Regularity may be beautiful, but it excludes the sublime. What he wished for was something like Lloyd's list.

Comets—due 3; arrived 1. *Mercury*, when last seen, appeared to be distressed; but made no signals. *Pallas* and *Vesta*, not heard of for some time; supposed to have foundered. *Moon*, spoken last night through a heavy bank of clouds; out sixteen days: all right.

Now this poor man's misfortune was, to have lived in the days of mere planetary astronomy. At present, when our own little system, with all its grandeurs, has dwindled by comparison to a subordinate province, if any man is bold enough to say so, a poor shivering unit amongst myriads that are brighter, we ought no longer to talk of astronomy, but of *the astronomies*. There is the planetary, the cometary, the sidereal, perhaps also others; as, for instance, even yet the nebular; because, though Lord Rosse has smitten it with the son of Amram's rod, has made it open, and cloven a path through it, yet other and more fearful *nebulæ* may loom in sight, (if further improvements should be effected in the telescope,) that may puzzle even Lord Rosse. And when he tells his *famulus*—'Fire a shot at that strange fellow, and make him show his colors,' possibly the mighty stranger may disdain the summons. That would be vexatious: we should all be incensed at *that*. But no matter. What's a *nebula*, what's a world, more or less? In the spiritual heavens are many mansions: in the starry heavens, that are now unfolding and preparing to unfold before us, are many vacant areas upon which the astronomer may pitch his secret pavilion. He may dedicate himself to the service of the *Double Suns*; he has my license to devote his whole time to the quadruple system of suns in *Lyra*. Swammerdam spent his life in a ditch watching frogs and tadpoles; why may not an astronomer give nine lives, if he had them, to the watching of that awful appearance in *Hercules*, which pretends to some rights over our own unoffending system? Why may he not mount guard with public approbation, for the next fifty years, upon the zodiacal light, the interplanetary ether, and other rarities, which the professional body of astronomers would naturally keep (if they could) for their own private enjoyment? There is no want of variety now, nor in fact of irregularity: for the most exquisite clock-work, which from enormous distance *seems* to go wrong, virtually for us *does* go wrong; so that our friend of the last century, who complained of the solar system, would not need to do so any longer. There are anomalies enough to keep him cheerful. There are now even things to alarm us; for anything in the starry worlds that look suspicious, anything that ought *not* to be there, is, for all purposes of frightening us, as good as a ghost.

But of all the novelties that excite my own interest in the expanding astronomy of recent times, the most delightful and promising are those charming little pyrotechnic planetoids,[Footnote: *'Pyrotechnic Planetoids:'*— The reader will understand me as alluding to the periodic shooting stars. It is now well known, that as, upon our own poor little earthly ocean, we fall in with certain phenomena as we approach certain latitudes; so also upon the great ocean navigated by our Earth, we fall in with prodigious showers of these meteors at periods no longer uncertain, but fixed as jail-deliveries. 'These remarkable showers of meteors,' says Dr. Nichol, 'observed at different periods in August and November, seem to demonstrate the fact, that, at these periods, we have come in contact with two streams of such planetoids then intersecting the earth's orbit.' If they intermit, it is only because they are shifting their nodes, or points of intersection.] that variegate our annual course. It always struck me as most disgusting, that, in going round the sun, we must be passing continually over old roads, and yet we had no means of establishing an acquaintance with them: they might as well be new for every trip. Those chambers of ether, through which we are tearing along night and day, (for *our* train stops at no stations,) doubtless, if we could put some mark upon them, must be old fellows perfectly liable to recognition. I suppose, *they* never have notice to quit. And yet, for want of such a mark, though all our lives flying past them and through them, we can never challenge them as known. The same thing happens in the desert: one monotonous iteration of sand, sand, sand, unless where some miserable fountain stagnates, forbids all approach to familiarity: nothing is circumstantiated or differenced: travel it for three generations, and you are no nearer to identification of its parts: so that it amounts to travelling through an abstract idea. For the desert, really I suspect the thing is hopeless: but, as regards our planetary orbit, matters are mending: for the last six or seven years I have heard of these fiery showers, but indeed I cannot say how much earlier they were first noticed,[Footnote: Somewhere I have seen it remarked, that if, on a public road, you meet a party of four women, it is at least fifty to one that they are all laughing; whereas, if you meet an equal party of my own unhappy sex, you may wager safely that they are talking gravely, and that one of them is uttering the word *money*. Hence it must be, viz, because our sisters are too much occupied with the playful things of this earth, and our brothers with its gravities, that neither party sufficiently watches the skies. And *that* accounts for a fact which often has struck myself, viz., that, in cities, on bright moonless nights, when some brilliant skirmishings of the Aurora are exhibiting, or even a luminous arch, which is a broad ribbon of snowy light that spans the skies, positively unless I myself say to people—'Eyes upwards!' not one in a hundred, male or female, but fails to see the show, though it may be seen *gratis*, simply because their eyes are too uniformly reading the earth. This downward direction of the eyes, however, must have been worse in former ages: because else it never *could* have happened that, until Queen Anne's days, nobody ever hinted in a book that there *was* such a thing, or *could* be such a thing, as the Aurora Borealis; and in fact Halley had the credit of discovering it.] as celebrating two annual festivals—one in August, one in November. You are a little too late, reader, for seeing this year's summer festival; but that's no reason why you should not engage a good seat for the November meeting; which, if I recollect, is about the 9th, or the Lord Mayor's day, and on the whole better worth seeing. For anything *we* know, this may be a great day in the earth's earlier history; she may have put forth her original rose on this day, or tried her hand at a primitive specimen of wheat; or she may, in fact, have survived some gunpowder plot about this time; so that the meteoric appearance may be a kind congratulating *feu-de-joye*, on the anniversary of the happy event. What it is that the 'cosmogony man' in the 'Vicar of Wakefield' would have thought of such novelties, whether he would have favored us with his usual opinion upon such topics, viz., that *anarchon ara kai ateleutaion to pan,* or have sported a new one exclusively for this occasion, may be doubtful. What it is that astronomers think, who are a kind of 'cosmogony men,' the reader may learn from Dr. Nichol, Note B.

In taking leave of a book and a subject so well fitted to draw out the highest mode of that grandeur, which *can* connect itself with the external, (a grandeur capable of drawing down a spiritual being to earth, but not of raising an earthly being to heaven,) I would wish to contribute my own brief word of homage to this grandeur by recalling from a fading remembrance of twenty-five years back a short *bravura* of John Paul Richter. I call it a *bravura*, as being intentionally a passage of display and elaborate execution; and in this sense I may call it partly 'my own,' that at twenty-five years' distance, (after one single reading,) it would not have been possible for any man to report a passage of this length without greatly disturbing [Footnote: *'Disturbing;'*—neither perhaps should I much have sought to avoid alterations if the original had been lying before me: for it takes the shape of a dream; and this most brilliant of all German writers wanted in that field the severe simplicity, that horror of the *too much*, belonging to Grecian architecture, which is essential to the perfection of a dream considered as a work of art. He was too elaborate, to realize the grandeur of the shadowy.] the texture of the composition: by altering, one makes it partly one's own; but it is right to mention, that the sublime turn at the end belongs entirely to John Paul.

'God called up from dreams a man into the vestibule of heaven, saying,—"Come thou hither, and see the glory of my house." And to the servants that stood around his throne he said,—"Take him, and undress him from his robes of flesh: cleanse his vision, and put a new breath into his nostrils: only touch not with any change his human heart—the heart that weeps and trembles." It was done; and, with a mighty angel for his guide, the man stood ready for his infinite voyage; and from the terraces of heaven, without sound or farewell, at once they wheeled away into endless space. Sometimes with the solemn flight of angel wing they fled through Zaarrahs of darkness, through wildernesses of death, that divided the worlds of life: sometimes they swept over frontiers, that were quickening under prophetic motions from God. Then, from a distance that is counted only in heaven, light dawned for a time through a sleepy film: by unutterable pace the light swept to *them*, they by unutterable pace to the light: in a moment the rushing of planets was upon them: in a moment the blazing of suns was around them. Then came eternities of twilight, that revealed, but were not revealed. To the right hand and to the left towered mighty constellations, that by self-repetitions and answers from afar, that by counter-positions, built up triumphal gates, whose architraves, whose archways—horizontal, upright—rested, rose—at altitudes, by spans—that seemed ghostly from infinitude. Without measure were the architraves, past number were the archways, beyond memory the gates. Within were stairs that scaled the eternities above, that descended to the eternities below: above was below, below was above, to the man stripped of gravitating body: depth was swallowed up in height insurmountable, height was swallowed up in depth unfathomable. Suddenly as thus they rode from infinite to infinite, suddenly as thus they tilted over abysmal worlds, a mighty cry arose—that systems more mysterious, that worlds more billowy,—other heights, and other depths,—were coming, were nearing, were at hand. Then the man sighed, and stopped, shuddered and wept. His over-laden heart uttered itself in tears; and he said,—"Angel, I will go no farther. For the spirit of man aches with this infinity. Insufferable is the glory of God. Let me lie down in the grave from the persecutions of the infinite; for end, I see, there is none." And from all the listening stars that shone around issued a choral voice, "The man speaks truly: end there is none, that ever yet we heard of." "End is there none?" the angel solemnly demanded: "Is there indeed no end? And is this the sorrow that kills you?" But no voice answered, that he might answer himself. Then the angel threw up his glorious hands to the heaven of heavens; saying, "End is there none to the universe of God? Lo! also there is no Beginning."'

NOTE.—On throwing his eyes hastily over the preceding paper, the writer becomes afraid that some readers may give such an interpretation to a few playful expressions upon the age of our earth, &c., as to class him with those who use geology, cosmology, &c., for purposes of attack, or insinuation against the Scriptures. Upon this point, therefore, he wishes to make a firm explanation of his own opinions, which, (whether right or wrong,) will liberate him, once and for all, from any such jealousy.

It is sometimes said, that the revealer of a true religion, does not come amongst men for the sake of teaching truths in science, or correcting errors in science. Most justly is this said: but often in terms far too feeble. For generally these terms are such as to imply, that, although no function of his mission, it was yet open to him—although not pressing with the force of an obligation upon the revealer, it was yet at his discretion—if not to correct other men's errors, yet at least in his own person to speak with scientific precision. I contend that it was *not*. I contend, that to have uttered the truths of astronomy, of geology, &c., at the era of new-born Christianity, was not only *below* the purposes of a religion, but would have been *against* them. Even upon errors of a far more important class than any errors in science can ever be,—superstitions, for instance, that degraded the very idea of God; prejudices and false usages, that laid waste human happiness, (such as slavery and many hundreds of other abuses that might be mentioned,) the rule evidently acted upon by the Founder of Christianity was this—Given the purification of the fountain, once assumed that the fountains of truth are cleansed, all these derivative currents of evil will cleanse themselves. And the only exceptions, which I remember, to this rule, are two cases in which, from the personal appeal made to his decision, Christ would have made himself a party to wretched delusions, if he had not condescended to expose their folly. But, as a general rule, the branches of error were disregarded, and the roots only attacked. If, then, so lofty a station was taken with regard even to such errors as had moral and spiritual relations, how much more with regard to the comparative trifles, (as in the ultimate relations of human nature they are,) of merely human science! But, for my part, I go further, and assert, that upon three reasons it was impossible for any messenger from God, (or offering himself in that character,) for a moment to have descended into the communication of truth merely scientific, or economic, or worldly. And the reasons are these: *First*, Because it would have degraded his mission, by lowering it to the base level of a collision with human curiosity, or with petty and transitory interests. *Secondly*, Because it would have ruined his mission; would utterly have prostrated the free agency and the proper agency of that mission. He that, in those days, should have proclaimed the true theory of the Solar System and the heavenly forces, would have been shut up at once—as a lunatic likely to become dangerous. But suppose him to have escaped *that*; still, as a divine teacher, he has no liberty of caprice. He must stand to the promises of his own acts. Uttering the first truth of a science, he is pledged to the second: taking the main step, he is committed to all which follow. He is thrown at once upon the endless controversies which science in every stage provokes, and in none more than in the earliest. Or, if he retires as from a scene of contest that he had not anticipated, he retires as one confessing a human precipitance and a human oversight, weaknesses, venial in others, but fatal to the pretensions of a divine teacher. Starting besides from such pretensions, he could not (as others might) have the privilege of selecting arbitrarily or partially. If upon one science, then upon all,—if upon science, then upon, art,—if upon art and science, then upon *every* branch of social economy, upon *every* organ of civilization, his reformations and advances are equally due; due as to all, if due as to any. To move in one direction, is constructively to undertake for all. Without power to retreat, he has thus thrown the intellectual interests of his followers into a channel utterly alien to the purposes of a spiritual mission.

Thus far he has simply failed: but next comes a worse result; an evil, not negative but positive. Because, *thirdly*, to apply the light of a revelation for the benefit of a merely human science, which is virtually done by so applying the illumination of an *inspired* teacher, is—to assault capitally the scheme of God's discipline and training for man. To improve by *heavenly* means, if but in one solitary science—to lighten, if but in one solitary section, the condition of difficulty which had been designed for the strengthening and training of human faculties, is *pro tanto* to disturb—to cancel—to contradict a previous purpose of God, made known by silent indications from the beginning of the world. Wherefore did God give to man the powers for contending with scientific difficulties? Wherefore did he lay a secret train of continual occasions, that should rise, by intervals, through thousands of generations, for provoking and developing those activities in man's intellect, if, after all, he is to send a messenger of his own, more than human, to intercept and strangle all these great purposes? When, therefore, the persecutors of Galileo, alleged that Jupiter, for instance, could not move in the way alleged, because then the Bible would have proclaimed it,—as they thus threw back upon God the burthen of discovery, which he had thrown upon Galileo, why did they not, by following out their own logic, throw upon the Bible the duty of discovering the telescope, or discovering the satellites of Jupiter? And, as no such discoveries were there, why did they not, by parity of logic, and for mere consistency, deny the telescope as a fact, deny the Jovian planets as facts? But this it is to mistake the very meaning and purposes of a revelation. A revelation is not made for the purpose of showing to idle men that which they may show to themselves, by faculties already given to them, if only they will exert those faculties, but for the purpose of showing *that* which the moral darkness of man will not, without supernatural light, allow him to perceive. With disdain, therefore, must every considerate person regard the notion,—that God could wilfully interfere with his own plans, by accrediting ambassadors to reveal astronomy, or any other science, which he has commanded men to cultivate *without* revelation, by endowing them with all the natural powers for doing so.

Even as regards astronomy, a science so nearly allying itself to religion by the loftiness and by the purity of its contemplations, Scripture is nowhere the *parent* of any doctrine, nor so much as the silent sanctioner of any doctrine. Scripture cannot become the author of falsehood,—though it were as to a trifle, cannot become a party to falsehood. And it is made impossible for Scripture to teach falsely, by the simple fact that Scripture, on such subjects, will not condescend to teach at all. The Bible adopts the erroneous language of men, (which at any rate it must do, in order to make itself understood,) not by way of sanctioning a theory, but by way of using a fact. The Bible *uses* (postulates) the phenomena of day and night, of summer and winter, and expresses them, in relation to their causes, as *men* express them, men, even, that are scientific astronomers. But the results, which are all that concern Scripture, are equally true, whether accounted for by one hypothesis which is philosophically just, or by another which is popular and erring.

Now, on the other hand, in geology and cosmology, the case is still stronger. *Here* there is no opening for a compliance even with popular language. *Here*, where there is no such stream of apparent phenomena running counter (as in astronomy) to the real phenomena, neither is there any popular language opposed to the scientific. The whole are abstruse speculations, even as regards their objects, not dreamed of as possibilities, either in their true aspects or their false aspects, till modern times. The Scriptures, therefore, nowhere allude to such sciences, either under the shape of histories, applied to processes current and in movement, or under the shape of theories applied to processes past and accomplished.

The Mosaic cosmogony, indeed, gives the succession of natural births; and that succession will doubtless be more and more confirmed and illustrated as geology advances. But as to the time, the duration, of this cosmogony, it is the idlest of notions that the Scriptures either have or could have condescended to human curiosity upon so awful a prologue to the drama of this world. Genesis would no more have indulged so mean a passion with respect to the mysterious inauguration of the world, than the Apocalypse with respect to its mysterious close. 'Yet the six *days* of Moses!' Days! But is any man so little versed in biblical language as not to know that (except in the merely historical parts of the Jewish records) every section of time has a secret and separate acceptation in the Scriptures? Does an *æon*, though a Grecian word, bear scripturally [either in Daniel or in Saint John] any sense known to Grecian ears? Do the seventy *weeks* of the prophet mean weeks in the sense of human calendars? Already the Psalms, (xc) already St. Peter, (2d Epist.) warn us of a peculiar sense attached to the word *day* in divine ears? And who of the innumerable interpreters understands the twelve hundred and odd days in Daniel, or his two thousand and odd days, to mean, by possibility, periods of twenty-four hours? Surely the theme of Moses was as mystical, and as much entitled to the benefit of mystical language, as that of the prophets.

The sum of the matter is this:—God, by a Hebrew prophet, is sublimely described as *the Revealer*; and, in variation of his own expression, the same prophet describes him as the Being 'that knoweth the darkness.' Under no idea can the relations of God to man be more grandly expressed. But of what is he the revealer? Not surely of those things which he has enabled man to reveal for himself, and which he has commanded him so to reveal, but of those things which, were it not through special light from heaven, must eternally remain sealed up in the inaccessible darkness. On this principle we should all laugh at a revealed cookery. But essentially the same ridicule applies to a revealed astronomy, or a revealed geology. As a fact, there *is* no such astronomy or geology: as a possibility, by the *a priori* argument which I have used, (viz., that a revelation on such fields, would contradict *other* machineries of providence,) there *can* be no such astronomy or geology. Consequently there *can* be none such in the Bible. Consequently there *is* none. Consequently there can be no schism or feud upon *these* subjects between the Bible and the philosophies outside. Geology is a field left open, with the amplest permission from above, to the widest and wildest speculations of man.

MODERN SUPERSTITION

It is said continually—that the age of miracles is past. We deny that it is so in any sense which implies this age to differ from all other generations of man except one. It is neither past, nor ought we to wish it past. Superstition is no vice in the constitution of man: it is not true that, in any philosophic view, *primus in orbe deos fecit timor*—meaning by *fecit* even so much as *raised into light*. As Burke remarked, the *timor* at least must be presumed to preexist, and must be accounted for, if not the gods. If the fear created the gods, what created the fear? Far more true, and more just to the grandeur of man, it would have been to say—*Primus in orbe deos fecit sensus infiniti*. Even in the lowest Caffre, more goes to the sense of a divine being than simply his wrath or his power. Superstition, indeed, or the sympathy with the invisible, is the great test of man's nature, as an earthly combining with a celestial. In superstition lies the possibility of religion. And though superstition is often injurious, degrading, demoralizing, it is so, not as a form of corruption or degradation, but as a form of non-development. The crab is harsh, and for itself worthless. But it is the germinal form of innumerable finer fruits: not apples only the most exquisite, and pears; the peach and the nectarine are said to have radiated from this austere stock when cultured, developed, and transferred to all varieties of climate. Superstition will finally pass into pure forms of religion as man advances. It would be matter of lamentation to hear that superstition had at all decayed until man had made corresponding steps in the purification and development of his intellect as applicable to religious faith. Let us hope that this is not so. And, by way of judging, let us throw a hasty eye over the modes of popular superstition. If these manifest their vitality, it will prove that the popular intellect does not go along with the bookish or the worldly (philosophic we cannot call it) in pronouncing the miraculous extinct. The popular feeling is all in all.

This function of miraculous power, which is most widely diffused through Pagan and Christian ages alike, but which has the least root in the solemnities of the imagination, we may call the *Ovidian*. By way of distinction, it may be so called; and with some justice, since Ovid in his *Metamorphoses* gave the first elaborate record of such a tendency in human superstition. It is a movement of superstition under the domination of human affections; a mode of spiritual awe which seeks to reconcile itself with human tenderness or admiration; and which represents supernatural power as expressing itself by a sympathy with human distress or passion concurrently with human sympathies, and as supporting that blended sympathy by a symbol incarnated with the fixed agencies of nature. For instance, a pair of youthful lovers perish by a double suicide originating in a fatal mistake, and a mistake operating in each case through a noble self-oblivion. The tree under which their meeting has been concerted, and which witnesses their tragedy, is supposed ever afterwards to express the divine sympathy with this catastrophe in the gloomy color of its fruit:—

> 'At tu, quæ ramis (arbor!) miserabile corpus
> Nunc tegis unius, mox es tectura duorum,
> Signa tene cædis:—pullosque et luctibus aptos
> Semper habe fructus—gemini monumenta cruoris:'

Such is the dying adjuration of the lady to the tree. And the fruit becomes from that time a monument of a double sympathy—sympathy from man, sympathy from a dark power standing behind the agencies of nature, and speaking through them. Meantime the object of this sympathy is understood to be not the individual catastrophe, but the universal case of unfortunate love exemplified in this particular romance. The inimitable grace with which Ovid has delivered these early traditions of human tenderness, blending with human superstition, is notorious; the artfulness of the pervading connection, by which every tale in the long succession is made to arise spontaneously out of that which precedes, is absolutely unrivalled; and this it was, with his luxuriant gayety, which procured for him a preference, even with Milton, a poet so opposite by intellectual constitution. It is but reasonable, therefore, that this function of the miraculous should bear the name of *Ovidian*. Pagan it was in its birth; and to paganism its titles ultimately ascend. Yet we know that in the transitional state through the centuries succeeding to Christ, during which paganism and Christianity were slowly descending and ascending, as if from two different strata of the atmosphere, the two powers interchanged whatsoever they could. (See Conyer's Middleton; and see Blount of our own days.) It marked the earthly nature of paganism, that it could borrow little or nothing by organization: it was fitted to no expansion. But the true faith, from its vast and comprehensive adaptation to the nature of man, lent itself to many corruptions—some deadly in their tendencies, some harmless. Amongst these last was the Ovidian form of connecting the unseen powers moving in nature with human sympathies of love or reverence. The legends of this kind are universal and endless. No land, the most austere in its Protestantism, but has adopted these superstitions: and everywhere by those even who reject them they are entertained with some degree of affectionate respect.

That the ass, which in its very degradation still retains an under-power of sublimity, [Footnote: '*An under-power of sublimity*.'—Everybody knows that Homer compared the Telamonian Ajax, in a moment of heroic endurance, to an ass. This, however, was only under a momentary glance from a peculiar angle of the case. But the Mahometan, too solemn, and also perhaps too stupid to catch the fanciful colors of things, absolutely by choice, under the Bagdad Caliphate, decorated a most favorite hero with the title of the *Ass*— which title is repeated with veneration to this day. The wild ass is one of the few animals which has the reputation of never flying from an enemy.] or of sublime suggestion through its ancient connection with the wilderness, with the Orient, with Jerusalem, should have been honored amongst all animals, by the visible impression upon its back of Christian symbols— seems reasonable even to the infantine understanding when made acquainted with its meekness, its patience, its suffering life, and its association with the founder of Christianity in one great triumphal solemnity. The very man who brutally abuses it, and feels a hardhearted contempt for its misery and its submission, has a semi-conscious feeling that the same qualities were possibly those which recommended it to a distinction, [Footnote: '*Which recommended it to a distinction*.'—It might be objected that the Oriental ass was often a superb animal; that it is spoken of prophetically as such; and that historically the Syrian ass is made known to us as having been used in the prosperous ages of Judea for the riding of princes. But this is no objection. Those circumstances in the history of the ass were requisite to establish its symbolic propriety in a great symbolic pageant of triumph. Whilst, on the other hand, the individual animal, there is good reason to think, was marked by all the qualities of the general race as a suffering and unoffending tribe in the animal creation. The asses on which princes rode were of a separate color, of a peculiar breed, and improved, like the English racer, by continual care.] when all things were valued upon a scale inverse to that of the world. Certain it is, that in all Christian lands the legend about the ass is current amongst the rural population. The haddock, again, amongst marine animals, is supposed, throughout all maritime Europe, to be a privileged fish; even in austere Scotland, every child can point out the impression of St. Peter's thumb, by which from age to age it is distinguished from fishes having otherwise an external resemblance. All domesticated cattle, having the benefit of man's guardianship and care, are believed throughout England and Germany to go down upon their knees at one particular moment of Christmas eve, when the fields are covered with darkness, when no eye looks down but that of God, and when the exact anniversary hour revolves of the angelic song, once rolling over the fields and flocks of Palestine. [Footnote: Mahometanism, which everywhere pillages Christianity, cannot but have its own face at times glorified by its stolen jewels. This solemn hour of jubilation, gathering even the brutal natures into its fold, recalls accordingly the Mahometan legend (which the reader may remember is one of those incorporated into Southey's *Thalaba*) of a great hour revolving once in every year, during which the gates of Paradise were thrown open to their utmost extent, and gales of happiness issued forth upon the total family of man.] The Glastonbury Thorn is a more local superstition; but at one time the legend was as widely diffused as that of Loretto, with the angelic translation of its sanctities: on Christmas morning, it was devoutly believed by all Christendom, that this holy thorn put forth its annual blossoms. And with respect to the aspen tree, which Mrs. Hemans very naturally mistook for a Welsh legend, having first heard it in Denbighshire, the popular faith is universal—that it shivers mystically in sympathy with the horror of that mother tree in Palestine which was compelled to furnish materials for the cross. Neither would it in this case be any objection, if a passage were produced from Solinus or Theophrastus, implying that the aspen tree had always shivered—for the tree might presumably be penetrated by remote presentiments, as well as by remote remembrances. In so vast a case the obscure sympathy should stretch, Janus-like, each way. And an objection of the same kind to the rainbow, considered as the sign or seal by which God attested his covenant in bar of all future deluges, may be parried in something of the same way. It was not then first created—true: but it was then first selected by preference, amongst a multitude of natural signs as yet unappropriated, and then first charged with the new function of a message and a ratification to man. Pretty much the same theory, that is, the same way of accounting for the natural existence without disturbing the supernatural functions, may be applied to the great constellation of the other hemisphere, called the Southern Cross. It is viewed popularly in South America, and the southern parts of our northern hemisphere, as the great banner, or gonfalon, held aloft by Heaven before the Spanish heralds of the true faith in 1492. To that superstitious and ignorant race it costs not an effort to suppose, that by some synchronizing miracle, the constellation had been then specially called into existence at the very moment when the first Christian procession, bearing a cross in their arms, solemnly stepped on shore from the vessels of Christendom. We Protestants know better: we understand the impossibility of supposing such a narrow and local reference in orbs, so transcendently vast as those composing the constellation—orbs removed from each other by such unvoyageable worlds of space, and having, in fact, no real reference to each other more than to any other heavenly bodies whatsoever. The unity of synthesis, by which they are composed into one figure of a cross, we know to be a mere accidental result from an arbitrary synthesis of human fancy. Take such and such stars, compose them into letters, and they will spell such a word. But still it was our own choice—a synthesis of our own fancy, originally to combine them in this way. They might be divided from each other, and otherwise combined. All this is true: and yet, as the combination does spontaneously offer itself [Footnote: '*Does spontaneously offer itself.*'—Heber (Bishop of Calcutta) complains that this constellation is not composed of stars answering his expectation in point of magnitude. But he admits that the dark barren space around it gives to this inferior magnitude a very advantageous relief.] to every eye, as the glorious cross does really glitter for ever through the silent hours of a vast hemisphere, even they who are not superstitious, may willingly yield to the belief—that, as the rainbow was laid in the very elements and necessities of nature, yet still bearing a pre-dedication to a service which would not be called for until many ages had passed, so also the mysterious cipher of man's imperishable hopes may have been entwined and enwreathed with the starry heavens from their earliest creation, as a prefiguration—as a silent heraldry of hope through one period, and as a heraldry of gratitude through the other.

All these cases which we have been rehearsing, taking them in the fullest literality, agree in this general point of union—they are all silent incarnations of miraculous power—miracles, supposing them to have been such originally, locked up and embodied in the regular course of nature, just as we see lineaments of faces and of forms in petrifactions, in variegated marbles, in spars, or in rocky strata, which our fancy interprets as once having been real human existences; but which are now confounded with the substance of a mineral product. Even those who are most superstitious, therefore, look upon cases of this order as occupying a midway station between the physical and the hyperphysical, between the regular course of nature and the providential interruption of that course. The stream of the miraculous is here confluent with the stream of the natural. By such legends the credulous man finds his superstition but little nursed; the incredulous finds his philosophy but little revolted. Both alike will be willing to admit, for instance, that the apparent act of reverential thanksgiving, in certain birds, when drinking, is caused and supported by a physiological arrangement; and yet, perhaps, both alike would bend so far to the legendary faith as to allow a child to believe, and would perceive a pure childlike beauty in believing, that the bird was thus rendering a homage of deep thankfulness to the universal Father, who watches for the safety of sparrows, and sends his rain upon the just and upon the unjust. In short, the faith in this order of the physico-miraculous is open alike to the sceptical and the non-sceptical: it is touched superficially with the coloring of superstition, with its tenderness, its humility, its thankfulness, its awe; but, on the other hand, it is not therefore tainted with the coarseness, with the silliness, with the credulity of superstition. Such a faith reposes upon the universal signs diffused through nature, and blends with the mysterious of natural grandeurs wherever found—with the mysterious of the starry heavens, with the mysterious of music, and with that infinite form of the mysterious for man's dimmest misgivings—

'*Whose dwelling is the light of setting suns.*'

But, from this earliest note in the ascending scale of superstitious faith, let us pass to a more alarming key. This first, which we have styled (in equity as well as for distinction) the *Ovidian*, is too ærial, too allegoric, almost to be susceptible of much terror. It is the mere *fancy*, in a mood half-playful, half-tender, which submits to the belief. It is the feeling, the sentiment, which creates the faith; not the faith which creates the feeling. And thus far we see that modern feeling and Christian feeling has been to the full as operative as any that is peculiar to paganism; judging by the Romish *Legenda*, very much more so. The Ovidian illustrations, under a false superstition, are entitled to give the designation, as being the first, the earliest, but not at all as the richest. Besides that, Ovid's illustrations emanated often from himself individually, not from the popular mind of his country; ours of the same classification uniformly repose on large popular traditions from the whole of Christian antiquity. These again are agencies of the supernatural which can never have a private or personal application; they belong to all mankind and to all generations. But the next in order are more solemn; they become terrific by becoming personal. These comprehend all that vast body of the marvellous which is expressed by the word *Ominous*. On this head, as dividing itself into the ancient and modern, we will speak next.

Everybody is aware of the deep emphasis which the Pagans laid upon words and upon names, under this aspect of the ominous. The name of several places was formally changed by the Roman government, solely with a view to that contagion of evil which was thought to lurk in the syllables, if taken significantly. Thus, the town of Maleventum, (Ill-come, as one might render it,) had its name changed by the Romans to Beneventum, (or Welcome.) *Epidamnum* again, the Grecian Calais, corresponding to the Roman Dover of Brundusium, was a name that would have startled the stoutest-hearted Roman 'from his propriety.' Had he suffered this name to escape him inadvertently, his spirits would have forsaken him—he would have pined away under a certainty of misfortune, like a poor Negro of Koromantyn who is the victim of Obi.[Footnote: '*The victim of Obi.*'—It seems worthy of notice, that this magical fascination is generally called Obi, and the magicians Obeah men, throughout Guinea, Negroland, &c.; whilst the Hebrew or Syriac word for the rites of necromancy, was *Ob* or *Obh*, at least when ventriloquism was concerned.] As a Greek word, which it was, the name imported no ill; but for a Roman to say *Ibo Epidamnum*, was in effect saying, though in a hybrid dialect, half-Greek half-Roman, 'I will go to ruin.' The name was therefore changed to Dyrrachium; a substitution which quieted more anxieties in Roman hearts than the erection of a light-house or the deepening of the harbor mouth. A case equally strong, to take one out of many hundreds that have come down to us, is reported by Livy. There was an officer in a Roman legion, at some period of the Republic, who bore the name either of Atrius Umber or Umbrius Ater: and this man being ordered on some expedition, the soldiers refused to follow him. They did right. We remember that Mr. Coleridge used facetiously to call the well-known sister of Dr. Aikin, Mrs. Barbauld, 'that pleonasm of nakedness'— the idea of nakedness being reduplicated and reverberated in the *bare* and the *bald*. This Atrius Umber might be called 'that pleonasm of darkness;' and one might say to him, in the words of Othello, 'What needs this iteration?' To serve under the Gloomy was enough to darken the spirit of hope; but to serve under the Black Gloomy was really rushing upon destruction. Yet it will be alleged that Captain Death was a most favorite and heroic leader in the English navy; and that in our own times, Admiral Coffin, though an American by birth, has not been unpopular in the same service. This is true: and all that can be said is, that these names were two-edged swords, which might be made to tell against the enemy as well as against friends. And possibly the Roman centurion might have turned his name to the same account, had he possessed the great Dictator's presence of mind; for he, when landing in Africa, having happened to stumble—an omen of the worst character, in Roman estimation—took out its sting by following up his own oversight, as if it had been intentional, falling to the ground, kissing it, and ejaculating that in this way he appropriated the soil.

Omens of every class were certainly regarded, in ancient Rome, with a reverence that can hardly be surpassed. But yet, with respect to these omens derived from names, it is certain that our modern times have more memorable examples on record. Out of a large number which occur to us, we will cite two:—The present King of the French bore in his boyish days a title which he would not have borne, but for an omen of bad augury attached to his proper title. He was called the Duc de Chartres before the Revolution, whereas his proper title was Duc de Valois. And the origin of the change was this:—The Regent's father had been the sole brother of Louis Quatorze. He married for his first wife our English princess Henrietta, the sister of Charles II., (and through her daughter, by the way, it is that the house of Savoy, *i.e.* of Sardinia, has pretensions to the English throne.) This unhappy lady, it is too well established, was poisoned. Voltaire, amongst many others, has affected to doubt the fact; for which in his time there might be some excuse. But since then better evidences have placed the matter beyond all question. We now know both the fact, and the how, and the why. The Duke, who probably was no party to the murder of his young wife, though otherwise on bad terms with her, married for his second wife a coarse German princess, homely in every sense, and a singular contrast to the elegant creature whom he had lost. She was a daughter of the Bavarian Elector; ill-tempered by her own confession, self-willed, and a plain speaker to excess; but otherwise a woman of honest German principles. Unhappy she was through a long life; unhappy through the monotony as well as the malicious intrigues of the French court; and so much so, that she did her best (though without effect) to prevent her Bavarian niece from becoming dauphiness. She acquits her husband, however, in the memoirs which she left behind, of any intentional share in her unhappiness; she describes him constantly as a well-disposed prince. But whether it were, that often walking in the dusk through the numerous apartments of that vast mansion which her husband had so much enlarged, naturally she turned her thoughts to the injured lady who had presided there before herself; or whether it arose from the inevitable gloom which broods continually over mighty palaces, so much is known for certain, that one evening, in the twilight, she met, at a remote quarter of the reception-rooms, something that she conceived to be a spectre. What she fancied to have passed on that occasion, was never known except to her nearest friends; and if she made any explanations in her memoirs, the editor has thought fit to suppress them. She mentions only, that in consequence of some ominous circumstances relating to the title of *Valois*, which was the proper second title of the Orleans family, her son, the Regent, had assumed in his boyhood that of Duc de Chartres. His elder brother was dead, so that the superior title was open to him; but, in consequence of those mysterious omens, whatever they might be, which occasioned much whispering at the time, the great title of Valois was laid aside for ever as of bad augury; nor has it ever been resumed through a century and a half that have followed that mysterious warning; nor will it be resumed unless the numerous children of the present Orleans branch should find themselves distressed for ancient titles; which is not likely, since they enjoy the honors of the elder house, and are now the *children of France* in a technical sense.

Here we have a great European case of state omens in the eldest of Christian houses. The next which we shall cite is equally a state case, and carries its public verification along with itself. In the spring of 1799, when Napoleon was lying before Acre, he became anxious for news from Upper Egypt, whither he had despatched Dessaix in pursuit of a distinguished Mameluke leader. This was in the middle of May. Not many days after, a courier arrived with favorable despatches—favorable in the main, but reporting one tragical occurrence on a small scale that, to Napoleon, for a superstitious reason, outweighed the public prosperity. A *djerme*, or Nile boat of the largest class, having on board a large party of troops and of wounded men, together with most of a regimental band, had run ashore at the village of Benouth. No case could be more hopeless. The neighboring Arabs were of the Yambo tribe—of all Arabs the most ferocious. These Arabs and the Fellahs (whom, by the way, many of our countrymen are so ready to represent as friendly to the French and hostile to ourselves,) had taken the opportunity of attacking the vessel. The engagement was obstinate; but at length the inevitable catastrophe could be delayed no longer. The commander, an Italian named Morandi, was a brave man; any fate appeared better than that which awaited him from an enemy so malignant. He set fire to the powder magazine; the vessel blew up; Morandi perished in the Nile; and all of less nerve, who had previously reached the shore in safety, were put to death to the very last man, with cruelties the most detestable, by their inhuman enemies. For all this Napoleon cared little; but one solitary fact there was in the report which struck him with consternation. This ill-fated *djerme*—what was it called? It was called *L'Italie*; and in the name of the vessel Napoleon read an augury of the fate which had befallen the Italian territory. Considered as a dependency of France, he felt certain that Italy was lost; and Napoleon was inconsolable. But what possible connection, it was asked, can exist between this vessel on the Nile and a remote peninsula of Southern Europe? 'No matter,' replied Napoleon; 'my presentiments never deceive me. You will see that all is ruined. I am satisfied that my Italy, my conquest, is lost to France!' So, indeed, it was. All European news had long been intercepted by the English cruisers; but immediately after the battle with the Vizier in July 1799, an English admiral first informed the French army of Egypt that Massena and others had lost all that Bonaparte had won in 1796. But it is a strange illustration of human blindness, that this very subject of Napoleon's lamentation—this very campaign of 1799—it was, with its blunders and its long equipage of disasters, that paved the way for his own elevation to the Consulship, just seven calendar months from the receipt of that Egyptian despatch; since most certainly, in the struggle of Brumaire 1799, doubtful and critical through every stage, it was the pointed contrast between *his* Italian campaigns and those of his successors which gave effect to Napoleon's pretensions with the political combatants, and which procured them a ratification amongst the people. The loss of Italy was essential to the full effect of Napoleon's previous conquest. That and the imbecile characters of Napoleon's chief military opponents were the true keys to the great revolution of Brumaire. The stone which he rejected became the keystone of the arch. So that, after all, he valued the omen falsely;

though the very next news from Europe, courteously communicated by his English enemies, showed that he had interpreted its meaning rightly.

These omens, derived from names, are therefore common to the ancient and the modern world. But perhaps, in strict logic, they ought to have been classed as one subdivision or variety under a much larger head, viz. words generally, no matter whether proper names or appellatives, as operative powers and agencies, having, that is to say, a charmed power against some party concerned from the moment that they leave the lips.

Homer describes prayers as having a separate life, rising buoyantly upon wings, and making their way upwards to the throne of Jove. Such, but in a sense gloomy and terrific, is the force ascribed under a widespread superstition, ancient and modern, to words uttered on critical occasions; or to words uttered at any time, which point to critical occasions. Hence the doctrine of *euphaemismos*, the necessity of abstaining from strong words or direct words in expressing fatal contingencies. It was shocking, at all times of paganism, to say of a third person—'If he should die;' or to suppose the case that he might be murdered. The very word *death* was consecrated and forbidden. *Si quiddam humanum passus fuerit* was the extreme form to which men advanced in such cases. And this scrupulous feeling, originally founded on the supposed efficacy of words, prevails to this day. It is a feeling undoubtedly supported by good taste, which strongly impresses upon us all the discordant tone of all impassioned subjects, (death, religion, &c.,) with the common key of ordinary conversation. But good taste is not in itself sufficient to account for a scrupulousness so general and so austere. In the lowest classes there is a shuddering recoil still felt from uttering coarsely and roundly the anticipation of a person's death. Suppose a child, heir to some estate, the subject of conversation—the hypothesis of his death is put cautiously, under such forms as, 'If anything but good should happen;' 'if any change should occur;' 'if any of us should chance to miscarry;' and so forth. Always a modified expression is sought—always an indirect one. And this timidity arises under the old superstition still lingering amongst men, like that ancient awe, alluded to by Wordsworth, for the sea and its deep secrets—feelings that have not, no, nor ever will, utterly decay. No excess of nautical skill will ever perfectly disenchant the great abyss from its terrors—no progressive knowledge will ever medicine that dread misgiving of a mysterious and pathless power given to words of a certain import, or uttered in certain situations, by a parent, to persecuting or insulting children; by the victim of horrible oppression, when laboring in final agonies; and by others, whether cursing or blessing, who stand central to great passions, to great interests, or to great perplexities.

And here, by way of parenthesis, we may stop to explain the force of that expression, so common in Scripture, '*Thou hast said it.*' It is an answer often adopted by our Saviour; and the meaning we hold to be this: Many forms in eastern idioms, as well as in the Greek occasionally, though meant *interrogatively*, are of a nature to convey a direct categorical *affirmation*, unless as their meaning is modified by the cadence and intonation. *Art thou*, detached from this vocal and accentual modification, is equivalent to *thou art*. Nay, even apart from this accident, the popular belief authorized the notion, that simply to have uttered any great thesis, though unconsciously — simply to have united verbally any two great ideas, though for a purpose the most different or even opposite, had the mysterious power of realizing them in act. An exclamation, though in the purest spirit of sport, to a boy, '*You shall be our imperator,*' was many times supposed to be the forerunner and fatal mandate for the boy's elevation. Such words executed themselves. To connect, though but for denial or for mockery, the ideas of Jesus and the Messiah, furnished an augury that eventually they would be found to coincide, and to have their coincidence admitted. It was an *argumentum ad hominem*, and drawn from a popular faith.

But a modern reader will object the want of an accompanying design or serious meaning on the part of him who utters the words—he never meant his words to be taken seriously—nay, his purpose was the very opposite. True: and precisely that is the reason why his words are likely to operate effectually, and why they should be feared. Here lies the critical point which most of all distinguishes this faith. Words took effect, not merely in default of a serious use, but exactly in consequence of that default. It was the chance word, the stray word, the word uttered in jest, or in trifling, or in scorn, or unconsciously, which took effect; whilst ten thousand words, uttered with purpose and deliberation, were sure to prove inert. One case will illustrate this:—Alexander of Macedon, in the outset of his great expedition, consulted the oracle at Delphi. For the sake of his army, had he been even without personal faith, he desired to have his enterprise consecrated. No persuasions, however, would move the priestess to enter upon her painful and agitating duties for the sake of obtaining the regular answer of the god. Wearied with this, Alexander seized the great lady by the arm, and using as much violence as was becoming to the two characters—of a great prince acting and a great priestess suffering—he pushed her gently backwards to the tripod on which, in her professional character, she was to seat herself. Upon this, in the hurry and excitement of the moment, the priestess exclaimed, *O pai, anixaitos ei—O son, thou art irresistible*; never adverting for an instant to his martial purposes, but simply to his personal importunities. The person whom she thought of as incapable of resistance, was herself, and all she meant *consciously* was—O son, I can refuse nothing to one so earnest. But mark what followed: Alexander desisted at once—he asked for no further oracle—he refused it, and exclaimed joyously:—'Now then, noble priestess, farewell; I have the oracle—I have your answer, and better than any which you could deliver from the tripod. I am invincible—so you have declared, you cannot revoke it. True, you thought not of Persia—you thought only of my importunity. But that very fact is what ratifies your answer. In its blindness I recognise its truth. An oracle from a god might be distorted by political ministers of the god, as in time past too often has been suspected. The oracle has been said to *Medize*, and in my own father's time to *Philippize*. But an oracle delivered unconsciously, indirectly, blindly, that is the oracle which cannot deceive.' Such was the all-famous oracle which Alexander accepted—such was the oracle on which he and his army reposing went forth 'conquering and to conquer.'

Exactly on this principle do the Turks act, in putting so high a value on the words of idiots. Enlightened Christians have often wondered at their allowing any weight to people bereft of understanding. But that is the very reason for allowing them weight: that very defect it is which makes them capable of being organs for conveying words from higher intelligences. A fine human intelligence cannot be a passive instrument—it cannot be a mere tube for conveying the words of inspiration: such an intelligence will intermingle ideas of its own, or otherwise modify what is given, and pollute what is sacred.

It is also on this principle that the whole practice and doctrine of Sortilegy rest. Let us confine ourselves to that mode of sortilegy which is conducted by throwing open privileged books at random, leaving to chance the page and the particular line on which the oracular functions are thrown. The books used have varied with the caprice or the error of ages. Once the Hebrew Scriptures had the preference. Probably they were laid aside, not because the reverence for their authority decayed, but because it increased. In later times Virgil has been the favorite. Considering the very limited range of ideas to which Virgil was tied by his theme—a colonizing expedition in a barbarous age, no worse book could have been selected: [Footnote: *'No worse book could have been selected.'* —The probable reason for making so unhappy a choice seems to have been that Virgil, in the middle ages, had the character of a necromancer, a diviner, &c. This we all know from Dante. Now, the original reason for this strange translation of character and functions we hold to have arisen from the circumstance of his maternal grandfather having borne the name of *Magus*. People in those ages held that a powerful enchanter, exorciser, &c., must have a magician amongst his *cognati*; the power must run in the blood, which on the maternal side could be undeniably ascertained. Under this preconception, they took Magus not for a proper name, but for a professional designation. Amongst many illustrations of the magical character sustained by Virgil in the middle ages, we may mention that a writer, about the year 1200, or the era of our Robin Hood, published by Montfaucon, and cited by Gibbon in his last volume, says of Virgil, —that *'Captus a Romanis invisibiliter exiit, ivitque Neapopolim.'*] so little indeed does the AEneid exhibit of human life in its multiformity, that much tampering with the text is required to bring real cases of human interest and real situations within the scope of any Virgilian sentence, though aided by the utmost latitude of accommodation. A king, a soldier, a sailor, &c., might look for correspondences to their own circumstances; but not many others. Accordingly, everybody remembers the remarkable answer which Charles I. received at Oxford from this Virgilian oracle, about the opening of the Parliamentary war. But from this limitation in the range of ideas it was that others, and very pious people too, have not thought it profane to resume the old reliance on the Scriptures. No case, indeed, can try so severely, or put upon record so conspicuously, this indestructible propensity for seeking light out of darkness—this thirst for looking into the future by the aid of dice, real or figurative, as the fact of men eminent for piety having yielded to the temptation. We give one instance—the instance of a person who, in *practical* theology, has been, perhaps, more popular than any other in any church. Dr. Doddridge, in his earlier days, was in a dilemma both of conscience and of taste as to the election he should make between two situations, one in possession, both at his command. He was settled at Harborough, in Leicestershire, and was 'pleasing himself with the view of a continuance' in that situation. True, he had received an invitation to Northampton; but the reasons against complying seemed so strong, that nothing was wanting but the civility of going over to Northampton, and making an apologetic farewell. On the last Sunday in November of the year 1729, the doctor went and preached a sermon in conformity with those purposes. 'But,' says he, 'on the morning of that day an incident happened, which affected me greatly.' On the night previous, it seems, he had been urged very importunately by his Northampton friends to undertake the vacant office. Much personal kindness had concurred with this public importunity: the good doctor was affected; he had prayed fervently, alleging in his prayer, as the reason which chiefly weighed with him to reject the offer, that it was far beyond his forces, and chiefly because he was too young [Footnote: *'Because he was too young'*—Dr. Doddridge was born in the summer of 1702; consequently he was at this era of his life about twenty-seven years old, and consequently not so obviously entitled to the excuse of youth. But he pleaded his youth, not with a view to the exertions required, but to the *auctoritas* and responsibilities of the situation.] and had no assistant. He goes on thus:—'As soon as ever this address' (meaning the prayer) 'was ended, I passed through a room of the house in which I lodged, where a child was reading to his mother, and the only words I heard distinctly were these, *And as thy days, so shall thy strength be.*' This singular coincidence between his own difficulty and a scriptural line caught at random in passing hastily through a room, (but observe, a line insulated from the context, and placed in high relief to his ear,) shook his resolution. Accident co-operated; a promise to be fulfilled at Northampton, in a certain contingency, fell due at the instant; the doctor was detained, this detention gave time for further representations; new motives arose, old difficulties were removed, and finally the doctor saw, in all this succession of steps, the first of which, however, lay in the *Sortes Biblicæ*, clear indications of a providential guidance. With that conviction he took up his abode at Northampton, and remained there for the next thirty-one years, until he left it for his grave at Lisbon; in fact, he passed at Northampton the whole of his public life. It must, therefore, be allowed to stand upon the records of sortilege, that in the main direction of his life—not, indeed, as to its spirit, but as to its form and local connections—a Protestant divine of much merit, and chiefly in what regards practice, and of the class most opposed to superstition, took his determining impulse from a variety of the *Sortes Virgilianæ*.

This variety was known in early times to the Jews—as early, indeed, as the era of the Grecian Pericles, if we are to believe the Talmud. It is known familiarly to this day amongst Polish Jews, and is called *Bathcol*, or the *daughter of a voice*; the meaning of which appellation is this:—The *Urim and Thummim*, or oracle in the breast-plate of the high priest, spoke directly from God. It was, therefore, the original or mother-voice. But about the time of Pericles, that is, exactly one hundred years before the time of Alexander the Great, the light of prophecy was quenched in Malachi or Haggai; and the oracular jewels in the breast-plate became simultaneously dim. Henceforwards the mother-voice was heard no longer: but to this succeeded an imperfect or daughter-voice, (*Bathcol*,) which lay in the first words happening to arrest the attention at a moment of perplexity. An illustration, which has been often quoted from the Talmud, is to the following effect:— Rabbi Tochanan, and Rabbi Simeon Ben Lachish, were anxious about a friend, Rabbi Samuel, six hundred miles distant on the Euphrates. Whilst talking earnestly together on this subject in Palestine, they passed a school; they paused to listen: it was a child reading the first book of Samuel; and the words which they caught were these—*And Samuel died*. These words they received as a *Bath-col*: and the next horseman from the Euphrates brought word accordingly that Rabbi Samuel had been gathered to his fathers at some station on the Euphrates.

Here is the very same case, the same *Bath-col* substantially, which we have cited from Orton's *Life of Doddridge*. And Du Cange himself notices, in his Glossary, the relation which this bore to the Pagan *Sortes*. 'It was,' says he, 'a fantastical way of divination, invented by the Jews, not unlike the *Sortes Virgilianæ* of the heathens. For, as with them the first words they happened to dip into in the works of that poet were a kind of oracle whereby they predicted future events,—so, with the Jews, when they appealed to *Bath-col*, the first words they heard from any one's mouth were looked upon as a voice from Heaven directing them in the matter they inquired about.'

If the reader imagines that this ancient form of the practical miraculous is at all gone out of use, even the example of Dr. Doddridge may satisfy him to the contrary. Such an example was sure to authorize a large imitation. But, even apart from that, the superstition is common. The records of conversion amongst felons and other ignorant persons might be cited by hundreds upon hundreds to prove that no practice is more common than that of trying the spiritual fate, and abiding by the import of any passage in the Scriptures which may first present itself to the eye. Cowper, the poet, has recorded a case of this sort in his own experience. It is one to which all the unhappy are prone. But a mode of questioning the oracles of darkness, far more childish, and, under some shape or other, equally common amongst those who are prompted by mere vacancy of mind, without that determination to sacred fountains which is impressed by misery, may be found in the following extravagant silliness of Rousseau, which we give in his own words—a case for which he admits that he himself would have *shut up* any other man (meaning in a lunatic hospital) whom he had seen practising the same absurdities:—

'Au milieu de mes études et d'une vie innocente autant qu'on la puisse mener, et malgré tout ce qu'on m'avoit pu dire, la peur de l'Enfer m'agitoit encore. Souvent je me demandois—En quel état suis-je? Si je mourrois à l'instant même, *serois-je damné*? Selon mes Jansénistes, [he had been reading the books of the Port Royal,] la chose est indubitable: mais, selon ma conscience, il me paroissoit que non. Toujours craintif et flottant dans cette cruelle incertitude, j'avois recours (pour en sortir) aux expédients les plus risibles, et pour lesquels je ferois volontiers enfermer un homme si je lui en voyois faire autant. ... Un jour, rêvant à ce triste sujet, je m'exerçois machinalement à lancer les pierres contre les troncs des arbres; et cela avec mon addresse ordinaire, c'est-à-dire sans presque jamais en toucher aucun. Tout au milieu de ce bel exercice, je m'avisai de faire une espèce de pronostic pour calmer mon inquiétude. Je me dis—je m'en vais jeter cette pierre contre l'arbre qui est vis-à-vis de moi: si je le touche, signe de salut: si je le manque, signe de damnation. Tout en disant ainsi, je jette ma pierre d'une main tremblante, et avec un horrible battement de coeur, mais si heureusement qu'elle va frapper au beau-milieu de l'arbre: ce qui véritablement n'étoit pas difficile: car j'avois eu soin de le choisir fort gros et fort près. *Depuis lors je n'ai plus doubté de mon salut.* Je ne sais, en me rappelant ce trait, si je dois rire ou gémir sur moimême.'—*Les Confessions, Partie I. Livre VI.*

Now, really, if Rousseau thought fit to try such tremendous appeals by taking 'a shy' at any random object, he should have governed his sortilegy (for such it may be called) with something more like equity. Fair play is a jewel: and in such a case, a man is supposed to play against an adverse party hid in darkness. To shy at a cow within six feet distance gives no chance at all to his dark antagonist. A pigeon rising from a trap at a suitable distance might be thought a *sincere* staking of the interest at issue: but, as to the massy stem of a tree 'fort gros et fort près'—the sarcasm of a Roman emperor applies, that to miss under such conditions implied an original genius for stupidity, and to hit was no trial of the case. After all, the sentimentalist had youth to plead in apology for this extravagance. He was hypochondriacal; he was in solitude; and he was possessed by gloomy imaginations from the works of a society in the highest public credit. But most readers will be aware of similar appeals to the mysteries of Providence, made in public by illustrious sectarians, speaking from the solemn station of a pulpit. We forbear to quote cases of this nature, though really existing in print, because we feel that the blasphemy of such anecdotes is more revolting and more painful to pious minds than the absurdity is amusing. Meantime it must not be forgotten, that the principle concerned, though it may happen to disgust men when associated with ludicrous circumstances, is, after all, the very same which has latently governed very many modes of ordeal, or judicial inquiry; and which has been adopted, blindly, as a moral rule, or canon, equally by the blindest of the Pagans, the most fanatical of the Jews, and the most enlightened of the Christians. It proceeds upon the assumption that man by his actions puts a question to Heaven; and that Heaven answers by the event. Lucan, in a well known passage, takes it for granted that the cause of Cæsar had the approbation of the gods. And why? Simply from the event. It was notoriously the triumphant cause. It was victorious, (*victrix* causa Deis placuit; sed *victa* Catoni.) It was the '*victrix* causa;' and, *as such*, simply because it was 'victrix,' it had a right in his eyes to postulate the divine favor as mere matter of necessary interference: whilst, on the other hand, the *victa causa*, though it seemed to Lucan sanctioned by human virtue in the person of Cato, stood unappealably condemned. This mode of reasoning may strike the reader as merely Pagan. Not at all. In England, at the close of the Parliamentary war, it was generally argued—that Providence had decided the question against the Royalists by the mere fact of the issue. Milton himself, with all his high-toned morality, uses this argument as irrefragable: which is odd, were it only on this account—that the issue ought necessarily to have been held for a time as merely hypothetic, and liable to be set aside by possible counter-issues through one generation at the least. But the capital argument against such doctrine is to be found in the New Testament. Strange that Milton should overlook, and strange that moralists in general have overlooked, the sudden arrest given to this dangerous but most prevalent mode of reasoning by the Founder of our faith. He first, he last, taught to his astonished disciples the new truth—at that time the astounding truth—that no relation exists between the immediate practical events of things on the one side, and divine sentences on the other. There was no presumption, he teaches them, against a man's favor with God, or that of his parents, because he happened to be afflicted to extremity with bodily disease. There was no shadow of an argument for believing a party of men criminal objects of heavenly wrath because upon them, by fatal preference, a tower had fallen, and because *their* bodies were exclusively mangled. How little can it be said that Christianity has yet developed the fulness of its power, when kings and senates so recently acted under a total oblivion of this great though novel Christian doctrine, and would do so still, were it not that religious arguments have been banished by the progress of manners from the field of political discussion.

But, quitting this province of the ominous, where it is made the object of a direct personal inquest, whether by private or by national trials, or the sortilege of events, let us throw our eyes over the broader field of omens, as they offer themselves spontaneously to those who do not seek, or would even willingly evade them. There are few of these, perhaps none, which are not universal in their authority, though every land in turn fancies them (like its proverbs) of local prescription and origin. The death-watch extends from England to Cashmere, and across India diagonally to the remotest nook of Bengal, over a three thousand miles' distance from the entrance of the Indian Punjaub. A hare crossing a man's path on starting in the morning, has been held in all countries alike to prognosticate evil in the course of that day. Thus, in the *Confessions of a Thug*, (which is partially built on a real judicial document, and everywhere conforms to the usages of Hindostan,) the hero of the horrid narrative [Footnote: '*The hero of the horrid narrative.*'—Horrid it certainly is; and one incident in every case gives a demoniacal air of coolness to the hellish atrocities, viz the regular forwarding of the *bheels*, or grave-diggers. But else the tale tends too much to monotony; and for a reason which ought to have checked the author in carrying on the work to three volumes, namely, that although there is much dramatic variety in the circumstances of the several cases, there is none in the catastrophes. The brave man and the coward, the erect spirit fighting to the last, and the poor creature that despairs from the first,—all are confounded in one undistinguishing end by sudden strangulation. This was the original defect of the plan. The sudden surprise, and the scientific noosing as with a Chilian *lasso*, constituted in fact a main feature of Thuggee. But still, the gradual theatrical arrangement of each Thug severally by the side of a victim, must often have roused violent suspicion, and that in time to intercept the suddenness of the murder. Now, for the sake of the dramatic effect, this interception ought more often to have been introduced, else the murders are but so many blind surprises as if in sleep.] charges some disaster of his own upon having neglected such an omen of the morning. The same belief operated in Pagan Italy. The same omen announced to Lord Lindsay's Arab attendants in the desert the approach of some disaster, which partially happened in the morning. And a Highlander of the 42d Regiment, in his printed memoirs, notices the same harbinger of evil as having crossed his own path on a day of personal disaster in Spain.

Birds are even more familiarly associated with such ominous warnings. This chapter in the great volume of superstition was indeed cultivated with unusual solicitude amongst the Pagans—*ornithomancy* grew into an elaborate science. But if every rule and distinction upon the number and the position of birds, whether to the right or the left, had been collected from our own village matrons amongst ourselves, it would appear that no more of this Pagan science had gone to wreck than must naturally follow the difference between a believing and a disbelieving government. Magpies are still of awful authority in village life, according to their number, &c.; for a striking illustration of which we may refer the reader to Sir Walter Scott's *Demonology*, reported not at second-hand, but from Sir Walter's personal communication with some seafaring fellow-traveller in a stage-coach.

Among the ancient stories of the same class is one which we shall repeat—having reference to that Herod Agrippa, grandson of Herod the Great, before whom St. Paul made his famous apology at Cæsarea. This Agrippa, overwhelmed by debts, had fled from Palestine to Rome in the latter years of Tiberius. His mother's interest with the widow of Germanicus procured him a special recommendation to her son Caligula. Viewing this child and heir of the popular Germanicus as the rising sun, Agrippa had been too free in his language. True, the uncle of Germanicus was the reigning prince; but he was old, and breaking up. True, the son of Germanicus was not yet on the throne; but he soon would be; and Agrippa was rash enough to call the Emperor a *superannuated old fellow,* and even to wish for his death. Sejanus was now dead and gone; but there was no want of spies: and a certain Macro reported his words to Tiberius. Agrippa was in consequence arrested; the Emperor himself condescending to point out the noble Jew to the officer on duty. The case was a gloomy one, if Tiberius should happen to survive much longer: and the story of the omen proceeds thus:—'Now Agrippa stood in his bonds before the Imperial palace, and in his affliction leaned against a certain tree, upon the boughs of which it happened that a bird had alighted which the Romans call *bubo,* or the owl. All this was steadfastly observed by a German prisoner, who asked a soldier what might be the name and offence of that man habited in purple. Being told that the man's name was Agrippa, and that he was a Jew of high rank, who had given a personal offence to the Emperor, the German asked permission to go near and address him; which being granted, he spoke thus:—"This disaster, I doubt not, young man, is trying to your heart; and perhaps you will not believe me when I announce to you beforehand the providential deliverance which is impending. However, this much I will say—and for my sincerity let me appeal to my native gods, as well as to the gods of this Rome, who have brought us both into trouble—that no selfish objects prompt me to this revelation—for a revelation it is—and to the following effect:—It is fated that you shall not long remain in chains. Your deliverance will be speedy; you shall be raised to the very highest rank and power; you shall be the object of as much envy as now you are of pity; you shall retain your prosperity till death; and you shall transmit that prosperity to your children. But"—and there the German paused. Agrippa was agitated; the bystanders were attentive; and after a time, the German, pointing solemnly to the bird, proceeded thus:—"But this remember heedfully—that, when next you see the bird which now perches above your head, you will have only five days longer to live! This event will be surely accomplished by that same mysterious god who has thought fit to send the bird as a warning sign; and you, when you come to your glory, do not forget me that foreshadowed it in your humiliation."' The story adds, that Agrippa affected to laugh when the German concluded; after which it goes on to say, that in a few weeks, being delivered by the death of Tiberius; being released from prison by the very prince on whose account he had incurred the risk; being raised to a tetrarchy, and afterwards to the kingdom of all Judea; coming into all the prosperity which had been promised to him by the German; and not losing any part of his interest at Rome through the assassination of his patron Caligula—he began to look back respectfully to the words of the German, and forwards with anxiety to the second coming of the bird. Seven years of sunshine had now slipped away as silently as a dream. A great festival, shows and vows, was on the point of being celebrated in honor of

Claudius Cæsar, at Strato's Tower, otherwise called Cæsarea, the Roman metropolis of Palestine. Duty and policy alike required that the king of the land should go down and unite in this mode of religious homage to the emperor. He did so; and on the second morning of the festival, by way of doing more conspicuous honor to the great solemnity, he assumed a very sumptuous attire of silver armor, burnished so highly as to throw back a dazzling glare from the sun's morning beams upon the upturned eyes of the vast multitude around him. Immediately from the sycophantish part of the crowd, of whom a vast majority were Pagans, ascended a cry of glorification as to some manifestation of Deity. Agrippa, gratified by this success of his new apparel, and by this flattery, not unusual in the case of kings, had not the firmness (though a Jew, and conscious of the wickedness, greater in himself than in the heathen crowd,) to reject the blasphemous homage. Voices of adoration continued to ascend; when suddenly, looking upward to the vast awnings prepared for screening the audience from the noonday heats, the king perceived the same ominous bird which he had seen at Rome in the day of his affliction, seated quietly, and looking down upon himself. In that same moment an icy pang shot through his intestines. He was removed into the palace; and at the end of five days, completely worn out by pain, Agrippa expired in the 54th year of his age, and the seventh of his sovereign power.

Whether the bird, here described as an owl, was really such, may be doubted, considering the narrow nomenclature of the Romans for all zoological purposes, and the total indifference of the Roman mind to all distinctions in natural history which are not upon the very largest scale. We should much suspect that the bird was a magpie. Meantime, speaking of ornithoscopy in relation to Jews, we remember another story in that subdivision of the subject which it may be worth while repeating; not merely on its own account, as wearing a fine oriental air, but also for the correction which it suggests to a very common error.

In some period of Syrian warfare, a large military detachment was entering at some point of Syria from the desert of the Euphrates. At the head of the whole array rode two men of some distinction: one was an augur of high reputation, the other was a Jew called Mosollam, a man of admirable beauty, a matchless horseman, an unerring archer, and accomplished in all martial arts. As they were now first coming within enclosed grounds, after a long march in the wilderness, the augur was most anxious to inaugurate the expedition by some considerable omen. Watching anxiously, therefore, he soon saw a bird of splendid plumage perching on a low wall. 'Halt!' he said to the advanced guard: and all drew up in a line. At that moment of silence and expectation, Mosollam, slightly turning himself in his saddle, drew his bow-string to his ear; his Jewish hatred of Pagan auguries burned within him; his inevitable shaft went right to its mark, and the beautiful bird fell dead. The augur turned round in fury. But the Jew laughed at him. 'This bird, you say, should have furnished us with omens of our future fortunes. But had he known anything of his own, he would never have perched where he did, or have come within the range of Mosollam's archery. How should that bird know our destiny, who did not know that it was his own to be shot by Mosollam the Jew?'

Now, this is a most common but a most erroneous way of arguing. In a case of this kind, the bird was not supposed to have any conscious acquaintance with futurity, either for his own benefit or that of others. But even where such a consciousness may be supposed, as in the case of oneiromancy, or prophecy by means of dreams, it must be supposed limited, and the more limited in a personal sense as they are illimitable in a sublime one. Who imagines that, because a Daniel or Ezekiel foresaw the grand revolutions of the earth, therefore they must or could have foreseen the little details of their own ordinary life? And even descending from that perfect inspiration to the more doubtful power of augury amongst the Pagans, (concerning which the most eminent of theologians have held very opposite theories,) one thing is certain, that, so long as we entertain such pretensions, or discuss them at all, we must take them with the principle of those who professed such arts, not with principles of our own arbitrary invention.

One example will make this clear:—There are in England [Footnote: 'There are in England'—Especially in Somersetshire, and for twenty miles round Wrington, the birthplace of Locke. Nobody sinks for wells without their advice. We ourselves knew an amiable and accomplished Scottish family, who, at an estate called Belmadrothie, in memory of a similar property in Ross shire, built a house in Somersetshire, and resolved to find water without help from the jowser. But after sinking to a greater depth than ever had been known before, and spending nearly £200, they were finally obliged to consult the jowser, who found water at once.] a class of men who practise the Pagan rhabdomancy in a limited sense. They carry a rod or rhabdos (*rhabdos*) of willow: this they hold horizontally; and by the bending of the rod towards the ground they discover the favorable places for sinking wells; a matter of considerable importance in a province so ill-watered as the northern district of Somersetshire, &c. These people are locally called *jowsers*; and it is probable, that from the suspicion with which their art has been usually regarded amongst people of education, as a mere legerdemain trick of Dousterswivel's, is derived the slang word to *chouse* for *swindle*. Meantime, the experimental evidences of a real practical skill in these men, and the enlarged compass of speculation in these days, have led many enlightened people to a Stoic *epochey*, or suspension of judgment, on the reality of this somewhat mysterious art. Now, in the East, there are men who make the same pretensions in a more showy branch of the art. It is not water, but treasures which they profess to find by some hidden kind of rhabdomancy. The very existence of treasures with us is reasonably considered a thing of improbable occurrence. But in the unsettled East, and with the low valuation of human life wherever Mahometanism prevails, insecurity and other causes must have caused millions of such deposits in every century to have perished as to any knowledge of survivors. The sword has been moving backwards and forwards, for instance, like a weaver's shuttle, since the time of Mahmoud the Ghaznevide, [Footnote: Mahmood of Ghizni, which, under the European name of Ghaznee, was so recently taken in one hour by our Indian army under Lord Keane Mahmood was the first Mahometan invader of Hindostan.] in Anno Domini 1000, in the vast regions between the Tigris, the Oxus, and the Indus. Regularly as it approached, gold and jewels must have sunk by whole harvests into the ground. A certain per centage has been doubtless recovered: a larger per centage has disappeared for ever. Hence naturally the jealousy of barbarous Orientals that we Europeans, in groping amongst pyramids, sphynxes, and tombs, are looking for buried treasures. The wretches are not so wide astray in what they believe as in what they disbelieve. The treasures do really exist which they fancy; but then also the other treasures in the glorious antiquities have that existence for our sense of beauty which to their brutality is inconceivable. In these circumstances, why should it surprise us that men will pursue the science of discovery as a regular trade? Many discoveries of treasure are doubtless made continually, which, for obvious reasons, are communicated to nobody. Some proportion there must be between the sowing of such grain as diamonds or emeralds, and the subsequent reaping, whether by accident or by art. For, with regard to the last, it is no more impossible, *prima fronte*, that a substance may exist having an occult sympathy with subterraneous water or subterraneous gold, than that the magnet should have a sympathy (as yet occult) with the northern pole of our planet.

The first flash of careless thought applied to such a case will suggest, that men holding powers of this nature need not offer their services for hire to others. And this, in fact, is the objection universally urged by us Europeans as decisive against their pretensions. Their knavery, it is fancied, stands self-recorded; since, assuredly, they would not be willing to divide their subterranean treasures, if they knew of any. But the men are not in such self-contradiction as may seem. Lady Hester Stanhope, from the better knowledge she had acquired of Oriental opinions, set Dr. Madden right on this point. The Oriental belief is that a fatality attends the appropriator of a treasure in any case where he happens also to be the discoverer. Such a person, it is held, will die soon, and suddenly—so that he is compelled to seek his remuneration from the wages or fees of his employers, not from the treasure itself.

Many more secret laws are held sacred amongst the professors of that art than that which was explained by Lady Hester Stanhope. These we shall not enter upon at present: but generally we may remark, that the same practices of subterranean deposits, during our troubled periods in Europe, led to the same superstitions. And it may be added, that the same error has arisen in both cases as to some of these superstitions. How often must it have struck people of liberal feelings, as a scandalous proof of the preposterous value set upon riches by poor men, that ghosts should popularly be supposed to rise and wander for the sake of revealing the situations of buried treasures. For ourselves, we have been accustomed to view this popular belief in the light of an argument for pity rather than for contempt towards poor men, as indicating the extreme pressure of that necessity which could so have demoralized their natural sense of truth. But certainly, in whatever feelings originating, such popular superstitions as to motives of ghostly missions did seem to argue a deplorable misconception of the relation subsisting between the spiritual world and the perishable treasures of this perishable world. Yet, when we look into the Eastern explanations of this case, we find that it is meant to express, not any overvaluation of riches, but the direct contrary passion. A human spirit is punished—such is the notion—punished in the spiritual world for excessive attachment to gold, by degradation to the office of its guardian; and from this office the tortured spirit can release itself only by revealing the treasure and transferring the custody. It is a penal martyrdom, not an elective passion for gold, which is thus exemplified in the wanderings of a treasure-ghost.

But, in a field where of necessity we are so much limited, we willingly pass from the consideration of these treasure or *khasne* phantoms (which alone sufficiently ensure a swarm of ghostly terrors for all Oriental ruins of cities,) to the same marvellous apparitions, as they haunt other solitudes even more awful than those of ruined cities. In this world there are two mighty forms of perfect solitude—the ocean and the desert: the wilderness of the barren sands, and the wilderness of the barren waters. Both are the parents of inevitable superstitions—of terrors, solemn, ineradicable, eternal. Sailors and the children of the desert are alike overrun with spiritual hauntings, from accidents of peril essentially connected with those modes of life, and from the eternal spectacle of the infinite. Voices seem to blend with the raving of the sea, which will for ever impress the feeling of beings more than human: and every chamber of the great wilderness which, with little interruption, stretches from the Euphrates to the western shores of Africa, has its own peculiar terrors both as to sights and sounds. In the wilderness of Zin, between Palestine and the Red Sea, a section of the desert well known in these days to our own countrymen, bells are heard daily pealing for matins, or for vespers, from some phantom convent that no search of Christian or of Bedouin Arab has ever been able to discover. These bells have sounded since the Crusades. Other sounds, trumpets, the *Alala* of armies, &c., are heard in other regions of the Desert. Forms, also, are seen of more people than have any right to be walking in human paths: sometimes forms of avowed terror; sometimes, which is a case of far more danger, appearances that mimic the shapes of men, and even of friends or comrades. This is a case much dwelt on by the old travellers, and which throws a gloom over the spirits of all Bedouins, and of every cafila or caravan. We all know what a sensation of loneliness or 'eeriness' (to use an expressive term of the ballad poetry) arises to any small party assembling in a single room of a vast desolate mansion: how the timid among them fancy continually that they hear some remote door opening, or trace the sound of suppressed footsteps from some distant staircase. Such is the feeling in the desert, even in the midst of the caravan. The mighty solitude is seen: the dread silence is anticipated which will succeed to this brief transit of men, camels, and horses. Awe prevails even in the midst of society: but, if the traveller should loiter behind from fatigue, or be so imprudent as to ramble aside—should he from any cause once lose sight of his party, it is held that his chance is small of recovering their traces. And why? Not chiefly from the want of footmarks where the wind effaces all impressions in half an hour, or of eyemarks where all is one blank ocean of sand, but much more from the sounds or the visual appearances which are supposed to beset and to seduce all insulated wanderers.

Everybody knows the superstitions of the ancients about the *Nympholeptoi*, or those who had seen Pan. But far more awful and gloomy are the existing superstitions, throughout Asia and Africa, as to the perils of those who are phantom-haunted in the wilderness. The old Venetian traveller Marco Polo states them well: he speaks, indeed, of the Eastern or Tartar deserts; the steppes which stretch from European Russia to the footsteps of the Chinese throne; but exactly the same creed prevails amongst the Arabs, from Bagdad to Suez and Cairo—from Rosetta to Tunis—Tunis to Timbuctoo or Mequinez. 'If, during the daytime,' says he, 'any person should remain behind until the caravan is no longer in sight, he hears himself unexpectedly called to by name, and in a voice with which he is familiar. Not doubting that the voice proceeds from some of his comrades, the unhappy man is beguiled from the right direction; and soon finding himself utterly confounded as to the path, he roams about in distraction until he perishes miserably. If, on the other hand, this perilous separation of himself from the caravan should happen at night, he is sure to hear the uproar of a great cavalcade a mile or two to the right or left of the true track. He is thus seduced on one side: and at break of day finds himself far removed from man. Nay, even at noon-day, it is well known that grave and respectable men to all appearance will come up to a particular traveller, will bear the look of a friend, and will gradually lure him by earnest conversation to a distance from the caravan; after which the sounds of men and camels will be heard continually at all points but the true one; whilst an insensible turning by the tenth of an inch at each separate step from the true direction will very soon suffice to set the traveller's face to the opposite point of the compass from that which his safety requires, and which his fancy represents to him as his real direction. Marvellous, indeed, and almost passing belief, are the stories reported of these desert phantoms, which are said at times to fill the air with choral music from all kinds of instruments, from drums, and the clash of arms: so that oftentimes a whole caravan are obliged to close up their open ranks, and to proceed in a compact line of march.'

Lord Lindsay, in his very interesting travels in Egypt, Edom, &c., agrees with Warton in supposing (and probably enough) that from this account of the desert traditions in Marco Polo was derived Milton's fine passage in Comus:—

> 'Of calling shapes, and beckoning shadows dire,
> And aery tongues that syllable men's names
> On sands, and shores, and desert wildernesses.'

But the most remarkable of these desert superstitions, as suggested by the mention of Lord Lindsay, is one which that young nobleman, in some place which we cannot immediately find, has noticed, but which he only was destined by a severe personal loss immediately to illustrate. Lord L. quotes from Vincent le Blanc an anecdote of a man in his own caravan, the companion of an Arab merchant, who disappeared in a mysterious manner. Four Moors, with a retaining fee of 100 ducats, were sent in quest of him, but came back *re infecta*. 'And 'tis uncertain,' adds Le Blanc, 'whether he was swallowed up in the sands, or met his death by any other misfortune; as it often happens, by the relation of a merchant then in our company, who told us, that two years before, traversing the same journey, a comrade of his, going a little aside from the company, saw three men who called him by his name; and one of them, to his thinking, favored very much his companion; and, as he was about to follow them, his real companion calling him to come back to his company, he found himself deceived by the others, and thus was saved. And all travellers in these parts hold, that in the deserts are many such phantasms seen, that strive to seduce the traveller.' Thus far it is the traveller's own fault, warned as he is continually by the extreme anxiety of the Arab leaders or guides, with respect to all who stray to any distance, if he is duped or enticed by these pseudo-men: though, in the case of Lapland dogs, who ought to have a surer instinct of detection for counterfeits, we know from Sir Capel de Broke and others, that they are continually wiled away by the wolves who roam about the nightly encampments of travellers. But there is a secondary disaster, according to the Arab superstition, awaiting those whose eyes are once opened to the discernment of these phantoms. To see them, or to hear them, even where the traveller is careful to refuse their lures, entails the certainty of death in no long time. This is another form of that universal faith which made it impossible for any man to survive a bodily commerce, by whatever sense, with a spiritual being. We find it in the Old Testament, where the expression, 'I have seen God and shall die,' means simply a supernatural being; since no Hebrew believed it possible for a nature purely human to sustain for a moment the sight of the Infinite Being. We find the same faith amongst ourselves, in case of *doppelgänger* becoming apparent to the sight of those whom they counterfeit; and in many other varieties. We modern Europeans, of course, laugh at these superstitions; though, as La Place remarks, (*Essai sur les Probabilités,*) any case, however apparently incredible, if it is a recurrent case, is as much entitled to a fair valuation as if it had been more probable beforehand.[Footnote: *'Is as much entitled to a fair valuation, under the lans of induction, as if it had been more probable beforehand'*—One of the cases which La Place notices as entitled to a grave consideration, but which would most assuredly be treated as a trivial phenomenon, unworthy of attention, by commonplace spectators, is—when a run of success, with no apparent cause, takes place on heads or tails, (*pile ou croix*) Most people dismiss such a case as pure accident. But La Place insists on its being duly valued as a fact, however unaccountable as an effect. So again, if in a large majority of experiences like those of Lord Lindsay's party in the desert, death should follow, such a phenomenon is as well entitled to its separate valuation as any other.] This being premised, we who connect superstition with the personal result, are more impressed by the disaster which happened to Lord Lindsay, than his lordship, who either failed to notice the *nexus* between the events, or possibly declined to put the case too forward in his reader's eye, from the solemnity of the circumstances, and the private interest to himself and his own family, of the subsequent event. The case was this:—Mr. William Wardlaw Ramsay, the companion (and we believe relative) of Lord Lindsay, a man whose honorable character, and whose intellectual accomplishments speak for themselves, in the posthumus memorabilia of his travels published by

Lord L., had seen an array of objects in the desert, which facts immediately succeeding demonstrated to have been a mere ocular *lusus,* or (according to Arab notions) phantoms. During the absence from home of an Arab sheikh, who had been hired as conductor of Lord Lindsay's party, a hostile tribe (bearing the name of Tellaheens) had assaulted and pillaged his tents. Report of this had reached the English travelling party; it was known that the Tellaheens were still in motion, and a hostile rencounter was looked for for some days. At length, in crossing the well known valley of the *Wady Araba,* that most ancient channel of communication between the Red Sea and Judea, &c., Mr. Ramsay saw, to his own entire conviction, a party of horse moving amongst some sand-hills. Afterwards it became certain, from accurate information, that this must have been a delusion. It was established, that no horseman *could* have been in that neighborhood at that time. Lord Lindsay records the case as an illustration of 'that spiritualized tone the imagination naturally assumes, in scenes presenting so little sympathy with the ordinary feelings of humanity;' and he reports the case in these pointed terms:—'Mr. Ramsay, a man of remarkably strong sight, and by no means disposed to superstitious credulity, distinctly saw a party of horse moving among the sand-hills; and I do not believe he was ever able to divest himself of that impression.' No—and, according to Arab interpretation, very naturally so; for, according to their faith, he really *had* seen the horsemen; phantom horseman certainly, but still objects of sight. The sequel remains to be told—by the Arabian hypothesis, Mr. Ramsay had but a short time to live—he was under a secret summons to the next world. And accordingly, in a few weeks after this, whilst Lord Lindsay had gone to visit Palmyra, Mr. Ramsay died at Damascus.

This was a case exactly corresponding to the Pagan *nympholepsis*—he had seen the beings whom it is not lawful to see and live. Another case of Eastern superstition, not less determined, and not less remarkably fulfilled, occurred some years before to Dr. Madden, who travelled pretty much in the same route as Lord Lindsay. The doctor, as a phrenologist, had been struck with the very singular conformation of a skull which he saw amongst many others on an altar in some Syrian convent. He offered a considerable sum in gold for it; but it was by repute the skull of a saint; and the monk with whom Dr. M. attempted to negotiate, not only refused his offers, but protested that even for the doctor's sake, apart from the interests of the convent, he could not venture on such a transfer: for that, by the tradition attached to it, the skull would endanger any vessel carrying it from the Syrian shore: the vessel might escape; but it would never succeed in reaching any but a Syrian harbor. After this, for the credit of our country, which stands so high in the East, and should be so punctiliously tended by all Englishmen, we are sorry to record that Dr. Madden (though otherwise a man of scrupulous honor) yielded to the temptation of substituting for the saint's skull another less remarkable from his own collection. With this saintly relic he embarked on board a Grecian ship; was alternately pursued and met by storms the most violent; larboard and starboard, on every quarter, he was buffeted; the wind blew from every point of the compass; the doctor honestly confesses that he often wished this baleful skull back in safety on the quiet altar from which he took it; and finally, after many days of anxiety, he was too happy in finding himself again restored to some oriental port, from which he secretly vowed never again to sail with a saint's skull, or with any skull, however remarkable phrenologically, not purchased in an open market.

Thus we have pursued, through many of its most memorable sections, the spirit of the miraculous as it moulded and gathered itself in the superstitions of Paganism; and we have shown that, in the modern superstitions of Christianity, or of Mahometanism, (often enough borrowed from Christian sources,) there is a pretty regular correspondence. Speaking with a reference to the strictly popular belief, it cannot be pretended for a moment, that miraculous agencies are slumbering in modern ages. For one superstition of that nature which the Pagans had, we can produce twenty. And if, from the collation of numbers, we should pass to that of quality, it is a matter of notoriety, that from the very philosophy of Paganism, and its slight root in the terrors or profounder mysteries of spiritual nature, no comparison could be sustained for a moment between the true religion and any mode whatever of the false. Ghosts we have purposely omitted, because that idea is so peculiarly Christian [Footnote: '*Because that idea is so peculiarly Christian*'—One reason, additional to the main one, why the idea of a ghost could not be conceived or reproduced by Paganism, lies in the fourfold resolution of the human nature at death, viz.—1. *corpus*; 2. *manes*; 3. *spiritus*; 4. *anima*. No reversionary consciousness, no restitution of the total nature, sentient and active, was thus possible. Pliny has a story which looks like a ghost story; but it is all moonshine—a mere *simulacrum*.] as to reject all counterparts or affinities from other modes of the supernatural. The Christian ghost is too awful a presence, and with too large a substratum of the real, the impassioned, the human, for our present purposes. We deal chiefly with the wilder and more ærial forms of superstition; not so far off from fleshly nature as the purely allegoric—not so near as the penal, the purgatorial, the penitential. In this middle class, 'Gabriel's hounds'— the 'phantom ship'—the gloomy legends of the charcoal burners in the German forests—and the local or epichorial superstitions from every district of Europe, come forward by thousands, attesting the high activity of the miraculous and the hyperphysical instincts, even in this generation, wheresoever the voice of the people makes itself heard.

But in Pagan times, it will be objected, the popular superstitions blended themselves with the highest political functions, gave a sanction to national counsels, and oftentimes gave their starting point to the very primary movements of the state. Prophecies, omens, miracles, all worked concurrently with senates or princes. Whereas in our days, says Charles Lamb, the witch who takes her pleasure with the moon, and summons Beelzebub to her sabbaths, nevertheless trembles before the beadle, and hides herself from the overseer. Now, as to the witch, even the horrid Canidia of Horace, or the more dreadful Erichtho of Lucan, seems hardly to have been much respected in any era. But for the other modes of the supernatural, they have entered into more frequent combinations with state functions and state movements in our modern ages than in the classical age of Paganism. Look at prophecies, for example: the Romans had a few obscure oracles afloat, and they had the Sibylline books under the state seal. These books, in fact, had been kept so long, that, like port wine superannuated, they had lost their flavor and body. [Footnote: *'Like port wine superannuated, the Sibylline books had lost their flavor and their body.'* —There is an allegoric description in verse, by Mr. Rogers, of an ice-house, in which winter is described as a captive, &c., which is memorable on this account, that a brother poet, on reading the passage, mistook it, (from not understanding the allegorical expressions,) either sincerely or maliciously, for a description of the house-dog. Now, this little anecdote seems to embody the poor Sibyl's history,—from a stern icy sovereign, with a petrific mace, she lapsed into an old toothless mastiff. She continued to snore in her ancient kennel for above a thousand years. The last person who attempted to stir her up with a long pole, and to extract from her paralytic dreaming some growls or snarls against Christianity, was Aurelian, in a moment of public panic. But the thing was past all tampering. The poor creature could neither be kicked nor coaxed into vitality.] On the other hand, look at France. Henry the historian, speaking of the fifteenth century, describes it as a national infirmity of the English to be prophecy-ridden. Perhaps there never was any foundation for this as an exclusive remark; but assuredly not in the next century. There had been with us British, from the twelfth century, Thomas of Ercildoune in the north, and many monkish local prophets for every part of the island; but latterly England had no terrific prophet, unless, indeed Nixon of the Vale Royal in Cheshire, who uttered his dark oracles sometimes with a merely Cestrian, sometimes with a national reference. Whereas in France, throughout the sixteenth century, every principal event was foretold successively, with an accuracy that still shocks and confounds us. Francis the First, who opens the century, (and by many is held to open the book of *modern history*, as distinguished from the middle or *feudal* history,) had the battle of Pavia foreshown to him, not by name, but in its results—by his own Spanish captivity—by the exchange for his own children upon a frontier river of Spain—finally, by his own disgraceful death, through an infamous disease conveyed to him under a deadly circuit of revenge. This king's son, Henry the Second, read some years *before* the event a description of that tournament, on the marriage of the Scottish Queen with his eldest son, Francis II., which proved fatal to himself, through the awkwardness of the Compte de Montgomery and his own obstinacy. After this, and we believe a little after the brief reign of Francis II., arose Nostradamus, the great prophet of the age. All the children of Henry II. and of Catharine de Medici, one after the other, died in circumstances of suffering and horror, and Nostradamus pursued the whole with ominous allusions. Charles IX., though the authorizer of the Bartholomew massacre, was the least guilty of his party, and the only one who manifested a dreadful remorse. Henry III., the last of the brothers, died, as the reader will remember, by assassination. And all these tragic successions of events are still to be read more or less dimly prefigured in verses of which we will not here discuss the dates. Suffice it, that many authentic historians attest the good faith of the prophets; and finally, with respect to the first of the Bourbon dynasty, Henry IV., who succeeded upon the assassination of his brother-in-law, we have the peremptory assurance of Sully and other Protestants, countersigned by writers both historical and controversial, that not only was he prepared, by many warnings, for his own tragical death—not only was the day, the hour prefixed—not only was an almanac sent to him, in which the bloody summer's day of 1610 was pointed out to his attention in bloody colors; but the mere record of the king's last afternoon shows beyond a doubt the extent and the punctual limitation of his anxieties. In fact, it is to this attitude of listening expectation in the king, and breathless waiting for the blow, that Schiller alludes in that fine speech of Wallenstein to his sister, where he notices the funeral knells that sounded continually in Henry's ears, and, above all, his prophetic instinct, that caught the sound from a far distance of his murderer's motions, and could distinguish, amidst all the tumult of a mighty capital, those stealthy steps

— —*'Which even then were seeking him*
Throughout the streets of Paris.'

We profess not to admire Henry the Fourth of France, whose secret character we shall, on some other occasion, attempt to expose. But his resignation to the appointments of Heaven, in dismissing his guards, as feeling that against a danger so domestic and so mysterious, all fleshly arms were vain, has always struck us as the most like magnanimity of anything in his very theatrical life.

Passing to our own country, and to the times immediately in succession, we fall upon some striking prophecies, not verbal but symbolic, if we turn from the broad highway of public histories, to the by-paths of private memories. Either Clarendon it is, in his Life (not his public history), or else Laud, who mentions an anecdote connected with the coronation of Charles I., (the son-in-law of the murdered Bourbon,) which threw a gloom upon the spirits of the royal friends, already saddened by the dreadful pestilence which inaugurated the reign of this ill-fated prince, levying a tribute of one life in sixteen from the population of the English metropolis. At the coronation of Charles, it was discovered that all London would not furnish the quantity of purple velvet required for the royal robes and the furniture of the throne. What was to be done? Decorum required that the furniture should be all *en suite*. Nearer than Genoa no considerable addition could be expected. That would impose a delay of 150 days. Upon mature consideration, and chiefly of the many private interests that would suffer amongst the multitudes whom such a solemnity had called up from the country, it was resolved to robe the King in *white* velvet. But this, as it afterwards occurred, was the color in which victims were arrayed. And thus, it was alleged, did the King's council establish an augury of evil. Three other ill omens, of some celebrity, occurred to Charles I., viz., on occasion of creating his son Charles a knight of the Bath, at Oxford some years after; and at the bar of that tribunal which sat in judgment upon him.

The reign of his second son, James II., the next reign that could be considered an unfortunate reign, was inaugurated by the same evil omens. The day selected for the coronation (in 1685) was a day memorable for England—it was St. George's day, the 23d of April, and entitled, even on a separate account, to be held a sacred day as the birthday of Shakspeare in 1564, and his deathday in 1616. The King saved a sum of sixty thousand pounds by cutting off the ordinary cavalcade from the Tower of London to Westminster. Even this was imprudent. It is well known that, amongst the lowest class of the English, there is an obstinate prejudice (though unsanctioned by law) with respect to the obligation imposed by the ceremony of coronation. So long as this ceremony is delayed, or mutilated, they fancy that their obedience is a matter of mere prudence, liable to be enforced by arms, but not consecrated either by law or by religion. The change made by James was, therefore, highly imprudent; shorn of its antique traditionary usages, the yoke of conscience was lightened at a moment when it required a double ratification. Neither was it called for on motives of economy, for James was unusually rich. This voluntary arrangement was, therefore, a bad beginning; but the accidental omens were worse. They are thus reported by Blennerhassett, (History of England to the end of George I., Vol. iv., p. 1760, printed at Newcastle-upon-Tyne: 1751.) 'The crown being too little for the King's head, was often in a tottering condition, and like to fall off.' Even this was observed attentively by spectators of the most opposite feelings. But there was another simultaneous omen, which affected the Protestant enthusiasts, and the superstitious, whether Catholic or Protestant, still more alarmingly. 'The same day the king's arms, pompously painted in the great altar window of a London church, suddenly fell down without apparent cause, and broke to pieces, whilst the rest of the window remained standing. Blennerhassett mutters the dark terrors which possessed himself and others.' 'These,' says he, 'were reckoned ill omens to the king.'

In France, as the dreadful criminality of the French sovereigns through the 17th century began to tell powerfully, and reproduce itself in the miseries and tumults of the French populace through the 18th century, it is interesting to note the omens which unfolded themselves at intervals. A volume might be written upon them. The French Bourbons renewed the picture of that fatal house which in Thebes offered to the Grecian observers the spectacle of dire auguries, emerging from darkness through three generations, à plusieurs reprises. Everybody knows the fatal pollution of the marriage pomps on the reception of Marie Antoinette in Paris; the numbers who perished are still spoken of obscurely as to the amount, and with shuddering awe for the unparalleled horrors standing in the background of the fatal reign—horrors

'That hush'd in grim repose, await their evening prey.'

But in the life of Goethe is mentioned a still more portentous (though more shadowy) omen in the pictorial decorations of the arras which adorned the pavilion on the French frontier; the first objects which met the Austrian Archduchess on being hailed as Dauphiness, was a succession of the most tragic groups from the most awful section of the Grecian theatre. The next alliance of the same kind between the same great empires, in the persons of Napoleon and the Archduchess Marie Louisa, was overshadowed by the same unhappy omens, and, as we all remember, with the same unhappy results, within a brief period of five years.

Or, if we should resort to the fixed and monumental rather than to these auguries of great nations—such, for instance, as were embodied in those Palladia, or protesting talismans, which capital cities, whether Pagan or Christian, glorified through a period of twenty-five hundred years, we shall find a long succession of these enchanted pledges, from the earliest precedent of Troy (whose palladium was undoubtedly a talisman) down to that equally memorable, and bearing the same name, at Western Rome.

We may pass, by a vast transition of two and a half millennia, to that great talisman of Constantinople, the triple serpent, (having perhaps an original reference to the Mosaic serpent of the wilderness, which healed the infected by the simple act of looking upon it, as the symbol of the Redeemer, held aloft upon the Cross for the deliverance from moral contagion.) This great consecrated talisman, venerated equally by Christian, by Pagan, and by Mahometan, was struck on the head by Mahomet the Second, on that same day, May 29th of 1453, in which he mastered by storm this glorious city, the bulwark of eastern Christendom, and the immediate rival of his own European throne at Adrianople. But mark the superfetation of omens—omen supervening upon omen, augury engrafted upon augury. The hour was a sad one for Christianity; just 720 years before the western horn of Islam had been rebutted in France by the Germans, chiefly under Charles Martel. But now it seemed as though another horn, even more vigorous, was preparing to assault Christendom and its hopes from the eastern quarter. At this epoch, in the very hour of triumph, when the last of the Cæsars had glorified his station, and sealed his testimony by martyrdom, the fanatical Sultan, riding to his stirrups in blood, and wielding that iron mace which had been his sole weapon, as well as cognizance, through the battle, advanced to the column, round which the triple serpent roared spirally upwards. He smote the brazen talisman; he shattered one head; he left it mutilated as the record of his great revolution; but crush it, destroy it, he did not—as a symbol prefiguring the fortunes of Mahometanism, his people noticed, that in the critical hour of fate, which stamped the Sultan's acts with efficacy through ages, he had been prompted by his secret genius only to 'scotch the snake,' not to crush it. Afterwards the fatal hour was gone by; and this imperfect augury has since concurred traditionally with the Mahometan prophecies about the Adrianople gate of Constantinople, to depress the ultimate hopes of Islam in the midst of all its insolence. The very haughtiest of the Mussulmans believe that the gate is already in existence, through which the red Giaours (the *Russi*) shall pass to the conquest of Stamboul; and that everywhere, in Europe at least, the hat of Frangistan is destined to surmount the turban—the crescent must go down before the cross.

COLERIDGE AND OPIUM-EATING

What is the deadest of things earthly? It is, says the world, ever forward and rash—'a door-nail!' But the world is wrong. There is a thing deader than a door-nail, viz., Gillman's Coleridge, Vol. I. Dead, more dead, most dead, is Gillman's Coleridge, Vol. I.; and this upon more arguments than one. The book has clearly not completed its elementary act of respiration; the *systole* of Vol. I. is absolutely useless and lost without the *diastole* of that Vol. II., which is never to exist. That is one argument, and perhaps this second argument is stronger. Gillman's Coleridge, Vol. I., deals rashly, unjustly, and almost maliciously, with some of our own particular friends; and yet, until late in this summer, *Anno Domini* 1844, we—that is, neither ourselves nor our friends—ever heard of its existence. Now a sloth, even without the benefit of Mr. Waterton's evidence to his character, will travel faster than that. But malice, which travels fastest of all things, must be dead and cold at starting, when it can thus have lingered in the rear for six years; and therefore, though the world was so far right, that people *do* say, 'Dead as a door-nail,' yet, henceforward, the weakest of these people will see the propriety of saying—'Dead as Gillman's Coleridge.'

The reader of experience, on sliding over the surface of this opening paragraph, begins to think there's mischief singing in the upper air. 'No, reader, not at all. We never were cooler in our days. And this we protest, that, were it not for the excellence of the subject, *Coleridge and Opium-Eating*, Mr. Gillman would have been dismissed by us unnoticed. Indeed, we not only forgive Mr. Gillman, but we have a kindness for him; and on this account, that he was good, he was generous, he was most forbearing, through twenty years, to poor Coleridge, when thrown upon his hospitality. An excellent thing *that*, Mr. Gillman, till, noticing the theme suggested by this unhappy Vol. I., we are forced at times to notice its author, Nor is this to be regretted. We remember a line of Horace never yet properly translated, viz:—

'Nec scutica dignum horribili sectere flagello.'

The true translation of which, as we assure the unlearned reader, is—'Nor must you pursue with the horrid knout of Christopher that man who merits only a switching.' Very true. We protest against all attempts to invoke the exterminating knout; for *that* sends a man to the hospital for two months; but you see that the same judicious poet, who dissuades an appeal to the knout, indirectly recommends the switch, which, indeed, is rather pleasant than otherwise, amiably playful in some of its little caprices, and in its worst, suggesting only a pennyworth of diachylon.

We begin by professing, with hearty sincerity, our fervent admiration of the extraordinary man who furnishes the theme for Mr. Gillman's *coup-d'essai* in biography. He was, in a literary sense, our brother—for he also was amongst the contributors to *Blackwood*—and will, we presume, take his station in that Blackwood gallery of portraits, which, in a century hence, will possess more interest for intellectual Europe than any merely martial series of portraits, or any gallery of statesmen assembled in congress, except as regards one or two leaders; for defunct major-generals, and secondary diplomatists, when their date is past, awake no more emotion than last year's advertisements, or obsolete directories; whereas those who, in a stormy age, have swept the harps of passion, of genial wit, or of the wrestling and gladiatorial reason, become more interesting to men when they can no longer be seen as bodily agents, than even in the middle chorus of that intellectual music over which, living, they presided.

Of this great camp Coleridge was a leader, and fought amongst the *primipili*; yet, comparatively, he is still unknown. Heavy, indeed, are the arrears still due to philosophic curiosity on the real merits, and on the separate merits, of Samuel Taylor Coleridge. Coleridge as a poet—Coleridge as a philosopher! How extensive are those questions, if those were all! and upon neither question have we yet any investigation—such as, by compass of views, by research, or even by earnestness of sympathy with the subject, can, or ought to satisfy, a philosophic demand. Blind is that man who can persuade himself that the interest in Coleridge, taken as a total object, is becoming an obsolete interest. We are of opinion that even Milton, now viewed from a distance of two centuries, is still inadequately judged or appreciated in his character of poet, of patriot and partisan, or, finally, in his character of accomplished scholar. But, if so, how much less can it be pretended that satisfaction has been rendered to the claims of Coleridge? for, upon Milton, libraries have been written. There has been time for the malice of men, for the jealousy of men, for the enthusiasm, the scepticism, the adoring admiration of men, to expand themselves! There has been room for a Bentley, for an Addison, for a Johnson, for a wicked Lauder, for an avenging Douglas, for an idolizing Chateaubriand; and yet, after all, little enough has been done towards any comprehensive estimate of the mighty being concerned. Piles of materials have been gathered to the ground; but, for the monument which should have risen from these materials, neither the first stone has been laid, nor has a qualified architect yet presented his credentials. On the other hand, upon Coleridge little, comparatively, has yet been written, whilst the separate characters on which the judgment is awaited, are more by one than those which Milton sustained. Coleridge, also, is a poet; Coleridge, also, was mixed up with the fervent politics of his age— an age how memorably reflecting the revolutionary agitations of Milton's age. Coleridge, also, was an extensive and brilliant scholar. Whatever might be the separate proportions of the two men in each particular department of the three here noticed, think as the reader will upon that point, sure we are that either subject is ample enough to make a strain upon the amplest faculties. How alarming, therefore, for any *honest* critic, who should undertake this later subject of Coleridge, to recollect that, after pursuing him through a zodiac of splendors corresponding to those of Milton in kind, however different in degree—after weighing him as a poet, as a philosophic politician, as a scholar, he will have to wheel after him into another orbit, into the unfathomable *nimbus* of transcendental metaphysics. Weigh him the critic must in the golden balance of philosophy the most abstruse—a balance which even itself requires weighing previously, or he will have done nothing that can be received for an estimate of the composite Coleridge. This astonishing man, be it again remembered, besides being an exquisite poet, a profound political speculator, a philosophic student of literature through all its chambers and recesses, was also a circumnavigator on the most pathless waters of scholasticism and metaphysics. He had sounded, without guiding charts, the secret deeps of Proclus and Plotinus; he had laid down buoys on the twilight, or moonlight, ocean of Jacob Boehmen; [Footnote: 'JACOB BOEHMEN.' We ourselves had the honor of presenting to Mr. Coleridge, Law's English version of Jacob—a set of huge quartos. Some months afterwards we saw this work lying open, and one volume at least overflowing, in parts, with the commentaries and the *corollaries* of Coleridge. Whither has this work, and so many others swathed about with Coleridge's MS. notes, vanished from the world?] he had cruised over the broad Atlantic of Kant and Schelling, of Fichte and Oken. Where is the man who shall be equal to these things? We at least make no such adventurous effort; or, if ever we should presume to do so, not at present. Here we design only to make a coasting voyage of survey round the headlands and most conspicuous seamarks of our subject, as they are brought forward by Mr. Gillman, or collaterally suggested by our own reflections; and especially we wish to say a word or two on Coleridge as an opium-eater.

Naturally the first point to which we direct our attention, is the history and personal relations of Coleridge. Living with Mr. Gillman for nineteen years as a domesticated friend, Coleridge ought to have been known intimately. And it is reasonable to expect, from so much intercourse, some additions to our slender knowledge of Coleridge's adventures, (if we may use so coarse a word,) and of the secret springs at work in those early struggles of Coleridge at Cambridge, London, Bristol, which have been rudely told to the world, and repeatedly told, as showy romances, but never rationally explained.

The anecdotes, however, which Mr. Gillman has added to the personal history of Coleridge, are as little advantageous to the effect of his own book as they are to the interest of the memorable character which he seeks to illustrate. Always they are told without grace, and generally are suspicious in their details. Mr. Gillman we believe to be too upright a man for countenancing any untruth. He has been deceived. For example, will any man believe this? A certain 'excellent equestrian' falling in with Coleridge on horseback, thus accosted him—'Pray, Sir, did you meet a tailor along the road?' 'A tailor!' answered Coleridge; 'I did meet a person answering such a description, who told me he had dropped his goose; that if I rode a little further I should find it; and I guess he must have meant you.' In Joe Miller this story would read, perhaps, sufferably. Joe has a privilege; and we do not look too narrowly into the mouth of a Joe-Millerism. But Mr. Gillman, writing the life of a philosopher, and no jest-book, is under a different law of decorum. That retort, however, which silences the jester, it may seem, must be a good one. And we are desired to believe that, in this case, the baffled assailant rode off in a spirit of benign candor, saying aloud to himself, like the excellent philosopher that he evidently was, 'Caught a Tartar!'

But another story of a sporting baronet, who was besides a Member of Parliament, is much worse, and altogether degrading to Coleridge. This gentleman, by way of showing off before a party of ladies, is represented as insulting Coleridge by putting questions to him on the qualities of his horse, so as to draw the animal's miserable defects into public notice, and then closing his display by demanding what he would take for the horse 'including the rider.' The supposed reply of Coleridge might seem good to those who understand nothing of true dignity; for, as an *impromptu*, it was smart and even caustic. The baronet, it seems, was reputed to have been bought by the minister; and the reader will at once divine that the retort took advantage of that current belief, so as to throw back the sarcasm, by proclaiming that neither horse nor rider had a price placarded in the market at which any man could become their purchaser. But this was not the temper in which Coleridge either did reply, or could have replied. Coleridge showed, in the *spirit* of his manner, a profound sensibility to the nature of a gentleman; and he felt too justly what it became a self-respecting person to say, ever to have aped the sort of flashy fencing which might seem fine to a theatrical blood.

Another story is self-refuted: 'A hired partisan' had come to one of Coleridge's political lectures with the express purpose of bringing the lecturer into trouble; and most preposterously he laid himself open to his own snare by refusing to pay for admission. Spies must be poor artists who proceed thus. Upon which Coleridge remarked—'That, before the gentleman kicked up a dust, surely he would down with the dust.' So far the story will not do. But what follows is possible enough. The *same* 'hired' gentleman, by way of giving unity to the tale, is described as having hissed. Upon this a cry arose of 'Turn him out!' But Coleridge interfered to protect him; he insisted on the man's right to hiss if he thought fit; it was legal to hiss; it was natural to hiss; 'for what is to be expected, gentlemen, when the cool waters of reason come in contact with red-hot aristocracy, but a hiss?' *Euge!*

Amongst all the anecdotes, however of this splendid man, often trivial, often incoherent, often unauthenticated, there is one which strikes us as both true and interesting; and we are grateful to Mr. Gillman for preserving it. We find it introduced, and partially authenticated, by the following sentence from Coleridge himself:—'From eight to fourteen I was a playless day-dreamer, a *helluo librorum*; my appetite for which was indulged by a singular incident. A stranger, who was struck by my conversation, made me free of a circulating library in King's Street, Cheapside.' The more circumstantial explanation of Mr. Gillman is this: 'The incident indeed was singular. Going down the Strand, in one of his day-dreams, fancying himself swimming across the Hellespont, thrusting his hands before him as in the act of swimming, his hand came in contact with a gentleman's pocket. The gentleman seized his hand, turning round, and looking at him with some anger—"What! so young, and yet so wicked?" at the same time accused him of an attempt to pick his pocket. The frightened boy sobbed out his denial of the intention, and explained to him how he thought himself Leander swimming across the Hellespont. The gentleman was so struck and delighted with the novelty of the thing, and with the simplicity and intelligence of the boy, that he subscribed, as before stated, to the library; in consequence of which Coleridge was further enabled to indulge his love of reading.'

We fear that this slovenly narrative is the very perfection of bad story-telling. But the story itself is striking, and, by the very oddness of the incidents, not likely to have been invented. The effect, from the position of the two parties—on the one side, a simple child from Devonshire, dreaming in the Strand that he was swimming over from Sestos to Abydos, and, on the other, the experienced man, dreaming only of this world, its knaves and its thieves, but still kind and generous—is beautiful and picturesque. *Oh! si sic omnia!*

But the most interesting to us of the *personalities* connected with Coleridge are his feuds and his personal dislikes. Incomprehensible to us is the war of extermination which Coleridge made upon the political economists. Did Sir James Steuart, in speaking of vine-dressers, (not *as* vine-dressers, but generally as cultivators,) tell his readers, that, if such a man simply replaced his own consumption, having no surplus whatever or increment for the public capital, he could not be considered a useful citizen? Not the beast in the Revelation is held up by Coleridge as more hateful to the spirit of truth than the Jacobite baronet. And yet we know of an author—viz., one S. T. Coleridge—who repeated that same doctrine without finding any evil in it. Look at the first part of the *Wallenstein*, where Count Isolani having said, 'Pooh! we are *all* his subjects,' *i. e.*, soldiers, (though unproductive laborers,) not less than productive peasants, the emperor's envoy replies—'Yet with a difference, general;' and the difference implies Sir James's scale, his vine-dresser being the equatorial case between the two extremes of the envoy. Malthus again, in his population-book, contends for a mathematic difference between animal and vegetable life, in respect to the law of increase, as though the first increased by geometrical ratios, the last by arithmetical! No proposition more worthy of laughter; since both, when permitted to expand, increase by geometrical ratios, and the latter by much higher ratios. Whereas, Malthus persuaded himself of his crotchet simply by refusing the requisite condition in the vegetable case, and granting it in the other. If you take a few grains of wheat, and are required to plant all successive generations of their produce in the same flower-pot for ever, of course you neutralize its expansion by your own act of arbitrary limitation. [Footnote: Malthus would have rejoined by saying—that the flowerpot limitation was the actual limitation of nature in our present circumstances. In America it is otherwise, he would say, but England is the very flowerpot you suppose; she is a flowerpot which cannot be multiplied, and cannot even be enlarged. Very well, so be it (which we say in order to waive irrelevant disputes). But then the true inference will be—not that vegetable increase proceeds under a different law from that which governs animal increase, but that, through an accident of position, the experiment cannot be tried in England. Surely the levers of Archimedes, with submission to Sir Edward B. Lytton, were not the less levers because he wanted the *locum standi*. It is proper, by the way, that we should inform the reader of this generation where to look for Coleridge's skirmishings with Malthus. They are to be found chiefly in the late Mr. William Hazlitt's work on that subject: a work which Coleridge so far claimed as to assert that it had been substantially made up from his own conversation.] But so you would do, if you tried the case of *animal* increase by still exterminating all but one replacing couple of parents. This is not to try, but merely a pretence of trying, one order of powers against another. That was folly. But Coleridge combated this idea in a manner so obscure, that nobody understood it. And leaving these speculative conundrums, in coming to the great practical interests afloat in the Poor Laws, Coleridge did so little real work, that he left, as a *res integra*, to Dr. Alison, the capital argument that legal and *adequate* provision for the poor, whether impotent poor or poor accidentally out of work, does not extend pauperism—no, but is the one great resource for putting it down. Dr. Alison's overwhelming and *experimental* manifestations of that truth have prostrated Malthus and his generation for ever. This comes of not attending to the Latin maxim—'*Hoc* age'—mind the object before you. Dr. Alison, a wise man, '*hoc* egit:' Coleridge '*aliud* egit.' And we see the result. In a case which suited him, by interesting his peculiar feeling, Coleridge could command

'*Attention full ten times as much as there needs.*'

But search documents, value evidence, or thresh out bushels of statistical tables, Coleridge could not, any more than he could ride with Elliot's dragoons.

Another instance of Coleridge's inaptitude for such studies as political economy is found in his fancy, by no means 'rich and rare,' but meagre and trite, that taxes can never injure public prosperity by mere excess of quantity; if they injure, we are to conclude that it must be by their quality and mode of operation, or by their false appropriation, (as, for instance, if they are sent out of the country and spent abroad.) Because, says Coleridge, if the taxes are exhaled from the country as vapors, back they come in drenching showers. Twenty pounds ascend in a Scotch mist to the Chancellor of the Exchequer from Leeds; but does it evaporate? Not at all: By return of post down comes an order for twenty pounds' worth of Leeds cloth, on account of Government, seeing that the poor men of the — —th regiment want new gaiters. True; but of this return twenty pounds, not more than four will be profit, *i.e.*, surplus accruing to the public capital; whereas, of the original twenty pounds, every shilling was surplus. The same unsound fancy has been many times brought forward; often in England, often in France. But it is curious, that its first appearance upon any stage was precisely two centuries ago, when as yet political economy slept with the pre-Adamites, viz., in the Long Parliament. In a quarto volume of the debates during 1644-45, printed as an independent work, will be found the same identical doctrine, supported very sonorously by the same little love of an illustration from the see-saw of mist and rain.

Political economy was not Coleridge's forte. In politics he was happier. In mere personal politics, he (like every man when reviewed from a station distant by forty years) will often appear to have erred; nay, he will be detected and nailed in error. But this is the necessity of us all. Keen are the refutations of time. And absolute results to posterity are the fatal touchstone of opinions in the past. It is undeniable, besides, that Coleridge had strong personal antipathies, for instance, to Messrs. Pitt and Dundas. Yet *why*, we never could understand. We once heard him tell a story upon Windermere, to the late Mr. Curwen, then M. P. for Workington, which was meant, apparently, to account for this feeling. The story amounted to this; that, when a freshman at Cambridge, Mr. Pitt had wantonly amused himself at a dinner party in Trinity, in smashing with filberts (discharged in showers like grape-shot) a most costly dessert set of cut glass, from which Samuel Taylor Coleridge argued a principle of destructiveness in his *cerebellum*. Now, if this dessert set belonged to some poor suffering Trinitarian, and not to himself, we are of opinion that he was faulty, and ought, upon his own great subsequent maxim, to have been coerced into 'indemnity for the past, and security for the future.' But, besides that this glassy *mythus* belongs to an æra fifteen years earlier than Coleridge's so as to justify a shadow of scepticism, we really cannot find, in such an *escapade* under the boiling blood of youth, any sufficient justification of that withering malignity towards the name of Pitt, which runs through Coleridge's famous *Fire, Famine, and Slaughter*. As this little viperous *jeu-d'esprit* (published anonymously) subsequently became the subject of a celebrated after-dinner discussion in London, at which Coleridge (*comme de raison*) was the chief speaker, the reader of this generation may wish to know the question at issue; and in order to judge of *that*, he must know the outline of this devil's squib. The writer brings upon the scene three pleasant young ladies, viz., Miss Fire, Miss Famine, and Miss Slaughter. 'What are you up to? What's the row?'—we may suppose to be the introductory question of the poet. And the answer of the ladies makes us aware that they are fresh from larking in Ireland, and in France. A glorious spree they had; lots of fun; and laughter *a discretion*. At all times *gratus puellæ risus ab angulo*; so that we listen to their little gossip with interest. They had been setting men, it seems, by the ears; and the drollest little atrocities they do certainly report. Not but we have seen better in the Nenagh paper, so far as Ireland is concerned. But the pet little joke was in La Vendee. Miss Famine, who is the girl for our money, raises the question—whether any of them can tell the name of the leader and prompter to these high jinks of hell—if so, let her whisper it.

> 'Whisper it, sister, so and so,
> In a dark hint—distinct and low.'

Upon which the playful Miss Slaughter replies:—

'Letters four do form his name.
He came by stealth and unlock'd my den;
And I have drunk the blood since then
Of thrice three hundred thousand men.'

Good: but the sting of the hornet lies in the conclusion. If this quadriliteral man had done so much for *them*, (though really, we think, 6s. 8d. might have settled his claim,) what, says Fire, setting her arms a-kimbo, would they do for *him*? Slaughter replies, rather crustily, that, as far as a good kicking would go—or (says Famine) a little matter of tearing to pieces by the mob— they would be glad to take tickets at his benefit. 'How, you bitches!' says Fire, 'is that all?

'I alone am faithful; I
Cling to him everlastingly.'

The sentiment is diabolical. And the question argued at the London dinner-table was—Could the writer have been other than a devil? The dinner was at the late excellent Mr. Sotheby's, known advantageously in those days as the translator of Wieland's *Oberon*. Several of the great guns amongst the literary body were present; in particular, Sir Walter Scott; and he, we believe, with his usual good-nature, took the apologetic side of the dispute. In fact, he was in the secret. Nobody else, barring the author, knew at first whose good name was at stake. The scene must have been high. The company kicked about the poor diabolic writer's head as if it had been a tennis-ball. Coleridge, the yet unknown criminal, absolutely perspired and fumed in pleading for the defendant; the company demurred; the orator grew urgent; wits began to *smoke* the case, as active verbs; the advocate to *smoke*, as a neuter verb; the 'fun grew fast and furious;' until at length *delinquent arose*, burning tears in his eyes, and confessed to an audience, (now bursting with stifled laughter, but whom he supposed to be bursting with fiery indignation,) 'Lo! I am he that wrote it.'

For our own parts, we side with Coleridge. Malice is not always of the heart. There is a malice of the understanding and the fancy. Neither do we think the worse of a man for having invented the most horrible and old-woman-troubling curse that demons ever listened to. We are too apt to swear horribly ourselves; and often have we frightened the cat, to say nothing of the kettle, by our shocking [far too shocking!] oaths.

There were other celebrated men whom Coleridge detested, or seemed to detest—Paley, Sir Sidney Smith, Lord Hutchinson, (the last Lord Donoughmore,) and Cuvier. To Paley it might seem as if his antipathy had been purely philosophic; but we believe that partly it was personal; and it tallies with this belief, that, in his earliest political tracts, Coleridge charged the archdeacon repeatedly with his own joke, as if it had been a serious saying, viz.—'That he could not afford to keep a conscience;' such luxuries, like a carriage, for instance, being obviously beyond the finances of poor men.

With respect to the philosophic question between the parties, as to the grounds of moral election, we hope it is no treason to suggest that both were perhaps in error. Against Paley, it occurs at once that he himself would not have made consequences the *practical* test in valuing the morality of an act, since these can very seldom be traced at all up to the final stages, and in the earliest stages are exceedingly different under different circumstances; so that the same act, tried by its consequences, would bear a fluctuating appreciation. This could not have been Paley's *revised* meaning. Consequently, had he been pressed by opposition, it would have come out, that by *test* he meant only *speculative* test: a very harmless doctrine certainly, but useless and impertinent to any purpose of his system. The reader may catch our meaning in the following illustration. It is a matter of general belief, that happiness, upon the whole, follows in a higher degree from constant integrity, than from the closest attention to self-interest. Now happiness is one of those consequences which Paley meant by final or remotest. But we could never use this idea as an exponent of integrity, or interchangeable criterion, because happiness cannot be ascertained or appreciated except upon long tracts of time, whereas the particular act of integrity depends continually upon the election of the moment. No man, therefore, could venture to lay down as a rule, Do what makes you happy; use this as your test of actions, satisfied that in that case always you will do the thing which is right. For he cannot discern independently what *will* make him happy; and he must decide on the spot. The use of the *nexus* between morality and happiness must therefore be inverted; it is not practical or prospective, but simply retrospective; and in that form it says no more than the good old rules hallowed in every cottage. But this furnishes no practical guide for moral election which a man had not, before he ever thought of this *nexus*. In the sense in which it is true, we need not go to the professor's chair for this maxim; in the sense in which it would serve Paley, it is absolutely false.

On the other hand, as against Coleridge, it is certain that many acts could be mentioned which are judged to be good or bad only because their consequences are known to be so, whilst the great catholic acts of life are entirely (and, if we may so phrase it, haughtily) independent of consequences. For instance, fidelity to a trust is a law of immutable morality subject to no casuistry whatever. You have been left executor to a friend — you are to pay over his last legacy to X, though a dissolute scoundrel; and you are to give no shilling of it to the poor brother of X, though a good man, and a wise man, struggling with adversity. You are absolutely excluded from all contemplation of results. It was your deceased friend's right to make the will; it is yours simply to see it executed. Now, in opposition to this primary class of actions stands another, such as the habit of intoxication, which are known to be wrong only by observing the consequences. If drunkenness did not terminate, after some years, in producing bodily weakness, irritability in the temper, and so forth, it would *not* be a vicious act. And accordingly, if a transcendent motive should arise in favor of drunkenness, as that it would enable you to face a degree of cold, or contagion, else menacing to life, a duty would arise, *pro hac vice*, of getting drunk. We had an amiable friend who suffered under the infirmity of cowardice; an awful coward he was when sober; but, when very drunk, he had courage enough for the Seven Champions of Christendom, Therefore, in an emergency, where he knew himself suddenly loaded with the responsibility of defending a family, we approved highly of his getting drunk. But to violate a trust could never become right under any change of circumstances. Coleridge, however, altogether overlooked this distinction: which, on the other hand, stirring in Paley's mind, but never brought out to distinct consciousness, nor ever investigated, nor limited, has undermined his system. Perhaps it is not very important how a man *theorizes* upon morality; happily for us all, God has left no man in such questions practically to the guidance of his understanding; but still, considering that academic bodies *are* partly instituted for the support of speculative truth as well as truth practical, we must think it a blot upon the splendor of Oxford and Cambridge that both of them, in a Christian land, make Paley the foundation of their ethics; the alternative being Aristotle. And, in our mind, though far inferior as a moralist to the Stoics, Aristotle is often less of a pagan than Paley.

Coleridge's dislike to Sir Sidney Smith and the Egyptian Lord Hutchinson fell under the category of Martial's case.

'Non amo te, Sabidi, nec possum dicere quare,
Hoc solum novi—non amo te, Sabidi.'

Against Lord Hutchinson, we never heard him plead anything of moment, except that he was finically Frenchified in his diction; of which he gave this instance—that having occasion to notice a brick wall, (which was literally *that*, not more and not less,) when reconnoitring the French defences, he called it a *revêtement*. And we ourselves remember his using the French word *gloriole* rather ostentatiously; that is, when no particular emphasis attached to the case. But every man has his foibles; and few, perhaps, are less conspicuously annoying than this of Lord Hutchinson's. Sir Sidney's crimes were less distinctly revealed to our mind. As to

Cuvier, Coleridge's hatred of *him* was more to our taste; for (though quite unreasonable, we fear) it took the shape of patriotism. He insisted on it, that our British John Hunter was the genuine article, and that Cuvier was a humbug. Now, speaking privately to the public, we cannot go quite so far as *that*. But, when publicly we address that most respectable character, *en grand costume*, we always mean to back Coleridge. For we are a horrible John Bull ourselves. As Joseph Hume observes, it makes no difference to us— right or wrong, black or white—when our countrymen are concerned. And John Hunter, notwithstanding he had a bee in his bonnet, [Footnote: *Vide*, in particular, for the most exquisite specimen of pigheadedness that the world can furnish, his perverse evidence on the once famous case at the Warwick assizes, of Captain Donelan for poisoning his brother-in-law, Sir Theodosius Boughton.] was really a great man; though it will not follow that Cuvier must, therefore, have been a little one. We do not pretend to be acquainted with the tenth part of Cuvier's performances; but we suspect that Coleridge's range in that respect was not much greater than our own.

Other cases of monomaniac antipathy we might revive from our recollections of Coleridge, had we a sufficient motive. But in compensation, and by way of redressing the balance, he had many strange likings—equally monomaniac—and, unaccountably, he chose to exhibit his whimsical partialities by dressing up, as it were, in his own clothes, such a set of scarecrows as eye has not beheld. Heavens! what an ark of unclean beasts would have been Coleridge's private *menagerie* of departed philosophers, could they all have been trotted out in succession! But did the reader feel them to be the awful bores which, in fact, they were? No; because Coleridge had blown upon these withered anatomies, through the blowpipe of his own creative genius, a stream of gas that swelled the tissue of their antediluvian wrinkles, forced color upon their cheeks, and splendor upon their sodden eyes. Such a process of ventriloquism never *has* existed. He spoke by their organs. They were the tubes; and he forced through their wooden machinery his own Beethoven harmonies.

First came Dr. Andrew Bell. We knew him. Was he dull? Is a wooden spoon dull? Fishy were his eyes; torpedinous was his manner; and his main idea, out of two which he really had, related to the moon—from which you infer, perhaps, that he was lunatic. By no means. It was no craze, under the influence of the moon, which possessed him; it was an idea of mere hostility to the moon. The Madras people, like many others, had an idea that she influenced the weather. Subsequently the Herschels, senior and junior, systematized this idea; and then the wrath of Andrew, previously in a crescent state, actually dilated to a plenilunar orb. The Westmoreland people (for at the lakes it was we knew him) expounded his condition to us by saying that he was 'maffled;' which word means 'perplexed in the extreme.' His wrath did not pass into lunacy; it produced simple distraction; an uneasy fumbling with the idea; like that of an old superannuated dog who longs to worry, but cannot for want of teeth. In this condition you will judge that he was rather tedious. And in this condition Coleridge took him up. Andrew's other idea, because he *had* two, related to education. Perhaps six-sevenths of that also came from Madras. No matter, Coleridge took *that* up; Southey also; but Southey with his usual temperate fervor. Coleridge, on the other hand, found celestial marvels both in the scheme and in the man. Then commenced the apotheosis of Andrew Bell: and because it happened that his opponent, Lancaster, between ourselves, really *had* stolen his ideas from Bell, what between the sad wickedness of Lancaster and the celestial transfiguration of Bell, gradually Coleridge heated himself to such an extent, that people, when referring to that subject, asked each other, 'Have you heard Coleridge lecture on *Bel and the Dragon*?'

The next man glorified by Coleridge was John Woolman, the Quaker. Him, though we once possessed his works, it cannot be truly affirmed that we ever read. Try to read John, we often did; but read John we did not. This, however, you say, might be our fault, and not John's. Very likely. And we have a notion that now, with our wiser thoughts, we *should* read John, if he were here on this table. It is certain that he was a good man, and one of the earliest in America, if not in Christendom, who lifted up his hand to protest against the slave-trade. But still, we suspect, that had John been all that Coleridge represented, he would not have repelled us from reading his travels in the fearful way that he did. But, again, we beg pardon, and entreat the earth of Virginia to lie light upon the remains of John Woolman; for he was an Israelite, indeed, in whom there was no guile.

The third person raised to divine honors by Coleridge was Bowyer, the master of Christ's Hospital, London—a man whose name rises into the nostrils of all who knew him with the gracious odor of a tallow-chandler's melting-house upon melting day, and whose memory is embalmed in the hearty detestation of all his pupils. Coleridge describes this man as a profound critic. Our idea of him is different. We are of opinion that Bowyer was the greatest villain of the eighteenth century. We may be wrong; but we cannot be *far* wrong. Talk of knouting indeed! which we did at the beginning of this paper in the mere playfulness of our hearts—and which the great master of the knout, Christopher, who visited men's trespasses like the Eumenides, never resorted to but in love for some great idea which had been outraged; why, this man knouted his way through life, from bloody youth up to truculent old age. Grim idol! whose altars reeked with children's blood, and whose dreadful eyes never smiled except as the stern goddess of the Thugs smiles, when the sound of human lamentations inhabits her ears. So much had the monster fed upon this great idea of 'flogging,' and transmuted it into the very nutriment of his heart, that he seems to have conceived the gigantic project of flogging all mankind; nay worse, for Mr. Gillman, on Coleridge's authority, tells us the following anecdote:—'"*Sirrah, I'll flog you*," were words so familiar to him, that on one occasion some *female* friend of one of the boys,' (who had come on an errand of intercession,) 'still lingering at the door, after having been abruptly told to go, Bowyer exclaimed—"Bring that woman here, and I'll flog her."'

To this horrid incarnation of whips and scourges, Coleridge, in his *Biographia Literaria*, ascribes ideas upon criticism and taste, which every man will recognise as the intense peculiarities of Coleridge. Could these notions really have belonged to Bowyer, then how do we know but he wrote *The Ancient Mariner*? Yet, on consideration, no. For even Coleridge admitted that, spite of his fine theorizing upon composition, Mr. Bowyer did not prosper in the practice. Of which he gave us this illustration; and as it is supposed to be the only specimen of the Bowyeriana which now survives in this sublunary world, we are glad to extend its glory. It is the most curious example extant of the melodious in sound:—

"'Twas thou that smooth'd'st the rough-rugg'd bed of pain.'

'Smooth'd'st!' Would the teeth of a crocodile not splinter under that word? It seems to us as if Mr. Bowyer's verses ought to be boiled before they can be read. And when he says, 'Twas thou, what is the wretch talking to? Can he be apostrophizing the knout? We very much fear it. If so, then, you see (reader!) that, even when incapacitated by illness from operating, he still adores the image of his holy scourge, and invokes it as alone able to smooth 'his rough-rugg'd bed.' Oh, thou infernal Bowyer! upon whom even Trollope (*History of Christ's Hospital*) charges 'a discipline *tinctured* with more than due severity;'—can there be any partners found for thee in a quadrille, except Draco, the bloody lawgiver, Bishop Bonner, and Mrs. Brownrigg?

The next pet was Sir Alexander Ball. Concerning Bowyer, Coleridge did not talk much, but chiefly wrote; concerning Bell, he did not write much, but chiefly talked. Concerning Ball, however, he both wrote and talked. It was in vain to muse upon any plan for having Ball blackballed, or for rebelling against Bell. Think of a man, who had fallen into one pit called Bell; secondly, falling into another pit called Ball. This was too much. We were obliged to quote poetry against them:—

'Letters four do form his name;
He came by stealth and unlock'd my den;
And the nightmare I have felt since then

Of thrice three hundred thousand men.'

Not that we insinuate any disrespect to Sir Alexander Ball. He was about the foremost, we believe, in all good qualities, amongst Nelson's admirable captains at the Nile. He commanded a seventy-four most effectually in that battle; he governed Malta as well as Sancho governed Barataria; and he was a true practical philosopher—as, indeed, was Sancho. But still, by all that we could ever learn, Sir Alexander had no taste for the abstract upon any subject; and would have read, as mere delirious wanderings, those philosophic opinions which Coleridge fastened like wings upon his respectable, but astounded, shoulders.

We really beg pardon for having laughed a little at these crazes of Coleridge. But laugh we did, of mere necessity, in those days, at Bell and Ball, whenever we did not groan. And, as the same precise alternative offered itself now, viz., that, in recalling the case, we must reverberate either the groaning or the laughter, we presumed the reader would vote for the last. Coleridge, we are well convinced, owed all these wandering and exaggerated estimates of men—these diseased impulses, that, like the *mirage*, showed lakes and fountains where in reality there were only arid deserts, to the derangements worked by opium. But now, for the sake of change, let us pass to another topic. Suppose we say a word or two on Coleridge's accomplishments as a scholar. We are not going to enter on so large a field as that of his scholarship in connection with his philosophic labors, scholarship in the result; not this, but scholarship in the means and machinery, range of *verbal* scholarship, is what we propose for a moment's review.

For instance, what sort of a German scholar was Coleridge? We dare say that, because in his version of the *Wallenstein* there are some inaccuracies, those who may have noticed them will hold him cheap in this particular pretension. But, to a certain degree, they will be wrong. Coleridge was not *very* accurate in anything but in the use of logic. All his philological attainments were imperfect. He did not talk German; or so obscurely—and, if he attempted to speak fast, so erroneously—that in his second sentence, when conversing with a German lady of rank, he contrived to assure her that in his humble opinion she was a — —. Hard it is to fill up the hiatus decorously; but, in fact, the word very coarsely expressed that she was no better than she should be. Which reminds us of a parallel misadventure to a German, whose colloquial English had been equally neglected. Having obtained an interview with an English lady, he opened his business (whatever it might be) thus—'High-born madam, since your husband have kicked de bucket'——'Sir!' interrupted the lady, astonished and displeased. 'Oh, pardon!—nine, ten thousand pardon! Now, I make new beginning—

quite oder beginning. Madam, since your husband have cut his stick'——It may be supposed that this did not mend matters; and, reading that in the lady's countenance, the German drew out an octavo dictionary, and said, perspiring with shame at having a second time missed fire,—'Madam, since your husband have gone to kingdom come'——This he said beseechingly; but the lady was past propitiation by this time, and rapidly moved towards the door. Things had now reached a crisis; and, if something were not done quickly, the game was up. Now, therefore, taking a last hurried look at his dictionary, the German flew after the lady, crying out in a voice of despair— 'Madam, since your husband, your most respected husband, have hopped de twig'——This was his sheet-anchor; and, as this also *came home,* of course the poor man was totally wrecked. It turned out that the dictionary he had used (Arnold's, we think,)—a work of a hundred years back, and, from mere ignorance, giving slang translations from Tom Brown, L'Estrange, and other jocular writers—had put down the verb *sterben (to die)* with the following worshipful series of equivalents—1. To kick the bucket; 2. To cut one's stick; 3. To go to kingdom come; 4. To hop the twig.

But, though Coleridge did not pretend to any fluent command of conversational German, he read it with great ease. His knowledge of German literature was, indeed, too much limited by his rare opportunities for commanding anything like a well-mounted library. And particularly it surprised us that Coleridge knew little or nothing of John Paul (Richter). But his acquaintance with the German philosophic masters was extensive. And his valuation of many individual German words or phrases was delicate and sometimes profound.

As a Grecian, Coleridge must be estimated with a reference to the state and standard of Greek literature at that time and in this country. Porson had not yet raised our ideal. The earliest laurels of Coleridge were gathered, however, in that field. Yet no man will, at this day, pretend that the Greek of his prize ode is sufferable. Neither did Coleridge ever become an accurate Grecian in later times, when better models of scholarship, and better aids to scholarship, had begun to multiply. But still we must assert this point of superiority for Coleridge, that, whilst he never was what may be called a well-mounted scholar in any department of verbal scholarship, he yet displayed sometimes a brilliancy of conjectural sagacity, and a felicity of philosophic investigation, even in this path, such as better scholars do not often attain, and of a kind which cannot be learned from books. But, as respects his accuracy, again we must recall to the reader the state of Greek literature in England during Coleridge's youth; and, in all equity, as a means of placing Coleridge in the balances, specifically we must recall the state of Greek metrical composition at that period.

To measure the condition of Greek literature even in Cambridge, about the initial period of Coleridge, we need only look back to the several translations of Gray's *Elegy* by three (if not four) of the reverend gentlemen at that time attached to Eton College. Mathias, no very great scholar himself in this particular field, made himself merry, in his *Pursuits of Literature*, with these Eton translations. In that he was right. But he was *not* right in praising a contemporary translation by Cook, who (we believe) was the immediate predecessor of Porson in the Greek chair. As a specimen of this translation, [Footnote: It was printed at the end of Aristotle's *Poetics*, which Dr. Cook edited.] we cite one stanza; and we cannot be supposed to select unfairly, because it is the stanza which Mathias praises in extravagant terms. "Here," says he, "Gray, Cook, and Nature, do seem to contend for the mastery." The English quatrain must be familiar to every body:—

> *"The boast of heraldry, the pomp of pow'r,*
> *And all that beauty, all that wealth e'er gave,*
> *Await alike the inevitable hour:*
> *The paths of glory lead but to the grave."*

And the following, we believe, though quoting from a thirty-three years' recollection of it, is the exact Greek version of Cook:—

> *'A charis eugenon, charis a basilaeidos achas*
> *Lora tuchaes chryseaes, Aphroditaes kala ta dora,*
> *Paith ama tauta tethiake, kai eiden morsimon amar*
> *Proon kle olole, kai ocheto xunon es Adaen.'*

Now really these verses, by force of a little mosaic tesselation from genuine Greek sources, pass fluently over the tongue; but can they be considered other than a *cento*? Swarms of English schoolboys, at this day, would not feel very proud to adopt them. In fact, we remember (at a period say twelve years later than this) some iambic verses, which were really composed by a boy, viz., a son of Dr. Prettyman, (afterwards Tomline,) Bishop of Winchester, and, in earlier times, private tutor to Mr. Pitt; they were published by Middleton, first Bishop of Calcutta, in the preface to his work on the Greek article; and for racy idiomatic Greek, self-originated, and not a mere mocking-bird's iteration of alien notes, are so much superior to all the attempts of these sexagenarian doctors, as distinctly to mark the growth of a new era and a new generation in this difficult accomplishment, within the first decennium of this century. It is singular that only one blemish is suggested by any of the contemporary critics in Dr. Cook's verses, viz., in the word *xunon*, for which this critic proposes to substitute *ooinon*, to prevent, as he observes, the last syllable of *ocheto* from being lengthened by the *x*. Such considerations as these are necessary to the *trutinæ castigatio,* before we can value Coleridge's place on the scale of his own day; which day, *quoad hoc*, be it remembered, was 1790.

As to French, Coleridge read it with too little freedom to find pleasure in French literature. Accordingly, we never recollect his referring for any purpose, either of argument or illustration, to a French classic. Latin, from his regular scholastic training, naturally he read with a scholar's fluency; and indeed, he read constantly in authors, such as Petrarch, Erasmus, Calvin, &c., whom he could not then have found in translations. But Coleridge had not cultivated an acquaintance with the delicacies of classic Latinity. And it is remarkable that Wordsworth, educated most negligently at Hawkshead school, subsequently by reading the lyric poetry of Horace, simply for his own delight as a student of composition, made himself a master of Latinity in its most difficult form; whilst Coleridge, trained regularly in a great Southern school, never carried his Latin to any classical polish.

There is another accomplishment of Coleridge's, less broadly open to the judgment of this generation, and not at all of the next—viz., his splendid art of conversation, on which it will be interesting to say a word. Ten years ago, when the music of this rare performance had not yet ceased to vibrate in men's ears, what a sensation was gathering amongst the educated classes on this particular subject! What a tumult of anxiety prevailed to 'hear Mr. Coleridge'—or even to talk with a man who *had* heard him! Had he lived till this day, not Paganini would have been so much sought after. That sensation is now decaying; because a new generation has emerged during the ten years since his death. But many still remain whose sympathy (whether of curiosity in those who did *not* know him, or of admiration in those who *did*) still reflects as in a mirror the great stir upon this subject which then was moving in the world. To these, if they should inquire for the great distinguishing principle of Coleridge's conversation, we might say that it was the power of vast combination 'in linked sweetness long drawn out.' He gathered into focal concentration the largest body of objects, *apparently* disconnected, that any man ever yet, by any magic, could assemble, or, *having* assembled, could manage. His great fault was, that, by not opening sufficient spaces for reply or suggestion, or collateral notice, he not only narrowed his own field, but he grievously injured the final impression. For when men's minds are purely passive, when they are not allowed to re-act, then it is that they collapse most, and that their sense of what is said must ever be feeblest. Doubtless there must have been great conversational masters elsewhere, and at many periods; but in this lay Coleridge's characteristic advantage, that he was a great natural power, and also a great artist. He was a power in the art, and he carried a new art into the power.

But now, finally—having left ourselves little room for more—one or two words on Coleridge as an opium-eater.

We have not often read a sentence falling from a wise man with astonishment so profound, as that particular one in a letter of Coleridge's to Mr. Gillman, which speaks of the effort to wean one's-self from opium as a trivial task. There are, we believe, several such passages. But we refer to that one in particular which assumes that a single 'week' will suffice for the whole process of so mighty a revolution. Is indeed leviathan *so* tamed? In that case the quarantine of the opium-eater might be finished within Coleridge's time, and with Coleridge's romantic ease. But mark the contradictions of this extraordinary man. Not long ago we were domesticated with a venerable rustic, strong-headed, but incurably obstinate in his prejudices, who treated the whole body of medical men as ignorant pretenders, knowing absolutely nothing of the system which they professed to superintend. This, you will remark, is no very singular case. No; nor, as we believe, is the antagonist case of ascribing to such men magical powers. Nor, what is worse still, the co-existence of both cases in the same mind, as in fact happened here. For this same obstinate friend of ours, who treated all medical pretensions as the mere jest of the universe, every 'third day was exacting from his own medical attendants some exquisite *tour-de-force*, as that they should know or should do something, which, if they *had* known or done, all men would have suspected them reasonably of magic. He rated the whole medical body as infants; and yet what he exacted from them every third day as a matter of course, virtually presumed them to be the only giants within the whole range of science. Parallel and equal is the contradiction of Coleridge. He speaks of opium excess, his own excess, we mean—the excess of twenty-five years—as a thing to be laid aside easily and for ever within seven days; and yet, on the other hand, he describes it pathetically, sometimes with a frantic pathos, as the scourge, the curse, the one almighty blight which had desolated his life.

This shocking contradiction we need not press. All readers will see *that*. But some will ask—Was Mr. Coleridge right in either view? Being so atrociously wrong in the first notion, (viz., that the opium of twenty-five years was a thing easily to be forsworn,) where a child could know that he was wrong, was he even altogether right, secondly, in believing that his own life, root and branch, had been withered by opium? For it will not follow, because, with a relation to happiness and tranquillity, a man may have found opium his curse, that therefore, as a creature of energies and great purposes, he must have been the wreck which he seems to suppose. Opium gives and takes away. It defeats the *steady* habit of exertion, but it creates spasms of irregular exertion; it ruins the natural power of life, but it develops preternatural paroxysms of intermitting power. Let us ask of any man who holds that not Coleridge himself but the world, as interested in Coleridge's usefulness, has suffered by his addiction to opium; whether he is aware of the way in which opium affected Coleridge; and secondly, whether he is aware of the actual contributions to literature—how large they were—which Coleridge made *in spite* of opium. All who were intimate with Coleridge must remember the fits of genial animation which were created continually in his manner and in his buoyancy of thought by a recent or by an *extra* dose of the omnipotent drug. A lady, who knew nothing experimentally of opium, once told us, that she 'could tell when Mr. Coleridge had taken too much opium by his shining countenance.' She was right; we know that mark of opium excesses well, and the cause of it; or at least we believe the cause to lie in the quickening of the insensible perspiration which accumulates and glistens on the face. Be that as it may, a criterion it was that could not deceive us as to the condition of Coleridge. And uniformly in that condition he made his most effective intellectual displays. It is true that he might not be happy under this fiery animation, and we fully believe that he was not. Nobody is happy under laudanum except for a very short term of years. But in what way did that operate upon his exertions as a writer? We are of opinion that it killed Coleridge as a poet. 'The harp of Quantock' was silenced for ever by the torment of opium. But proportionably it roused and stung by misery his metaphysical instincts into more spasmodic life. Poetry can flourish only in the atmosphere of happiness. But subtle and perplexed investigations of difficult problems are amongst the commonest resources for beguiling the sense of misery. And for this we have the direct authority of Coleridge himself speculating on his own case. In the beautiful though unequal ode entitled *Dejection*, stanza six, occurs the following passage:

> 'For not to think of what I needs must feel,
> But to be still and patient all I can;
> And haply by abstruse research to steal
> From my own nature all the natural man—
> This was my sole resource, my only plan;
> Till that, which suits a part, infects the whole,
> And now is almost grown the habit of my soul.'

Considering the exquisite quality of some poems which Coleridge has composed, nobody can grieve (or *has* grieved) more than ourselves, at seeing so beautiful a fountain choked up with weeds. But had Coleridge been a happier man, it is our fixed belief that we should have had far less of his philosophy, and perhaps, but not certainly, might have had more of his general literature. In the estimate of the public, doubtless, *that* will seem a bad exchange. Every man to his taste. Meantime, what we wish to show is, that the loss was not absolute, but merely relative.

It is urged, however, that, even on his philosophic speculations, opium operated unfavorably in one respect, by often causing him to leave them unfinished. This is true. Whenever Coleridge (being highly charged, or saturated, with opium) had written with distempered vigor upon any question, there occurred soon after a recoil of intense disgust, not from his own paper only, but even from the subject. All opium-eaters are tainted with the infirmity of leaving works unfinished, and suffering reactions of disgust. But Coleridge taxed himself with that infirmity in verse before he could at all have commenced opium-eating. Besides, it is too much assumed by Coleridge and by his biographer, that to leave off opium was of course to regain juvenile health. But all opium-eaters make the mistake of supposing every pain or irritation which they suffer to be the product of opium. Whereas a wise man will say, suppose you *do* leave off opium, that will not deliver you from the load of years (say sixty-three) which you carry on your back. Charles Lamb, another man of true genius, and another head belonging to the Blackwood Gallery, made that mistake in his *Confessions of a Drunkard*. 'I looked back,' says he, 'to the time when always, on waking in the morning, I had a song rising to my lips.' At present, it seems, being a drunkard, he has no such song. Ay, dear Lamb, but note this, that the drunkard was fifty-six years old, the songster was twenty-three. Take twenty-three from fifty-six, and we have some reason to believe that thirty-three will remain; which period of thirty-three years is a pretty good reason for not singing in the morning, even if brandy has been out of the question.

It is singular, as respects Coleridge, that Mr. Gillman never says one word upon the event of the great Highgate experiment for leaving off laudanum, though Coleridge came to Mr. Gillman's for no other purpose; and in a week, this vast creation of new earth, sea, and all that in them is, was to have been accomplished. We *rayther* think, as Bayley junior observes, that the explosion must have hung fire. But *that* is a trifle. We have another pleasing hypothesis on the subject. Mr. Wordsworth, in his exquisite lines written on a fly-leaf of his own *Castle of Indolence*, having described Coleridge as 'a noticeable man with large grey eyes,' goes on to say, 'He' (viz., Coleridge) 'did that other man entice' to view his imagery. Now we are sadly afraid that 'the noticeable man with large grey eyes' did entice 'that other man,' viz., Gillman, to commence opium-eating. This is droll; and it makes us laugh horribly. Gillman should have reformed *him*; and lo! *he* corrupts Gillman. S. T. Coleridge visited Highgate by way of being converted from the heresy of opium; and the issue is—that, in two months' time, various grave men, amongst whom our friend Gillman marches first in great pomp, are found to have faces shining and glorious as that of AEsculapius; a fact of which we have already explained the secret meaning. And scandal says (but then what will not scandal say?) that a hogshead of opium goes up daily through Highgate tunnel. Surely one corroboration of our hypothesis may be found in the fact, that Vol. I. of Gillman's Coleridge is for ever to stand unpropped by Vol. II. For we have already observed, that opium-eaters, though good fellows upon the whole, never finish anything.

What then? A man has a right never to finish anything. Certainly he has; and by Magna Charta. But he has no right, by Magna Charta or by Parva Charta, to slander decent men, like ourselves and our friend the author of the *Opium Confessions*. Here it is that our complaint arises against Mr. Gillman. If he has taken to opium-eating, can we help *that*? If *his* face shines, must our faces be blackened? He has very improperly published some intemperate passages from Coleridge's letters, which ought to have been considered confidential, unless Coleridge had left them for publication, charging upon the author of the *Opium Confessions* a reckless disregard of the temptations which, in that work, he was scattering abroad amongst men. Now this author is connected with ourselves, and we cannot neglect his defence, unless in the case that he undertakes it himself.

We complain, also, that Coleridge raises (and is backed by Mr. Gillman in raising) a distinction perfectly perplexing to us, between himself and the author of the *Opium Confessions* upon the question—Why they severally began the practice of opium-eating? In himself, it seems, this motive was to relieve pain, whereas the Confessor was surreptitiously seeking for pleasure. Ay, indeed—where did he learn *that*? We have no copy of the *Confessions* here, so we cannot quote chapter and verse; but we distinctly remember, that toothache is recorded in that book as the particular occasion which first introduced the author to the knowledge of opium. Whether afterwards, having been thus initiated by the demon of pain, the opium confessor did not apply powers thus discovered to purposes of mere pleasure, is a question for himself; and the same question applies with the same cogency to Coleridge. Coleridge began in rheumatic pains. What then? This is no proof that he did not end in voluptuousness. For our parts, we are slow to believe that ever any man did, or could, learn the somewhat awful truth, that in a certain ruby-colored elixir, there lurked a divine power to chase away the genius of ennui, without subsequently abusing this power. To taste but once from the tree of knowledge, is fatal to the subsequent power of abstinence. True it is, that generations have used laudanum as an anodyne, (for instance, hospital patients,) who have not afterwards courted its powers as a voluptuous stimulant; but that, be sure, has arisen from no abstinence in *them*. There are, in fact, two classes of temperaments as to this terrific drug—those which are, and those which are not, preconformed to its power; those which genially expand to its temptations, and those which frostily exclude them. Not in the energies of the will, but in the qualities of the nervous organization, lies the dread arbitration of—Fall or stand: doomed thou art to yield; or, strengthened constitutionally, to resist. Most of those who have but a low sense of the spells lying couchant in opium, have practically none at all. For the initial fascination is for *them* effectually defeated by the sickness which nature has associated with the first stages of opium-eating. But to that other class, whose nervous sensibilities vibrate to their profoundest depths under the first touch of the angelic poison, even as a lover's ear thrills on hearing unexpectedly the voice of her whom he loves, opium is the Amreeta cup of beatitude. You know the *Paradise Lost*? and you remember, from the eleventh book, in its earlier part, that laudanum already existed in Eden—nay, that it was used medicinally by an archangel; for, after Michael had 'purged with euphrasy and rue' the eyes of Adam, lest he should be unequal to the mere *sight* of the great visions about to unfold their draperies before him, next he fortifies his fleshly spirits against the *affliction* of these visions, of which visions the first was death. And how?

'He from the well of life three drops instill'd.'

What was their operation?

'So deep the power of these ingredients pierced,
Even to the inmost seat of mental sight,
That Adam, now enforced to close his eyes,
Sank down, and all his spirits became entranced.
But him the gentle angel by the hand
Soon raised' — —

The second of these lines it is which betrays the presence of laudanum. It is in the faculty of mental vision, it is in the increased power of dealing with the shadowy and the dark, that the characteristic virtue of opium lies. Now, in the original higher sensibility is found some palliation for the *practice* of opium-eating; in the greater temptation is a greater excuse. And in this faculty of self-revelation is found some palliation for *reporting* the case to the world, which both Coleridge and his biographer have overlooked.

TEMPERANCE MOVEMENT

The most remarkable instance of a combined movement in society, which history, perhaps, will be summoned to notice, is that which, in our own days, has applied itself to the abatement of intemperance. Naturally, or by any *direct* process, the machinery set in motion would seem irrelevant to the object: if one hundred men unite to elevate the standard of temperance, they can do this with effect only by improvements in their own separate cases: each individual, for such an effort of self-conquest, can draw upon no resources but his own. One member in a combination of one hundred, when running a race, can hope for no cooperation from his ninety-nine associates. And yet, by a secondary action, such combinations are found eminently successful. Having obtained from every confederate a pledge, in some shape or other, that he will give them his support, thenceforwards they bring the passions of shame and self-esteem to bear upon each member's personal perseverance. Not only they keep alive and continually refresh in his thoughts the general purpose, which else might fade; but they also point the action of public contempt and of self-contempt at any defaulter much more potently, and with more acknowledged right to do so, when they use this influence under a license, volunteered, and signed, and sealed, by the man's own hand. They first conciliate his countenance through his intellectual perceptions of what is right; and next they sustain it through his conscience, (the strongest of his internal forces,) and even through the weakest of his human sensibilities. That revolution, therefore, which no combination of men can further by abating the original impulse of temptations, they often accomplish happily by maturing the secondary energies of resistance.

Already in their earliest stage, these temperance movements had obtained, both at home and abroad, a *national* range of grandeur. More than ten years ago, when M. de Tocqueville was resident in the United States, the principal American society counted two hundred and seventy thousand members: and in one single state (Pennsylvania) the annual diminution in the use of spirits had very soon reached half a million of gallons. Now a machinery must be so far good which accomplishes its end: the means are meritorious for so much as they effect. Even to strengthen a feeble resolution by the aid of other infirmities, such as shame or the very servility and cowardice of deference to public opinion, becomes prudent and laudable in the service of so great a cause. Nay, sometimes to make public profession of self-distrust by assuming the coercion of public pledges, may become an expression of frank courage, or even of noble principle, not fearing the shame of confession when it can aid the powers of victorious resistance. Yet still, so far as it is possible, every man sighs for a still higher victory over himself: a victory not tainted by bribes, and won from no impulses but those inspired by his own higher nature, and his own mysterious force of will; powers that in no man were fully developed.

This being so, it is well that from time to time every man should throw out any hints that have occurred to his experience,—suggesting such as may be new, renewing such as may be old, towards the encouragement or the information of persons engaged in so great a struggle. My own experience had never travelled in that course which could much instruct me in the miseries from wine, or in the resources for struggling with it. I had repeatedly been obliged indeed to lay it aside altogether; but in this I never found room for more than seven or ten days' struggle: excesses I had never practised in the use of wine; simply the habit of using it, and the collateral habits formed by excessive use of opium, had produced any difficulty at all in resigning it even on an hour's notice. From opium I derive my right of offering hints at all upon the subjects of abstinence in other forms. But the modes of suffering from the evil, and the separate modes of suffering from the effort of self-conquest, together with errors of judgment incident to such states of transitional torment, are all nearly allied, practically analogous as regards the remedies, even if characteristically distinguished to the inner consciousness. I make no scruple, therefore, of speaking as from a station of high experience and of most watchful attention, which never remitted even under sufferings that were at times absolutely frantic.

I. The first hint is one that has been often offered; viz., the diminution of the particular liquor used, by the introduction into each glass of some inert substance, ascertained in bulk, and equally increasing in amount from day to day. But this plan has often been intercepted by an accident: shot, or sometimes bullets, were the substances nearest at hand; an objection arose from too scrupulous a caution of chemistry as to the action upon lead of the vinous acid. Yet all objection of this kind might be removed at once, by using beads in a case where small decrements were wanted, and marbles, if it were thought advisable to use larger. Once for all, however, in cases deeply rooted, no advances ought ever to be made but by small stages: for the effect, which is insensible at first, by the tenth, twelfth, or fifteenth day, generally accumulates unendurably under any bolder deductions. I must not stop to illustrate this point; but certain it is, that by an error of this nature at the outset, most natural to human impatience under exquisite suffering, too generally the trial is abruptly brought to an end through the crisis of a passionate relapse.

II. Another object, and one to which the gladiator matched in single duel with intemperance, must direct a religious vigilance, is the *digestibility* of his food: it must be digestible not only by its original qualities, but also by its culinary preparation. In this last point we are all of us Manichæans: all of us yield a cordial assent to that Manichæan proverb, which refers the meats and the cooks of this world to two opposite fountains of light and of darkness. Oromasdes it is, or the good principle, that sends the food; Ahrimanes, or the evil principle, that everywhere sends the cooks. Man has been repeatedly described or even defined, as by differential privilege of his nature, 'A cooking animal.' Brutes, it is said, have faces,—man only has a countenance; brutes are as well able to eat as man,—man only is able to cook what he eats. Such are the romances of self-flattery. I, on the contrary, maintain, that six thousand years have not availed, in this point, to raise our race generally to the level of ingenious savages. The natives of the Society and the Friendly Isles, or of New Zealand, and other favored spots, had, and still have, an *art* of cookery, though very limited in its range: the French [Footnote: But judge not, reader, of French skill by the attempts of fourth-rate artists; and understand me to speak with respect of this skill, not as it is the tool of luxury, but as it is the handmaid of health.] have an art, and more extensive; but we English are about upon a level (as regards this science) with the ape, to whom an instinct whispers that chestnuts may be roasted; or with the aboriginal Chinese of Charles Lamb's story, to whom the experience of many centuries had revealed thus much, viz., that a dish very much beyond the raw flesh of their ancestors, might be had by burning down the family mansion, and thus roasting the pig-stye. Rudest of barbarous devices is English cookery, and not much in advance of this primitive Chinese step; a fact which it would not be worth while to lament, were it not for the sake of the poor trembling deserter from the banners of intoxication, who is thus, and by no other cause, so often thrown back beneath the yoke which he had abjured. Past counting are the victims of alcohol, that, having by vast efforts emancipated themselves for a season, are violently forced into relapsing by the nervous irritations of demoniac cookery. Unhappily for *them*, the horrors of indigestion are relieved for the moment, however ultimately strengthened, by strong liquors; the relief is immediate, and cannot fail to be perceived; but the aggravation, being removed to a distance, is not always referred to its proper cause. This is the capital rock and stumbling-block in the path of him who is hurrying back to the camps of temperance; and many a reader is likely to misapprehend the case through the habit he has acquired of supposing indigestion to lurk chiefly amongst *luxurious* dishes. But, on the contrary, it is amongst the plainest, simplest, and commonest dishes that such misery lurks, in England. Let us glance at three articles of diet, beyond all comparison of most ordinary occurrence, viz., potatoes, bread, and butcher's meat. The art of preparing potatoes for *human* use is utterly unknown, except in certain provinces of our empire, and amongst certain sections of the laboring class. In our great cities,—London, Edinburgh, &c.—the sort of things which you see offered at table under the name and reputation of potatoes, are such that, if you could suppose the company to be composed of Centaurs and Lapithæ, or any other quarrelsome people, it would become necessary for the police to interfere. The potato of cities is a very dangerous missile; and, if thrown with an accurate aim by an angry hand, will fracture any known skull. In volume and consistency, it is very like a paving-stone; only that, I should say, the paving-stone had the advantage in point of tenderness. And upon this horrid basis, which youthful ostriches would repent of swallowing, the trembling, palpitating invalid, fresh from the scourging of alcohol, is requested to build the superstructure of his dinner. The proverb says, that three flittings are as bad as a fire; and on that model I conceive that three potatoes, as they are found at many British dinner-tables, would be equal, in principle of ruin, to two glasses of vitriol. The same savage ignorance appears, and only not so often, in the bread of this island. Myriads of families eat it in that early stage of sponge which bread assumes during the process of baking; but less than sixty hours will not fit this dangerous article of human diet to be eaten. And those who are acquainted with the works of Parmentier, or other learned investigators of bread and of the baker's art, must be aware that this quality of sponginess (though quite equal to the ruin of the digestive organs) is but one in a legion of vices to which the article is liable. A German of much research wrote a book on the conceivable faults in a pair of shoes, which he found to be about six hundred and sixty-six, many of them, as he observed, requiring a very delicate process of study to find out; whereas the possible faults in bread, which are not less in number, require no study at all for the defection; they publish themselves through all varieties of misery. But the perfection of barbarism, as regards our island cookery, is reserved for animal food; and the two poles of Oromasdes and Ahrimanes are nowhere so conspicuously exhibited. Our insular sheep, for instance, are so far superior to any which the continent produces, that the present Prussian minister at our court is in the habit of questioning a man's right to talk of mutton as anything beyond a great idea, unless he can prove a residence in Great Britain. One sole case he cites of a dinner on the Elbe, when a particular leg of mutton really struck him as rivalling any which he had known in England. The mystery seemed inexplicable; but, upon inquiry, it turned out to be an importation from Leith. Yet this incomparable article, to produce which the skill of the feeder must co-operate with the peculiar bounty of nature, calls forth the most dangerous refinements of barbarism in its cookery. A Frenchman requires, as the primary qualification of flesh meat, that it should be tender. We English universally, but especially the Scots, treat that quality with indifference, or with bare toleration. What we require is, that it should be fresh, that is, recently killed, (in which state it cannot be digestible except by a crocodile;) and we present it at table in a transition state of leather, demanding the teeth of a tiger to rend it in pieces, and the stomach of a tiger to digest it.

With these habits amongst our countrymen, exemplified daily in the articles of widest use, it is evident that the sufferer from intemperance has a harder quarantine, in this island, to support during the effort of restoration, than he could have anywhere else in Christendom. In Persia, and, perhaps, there only on this terraqueous planet, matters might be even worse: for, whilst we English neglect the machinery of digestion, as a matter entitled to little consideration, the people of Teheran seem unaware that there *is* any such machinery. So, at least, one might presume, from cases on record, and especially from the reckless folly, under severe illness, from indigestion, of the three Persian princes, who visited this country, as stated by their official *mehmander*, Mr. Fraser. With us, the excess of ignorance, upon this subject, betrays itself oftenest in that vain-glorious answer made by the people, who at any time are admonished of the sufferings which they are preparing for themselves by these outrages upon the most delicate of human organs. They, for *their* parts, 'know not if they *have* a stomach; they know not what it is that dyspepsy means;' forgetting that, in thus vaunting their *strength* of stomach, they are, at the same time, proclaiming its coarseness; and showing themselves unaware that precisely those, whom such coarseness of organization reprieves from immediate and seasonable reaction of suffering, are the favorite subjects of that heavier reaction which takes the shape of *delirium tremens*, of palsy, and of lunacy. It is but a fanciful advantage which *they* enjoy, for whom the immediate impunity avails only to hide the final horrors which are gathering upon them from the gloomy rear. Better, by far, that more of immediate discomfort had guaranteed to them less of reversionary anguish. It may be safely asserted, that few, indeed, are the suicides amongst us to which the miseries of indigestion have not been a large concurring cause; and even where nothing so dreadful as *that* occurs, always these miseries are the chief hinderance of the self-reforming drunkard, and the commonest cause of his relapse. It is certain, also, that misanthropic gloom and bad temper besiege that class, by preference, to whom peculiar coarseness or obtuse sensibility of organization has denied the salutary warnings and early prelibations of punishment which, happily for most men, besiege the more direct and obvious frailties of the digestive apparatus.

The whole process and elaborate machinery of digestion are felt to be mean and humiliating when viewed in relation to our mere animal economy. But they rise into dignity, and assert their own supreme importance, when they arc studied from another station, viz., in relation to the intellect and temper; no man dares, *then*, to despise them: it is then seen that these functions of the human system form the essential basis upon which the strength and health of our higher nature repose; and that upon these functions, chiefly, the general happiness of life is dependent. All the rules of prudence, or gifts of experience that life can accumulate, will never do as much for human comfort and welfare as would be done by a stricter attention, and a wiser science, directed to the digestive system; in this attention lies the key to any perfect restoration for the victim of intemperance: and, considering the peculiar hostility to the digestive health which exists in the dietetic habits of our own country, it may be feared that nowhere upon earth has the reclaimed martyr to intemperance so difficult a combat to sustain; nowhere, therefore, is it so important to direct the attention upon an *artificial* culture of those resources which naturally, and by the established habits of the land, are surest to be neglected. The sheet anchor for the storm-beaten sufferer, who is laboring to recover a haven of rest from the agonies of intemperance, and who has had the fortitude to abjure the poison which ruined, but which also, for brief intervals, offered him his only consolation, lies, beyond all doubt, in a most anxious regard to everything connected with this supreme function of our animal economy. And, as few men that are not regularly trained to medical studies can have the complex knowledge requisite for such a duty, some printed guide should be sought of a regular professional order. Twenty years ago, Dr. Wilson Philip published a valuable book of this class, which united a wide range of practical directions as to the choice of diet, and as to the qualities and tendencies of all esculent articles likely to be found at British tables, with some ingenious speculations upon the still mysterious theory of digestion. These were derived from experiments made upon rabbits, and had originally been communicated by him to the Royal Society of London, who judged them worthy of publication in their Transactions. I notice them chiefly for the sake of remarking, that the rationale of digestion, as here suggested, explains the reason of a fact, which merely *as* a fact, had not been known until modern times, viz., the injuriousness to enfeebled stomachs of all fluid. Fifty years ago—and still lingering inveterately amongst nurses, and other ignorant persons— there prevailed a notion that 'slops' must be the proper resource of the valetudinarian; and the same erroneous notion appears in the common expression of ignorant wonder at the sort of breakfasts usual amongst women of rank in the times of Queen Elizabeth. 'What robust stomachs they must have had, to support such solid meals!' As to the question of fact, whether the stomachs were more or less robust in those days than at the present, there is no need to offer an opinion. But the question of principle concerned in scientific dietetics points in the very opposite direction. By how much the organs of digestion are feebler, by so much is it the more indispensable that solid food and animal food should be adopted. A robust stomach may be equal to the trying task of supporting a fluid, such as tea for breakfast; but for a feeble stomach, and still more for a stomach *enfeebled* by bad habits, broiled beef, or something equally solid and animal, but not too much subjected to the action of fire, is the only tolerable diet. This, indeed, is the one capital rule for a sufferer from habitual intoxication, who must inevitably labor under an impaired digestion; that as little as possible he should use of any liquid diet, and as little as possible of vegetable diet. Beef, and a little bread, (at the least sixty hours old,) compose the privileged bill of fare for his breakfast. But precisely it is, by the way, in relation to this earliest meal, that human folly has in one or two instances shown itself most ruinously inventive. The less variety there is at that meal, the more is the danger from any single luxury; and there is one, known by the name of 'muffins,' which has repeatedly manifested itself to be a plain and direct bounty upon suicide. Darwin, in his 'Zoonomia,' reports a case where an officer, holding the rank of lieutenant-colonel, could not tolerate a breakfast in which this odious article was wanting; but, as a savage retribution invariably supervened within an hour or two upon this act of insane sensuality, he came to a resolution that life was intolerable *with* muffins, but still more intolerable *without* muffins. He would stand the nuisance no longer; but yet, being a just man, he would give nature one final chance of reforming her dyspeptic atrocities. Muffins, therefore, being laid at one angle of the breakfast-table, and loaded pistols at another, with rigid equity the Colonel awaited the result. This was naturally pretty much as usual: and then, the poor man, incapable of retreating from his word of honor, committed suicide,—having previously left a line for posterity to the effect (though I forget the expression), 'That a muffinless world was no world for him: better no life at all than a life dismantled of muffins.'—Dr. Darwin was a showy philosopher, and fond of producing effect, so that some allowance must be made in construing the affair. Strictly speaking, it is probable that not the especial want of muffins, but the general torment of indigestion, was the curse from which the unhappy sufferer sought relief by suicide. And the Colonel was not the first by many a million, that has fled from the very same form of wretchedness, or from its effects upon the genial spirits, to the same gloomy refuge. It should never be forgotten that, although some other more overt vexation is generally assigned as the proximate cause of suicide, and often may be so as regards the immediate occasion, too generally this vexation borrowed its whole power to annoy, from the habitual atmosphere of irritation in which the system had been kept by indigestion. So that indirectly, and virtually, perhaps, all suicides may be traced to mismanaged digestion. Meantime, in alluding at all to so dreadful a subject as suicide, I do so only by way of giving deeper effect to the opinion expressed above, upon the chief cause of relapse into habits of intemperance amongst those who have once accomplished their deliverance. Errors of digestion, either from impaired powers, or from powers not so much enfeebled as deranged, is the one immeasurable source both of disease and of secret wretchedness to the human race. Life is laid waste by the eternal fretting of the vital forces, emanating from this one cause. And it may well be conceived, that if cases so endless, even of suicide, in every generation, are virtually traceable to this main root, much more must it be able to shake and undermine the yet palpitating frame of the poor fugitive from intemperance; since indigestion in every mode and variety of its changes irresistibly upholds the temptation to that form of excitement which, though one foremost cause of indigestion, is yet unhappily its sole immediate palliation.

III. Next, after the most vigorous attention, and a scientific attention to the digestive system, in power of operation, stands *exercise*. Here, however, most people have their own separate habits, with respect to the time of exercise, the duration, and the particular mode, on which a stranger cannot venture to intrude with his advice. Some will not endure the steady patience required for walking exercise; many benefit most by riding on horseback; and in days when roads were more rugged, and the springs of carriages less improved, I have known people who found most advantage in the vibrations communicated to the frame by a heavy rumbling carriage. For myself, under the ravages of opium, I have found walking the most beneficial exercise; besides that, it requires no previous notice or preparation of any kind; and this is a capital advantage in a state of drooping energies, or of impatient and unresting agitation. I may mention, as possibly an accident of my individual temperament, but possibly, also, no accident at all, that the relief obtained by walking was always most sensibly brought home to my consciousness, when some part of it (at least a mile and a half) has been performed before breakfast. In this there soon ceased to be any difficulty; for, whilst under the full oppression of opium, it was impossible for me to rise at any hour that could, by the most indulgent courtesy, be described as within the pale of morning, no sooner had there been established any considerable relief from this oppression, than the tendency was in the opposite direction; the difficulty became continually greater of sleeping even to a reasonable hour. Having once accomplished the feat of walking at nine A. M., I backed, in a space of seven or eight months, to eight o'clock, to seven, to six, five, four, three; until at this point a metaphysical fear fell upon me that I was actually backing into 'yesterday,' and should soon have no sleep at all. Below three, however, I did not descend; and, for a couple of years, three and a half hours' sleep was all that I could obtain in the twenty-four hours. From this no particular suffering arose, except the nervous impatience of lying in bed for one moment after awaking. Consequently, the habit of walking before breakfast became at length troublesome no longer as a most odious duty, but, on the contrary, as a temptation that could hardly be resisted on the wettest mornings. As to the quantity of the exercise, I found that six miles a day formed the *minimum* which would support permanently a particular standard of animal spirits, evidenced to myself by certain apparent symptoms. I averaged about nine and a half miles a day; but ascended on particular days to fifteen or sixteen, and more rarely to twenty-three or twenty-four; a quantity which did not produce fatigue, on the contrary it spread a sense of improvement through almost the whole week that followed; but usually, in the night immediately succeeding to such an exertion, I lost much of my sleep; a privation that, under the circumstances explained, deterred me from trying the experiment too often. For one or two years, I accomplished more than I have here claimed, viz., from six to seven thousand miles in the twelve months. Let me add to this slight abstract of my own experience, in a point where it is really difficult to offer any useful advice, (the tastes and habits of men varying so much in this chapter of exercise,) that one caution seems applicable to the case of all persons suffering from nervous irritability, viz., that a secluded space should be measured off accurately, in some private grounds not liable to the interruption or notice of chance intruders; for these annoyances are unendurable to the restless invalid; to be questioned upon trivial things is death to him; and the perpetual anticipation of such annoyances is little less distressing. Some plan must also be adopted for registering the number of rounds performed. I once walked for eighteen months in a circuit so confined that forty revolutions were needed to complete a mile. These I counted, at one time, by a rosary of beads; every tenth round being marked by drawing a blue bead, the other nine by drawing white beads. But this plan, I found in practice, more troublesome and inaccurate than that of using ten detached counters, stones, or anything else that was large enough and solid. These were applied to the separate bars of a garden chair; the first bar indicating of itself the first decade, the second bar the second decade, and so on. In fact, I used the chair in some measure as a Roman abacus, but on a still simpler plan; and as the chair offered sixteen bars, it followed, that on covering the last bar of the series with the ten markers, I perceived without any trouble of calculation the accomplishment of my fourth mile.

A necessity, more painful to me by far than that of taking continued exercise, arose out of a cause which applies, perhaps, with the same intensity only to opium cases, but must also apply in some degree to all cases of debilitation from morbid stimulation of the nerves, whether by means of wine, or opium, or distilled liquors. In travelling on the outside of mails, during my youthful days, for I could not endure the inside, occasionally, during the night-time, I suffered naturally from cold: no cloaks, &c. were always sufficient to relieve this; and I then made the discovery that opium, after an hour or so, diffuses a warmth deeper and far more permanent than could be had from any other known source. I mention this, to explain, in some measure, the awful passion of cold which for some years haunted the inverse process of laying aside the opium. It was a perfect frenzy of misery; cold was a sensation which then first, as a mode of torment, seemed to have been revealed. In the months of July and August, and not at all the less during the very middle watch of the day, I sate in the closest proximity to a blazing fire; cloaks, blankets, counterpanes, hearthrugs, horse-cloths, were piled upon my shoulders, but with hardly a glimmering of relief. At night, and after taking coffee, I felt a little warmer, and could sometimes afford to smile at the resemblance of my own case to that of Harry Gill. [Footnote: 'Harry Gill:'—Many readers, in this generation, may not be aware of this ballad as one amongst the early poems of Wordsworth. Thirty or forty years ago, it was the object of some insipid ridicule, which ought, perhaps, in another place, to be noticed. And, doubtless, this ridicule was heightened by the false impression that the story had been some old woman's superstitious fiction, meant to illustrate a supernatural judgment on hard-heartedness. But the story was a physiologic fact; and, originally, it had been brought forward in a philosophic work, by Darwin, who had the reputation of an irreligious man, and even of an infidel. A bold freethinker he certainly was: a Deist, and, by public repute, something more.] But, secretly, I was struck with awe at the revelation of powers so unsearchably new, lurking within old affections so familiarly known as cold. Upon the analogy of this case, it might be thought that nothing whatever had yet been truly and seriously felt by man; nothing searched or probed by human sensibilities, to a depth below the surface. If cold could give out mysteries of suffering so novel, all things in the world might be yet unvisited by the truth of human sensations. All experience, worthy of the name, was yet to begin. Meantime, the external phenomenon, by which the cold expressed itself, was a sense (but with little reality) of eternal freezing perspiration. From this I was never free; and at length, from finding one general ablution sufficient for one day, I was thrown upon the irritating necessity of repeating it more frequently than would seem credible, if stated. At this time, I used always hot water; and a thought occurred to me very seriously that it would be best to live constantly, and, perhaps, to sleep in a bath. What caused me to renounce this plan, was an accident that compelled me for one day to use cold water. This, first of all, communicated any lasting warmth; so that ever afterwards I used none *but* cold water. Now, to live in a *cold* bath, in our climate, and in my own state of preternatural sensibility to cold, was not an idea to dally with. I wish to mention, however, for the information of other sufferers in the same way, one change in the mode of applying the water, which led to a considerable and a sudden improvement in the condition of my feelings. I had endeavored to procure a child's battledore, as an easy means (when clothed with sponge) of reaching the interspace between the shoulders; which interspace, by the way, is a sort of Bokhara, so provokingly situated, that it will neither suffer itself to be reached from the north, in which direction even the Czar, with his long arms, has only singed his own fingers, and lost six thousand camels; nor at all better from the south, upon which line of approach the greatest potentate in Southern Asia, viz., No. —, in Leadenhall Street, has found it the best policy to pocket the little Khan's murderous defiances and persevering insults. There is no battledore long enough to reach him in either way. In my own difficulty, I felt almost as perplexed as the Honorable East India Company, when I found that no battledore was to be had; for no town was near at hand. In default of a battledore, therefore, my necessity threw my experiment upon a long hair-brush; and this, eventually, proved of much greater service than any sponge or any battledore; for, the friction of the brush caused an irritation on the surface of the skin, which, more than anything else, has gradually diminished the once continual misery of unrelenting frost; although even yet it renews itself most distressingly at uncertain intervals.

IV. I counsel the patient not to make the mistake of supposing that his amendment will necessarily proceed continuously, or by equal increments; because this, which is a common notion, will certainly lead to dangerous disappointments. How frequently I have heard people encouraging a self-reformer by such language as this:—'When you have got over the fourth day of abstinence, which suppose to be Sunday, then Monday will find you a trifle better; Tuesday better still,—though still it should be only by a trifle; and so on. You may, at least, rely on never going back; you may assure yourself of having seen the worst; and the positive improvements, if trifles separately, must soon gather into a sensible magnitude.' This may be true in a case of short standing: but, as a general rule, it is perilously delusive. On the contrary, the line of progress, if exhibited in a geometrical construction, would describe an ascending path upon the whole, but with frequent retrocessions into descending curves, which, compared with the point of ascent that had been previously gained and so vexatiously interrupted, would sometimes seem deeper than the original point of starting. This mortifying tendency I can report from experience many times repeated with regard to opium; and so unaccountably, as regarded all the previous grounds of expectation, that I am compelled to suppose it a tendency inherent in the very nature of all self-restorations for animal systems. They move perhaps necessarily *per saltum*, by, intermitting spasms, and pulsations of unequal energy.

V. I counsel the patient frequently to call back before his thoughts—when suffering sorrowful collapses, that seem unmerited by anything done or neglected—that such, and far worse, perhaps, must have been his experience, and with no reversion of hope behind, had he persisted in his intemperate indulgencies; *these* also suffer their own collapses, and (so far as things not co-present can be compared) by many degrees more shocking to the genial instincts.

VI. I exhort him to believe, that no movement on his own part, not the smallest conceivable, towards the restoration of his healthy state, can by possibility perish. Nothing in this direction is finally lost; but often it disappears and hides itself; suddenly, however, to reappear, and in unexpected strength, and much more hopefully; because such minute elements of improvement, by reappearing at a remoter stage, show themselves to have combined with other elements of the same kind: so that equally by their gathering tendency and their duration through intervals of apparent darkness, and below the current of what seemed absolute interruption, they argue themselves to be settled in the system. There is no good gift that does not come from God: almost his greatest is health, with the peace which it inherits; and man must reap *this* on the same terms as he was told to reap God's earliest gift, the fruits of the earth, viz.: 'in the sweat of his brow,' through labor, often through sorrow, through disappointment, but still through imperishable perseverance, and hoping under clouds, when all hope seems darkened.

VII. It is difficult, in selecting from many memoranda of warning and encouragement, to know which to prefer when the space disposable is limited. But it seems to me important not to omit this particular caution: The patient will be naturally anxious, as he goes on, frequently to test the amount of his advance, and its rate, if that were possible. But this he will see no mode of doing, except through tentative balancings of his feelings, and generally of the moral atmosphere around him, as to pleasure and hope, against the corresponding states, so far as he can recall them from his periods of intemperance. But these comparisons, I warn him, are fallacious, when made in this way; the two states are incommensurable on any plan of *direct* comparison. Some common measure must be found, and, *out of himself*; some positive fact, that will not bend to his own delusive feeling at the moment; as, for instance, in what degree he finds tolerable what heretofore was *not* so—the effort of writing letters, or transacting business, or undertaking a journey, or overtaking the arrears of labor, that had been once thrown off to a distance. If in these things he finds himself improved, by tests that cannot be disputed, he may safely disregard any sceptical whispers from a wayward sensibility which cannot yet, perhaps, have recovered its normal health, however much improved. His inner feelings may not yet point steadily to the truth, though they may vibrate in that direction. Besides, it is certain that sometimes very manifest advances, such as any medical man would perceive at a glance, carry a man through stages of agitation and discomfort. A far worse condition might happen to be less agitated, and so far more bearable. Now, when a man is positively suffering discomfort, when he is below the line of pleasurable feeling, he is no proper judge of his own condition, which he neither will nor can appreciate. Toothache extorts more groans than dropsy.

VIII. Another important caution is, not to confound with the effects of intemperance any other natural effects of debility from advanced years. Many a man, having begun to be intemperate at thirty, enters at sixty or upwards upon a career of self-restoration. And by self-restoration he understands a renewal of that state in which he was when first swerving from temperance. But that state, for his memory, is coincident with his state of youth. The two states are coadunated. In his recollections they are intertwisted too closely. But life, without any intemperance at all, would soon have untwisted them. Charles Lamb, for instance, at forty-five, and Coleridge at sixty, measured their several conditions by such tests as the loss of all disposition to involuntary murmuring of musical airs or fragments when rising from bed. Once they had sung when rising in the morning light; now they sang no more. The *vocal* utterance of joy, for *them*, was silenced for ever. But these are amongst the changes that life, stern power, inflicts at any rate; these would have happened, and above all, to men worn by the unequal irritations of too much thinking, and by those modes of care

> That kill the bloom before its time,
> And blanch without the owner's crime
> The most resplendent hair,

not at all the less had the one drunk no brandy, nor the other any laudanum. A man must submit to the conditions of humanity, and not quarrel with a cure as incomplete, because in his climacteric year of sixty-three, he cannot recover, entirely, the vivacities of thirty-five. If, by dipping seven times in Jordan, he had cleansed his whole leprosy of intemperance; if, by going down into Bethesda, he were able to mount again upon the pinions of his youth,—even then he might querulously say,—'But, after all these marvels in my favor, I suppose that one of these fine mornings I, like other people, shall have to bespeak a coffin.' Why, yes, undoubtedly he will, or somebody *for* him. But privileges so especial were not promised even by the mysterious waters of Palestine. Die he must. And counsels tendered to the intemperate do not hope to accomplish what might have been beyond the baths of Jordan or Bethesda. They do enough, if, being executed by efforts in the spirit of earnest sincerity, they make a life of *growing* misery moderately happy for the patient; and, through that great change, perhaps, more than moderately useful for others.

IX. One final remark I will make:—pointed to the case, not of the yet struggling patient, but of him who is fully re-established; and the more so, because I (who am no hypocrite, but, rather, frank to an infirmity) acknowledge, in myself, the trembling tendency at intervals, which would, if permitted, sweep round into currents that might be hard to overrule. After the absolute restoration to health, a man is very apt to say,—'Now, then, how shall I use my health? To what delightful purpose shall I apply it? Surely it is idle to carry a fine jewel in one's watch-pocket, and never to astonish the weak minds of this world, by wearing it and flashing it in their eyes.' 'But how?' retorts his philosophic friend; 'my good fellow, are you not using it at this moment? Breathing, for instance, talking to me, (though rather absurdly,) and airing your legs at a glowing fire?' 'Why, yes,' the other confesses, 'that is all true; but I am dull; and, if you will pardon my rudeness, even in spite of your too philosophic presence. It is painful to say so, but sincerely, if I had the power, at this moment, to turn you, by magic, into a bottle of old port wine, so corrupt is my nature, that really I fear lest the exchange might, for the moment, strike me as agreeable.' Such a mood, I apprehend, is apt to revolve upon many of us, at intervals, however firmly married to temperance. And the propensity to it has a root in certain analogies running through our nature. If the reader will permit me for a moment the use of what, without such an apology, might seem pedantic, I would call it the instinct of *focalizing*, which prompts such random desires. Feeling is diffused over the whole surface of the body; but light is focalized in the eye; sound in the ear. The organization of a sense or a pleasure seems diluted and imperfect, unless it is gathered by some machinery into one focus, or local centre. And thus it is that a general state of pleasurable feeling sometimes seems too superficially diffused, and one has a craving to intensify or brighten it by concentration through some sufficient stimulant.

I, for my part, have tried every thing in this world except 'bang,' which, I believe, is obtained from hemp. There are other preparations of hemp which have been found to give great relief from *ennui*; not ropes, but something lately introduced, which acts upon the system as the laughing gas (nitrous oxide) acts at times. One farmer in Mid-Lothian was mentioned to me, eight months ago, as having taken it, and ever since annoyed his neighbors by immoderate fits of laughter; so that in January it was agreed to present him to the sheriff as a nuisance. But, for some reason, the plan was laid aside; and now, eight months later, I hear that the farmer is laughing more rapturously than ever, continues in the happiest frame of mind, the kindest of creatures, and the general torment of his neighborhood. Now, I confess to having had a lurking interest in this extract of hemp, when first I heard of it: and at intervals a desire will continue to make itself felt for some deeper compression or centralization of the genial feelings than ordinary life affords. But old things will not avail, and new things I am now able to resist. Still, as the occasional craving does really arise in most men, it is well to notice it; and chiefly for the purpose of saying, that this dangerous feeling wears off by degrees; and oftentimes for long periods it intermits so entirely as to be even displaced by a profound disgust to all modes of artificial stimulation. At those times I have remarked that the pleasurable condition of health does *not* seem weakened by its want of centralization. It seems to form a thousand centres. This it is well to know; because there are many who would resist effectually, if they were aware of any natural change going on silently in favor of their own efforts, such as would finally ratify the success. Towards such a result they would gladly contribute by waiting and forbearing; whilst, under despondency as to this result, they might more easily yield to some chance temptation.

Finally, there is something to interest us in the *time* at which this temperance movement has begun to stir. Let me close with a slight notice of what chiefly impresses myself in the relation between this time and the other circumstances of the case. In reviewing history, we may see something more than mere convenience in distributing it into three chambers; ancient history, ending in the space between the Western Empire falling and Mahomet arising; modern history, from that time to this; and a new modern history arising at present, or from the French Revolution. Two great races of men, our own in a two-headed form—British and American, and secondly, the Russian, are those which, like rising deluges, already reveal their mission to overflow the earth. Both these races, partly through climate, or through derivation of blood, and partly through the contagion of habits inevitable to brothers of the same nation, are tainted carnally with the appetite for brandy, for slings, for juleps. And no fire racing through the forests of Nova

Scotia for three hundred miles in the direction of some doomed city, ever moved so fiercely as the infection of habits amongst the dense and fiery populations of republican North America.

But it is remarkable, that the whole *ancient* system of civilization, all the miracles of Greece and Rome, Persia and Egypt, moved by the machinery of races that were *not* tainted with any such popular *marasmus*. The taste was slightly sowed, as an *artificial* taste, amongst luxurious individuals, but never ran through the laboring classes, through armies, through cities The blood and the climate forbade it. In this earliest era of history, all the great races, consequently all the great empires, threw themselves, by accumulation, upon the genial climates of the south,—having, in fact, the magnificent lake of the Mediterranean for their general centre of evolutions. Round this lake, in a zone of varying depth, towered the whole grandeurs of the Pagan earth. But, in such climates, man is naturally temperate. He is so by physical coercion, and for the necessities of rest and coolness. The Spaniard, the Moor, or the Arab, has no merit in his temperance. The effort, for *him*, would be to form the taste for alcohol. He has a vast foreground of disgust to traverse before he can reach a taste so remote and alien. No need for resistance in his will where nature resists on his behalf. Sherbet, shaddocks, grapes, these were innocent applications to thirst. And the great republic of antiquity said to her legionary sons:—'Soldier, if you thirst, there is the river;—Nile, suppose, or Ebro. Better drink there cannot be. Of this you may take "at discretion." Or, if you wait till the *impedimenta* come up, you may draw your ration of *Posca*' What was *posca*? It was, in fact, acidulated water; three parts of superfine water to one part of the very best vinegar. Nothing stronger did Rome, that awful mother, allow to her dearest children, *i. e.*, her legions. Truest of blessings, that veiling itself in seeming sternness, drove away the wicked phantoms that haunt the couches of yet greater nations. 'The blessings of the evil genii,' says an Eastern proverb, 'these are curses.' And the stern refusals of wisely loving mothers,—these are the mightiest of gifts.

Now, on the other hand, our northern climates have universally the taste, latent if not developed, for powerful liquors. And through their blood, as also through the natural tendency of the imitative principle amongst compatriots, from these high latitudes the greatest of our modern nations propagate the contagion to their brothers, though colonizing warm climates. And it is remarkable that our modern preparations of liquors, even when harmless in their earliest stages, are fitted, like stepping-stones, for making the transition to higher stages that are *not* harmless. The weakest preparations from malt, lead, by graduated steps, to the strongest; until we arrive at the intoxicating porter of London, which, under its local name (so insidiously delusive) of *'beer,'* diffuses the most extensive ravages.

Under these marked circumstances of difference between the ruling races of antiquity and of our modern times, it now happens that the greatest era by far of human expansion is opening upon us. Two vast movements are hurrying into action by velocities continually accelerated—the great revolutionary movement from political causes concurring with the great physical movement in locomotion and social intercourse, from the gigantic (though still infant) powers of steam. No such Titan resources for modifying each other were ever before dreamed of by nations: and the next hundred years will have changed the face of the world. At the opening of such a crisis, had no third movement arisen of resistance to intemperate habits, there would have been ground for despondency as to the amelioration of the human race. But, as the case stands, the new principle of resistance nationally to bad habits, has arisen almost concurrently with the new powers of national intercourse; and henceforward by a change equally sudden and unlooked for, that new machinery, which would else most surely have multiplied the ruins of intoxication, has become the strongest agency for hastening its extirpation.

ON WAR

Few people need to be told—that associations exist up and down Christendom, having the ambitious object of abolishing war. Some go so far as to believe that this evil of war, so ubiquitous, so ancient and apparently so inalienable from man's position upon earth, is already doomed; that not the private associations only, but the prevailing voice of races the most highly civilized, may be looked on as tending to confederation against it; that sentence of extermination has virtually gone forth, and that all which remains is gradually to execute that sentence. Conscientiously I find myself unable to join in these views. The project seems to me the most romantic of all romances in the course of publication. Consequently, when asked to become a member in any such association, I have always thought it most respectful, because most sincere, to decline. Yet, as it is painful to refuse all marks of sympathy with persons whose motives one honors, I design at my death to bequeath half-a-crown to the chief association for extinguishing war; the said half-crown to be improved in all time coming for the benefit of the association, under the trusteeship of Europe, Asia, and America, but not of Africa. I really dare not trust Africa with money, she is not able as yet to take care of herself. This half-crown, a fund that will overshadow the earth before it comes to be wanted under the provisions of my will, is to be improved at any interest whatever—no matter what; for the vast period of the accumulations will easily make good any tardiness of advance, long before the time comes for its commencing payment; a point which will be soon understood from the following explanation, by any gentleman that hopes to draw upon it.

There is in Ceylon a granite *cippus*, or monumental pillar, of immemorial antiquity; and to this pillar a remarkable legend is attached. The pillar measures six feet by six, *i. e.* thirty-six square feet, on the flat tablet of its horizontal surface; and in height several *riyanas*, (which arc Ceylonese cubits of eighteen inches each,) but of these cubits, there are either eight or twelve; excuse me for having forgotten which. At first, perhaps, you will be angry, viz., when you hear that this simple difference of four cubits, or six feet, measures a difference for your expectations, whether you count your expectations in kicks or halfpence, that absolutely strikes horror into arithmetic. The singularity of the case is, that the very solemnity of the legend and the wealth of the human race in time, depend upon the cubical contents of the monument, so that a loss of one granite chip is a loss of a frightful infinity; yet, again, for that very reason, the loss of all *but* a chip, leaves behind riches so appallingly too rich, that everybody is careless about the four cubits. Enough is as good a feast. Two bottomless abysses take as much time for the diver as ten; and five eternities are as frightful to look down as four-and-twenty. In the Ceylon legend all turns upon the inexhaustible series of ages which this pillar guarantees. But, as one inexhaustible is quite enough for one race of men, and you are sure of more by ineffable excess than you can use in any private consumption of your own, you become generous; 'and between friends,' you say, in accepting my apologies for the doubtful error as to the four cubits, 'what signifies an infinity more or less?'

For the Ceylonese legend is this, that once in every hundred years an angel visits this granite pillar. He is dressed in a robe of white muslin, muslin of that kind which the Romans called *aura textilis*—woven, as might seem, from zephyrs or from pulses of the air, such in its transparency, such in its gossamer lightness. Does the angel touch the pillar with his foot? Oh no! Even *that* would be something, but even *that* is not allowed. In his soundless flight across it, he suffers the hem of his impalpable robe to sweep the surface as softly as a moon-beam. So much and no more of pollution he endures from contact with earthly objects. The lowest extremity of his dress, but with the delicacy of light, grazes the granite surface. And *that* is all the attrition which the sacred granite receives in the course of any one century, and this is all the progress which we, the poor children of earth, in any one century make towards the exhaustion of our earthly imprisonment. But, argues the subtle legend, even *that* attrition, when weighed in metaphysical scales, cannot be denied its value; it has detached from the pillar an atom (no matter that it is an invisible atom) of granite dust, the ratio of which atom to a grain avoirdupois, if expressed as a fraction of unity, would by its denominator stretch from the Accountant-General's office in London to the Milky Way. Now the total mass of the granite represents, on this scheme of payment, the total funded debt of man's race to Father Time and earthly corruption; all this intolerable score, chalked up to our debit, we by ourselves and our representatives have to rub off, before the granite will be rubbed away by the muslin robe of the proud flying angel, (who, if he were a good fellow, might just as well give a sly kick with his heel to the granite,) before time will be at an end, and the burden of flesh accomplished. But you hear it expressed in terms that will astonish Baron Rothschild, what is the progress in liquidation which we make for each particular century. A billion of centuries pays off a quantity equal to a pinch of snuff. Despair seizes a man in contemplating a single *coupon*, no bigger than a visiting card, of such a stock as this; and behold we have to keep on paying away until the total granite is reduced to a level with a grain of mustard-seed. But when that is accomplished, thank heaven, our last generation of descendants will be entitled to leave at Master Time's door a visiting card, which the meagre shadow cannot refuse to take, though he will sicken at seeing it; viz., a P. P. C. card, upon seeing which, the old thief is bound to give receipt in full for all debts and pretended arrears.

The reader perhaps knows of debts on both sides the Atlantic that have no great prospect of being paid off sooner than this in Ceylon.

And naturally, to match this order of debts, moving off so slowly, there are funds that accumulate as slowly. My own funded half-crown is an illustration. The half-crown will travel in the inverse order of the granite pillar. The pillar and the half-crown move upon opposite tacks; and there *is* a point of time (which it is for Algebra to investigate) when they will cross each other in the exact moment of their several bisections — my aspiring half-crown tending gradually towards the fixed stars, so that perhaps it might be right to make the man in the moon trustee for that part of the accumulations which rises above the optics of sublunary bankers; whilst the Ceylon pillar is constantly unweaving its own granite texture, and dwindling earthwards. It is probable that each of the parties will have reached its consummation about the same time. What is to be done with the mustard-seed, Ceylon has forgotten to say. But what is to be done with the half-crown and its surplus, nobody can doubt after reading my last will and testament. After reciting a few inconsiderable legacies to the three continents, and to the man in the moon, for any trouble they may have had in managing the hyperbolical accumulations, I go on to observe, that, when war is reported to have taken itself off for ever, 'and no mistake,' (because I foresee many false alarms of a perpetual peace,) a variety of inconveniences will arise to all branches of the United Service, including the Horse Marines. Clearly there can be no more half-pay; and even more clearly, there is an end to full-pay. Pensions are at an end for 'good service.' Allowances for wounds cannot be thought of, when all wounds shall have ceased except those from female eyes — for which the Horse Guards is too little advanced in civilization to make any allowance at all. Bargains there will be no more amongst auctions of old Government stores. Birmingham will be ruined, or so much of it as depended on rifles. And the great Scotch works on the river Carron will be hungering for beef, so far as Carron depended for beef upon carronades. Other arrears of evil will stretch after the extinction of war.

Now upon my half-crown fund (which will be equal to anything by the time it is wanted) I charge once and for ever the general relief of all these arrears—of the poverty, the loss, the bankruptcy, arising by reason of this *quietus* of final extinction applied to war. I charge the fund with a perpetual allowance of half-pay to all the armies of earth; or indeed, whilst my hand is in, I charge it with *full* pay. And I strictly enjoin upon my trustees and executors, but especially upon the man in the moon, if his unsocial lip has left him one spark of gentlemanly feeling, that he and they shall construe all claims liberally; nay, with that riotous liberality which is safe and becoming, when applied to a fund so inexhaustible. Yes, reader, my fund will be inexhaustible, because the period of its growth will be measured by the concurrent deposition of the Ceylon mustard-seed from the everlasting pillar.

Yet why, or on what principle? It is because I see, or imagine that I see, a twofold necessity for war—necessity in two different senses—1st, a physical necessity arising out of man's nature when combined with man's situation; a necessity under which war may be regarded, if you please, as a nuisance, but as a nuisance inalienable from circumstances essential to human frailty. 2dly, a moral necessity connected with benefits of compensation, such as continually lurk in evils acknowledged to be such—a necessity under which it becomes lawful to say, that war *ought* to exist as a balance to opposite tendencies of a still more evil character. War is the mother of wrong and spoliation: war is a scourge of God—granted; but, like other scourges in the divine economy, war purifies and redeems itself in its character of a counterforce to greater evils that could not otherwise be intercepted or redressed. In two different meanings we say that a thing is necessary; either in that case where it is inexorably forced on by some sad overruling principle which it is vain to fight against, though all good men mourn over its existence and view it as an unconditional evil; or secondly, in that case, where an instrument of sorrowful consequences to man is nevertheless invoked and postulated by man's highest moral interests, is nevertheless clamorously indicated as a blessing when looked at in relation to some antagonist cause of evil for which it offers the one only remedy or principle of palliation. The very evil and woe of man's condition upon earth may be oftentimes detected in the necessity of looking to some other woe as the pledge of its purification; so that what separately would have been hateful for itself, passes mysteriously into an object of toleration, of hope, or even of prayer, as a counter-venom to the taint of some more mortal poison. Poverty, for instance, is in both senses necessary for man. It is necessary in the same sense as thirst is necessary (*i. e.* inevitable) in a fever—necessary as one corollary amongst many others, from the eternal hollowness of all human efforts for organizing any perfect model of society—a corollary which, how gladly would all of us unite to cancel, but which our hearts suggest, which Scripture solemnly proclaims, to be ineradicable from the land. In this sense, poverty is a necessity over which we *mourn*,—as one of the dark phases that sadden the vision of human life. But far differently, and with a stern gratitude, we recognize another mode of necessity for this gloomy distinction—a call for poverty, when seen in relation to the manifold agencies by which it developes human energies, in relation to the trials by which it searches the power of patience and religion, in relation to the struggles by which it evokes the nobilities of fortitude; or again, amongst those who are not sharers in these trials and struggles, but sympathizing spectators, in relation to the stimulation by which it quickens wisdom that watches over the causes of this evil, or by which it vivifies the spirit of love that labors for its mitigation. War stands, or seems to stand, upon the same double basis of necessity; a primary necessity that belongs to our human degradations, a secondary one that towers by means of its moral relations into the region of our impassioned exaltations. The two propositions on which I take my stand are these. *First*, that there are nowhere latent in society any powers by which it can effectually operate on war for its extermination. The machinery is not there. The game is not within the compass of the cards. *Secondly*, that this defect of power is, though sincerely I grieve in avowing such a sentiment, and perhaps (if an infirm reader had his eye upon me) I might seem, in sympathy with his weakness, to blush—not a curse, no not at all, but on the whole a blessing from century to century, if it is an inconvenience from year to year. The Abolition Committees, it is to be feared, will be very angry at both propositions. Yet, Gentlemen, hear me—strike, but hear me. I believe that's a sort of plagiarism from Themistocles. But never mind. I have as good a right to the words, until translated back into Greek, as that most classical of yellow admirals. '*Pereant qui ante nos nostra dixerunt!*'

The first proposition is, that war *cannot* be abolished. The second, and more offensive—that war ought not to be abolished. First, therefore, concerning the first. One at a time. Sufficient for the page is the evil thereof! How came it into any man's heart, first of all, to conceive so audacious an idea as that of a conspiracy against war? Whence could he draw any vapor of hope to sustain his preliminary steps? And in framing his plot, which way did he set his face to look out for accomplices? Revolving this question in times past, I came to the conclusion—that, perhaps, this colossal project of a war against war, had been first put in motion under a misconception (natural enough, and countenanced by innumerable books) as to the true historical origin of wars in many notorious instances. If these had arisen on trivial impulses, a trivial resistance might have intercepted them. If a man has once persuaded himself, that long, costly, and bloody wars had arisen upon a point of ceremony, upon a personal pique, upon a hasty word, upon some explosion of momentary caprice; it is a natural inference, that strength of national will and public combinations for resistance, supposing such forces to have been trained, organized, and, from the circumstances of the particular nation, to be permanently disposable for action, might prove redundantly effective, when pointed against a few personal authors of war, so presumably weak, and so flexible to any stern counter-volition as those *must* be supposed, whose wars argued so much of vicious levity. The inference is unexceptionable: it is the premises that are unsound. Anecdotes of war as having emanated from a lady's tea-table or toilette, would authorize such inference as to the facilities of controlling them. But the anecdotes themselves are false, or false substantially. *All* anecdotes, I fear, are false. I am sorry to say so, but my duty to the reader extorts from me the disagreeable confession, as upon a matter specially investigated by myself, that all dealers in anecdotes are tainted with mendacity. Where is the Scotchman, said Dr. Johnson, who does not prefer Scotland to truth? but, however this may be, rarer than such a Scotchman, rarer than the phoenix, is that virtuous man, a monster he is, nay, he is an impossible man, who will consent to lose a prosperous anecdote on the consideration that it happens to be a lie. All history, therefore, being built partly, and some of it altogether, upon anecdotage, must be a tissue of lies. Such, for the most part, is the history of Suetonius, who may be esteemed the father of anecdotage; and being such, he (and not Herodotus) should have been honored with the title, *Father of Lies*. Such is the Augustan history, which is all that remains of the Roman empire; such is the vast series of French memoirs, now stretching through more than three entire centuries. Are these works, then, to be held cheap, because their truths to their falsehoods are in the ratio of one to five hundred? On the contrary, they are better, and more to be esteemed on that account; because, *now* they are admirable reading on a winter's night; whereas, written on the principle of sticking to the truth, they would have been as dull as ditch water. Generally, therefore, the dealers in anecdotage are to be viewed with admiration, as patriotic citizens, willing to sacrifice their own characters, lest their countrymen should find themselves short of amusement. I esteem them as equal to Codrus, Timoleon, William Tell, or to Milton, as regards the liberty of unlicensed printing. And I object to them only in the exceptional case of their being cited as authorities for an inference, or as vouchers for a fact. Universally, it may be received as a rule of unlimited application,—that when an anecdote involves a stinging repartee, or collision of ideas, fancifully and brilliantly related to each other by resemblance or contrast, then you may challenge it as false to a certainty. One illustration of which is—that pretty nearly every memorable *propos*, or pointed repartee, or striking *mot*, circulating at this moment in Paris or London, as the undoubted property of Talleyrand, (that eminent knave,) was ascribed at Vienna, ninety years ago, to the Prince de Ligne, and thirty years previously, to Voltaire, and so on, regressively, to many other wits (knaves or not); until, at length, if you persist in backing far enough, you find yourself amongst Pagans, with the very same repartee, &c., doing duty in pretty good Greek; [Footnote: This is *literally* true, more frequently than would be supposed. For instance, a jest often ascribed to Voltaire, and of late pointedly reclaimed for him by Lord Brougham, as being one that he (Lord B.) could swear to for *his*, so characteristic seemed the impression of Voltaire's mind upon the *tournure* of the sarcasm, unhappily for this waste of sagacity, may be found recorded by Fabricius in the *Bibliotheca Græca*, as the jest of a Greek who has been dead for about seventeen centuries. The man certainly *did* utter the jest; and 1750 years ago. But who it was that he stole it from is another question. To all appearance, and according to Lord Brougham's opinion, the party robbed must have been M. de Voltaire. I notice the case, however, of the Greek thefts and frauds committed upon so many of our excellent wits belonging to the 18th and 19th centuries, chiefly with a view to M. de Talleyrand—that rather middling bishop, but very eminent knave. He also has been extensively robbed by the Greeks of the 2d and 3d centuries. How else can you account for so many of his sayings being found amongst *their* pages? A thing you may ascertain in a moment, at any police office, by having the Greeks searched: for surely you would never think of searching a bishop. Most of the Talleyrand jewels will be found concealed amongst the goods of these unprincipled Greeks. But one, and the most famous in the whole jewel-case, sorry am I to confess, was nearly stolen from the Bishop, not by any Greek, but by an English writer, viz., Goldsmith, who must have been dying about the time that his Excellency, the diplomatist, had the goodness to be born. That famous *mot* about language, as a gift made to man for the purpose of *concealing* his thoughts, is lurking in Goldsmith's Essays. Think of *that!* Already, in his innocent childhood, whilst the Bishop was in petticoats, and almost before he had begun to curse and to swear plainly in French, an Irish vagabond had attempted to swindle him out of that famous witticism which has since been as good as a life-annuity to the venerable knave's literary fame.] sometimes, for instance in Hierocles, sometimes in Diogenes Lærtius, in Plutarch, or in Athenæus. Now the thing you know claimed by so many people, could not belong to all of them: *all* of them could not be the inventors. Logic and common sense unite in showing us that it must have belonged to the moderns, who had clearly been hustled and robbed by the ancients, so much more likely to commit a robbery than Christians, they being all Gentiles— Pagans—Heathen dogs. What do I infer from this? Why, that upon *any* solution of the case, hardly one worthy saying can be mentioned, hardly one jest, pun, or sarcasm, which has not been the occasion and subject of many falsehoods—as having been *au-(and men)-daciously* transferred from generation to generation, sworn to in every age as this man's property, or that man's, by people that must have known they were lying, until you retire from the investigation with a conviction, that under any system of chronology, the science of lying is the only one that has never drooped. Date from *Anno Domini*, or from the Julian era, patronize Olympiads, or patronize (as *I* do, from misanthropy, because nobody else *will*) the era of Nabonassar,— no matter, upon every road, thicker than mile-stones, you see records of human mendacity, or (which is much worse, in my opinion,) of human sympathy with other people's mendacity.

This digression, now, on anecdotes,[Footnote: The word 'Anecdotes,' first, I believe, came into currency about the middle of the 6th century, from the use made of it by Procopius. *Literally* it indicated nothing that could interest either public malice or public favor; it promised only *unpublished* notices of the Emperor Justinian, his wife Theodora, Narses, Belisarius, &c. But *why* had they been unpublished? Simply because scandalous and defamatory: and hence, from the interest which invested the case of an imperial court so remarkable, this oblique, secondary and purely accidental modification of the word came to influence its *general* acceptation. Simply to have been previously unpublished, no longer raised any statement into an anecdote: it now received a new integration it must be some fresh publication of *personal* memorabilia; and these having reference to *human* creatures, must always be presumed to involve more evil than good—much defamation true or false—much doubtful insinuation—much suggestion of things worse than could be openly affirmed. So arose the word: but the *thing* arose with Suetonius, that dear, excellent and hard-working 'father of lies.'] is what the learned call an *excursus*, and, I am afraid, too long by half; not strictly in proportion. But don't mind *that*. I'll make it all right by being too short upon something else, at the next opportunity; and then nobody can complain. Meantime, I argue, that as all brilliant or epigrammatic anecdotes are probably false, (a thing that hereafter I shall have much pleasure in making out to the angry reader's satisfaction,) but to a dead certainty those anecdotes, in particular, which bear marks in their construction that a rhetorical effect of art had been contemplated by the narrator,—we may take for granted, that the current stories ascribing modern wars (French and English) to accidents the most inconsiderable, are false even in a literal sense; but at all events they are so when valued philosophically, and brought out into their circumstantial relations. For instance, we have a French anecdote, from the latter part of the seventeenth century, which ascribes one bloody war to the accident of a little 'miff,' arising between the king and his minister upon some such trifle as the situation of a palace window. Again, from the early part of the eighteenth century, we have an English anecdote, ascribing consequences no less bloody to a sudden feud between two ladies, and that feud, (if I remember,) tracing itself up to a pair of gloves; so that, in effect, the war and the gloves form the two poles of the transaction. Harlequin throws a pair of Limerick gloves into a corn-mill; and the spectator is astonished to see the gloves immediately issuing from the hopper, well ground into seven armies of one hundred thousand men each, and with parks of artillery to correspond. In these two anecdotes, we recognize at once the able and industrious artist arranging his materials with a pious regard to theatrical effect. This man knows how to group his figures; well he understands where to plant his masses of light and shade; and what impertinence it would be in us spectators, the reader suppose and myself, to go behind the scenes for critical inquiry into daylight realities. All reasonable men see that, the less of such realities our artist had to work with, the more was his merit. I am one of those that detest all insidious attempts to rob men situated as this artist of their fair fame, by going about and whispering that perhaps the thing is true. Far from it! I sympathize with the poor trembling artist, and agree most cordially that the whole story is a lie; and he may rely upon my support at all times to the extent of denying that any vestige of truth probably lay at the foundations of his ingenious apologue. And what I say of the English fable, I am willing to say of the French one. Both, I dare say, were the rankest fictions. But next, what, after all, if they were *not*? For, in the rear of all discussion upon anecdotes, considered simply as true or *not* true, comes finally a *valuation* of those anecdotes in their moral relation, and as to the inferences which they will sustain. The story, for example, of the French minister Louvois, and the adroitness with which he fastened upon great foreign potentates, in the shape of war, that irritability of temper in his royal master which threatened to consume himself; the diplomatic address with which he transmuted suddenly a task so delicate as that of skirmishing daily in a Council Chamber with his own sovereign, into that far jollier mode of disputation where one replies to all objections of the very keenest logician, either with round shot or with grape; here is an anecdote, which (for my own part) I am inclined to view as pure gasconade. But suppose the story true, still it may happen that a better valuation of it may disturb the whole edifice of logical inferences by which it seemed to favor the speculations of the war abolitionists. Let us see. What *was* the logic through which such a tale as this could lend any countenance to the schemes of these abolitionists? That logic travelled in the following channel. Such a tale, or the English tale of the gloves, being supposed true, it would seem to follow, that war and the purposes of war were phenomena of chance growth, not attached to any instinct so ancient, and apparently so grooved into the dark necessities of our nature, as we had all taken for granted. Usually, we rank war with hunger, with cold, with sorrow, with death, afflictions of our human state that spring up as inevitably without separate culture and in defiance of all hostile culture, as verdure, as weeds, and as flowers that overspread in spring time a fertile soil without needing to be sown or watered—awful is the necessity, as it seems, of all such afflictions. Yet, again, if (as these anecdote simply) war could by possibility depend frequently on accidents of personal temperament, irritability in a sensual king, wounded sensibilities of pride between two sensitive ladies, there in a moment shone forth a light of hope upon the crusade against war.

If *personal* accidents could, to any serious extent, be amongst the causes of war, then it would become a hopeful duty to combine personal influences that should take an opposite direction. If casual causes could be supposed chiefly to have promoted war, how easy for a nation to arrange permanent and determinate causes against it! The logic of these anecdotes seemed to argue that the whole fountains of war were left to the government of chance and the windiest of levities; that war was not in reality roused into activity by the evil that resides in the human will, but on the contrary, by the simple defect of any will energetic enough or steady enough to merit that name. Multitudes of evils exist in our social system, simply because no steadiness of attention, nor action of combined will, has been converged upon them. War, by the silent evidence of these anecdotes, seemed to lie amongst that class of evils. A new era might be expected to commence in new views upon war; and the evil would be half conquered from the moment that it should be traced to a trivial or a personal origin.

All this was plausible, but false. The anecdotes, and all similar anecdotes, might be true, but were delusive. The logical vice in them was—that they substituted an occasion for a cause. The king's ill temper for instance, acting through the levity and impatience of the minister, might be the *causa occasionalis* of the war, but not its true *causa efficiens*. What *was*? Where do the true permanent causes of war, as distinguished from its proximate excitements, find their lodgment and abiding ground? They lie in the system of national competitions; in the common political system to which all individual nations are unavoidably parties; in the system of public forces distributed amongst a number of adjacent nations, with no internal principle for adjusting the equilibrium of these forces, and no supreme *Areopagus*, or court of appeal, for deciding disputes. Here lies the *matrix* of war, because an eternal *matrix* of disputes lies in a system of interests that are continually the same, and therefore the parents of rivalships too close, that are continually different, and so far the parents of alienation too wide. All war is an instinctive *nisus* for redressing the errors of equilibrium in the relative position of nations amongst nations. Every nation's duty, first, midst, and last, is to itself. No nation can be safe from continual (because insensible) losses of ground, but by continual jealousies, watchings, and ambitious strivings to mend its own position. Civilities and high-bred courtesies pass and ought to pass between nations; that is the graceful drapery which shrouds their natural, fierce, and tiger-like relations to each other. But the glaring eyes, which express this deep and inalienable ferocity, look out at intervals from below these gorgeous draperies; and sad it is to think that at intervals the acts and the temper suitable to those glaring eyes *must* come forward. Mr. Carter was on terms of the most exquisite dissimulation with his lions and tigers; but, as often as he trusted his person amongst them, if, in the midst of infinite politeness exchanged on all sides, he saw a certain portentous expression of mutiny kindling in the eyeball of any discontented tiger, all was lost, unless he came down instantly upon that tiger's skull with a blow from an iron bar, that suggested something like apoplexy. On such terms do nations meet in diplomacy; high consideration for each other does not conceal the basis of enmity on which they rest; not an enmity that belongs to their feelings, but to the necessities of their position. Every nation in negotiating has its right hand upon the hilt of its sword, and at intervals playfully unsheaths a little of its gleaming blade. As things stand at present, war and peace are bound together like the vicissitudes of day and night, of Castor and Pollux. It matters little which bucket of the two is going up at the moment, which going down. Both are steadfastly tied by a system of alternations to a revolving wheel; and a new war as certainly becomes due during the evolutions of a tedious peace, as a new peace may be relied on during the throes of a bloody war, to tranquillize its wounds. Consequently, when the arrogant Louvois carried a war to the credit of his own little account on the national leger of France, this coxcomb well knew that a war was at any rate due about that time. Really, says he, I must find out some little war to exhaust the *surplus* irritability of this person, or he'll be the death of me. But irritable or not irritable, with a puppy for his minister or not, the French king would naturally have been carried headlong into war by the mere system of Europe, within a very few months. So much had the causes of complaint reciprocally accumulated. The account must be cleansed, the court roll of grievances must be purged. With respect to the two English ladies again, it is still more evident that they could not have *caused* a war by pulling caps with each other, since the grounds of every war, what had caused it, and prolonged it, was sure to be angrily reviewed by Parliament at each annual exposition of the Finance Minister's Budget. These ladies, and the French coxcomb, could at the utmost have claimed a distinction—such as that which belonged to a particular Turkish gunner, the captain of a gun at Navarino, viz., that he, by firing the first shot without orders, did (as a matter of fact) let loose and unmuzzle the whole of that dreadful iron hurricane from four nations which instantly followed, but which (be it known to the gunner) could not have been delayed for fifty minutes longer, whether he had fired the unauthorized gun or not.

But now, let me speak to the second proposition of my two-headed thesis, viz., that war *ought* not to be abolished, if such an abolition were even possible. *Prima facie*, it seems a dreadful doctrine to claim a place for war as amongst the evils that are salutary to man; but conscientiously I hold it to be such. I hold with Wordsworth, but for reasons which may or may not be the same, since he has not stated *his*—

> 'That God's most dreaded instrument,
> In working out a pure intent,
> Is man—array'd for mutual slaughter:
> Yea, Carnage is his daughter.'

I am obliged to hold, that supposing so romantic a condition realized as the cessation of war, this change, unless other evils were previously abolished, or neutralized in a way still more romantic to suppose, would not be for the welfare of human nature, but would tend to its rapid degradation.

One, in fact, of the earliest aspects under which this moral necessity for war forces itself upon our notice, is its physical necessity. I mean to say that one of the earliest reasons why war *ought* to exist, is because under any mode of suppressing war, virtually it *will* exist. Banish war as now administered, and it will revolve upon us in a worse shape, that is, in a shape of predatory and ruffian war, more and more licentious, as it enjoys no privilege or sufferance, by the supposition, under the national laws. Will the causes of war die away because war is forbidden? Certainly not; and the only result of the prohibition would be to throw back the exercise of war from national into private and mercenary hands; and *that* is precisely the retrograde or inverse course of civilization; for, in the natural order of civilization, war passes from the hands of knights, barons, insulated cities, into those of the universal community. If, again, it is attempted to put down this lawless *guerilla* state by national forces, then the result will be to have established an interminable warfare of a mixed character, private and public, civil and foreign, infesting the frontiers of all states like a fever, and in substitution for the occasional and intermitting wars of high national police, administered with the dignified responsibility that belongs to supreme rank, with the humanity that belongs to conscious power, and with the diminishing havoc that belongs to increasing skill in the arts of destruction. Even as to this last feature in warfare, which in the war of brigands and *condottieri* would for many reasons instantly decay, no reader can fail to be aware of the marvels effected by the forces of inventive science that run along side by side with the advances of civilization; look back even to the grandest period of the humane Roman warfare, listen to the noblest and most merciful of all Roman captains, saying on the day of Pharsalia, (and saying of necessity,) 'Strike at their faces, cavalry,' —yes, absolutely directing his own troopers to plough up with their sabres the blooming faces of the young Roman nobility; and then pass to a modern field of battle, where all is finished by musquetry and artillery amidst clouds of smoke, no soldier recognizing his own desolations, or the ghastly ruin of his own right arm, so that war, by losing all its brutality, is losing half of its demoralization.

War, so far from ending, because war was forbidden and nationally renounced, on the contrary would transmigrate into a more fearful shape. As things are at present, (and, observe, they are always growing better,) what numbers of noble-minded men, in the persons of our officers (yes, and often of non-commissioned officers,) do we British, for example, disperse over battle-fields, that could not dishonor their glorious uniform by any countenance to an act of cruelty! They are eyes delegated from the charities of our domestic life, to overlook and curb the license of war. I remember, in Xenophon, some passage where he describes a class of Persian gentlemen, who were called the *ophthalmoi*, or *eyes* of the king; but for a very different purpose. These British officers may be called the *opthalmoi*, or eyes of our Sovereign Lady, that into every corner of the battle carry their scrutiny, lest any cruelty should be committed on the helpless, or any advantage taken of a dying enemy. But mark, such officers would be rare in the irregular troops succeeding to the official armies. And through this channel, amongst others, war, when cried down by act of Parliament, and precisely *because* it was cried down, would become more perilously effective for the degradation of human nature. Being itself dishonored, war would become the more effective as an instrument for the dishonoring of its agents. However, at length, we will suppose the impossible problem solved—war, we will assume, is at last put down.

At length there is no more war. Though by the way, let me whisper in your ear, (supposing you to be a Christian,) this would be a prelibation drawn prematurely from the cup of millennial happiness; and, strictly speaking, there is no great homage to religion, even thus far—in figuring *that* to be the purchase of man for himself, and through his own efforts, which is viewed by Scripture as a glory removed to the infinite and starry distance of a millennium, and as the *teleutaion epigeinaema*, the last crowning attainment of Christian truth, no longer *militant* on earth. Christianity it is, but Christianity when *triumphant*, and no longer in conflict with adverse, or thwarting, or limiting influences, which only can be equal to a revolution so mighty. But all this, for the sake of pursuing the assumption, let us agree to waive. In reality, there are two separate stations taken up by the war denouncers. One class hold, that an influence derived from political economy is quite equal to the flying leap by which man is to clear this unfathomable gulph of war, and to land his race for ever on the opposite shore of a self-sustaining peace. Simply, the contemplation of national debts, (as a burthen which never would have existed without war,) and a computation of the waste, havoc, unproductive labor, &c., attached to any single campaign—these, they imagine, might suffice, *per se*, for the extinction of war. But the other class cannot go along with a speculation so infirm. Reasons there are, in the opposite scale, tempting man into war,—which are far mightier than any motives addressed to his self-interest. Even straining her energies to the utmost, they regard all policy of the *purse* as adequate: anything short of religion, they are satisfied, must be incommensurate to a result so vast.

I myself certainly agree with this last class; but upon this arises a delusion, which I shall have some trouble in making the reader understand: and of this I am confident-that a majority, perhaps, in every given amount of readers, will share in the delusion; will part from me in the persuasion that the error I attempt to expose is no error at all, but that it is myself who am in the wrong. The delusion which I challenge as such, respects the very meaning and value of a sacrifice made to Christianity. What is it? what do we properly mean, by a concession or a sacrifice made to a spiritual power, such as Christianity? If a king and his people, impressed by the unchristian character of war, were to say, in some solemn act—'We, the parties undersigned, for the reasons stated in the body of this document, proclaim to all nations, that from and after Midsummer eve of the year 1850, this being the eve of St. John the Baptist, (who was the herald of Christ,) we will no more prosecute any interest of ours, unless the one sole interest of national defence, by means of war,—and this sacrifice we make as a concession and act of homage to Christianity,—would *that* vow, I ask, sincerely offered, and steadily observed, really be a sacrifice made to Christianity? Not at all. A sacrifice, that was truly such, to a spiritual religion, must be a sacrifice not verbally (though sincerely) dedicating itself to the religion, but a sacrifice wrought and accomplished by that religion, through and by its own spirit. Midsummer eve of 1850 could clearly make no spiritual change in the king or his people—such they would be on the morning after St. John's day, as on the morning before it—*i. e.*, filled with all elements (though possibly undeveloped) of strife, feud, pernicious ambition.

The delusion, therefore, which I charge upon this religious class of war denouncers is, that whilst they see and recognize this infinite imperfection of any influence which Christianity yet exercises upon the world, they nevertheless rely upon that acknowledged shadow for the accomplishment of what would, in such circumstances, be a real miracle; they rely upon that shadow, as truly and entirely as if it were already that substance which, in a vast revolution of ages, it will finally become. And they rely upon this mockery in *two* senses; first, for the *endurance* of the frail human resolution that would thaw in an hour before a great outrage, or provocation suited to the nobler infirmities of man. Secondly, which is the point I mainly aim at, assuming, for a moment, that the resolution *could* endure, amongst all mankind, we are all equally convinced, that an evil so vast is not likely to be checked or controlled, except by some very extraordinary power. Well, where *is* it? Show me that power. I know of none but Christianity. *There*, undoubtedly, is hope. But, in order that the hope may become rational, the power must become practical. And practical it is not in the extent required, until this Christianity, from being dimly appreciated by a section [Footnote *What* section, if you please? I, for my part, do not agree with those that geographically degrade Christianity as occupying but a trifle on the area of our earth. Mark this; all Eastern populations have dwindled upon better acquaintance. Persia that *ought* to have, at least, two hundred and fifty millions of people, and *would* have them under English government, and once was supposed to have at least one hundred millions, how many millions has she? *Eight!* This was ascertained by Napoleon's emissary in 1808, General Gardanne. Afghanistan has very little more, though some falsely count fourteen millions. There go two vast chambers of Mahometanism; not twenty millions between them. Hindostan may *really* have one hundred and twenty millions claimed for her. As to the Burman Empire, I, nor anybody else knows the truth. But, as to China, I have never for a moment been moved by those ridiculous estimates of the flowery people, which our simple countrymen copy. Instead of three hundred and fifty millions, a third of the human race upon the most exaggerated estimate, read eighty or one hundred millions at most. Africa, as it regards religion, counts for a cipher. Europe, America, and the half of Asia, as to space, are Christian. Consequently, the total *facit*, as regards Christianity, is not what many amiable infidels make it to be. My dears, your wish was father to that thought.] of this world, shall have been the law that overrides the whole. That consummation is not immeasurably distant. Even now, from considerations connected with China, with New Zealand, Borneo, Australia, we may say, that already the fields are white for harvest. But alas! the interval is brief between Christianity small, and Christianity great, as regards space or terraqueous importance, compared with that interval which separates Christianity formally professed, from Christianity thankfully acknowledged by universal man in beauty and power.

Here, therefore, is one spoke in the wheel for so vast a change as war dethroned, viz., that you see no cause, though you should travel round the whole horizon, adequate to so prodigious an effect. What could do it? Why, Christianity could do it. Aye, true; but man disarms Christianity. And no mock Christianity, no lip homage to Christianity, will answer.

But is war, then, to go on for ever? Are we never to improve? Are nations to conduct their intercourse eternally under the secret understanding that an unchristian solution of all irreconcileable feuds stands in the rear as the ultimate appeal? I answer that war, going on even for ever, may still be for ever amending its modes and its results upon human happiness; secondly, that we not only are under no fatal arrest in our process of improvement, but that, as regards war, history shows how steadily we *have* been improving; and, thirdly, that although war may be irreversible as the last resource, this last resource may constantly be retiring further into the rear. Let us speak to this last point. War is the last resource only, because other and more intellectual resources for solving disputes are not available. And *why* are they not? Simply, because the knowledge, and the logic, which ultimately will govern the case, and the very circumstances of the case itself in its details, as the basis on which this knowledge and logic are to operate, happen not to have been sufficiently developed. A code of law is not a spasmodic effort of gigantic talent in any one man or any one generation; it is a slow growth of accidents and occasions expanding with civilization; dependent upon time as a multiform element in its development; and presupposing often a concurrent growth of *analogous* cases towards the completion of its system. For instance, the law which regulates the rights of shipping, seafaring men, and maritime commerce—how slow was its development! Before such works as the *Consolato del Mare* had been matured, how wide must have been the experience, and how slow its accumulation! During that long period of infancy for law, how many must have been the openings for ignorant and unintentional injustice! How differently, again, will the several parties to any transaction construe the rights of the case! Discussion, without rules for guiding it, will but embitter the dispute. And in the absence of all guidance from the intellect, gradually weaving a *common* standard of international appeal, it is clear that nations *must* fight, and *ought* to fight. Not being convinced, it is base to pretend that you *are* convinced; and failing to be convinced by your neighbor's arguments, you confess yourself a poltroon (and moreover you *invite* injuries from every neighbor) if you pocket your wrongs. The only course in such a case is to thump your neighbor, and to thump him soundly for the present. This treatment is very serviceable to your neighbor's optics; he sees things in a new light after a sufficient course of so distressing a regimen. But mark, even in this case, war has no tendency to propagate war, but tends to the very opposite result. To thump is as costly, and in other ways as painful, as to *be* thumped. The evil to both sides arises in an undeveloped state of law. If rights were defined by a well considered code growing out of long experience, each party sees that this scourge of war would continually tend to limit itself. Consequently the very necessity of war becomes the strongest invitation to that system of judicial logic which forms its sole limitation. But all war whatsoever stands in these circumstances. It follows that all war whatever, unless on the brutal principle of a Spartan warfare, that made war its own sufficient object and self-justification, operates as a perpetual bounty offered to men upon the investigation and final adjudication of those disputed cases through which war prospers. Hence it is, viz., because the true boundaries of reciprocal rights are for ever ascertaining themselves more clearly, that war is growing less frequent. The fields open to injustice (which originally from pure ignorance are so vast) continually (through deeper and more expansive surveys by man's intellect—searching—reflecting—comparing) are narrowing themselves; narrowing themselves in this sense, that all nations under a common centre of religious civilization, as Christendom suppose, or Islamism, would not fight—no, and would not (by the national sense of wrong and right) be permitted to fight—in a cause *confessedly* condemned by equity as now developed. The causes of war that still remain, are causes on which international law is silent—that large arrear of cases as yet unsettled; or else they are cases in which though law speaks with an authentic voice, it speaks in vain, because the circumstances are doubtful; so that, if the law is fixed as a lamp nailed to a wall, yet the *incidence* of the law on the particular circumstances, becomes as doubtful as the light of the lamp upon objects that are capriciously moving. We see all this illustrated in a class of cases that powerfully illustrate the good and the bad in war, the why and the wherefore, as likewise the why *not*, and therefore I presume the wherefore *not*; and this class of cases belongs to the *lex vicinitatis*. In the Roman law this section makes a great figure. And speaking accurately, it makes a greater in our own. But the reason why this *law of neighborhood* seems to fill so much smaller a section in ours, is because in English law, being *positively* a longer section, *negatively* to the whole compass of our law, it is less. The Roman law would have paved a road to the moon. And what is *that* expressed in time? Let us see: a railway train, worked at the speed of the Great Western Express, accomplishes easily a thousand miles in twenty-four hours; consequently in two hundred and forty days or eight months it would run into the moon with its buffers, and break up the quarters of that Robinson Crusoe who (and without any Friday) is the only policeman that parades that little pensive appendage or tender to our fuming engine of an earth. But the English law—oh frightful reader, don't even think of such a question as its relation in space and time to the Roman law. That it would stretch to the fixed stars is plain, but to which of them,—don't now, dear persecuting reader, unsettle our brains by asking. Enough it is that both in Roman and English law the rights of neighborhood are past measuring. Has a man a right to play the German flute, where the partitions are slender, all day long in the house adjoining to yours? Or, supposing a beneficent jury (beneficent to *him*) finds this to be no legal nuisance, has he a right to play it ill? Or, because juries, when tipsy, will wink at anything, does the privilege extend to the jew's-harp? to the poker and tongs? to the marrowbones and cleavers? Or, without ranging through the whole of the *Spectator's* culinary music, will the bagpipes be found within benefit of jury law? *War to the knife* I say, before we'll submit to *that*. And if the law won't protect us against it, then we'll turn rebels.

Now this law of neighborhood, this *lex vicinitatis*, amongst the Romans, righted itself and settled itself, as amongst ourselves it continues to do, by means of actions or legal suits. If a man poisons us with smoke, we compel him by an action to eat his own smoke, or (if he chooses) to make his chimneys eat it. Here you see is a transmuted war; in a barbarous state, fire and sword would have avenged this invasion of smoke; but amongst civilized men, paper bullets in the form of *Qui tam* and *Scire facias*, beat off the enemy. And on the same principle, exactly as the law of international rights clears up its dark places, war gradually narrows its grounds, and the *jus gentium* defines itself through national attorneys, *i. e.*, diplomatists.

For instance, now I have myself seen a case where a man cultivating a flower-garden, and distressed for some deliverance from his rubbish of dead leaves, litter, straw, stones, took the desperate resolution of projecting the whole upon his neighbor's flower-garden. I, a chance spectator of the outrage, knew too much of this world to lodge any protest against it, on the principle of mere abstract justice; so it would have passed unnoticed, but for the accident that his injured neighbor unexpectedly raised up his head above the dividing wall, and reproached the aggressor with his unprincipled conduct. This aggressor, adding evil to evil, suggested as the natural remedy for his own wrong, that the sufferer should pass the nuisance onwards to the garden next beyond him; from which it might be posted forward on the same principle. The aggrieved man, however, preferred passing it back, without any discount to the original proprietor. Here now, is a ripe case, a *causa teterrima*, for war between the parties, and for a national war had the parties been nations. In fact, the very same injury, in a more aggravated shape, is perpetrated from time to time by Jersey upon ourselves, and would, upon a larger scale, right itself by war. Convicts are costly to maintain; and Jersey, whose national revenue is limited, being too well aware of this, does us the favor to land upon the coasts of Hampshire, Dorset, &c., all the criminals whom she cannot summarily send back to self-support, at each jail-delivery. 'What are we to do in England?' is the natural question propounded by the injured scoundrels, when taking leave of their Jersey escort. 'Anything you please,' is the answer: 'rise if you can, to be dukes: only never come back hither; since, dukes or *no* dukes, to the rest of Christendom, to *us* of the Channel Islands you will always be transported felons.' There is therefore a good right of action, *i.e.*, a good ground of war, against Jersey, on the part of Great Britain, since, besides the atrocious injury inflicted, this unprincipled little island has the audacity to regard our England, (all Europe looking on,) as existing only for the purposes of a sewer or cess-pool to receive *her* impurities. Some time back I remember a Scottish newspaper holding up the case as a newly discovered horror in the social system. But, in a quiet way Jersey has always been engaged in this branch of exportation, and rarely fails to 'run' a cargo of rogues upon our shore, once or so in the season. What amuses one besides, in this Scottish denunciation of the villany, is, that Scotland [Footnote: To banish them 'forth of the kingdom,' was the *euphuismus*; but the reality understood was—to carry the knaves, like foxes in a bag, to the English soil, and there unbag them for English use.] of old, pursued the very same mode of jail-delivery as to knaves that were not thought ripe enough for hanging: she carted them to the English border, unchained them, and hurried them adrift into the wilderness, saying—Now, boys, shift for yourselves, and henceforth plunder none but Englishmen.

What I deduce from all this is, that as the feuds arising between individuals under the relation of neighbors, are so far from tending to a hostile result, that, on the contrary, as coming under a rule of law already ascertained, or furnishing the basis for a new rule, they gradually tighten the cords which exclude all opening for quarrel; not otherwise is the result, and therefore the usefulness, of war amongst nations. All the causes of war, the occasions upon which it is likely to arise, the true and the ostensible motives, are gradually evolved, are examined, searched, valued, by publicists; and by such means, in the further progress of men, a comprehensive law of nations will finally be accumulated, not such as now passes for international law, (a worthless code that *has* no weight in the practice of nations, nor deserves any,) but one which will exhaust the great body of cases under which wars have arisen under the Christian era, and gradually collect a public opinion of Christendom upon the nature of each particular case. The causes that *have* existed for war are the causes that *will* exist; or, at least, they are the same under modifications that will simply vary the rule, as our law cases in the courts are every day circumstantiating the particular statute concerned. At this stage of advance, and when a true European opinion has been created, a 'sensus communis,' or community of feeling on the main classifications of wars, it will become possible to erect a real Areopagus, or central congress for all Christendom, not with any commission to suppress wars,—a policy which would neutralize itself by reacting as a fresh cause of war, since high-spirited nations would arm for the purpose of resisting such decrees; but with the purpose and the effect of oftentimes healing local or momentary animosities, and also by publishing the opinion of Europe, assembled in council, with the effect of taking away the shadow of dishonor from the act of retiring from war. Not to mention that the mere delay, involved in the waiting for the solemn opinion of congress, would always be friendly to pacific councils. But *would* the belligerents wait? That concession might be secured by general exchange of treaties, in the same way that the cooperation of so many nations has been secured to the suppression of the trade in slaves. And one thing is clear, that when all the causes of war, involving *manifest* injustice, are banished by the force of European opinion, focally converged upon the subject, the range of war will be prodigiously circumscribed. The costliness of war, which, for various reasons has been continually increasing since the feudal period, will operate as another limitation upon its field, concurring powerfully with the public declaration from a council of collective Christendom.

There is, besides, a distinct and separate cause of war, more fatal to the possibilities of peace in Europe than open injustice; and this cause being certainly in the hands of nations to deal with as they please, there is a tolerable certainty that a congress *sincerely* pacific would cut it up by the roots. It is a cause noticed by Kant in his Essay on Perpetual Peace, and with great sagacity, though otherwise that little work is not free from visionary self-delusions: and this cause lies in the diplomacy of Europe. Treaties of peace are so constructed, as almost always to sow the seeds of future wars. This seems to the inexperienced reader a matter of carelessness or laxity in the choice of expression; and sometimes it may have been so; but more often it has been done under the secret dictation of powerful courts—making peaces only as truces, anxious only for time to nurse their energies, and to keep open some plausible call for war. This is not only amongst the most extensive causes of war, but the very worst: because it gives a colorable air of justice, and almost of necessity to a war, which is, in fact, the most outrageously unjust, as being derived from a pretext silently prepared in former years, with mere subtlety of malice: it is a war growing out of occasions, forged beforehand, lest no occasions should spontaneously arise. Now, this cause of war could and would be healed by a congress, and through an easy reform in European diplomacy.[Footnote:

One great *nidus* of this insidious preparation for war under the very masque of peace, which Kant, from brevity, has failed to particularize, lies in the neglecting to make any provision for cases that are likely enough to arise. A, B, C, D, are all equally possible, but the treaty provides a specific course of action only for A, suppose. Then upon B or C arising, the high contracting parties, though desperately and equally pacific, find themselves committed to war actually by a treaty of lasting peace. Their pacific majesties sigh, and say—Alas! that it should be so, but really fight we must, for what says the treaty?]

It is the strongest confirmation of the power inherent in growing civilization, to amend war, and to narrow the field of war, if we look back for the records of the changes in this direction which have already arisen in generations before our own.

The most careless reviewer of history can hardly fail to read a rude outline of progress made by men in the rights, and consequently in the duties of war through the last twenty-five centuries. It is a happy circumstance for man—that oftentimes he is led by pure selfishness into reforms, the very same as high principle would have prompted; and in the next stage of his advance, when once habituated to an improved code of usages, he begins to find a gratification to his sensibilities, (partly luxurious sensibilities, but partly moral,) in what originally had been a mere movement of self-interest. Then comes a third stage, in which having thoroughly reconciled himself to a better order of things, and made it even necessary to his own comfort, at length he begins in his reflecting moments to perceive a moral beauty and a fitness in arrangements that had emanated from accidents of convenience, so that finally he generates a sublime pleasure of conscientiousness out of that which originally commenced in the meanest forms of mercenary convenience. A Roman lady of rank, out of mere voluptuous regard to her own comfort, revolted from the harsh clamors of eternal chastisements inflicted on her numerous slaves; she forbade them; the grateful slaves showed their love for her; gradually and unintentionally she trained her feelings, when thus liberated from a continual temptation to the sympathies with cruelty, into a demand for gentler and purer excitement. Her purpose had been one of luxury; but, by the benignity of nature still watching for ennobling opportunities, the actual result was a development given to the higher capacities of her heart. In the same way, when the brutal right (and in many circumstances the brutal duty) of inflicting death upon prisoners taken in battle, had exchanged itself for the profits of ransom or slavery, this relaxation of ferocity (though commencing in selfishness) gradually exalted itself into a habit of mildness, and some dim perception of a sanctity in human life. The very vice of avarice ministered to the purification of barbarism; and the very evil of slavery in its earliest form was applied to the mitigation of another evil—war conducted in the spirit of piratical outrage. The commercial instincts of men having worked one set of changes in war, a second set of changes was prompted by instincts derived from the arts of ornament and pomp. Splendor of arms, of banners, of equipages, of ceremonies, and the elaborate forms of intercourse with enemies through conferences, armistices, treaties of peace, &c., having tamed the savagery of war into connection with modes of intellectual grandeur, and with the endless restraints of superstition or scrupulous religion,—a permanent light of civilization began to steal over the bloody shambles of buccaneering warfare. Other modes of harmonizing influences arose more directly from the bosom of war itself. Gradually the mere practice of war, and the culture of war though merely viewed as a rude trade of bloodshed, ripened into an intellectual art. Were it merely with a view to more effectual carnage, this art (however simple and gross at first) opened at length into wide scientific arts, into strategies, into tactics, into castrametation, into poliorcetics, and all the processes through which the first rude efforts of martial cunning finally connect themselves with the exquisite resources of science. War, being a game in which each side forces the other into the instant adoption of all improvements through the mere necessities of self-preservation, became continually more intellectual.

It is interesting to observe the steps by which, were it only through impulses of self-conservation, and when searching with a view to more effectual destructiveness, war did and must refine itself from a horrid trade of butchery into a magnificent and enlightened science. Starting from no higher impulse or question than how to cut throats most rapidly, most safely, and on the largest scale, it has issued even at our own stage of advance into a science, magnificent, oftentimes ennobling, and cleansed from all horrors except those which (not being within man's power utterly to divorce from it) no longer stand out as reproaches to his humanity.

Meantime a more circumstantial review of war, in relation to its motives and the causes assigned for its justification, would expose a series of changes greater perhaps than the reader is aware of. Such a review, which would too much lengthen a single paper, may or may not form the subject of a second. And I will content myself with saying, as a closing remark, that this review will detect a principle of steady advance in the purification and elevation of war—such as must offer hope to those who believe in the possibility of its absolute extermination, and must offer consolation to those who (like myself) deny it.

THE LAST DAYS OF IMMANUEL KANT

I take it for granted that every person of education will acknowledge some interest in the personal history of Immanuel Kant. A great man, though in an unpopular path, must always be an object of liberal curiosity. To suppose a reader thoroughly indifferent to Kant, is to suppose him thoroughly unintellectual; and, therefore, though in reality he should happen *not* to regard him with interest, it is one of the fictions of courtesy to presume that he does. On this principle I make no apology to the reader for detaining him upon a short sketch of Kant's life and domestic habits, drawn from the authentic records of his friends and pupils. It is true, that, without any illiberality on the part of the public in this country, the *works* of Kant are not regarded with the same interest which has gathered about his *name*; and this may be attributed to three causes—first, to the language in which they are written; secondly, to the supposed obscurity of the philosophy which they teach, whether intrinsic or due to Kant's particular mode of expounding it; thirdly, to the unpopularity of all speculative philosophy, no matter how treated, in a country where the structure and tendency of society impress upon the whole activities of the nation a direction exclusively practical. But, whatever may be the immediate fortunes of his writings, no man of enlightened curiosity will regard the author himself without something of a profounder interest. Measured by one test of power, viz., by the number of books written directly for or against himself, to say nothing of those which he has indirectly modified, there is no philosophic writer whatsoever, if we except Aristotle, who can pretend to approach Kant in the extent of the influence which he has exercised over the minds of men. Such being his claims upon our notice, I repeat that it is no more than a reasonable act of respect to the reader—to presume in him so much interest about Kant as will justify a sketch of his life.

Immanuel Kant, [Footnote: By the paternal side, the family of Kant was of Scotch derivation; and hence it is that the name was written by Kant the father—*Cant*, that being a Scotch name, and still to be found in Scotland. But Immanuel, though he always cherished his Scotch descent, substituted a *K* for a *C*, in order to adapt it better to the analogies of the German language.] the second of six children, was born at Königsberg, in Prussia, a city at that time containing about fifty thousand inhabitants, on the 22d of

April, 1724. His parents were people of humble rank, and not rich even for their own station, but able (with some assistance from a near relative, and a trifle in addition from a gentleman, who esteemed them for their piety and domestic virtues,) to give their son Immanuel a liberal education. He was sent when a child to a charity school; and, in the year 1732, removed to the Royal (or Frederician) Academy. Here he studied the Greek and Latin classics, and formed an intimacy with one of his schoolfellows, David Ruhnken, (afterwards so well known to scholars under his Latin name of Ruhn-kenius,) which lasted until the death of the latter. In 1737, Kant lost his mother, a woman of excellent character, and of accomplishments and knowledge beyond her rank, who contributed to the future eminence of her illustrious son by the direction which she gave to his youthful thoughts, and by the elevated morals to which she trained him. Kant never spoke of her to the end of his life without the utmost tenderness, and acknowledgment of his great obligations to her maternal care. In 1740, at Michælmas, he entered the University of Königsberg. In 1746, when about twenty-two years old, he printed his first work, upon a question partly mathematical and partly philosophic, viz., the valuation of living forces. The question had been first moved by Leibnitz, in opposition to the Cartesians, and was here finally settled, after having occupied most of the great mathematicians of Europe for more than half a century. It was dedicated to the King of Prussia, but never reached him—having, in fact, never been published. [Footnote: To this circumstance we must attribute its being so little known amongst the philosophers and mathematicians of foreign countries, and also the fact that D'Alembert, whose philosophy was miserably below his mathematics, many years afterwards still continued to represent the dispute as a verbal one.] From this time until 1770, he supported himself as a private tutor in different families, or by giving private lectures in Königsberg, especially to military men on the art of fortification. In 1770, he was appointed to the Chair of Mathematics, which he exchanged soon after for that of Logic and Metaphysics. On this occasion, he delivered an inaugural disputation—[*De Mundi Sensibilis atque Intelligibilis Forma et Principiis*]—which is remarkable for containing the first germs of the Transcendental Philosophy. In 1781, he published his great work, the *Critik der Reinen Vernunft*, or *Investigation of the Pure Reason*. On February 12, 1804, he died.

These are the great epochs of Kant's life. But his was a life remarkable not so much for its incidents, as for the purity and philosophic dignity of its daily tenor; and of this the best impression will be obtained from Wasianski's account of his last years, checked and supported by the collateral testimonies of Jachmann, Rink, Borowski, and other biographers. We see him here struggling with the misery of decaying faculties, and with the pain, depression, and agitation of two different complaints, one affecting his stomach, and the other his head; over all which the benignity and nobility of his mind are seen victoriously eminent to the last. The principal defect of this and all other memoirs of Kant is, that they report too little of his conversation and opinions. And perhaps the reader will be disposed to complain, that some of the notices are too minute and circumstantial, so as to be at one time undignified, and at another unfeeling. As to the first objection, it may be answered, that biographical gossip of this sort, and ungentlemanly scrutiny into a man's private life, though not what a man of honor would choose to write, may be read without blame; and, where a great man is the subject, sometimes with advantage. With respect to the other objection, I know not how to excuse Mr. Wasianski for kneeling at the bed-side of his dying friend, to record, with the accuracy of a short-hand reporter, the last flutter of his pulse and the struggles of expiring nature, except by supposing that the idea of Kant, as a person belonging to all ages, in his mind transcended and extinguished the ordinary restraints of human sensibility, and that, under this impression, he gave *that* to his sense of a public duty which, it may be hoped, he would willingly have declined on the impulse of his private affections.

The following paper on The Last Days of Kant, is gathered from the German of Wasianski, Jachmann, Borowski, and others.

My knowledge of Professor Kant began long before the period to which this little memorial of him chiefly refers. In the year 1773, or 1774, I cannot exactly remember which, I attended his lectures. Afterwards, I acted as his amanuensis; and in that office was naturally brought into a closer connection with him than any other of his pupils; so that, without any request on my part, he granted me a general privilege of free admission to his class-room. In 1780 I took orders, and withdrew myself from all connection with the university. I still continued, however, to reside in Königsberg; but wholly forgotten, or wholly unnoticed at least, by Kant. Ten years afterwards, (that is to say, in 1790,) I met him by accident at a party given on occasion of the marriage of one of the professors. At table, Kant distributed his conversation and attentions pretty generally; but after the entertainment, when the company broke up into parties, he came and seated himself very obligingly by my side. I was at that time a florist—an amateur, I mean, from the passion I had for flowers; upon learning which, he talked of my favorite pursuit, and with very extensive information. In the course of our conversation, I was surprised to find that he was perfectly acquainted with all the circumstances of my situation. He reminded me of our previous connection; expressed his satisfaction at finding that I was happy; and was so good as to desire that, if my engagements allowed me,

I would now and then come and dine with him. Soon after this, he rose to take his leave; and, as our road lay the same way, he proposed to me that I should accompany him home. I did so, and received an invitation for the next week, with a general invitation for every week after, and permission to name my own day. At first I was unable to explain the distinction with which Kant had treated me; and I conjectured that some obliging friend had spoken of me in his hearing, somewhat more advantageously than I could pretend to deserve; but more intimate experience has convinced me that he was in the habit of making continual inquiries after the welfare of his former pupils, and was heartily rejoiced to hear of their prosperity. So that it appeared I was wrong in thinking he had forgotten me.

This revival of my intimacy with Professor Kant, coincided pretty nearly, in point of time, with a complete change in his domestic arrangements. Up to this period it had been his custom to eat at a *table d'hôte*. But he now began to keep house himself, and every day invited two friends to dine with him, and upon any little festival from five to eight; for he was a punctual observer of Lord Chesterfield's rule—that his dinner party, himself included, should not fall below the number of the Graces—nor exceed that of the Muses. In the whole economy of his household arrangements, and especially of his dinner parties, there was something peculiar and amusingly opposed to the usual conventional restraints of society; not, however, that there was any neglect of decorum, such as sometimes occurs in houses where there are no ladies to impress a better tone upon the manners. The invariable routine was this: The moment that dinner was ready, Lampe, the professor's old footman, stepped into the study with a certain measured air, and announced it. This summons was obeyed at the pace of double quick time—Kant talking all the way to the eating-room about the state of the weather [Footnote: His reason for which was, that he considered the weather one of the principal forces which act upon the health; and his own frame was exquisitely sensible to all atmospheric influences.]—a subject which he usually pursued during the earlier part of the dinner. Graver themes, such as the political events of the day, were never introduced before dinner, or at all in his study. The moment that Kant had taken his seat, and unfolded his napkin, he opened the business of dinner with a particular formula—'*Now, then, gentlemen!*' and the tone and air with which he uttered these words, proclaimed, in a way which nobody could mistake, relaxation from the toils of the morning, and determinate abandonment of himself to social enjoyment. The table was hospitably spread; three dishes, wine, &c., with a small second course, composed the dinner. Every person helped himself; and all delays of ceremony were so disagreeable to Kant, that he seldom failed to express his displeasure with anything of that sort, though not angrily. He was displeased also if people ate little; and treated it as affectation. The first man to help himself was in his eyes the politest guest; for so much the sooner came his own turn. For this hatred of delay, Kant had a special excuse, having always worked hard from an early hour in the morning, and eaten nothing until dinner. Hence it was, that in the latter period of his life, though less perhaps from actual hunger than from some uneasy sensation of habit or periodical irritation of stomach, he could hardly wait with patience for the arrival of the last person invited.

There was no friend of Kant's but considered the day on which he was to dine with him as a day of pleasure. Without giving himself the air of an instructor, Kant really was so in the very highest degree. The whole entertainment was seasoned with the overflow of his enlightened mind, poured out naturally and unaffectedly upon every topic, as the chances of conversation suggested it; and the time flew rapidly away, from one o'clock to four, five, or even later, profitably and delightfully. Kant tolerated no *calms*, which was the name he gave to the momentary pauses in conversation, or periods when its animation languished. Some means or other he always devised for restoring its tone of interest, in which he was much assisted by the tact with which he drew from every guest his peculiar tastes, or the particular direction of his pursuits; and on these, be they what they might, he was never unprepared to speak with knowledge, and the interest of an original observer. The local affairs of Königsberg must have been interesting indeed, before they could be allowed to occupy the attention at *his* table. And, what may seem still more singular, it was rarely or never that he directed the conversation to any branch of the philosophy founded by himself. Indeed he was perfectly free from the fault which besets so many *savans* and *literati*, of intolerance towards those whose pursuits had disqualified them for any particular sympathy with his own. His style of conversation was popular in the highest degree, and unscholastic; so much so, that any stranger who should have studied his works, and been unacquainted with his person, would have found it difficult to believe, that in this delightful companion he saw the profound author of the Transcendental Philosophy.

The subjects of conversation at Kant's table were drawn chiefly from natural philosophy, chemistry, meteorology, natural history, and above all, from politics. The news of the day, as reported in the public journals, was discussed with a peculiar vigilance of examination. With regard to any narrative that wanted dates of time and place, however otherwise plausible, he was uniformly an inexorable sceptic, and held it unworthy of repetition. So keen was his penetration into the interior of political events, and the secret policy under which they moved, that he talked rather with the authority of a diplomatic person who had access to cabinet intelligence, than as a simple spectator of the great scenes which were unfolding in Europe. At the time of the French Revolution, he threw out many conjectures, and what were then accounted paradoxical anticipations, especially in regard to military operations, which were as punctually fulfilled as his own memorable conjecture in regard to the hiatus in the planetary system between Mars and Jupiter,[Footnote: To which the author should have added—and in regard to the hiatus between the planetary and cometary systems, which was pointed out by Kant several years before his conjecture was established by the good telescope of Dr. Herschel. Vesta and Juno, further confirmations of Kant's conjecture, were discovered in June 1804, when Wasianski wrote.] the entire confirmation of which he lived to witness on the discovery of Ceres by Piazzi, in Palermo, and of Pallas, by Dr. Olbers, at Bremen. These two discoveries, by the way, impressed him much; and they furnished a topic on which he always talked with pleasure; though, according to his usual modesty, he never said a word of his own sagacity in having upon *à priori* grounds shown the probability of such discoveries many years before.

It was not only in the character of a companion that Kant shone, but also as a most courteous and liberal host, who had no greater pleasure than in seeing his guests happy and jovial, and rising with exhilarated spirits from the mixed pleasures—intellectual and liberally sensual—of his Platonic banquets. Chiefly, perhaps, with a view to the sustaining of this tone of genial hilarity, he showed himself somewhat of an artist in the composition of his dinner parties. Two rules there were which he obviously observed, and I may say invariably: the first was, that the company should be miscellaneous; this for the sake of securing sufficient variety to the conversation: and accordingly his parties presented as much variety as the world of Königsberg afforded, being drawn from all the modes of life, men in office, professors, physicians, clergymen, and enlightened merchants. His second rule was, to have a due balance of *young* men, frequently of *very* young men, selected from the students of the university, in order to impress a movement of gaiety and juvenile playfulness on the conversation; an additional motive for which, as I have reason to believe, was, that in this way he withdrew his mind from the sadness which sometimes overshadowed it, for the early deaths of some young friends whom he loved.

And this leads me to mention a singular feature in Kant's way of expressing his sympathy with his friends in sickness. So long as the danger was imminent, he testified a restless anxiety, made perpetual inquiries, waited with patience for the crisis, and sometimes could not pursue his customary labors from agitation of mind. But no sooner was the patient's death announced, than he recovered his composure, and assumed an air of stern tranquillity—almost of indifference. The reason was, that he viewed life in general, and therefore, that particular affection of life which we call sickness, as a state of oscillation and perpetual change, between which and the fluctuating sympathies of hope and fear, there was a natural proportion that justified them to the reason; whereas death, as a permanent state that admitted of no *more* or *less*, that terminated all anxiety, and for ever extinguished the agitation of suspense, he would not allow to be fitted to any state of feeling, but one of the same enduring and unchanging character. However, all this philosophic heroism gave way on one occasion; for many persons will remember the tumultuous grief which he manifested upon the death of Mr. Ehrenboth, a young man of very fine understanding and extensive attainments, for whom he had the greatest affection. And naturally it happened, in so long a life as his, in spite of his provident rule for selecting his social companions as much as possible amongst the young, that he had to mourn for many a heavy loss that could never be supplied to him.

To return, however, to the course of his day, immediately after the termination of his dinner party, Kant walked out for exercise; but on this occasion he never took any companion, partly, perhaps, because he thought it right, after so much convivial and colloquial relaxation, to pursue his meditations,[Footnote: Mr. Wasianski is wrong. To pursue his meditations under these circumstances, might perhaps be an inclination of Kant's to which he yielded, but not one which he would justify or erect into a maxim. He disapproved of eating alone, or *solipsismus convictorii*, as he calls it, on the principle, that a man would be apt, if not called off by the business and pleasure of a social party, to think too much or too closely, an exercise which he considered very injurious to the stomach during the first process of digestion. On the same principle he disapproved of walking or riding alone; the double exercise of thinking and bodily agitation, carried on at the same time, being likely, as he conceived, to press too hard upon the stomach.] and partly (as I happen to know) for a very peculiar reason, viz., that he wished to breathe exclusively through his nostrils, which he could not do if he were obliged continually to open his mouth in conversation. His reason for this was, that the atmospheric air, being thus carried round by a longer circuit, and reaching the lungs, therefore, in a state of less rawness, and at a temperature somewhat higher, would be less apt to irritate them. By a steady perseverance in this practice, which he constantly recommended to his friends, he flattered himself with a long immunity from coughs, colds, hoarseness, and every mode of defluxion; and the fact really was, that these troublesome affections attacked him very rarely. Indeed I myself, by only occasionally adopting his rule, have found my chest not so liable as formerly to such attacks.

At six o'clock he sat down to his library table, which was a plain ordinary piece of furniture, and read till dusk. During this period of dubious light, so friendly to thought, he rested in tranquil meditation on what he had been reading, provided the book were worth it; if not, he sketched his lecture for the next day, or some part of any book he might then be composing. During this state of repose he took his station winter and summer by the stove, looking through the window at the old tower of Lobenicht; not that he could be said properly to see it, but the tower rested upon his eye,— obscurely, or but half revealed to his consciousness. No words seemed forcible enough to express his sense of the gratification which he derived from this old tower, when seen under these circumstances of twilight and quiet reverie. The sequel, indeed, showed how important it was to his comfort; for at length some poplars in a neighboring garden shot up to such a height as to obscure the tower, upon which Kant became very uneasy and restless, and at length found himself positively unable to pursue his evening meditations. Fortunately, the proprietor of the garden was a very considerate and obliging person, who had, besides, a high regard for Kant; and, accordingly, upon a representation of the case being made to him, he gave orders that the poplars should be cropped. This was done, the old tower of Lobenicht was again unveiled, and Kant recovered his equanimity, and pursued his twilight meditations as before.

After the candles were brought, Kant prosecuted his studies till nearly ten o'clock. A quarter of an hour before retiring for the night, he withdrew his mind as much as possible from every class of thoughts which demanded any exertion or energy of attention, on the principle, that by stimulating and exciting him too much, such thoughts would be apt to cause wakefulness; and the slightest interference with his customary hour of falling asleep, was in the highest degree unpleasant to him. Happily, this was with him a very rare occurrence. He undressed himself without his servant's assistance, but in such an order, and with such a Roman regard to decorum and the *to prepon*, that he was always ready at a moment's warning to make his appearance without embarrassment to himself or to others. This done, he lay down on a mattress, and wrapped himself up in a quilt, which in summer was always of cotton,—in autumn, of wool; at the setting-in of winter he used both— and against very severe cold, he protected himself by one of eider-down, of which the part which covered his shoulders was not stuffed with feathers, but padded, or rather wadded closely with layers of wool. Long practice had taught him a very dexterous mode of *nesting* himself, as it were, in the bed-clothes. First of all, he sat down on the bedside; then with an agile motion he vaulted obliquely into his lair; next he drew one corner of the bedclothes under his left shoulder, and passing it below his back, brought it round so as to rest under his right shoulder; fourthly, by a particular *tour d'adresse*, he treated the other corner in the same way, and finally contrived to roll it round his whole person. Thus swathed like a mummy, or (as I used to tell him) self-involved like the silk-worm in its cocoon, he awaited the approach of sleep, which generally came on immediately. For Kant's health was exquisite; not mere negative health, or the absence of pain, but a state of positive pleasurable sensation, and a genial sense of the entire possession of all his activities. Accordingly, when packed up for the night in the way I have described, he would often ejaculate to himself (as he used to tell us at dinner)—'Is it possible to conceive a human being with more perfect health than myself?' In fact, such was the innocence of his life, and such the happy condition of his situation, that no uneasy passion ever arose to excite him— nor care to harass—nor pain to awake him. Even in the severest winter his sleeping-room was without a fire; only in his latter years he yielded so far to the entreaties of his friends as to allow of a very small one. All nursing or self-indulgence found no quarter with Kant. In fact, five minutes, in the coldest weather, sufficed to supersede the first chill of the bed, by the diffusion of a general glow over his person. If he had any occasion to leave his room in the night-time, (for it was always kept dark day and night, summer and winter,) he guided himself by a rope, which was duly attached to his bed-post every night, and carried into the adjoining apartment.

Kant never perspired, [Footnote: This appears less extraordinary, considering the description of Kant's person, given originally by Reichardt, about eight years after his death. 'Kant,' says this writer, 'was drier than dust both in body and mind. His person was small; and possibly a more meagre, arid, parched anatomy of a man, has not appeared upon this earth. The upper part of his face was grand; forehead lofty and serene, nose elegantly turned, eyes brilliant and penetrating; but below it expressed powerfully the coarsest sensuality, which in him displayed itself by immoderate addiction to eating and drinking.' This last feature of his temperament is here expressed much too harshly.] night or day. Yet it was astonishing how much heat he supported habitually in his study, and in fact was not easy if it wanted but one degree of this heat. Seventy-five degrees of Fahrenheit was the invariable temperature of this room in which he chiefly lived; and if it fell below that point, no matter at what season of the year, he had it raised artificially to the usual standard. In the heats of summer he went thinly dressed, and invariably in silk stockings; yet, as even this dress could not always secure him against perspiring when engaged in active exercise, he had a singular remedy in reserve. Retiring to some shady place, he stood still and motionless—with the air and attitude of a person listening, or in suspense—until his usual *aridity* was restored. Even in the most sultry summer night, if the slightest trace of perspiration had sullied his night-dress, he spoke of it with emphasis, as of an accident that perfectly shocked him.

On this occasion, whilst illustrating Kant's notions of the animal economy, it may be as well to add one other particular, which is, that for fear of obstructing the circulation of the blood, he never would wear garters; yet, as he found it difficult to keep up his stockings without them, he had invented for himself a most elaborate substitute, which I shall describe. In a little pocket, somewhat smaller than a watch-pocket, but occupying pretty nearly the same situation as a watch-pocket on each thigh, there was placed a small box, something like a watch-case, but smaller; into this box was introduced a watch-spring in a wheel, round about which wheel was wound an elastic cord, for regulating the force of which there was a separate contrivance. To the two ends of this cord were attached hooks, which hooks were carried through a small aperture in the pockets, and so passing down the inner and the outer side of the thigh, caught hold of two loops which were fixed on the off side and the near side of each stocking. As might be expected, so complex an apparatus was liable, like the Ptolemaic system of the heavens, to occasional derangements; however, by good luck, I was able to apply an easy remedy to these disorders which sometimes threatened to disturb the comfort, and even the serenity, of the great man.

Precisely at five minutes before five o'clock, winter or summer, Lampe, Kant's servant, who had formerly served in the army, marched into his master's room with the air of a sentinel on duty, and cried aloud in a military tone,—'Mr. Professor, the time is come.' This summons Kant invariably obeyed without one moment's delay, as a soldier does the word of command—never, under any circumstances, allowing himself a respite, not even under the rare accident of having passed a sleepless night. As the clock struck five, Kant was seated at the breakfast-table, where he drank what he called *one* cup of tea; and no doubt he thought it such; but the fact was, that in part from his habit of reverie, and in part also for the purpose of refreshing its warmth, he filled up his cup so often, that in general he is supposed to have drunk two, three, or some unknown number. Immediately after he smoked a pipe of tobacco, (the only one which he allowed himself through the entire day,) but so rapidly, that a pile of glowing embers remained unsmoked. During this operation he thought over his arrangements for the day, as he had done the evening before during the twilight. About seven he usually went to his lecture-room, and from that he returned to his writing-table. Precisely at three quarters before one he rose from his chair, and called aloud to the cook,—'It has struck three quarters.' The meaning of which summons was this:—Immediately after taking soup, it was his constant practice to swallow what he called a dram, which consisted either of Hungarian wine, of Rhenish, of a cordial, or (in default of these) of Bishop. A flask of this was brought up by the cook on the proclamation of the three quarters. Kant hurried with it to the eating-room, poured out his *quantum*, left it standing in readiness, covered, however, with paper, to prevent its becoming vapid, and then went back to his study, and awaited the arrival of his guests, whom to the latest period of his life he never received but in full dress.

Thus we come round again to dinner, and the reader has now an accurate picture of the course of Kant's day; the rigid monotony of which was not burthensome to him; and probably contributed, with the uniformity of his diet, and other habits of the same regularity, to lengthen his life. On this consideration, indeed, he had come to regard his health and his old age as in a great measure the product of his own exertions. He spoke of himself often under the figure of a gymnastic artist, who had continued for nearly fourscore years to support his balance upon the slack-rope of life, without once swerving to the right or to the left. In spite of every illness to which his constitutional tendencies had exposed him, he still kept his position in life triumphantly. However, he would sometimes observe sportively, that it was really absurd, and a sort of insult to the next generation for a man to live so long, because he thus interfered with the prospects of younger people.

This anxious attention to his health accounts for the great interest which he attached to all new discoveries in medicine, or to new ways of theorizing on the old ones. As a work of great pretension in both classes, he set the highest value upon the theory of the Scotch physician Brown, or (as it is usually called, from the Latin name of its author,) the Brunonian Theory. No sooner had Weikard adopted [Footnote: This theory was afterwards greatly modified in Germany; and, judging from the random glances which I throw on these subjects, I believe that in this recast it still keeps its ground in that country.] and made it known in Germany, than Kant became familiar with it. He considered it not only as a great step taken for medicine, but even for the general interests of man, and fancied that in this he saw something analogous to the course which human nature has held in still more important inquiries, viz.: first of all, a continual ascent towards the more and more elaborately complex, and then a treading back, on its own steps, towards the simple and elementary. Dr. Beddoes's Essays, also, for producing by art and curing pulmonary consumption, and the method of Reich for curing fevers, made a powerful impression upon him; which, however, declined as those novelties (especially the last) began to sink in credit. As to Dr. Jenner's discovery of vaccination, he was less favorably disposed to it; he apprehended dangerous consequences from the absorption of a brutal miasma into the human blood, or at least into the lymph; and at any rate he thought, that, as a guarantee against the variolous infection, it required a much longer probation. Groundless as all these views were, it was exceedingly entertaining to hear the fertility of argument and analogy which he brought forward to support them. One of the subjects which occupied him at the latter end of his life, was the theory and phenomena of galvanism, which, however, he never satisfactorily mastered. Augustin's book upon this subject was about the last that he read, and his copy still retains on the margin his, pencil-marks of doubts, queries and suggestions.

The infirmities of age now began to steal upon Kant, and betrayed themselves in more shapes than one. Connected with Kant's prodigious memory for all things that had any intellectual bearings, he had from youth labored under an unusual weakness of this faculty in relation to the common affairs of daily life. Some remarkable instances of this are on record, from the period of his childish days; and now, when his second childhood was commencing, this infirmity increased upon him very sensibly. One of the first signs was, that he began to repeat the same stories more than once on the same day. Indeed, the decay of his memory was too palpable to escape his own notice; and, to provide against it, and secure himself from all apprehension of inflicting tedium upon his guests, he began to write a syllabus, or list of themes, for each day's conversation, on cards, or the covers of letters, or any chance scrap of paper. But these memoranda accumulated so fast upon him, and were so easily lost, or not forthcoming at the proper moment, that I prevailed on him to substitute a blank-paper book, which I had directed to be made, and which still remains, with some affecting memorials of his own conscious weakness. As often happens, however, in such cases, he had a perfect memory for the remote events of his life, and could repeat with great readiness, and without once stumbling, very long passages from German or Latin poems, especially from the AEneid, whilst the very words that had been uttered but a moment before dropped away from his remembrance. The past came forward with the distinctness and liveliness of an immediate existence, whilst the present faded away into the obscurity of infinite distance.

Another sign of his mental decay was the weakness with which he now began to theorize. He accounted for everything by electricity. A singular mortality at this time prevailed amongst the cats of Vienna, Basle, Copenhagen, and other places. Cats being so eminently an electric animal, of course he attributed this epizootic to electricity. During the same period, he persuaded himself that a peculiar configuration of clouds prevailed; this he took as a collateral proof of his electrical hypothesis. His own headaches, too, which in all probability were a mere remote effect of old age, and a direct one of an inability [Footnote: Mr. Wasianski is quite in the wrong here. If the hindrances which nature presented to the act of thinking were now on the increase, on the other hand, the disposition to think, by his own acknowledgment, was on the wane. The power and the habit altering in proportion, there is no case made out of that disturbed equilibrium to which apparently he would attribute the headaches. But the fact is, that, if he had been as well acquainted with Kant's writings as with Kant personally, he would have known, that some affection of the head of a spasmodic kind was complained of by Kant at a time when nobody could suspect him of being in a decaying state.] to think as easily and as severely as formerly, he explained upon the same principle. And this was a notion of which his friends were not anxious to disabuse him, because, as something of the same character of weather (and therefore probably the same general tendency of the electric power) is found to prevail for whole cycles of years, entrance upon another cycle held out to him some prospect of relief. A delusion which secured the comforts of hope was the next best thing to an actual remedy; and a man who, in such circumstances, is cured of his delusion, '*cui demptus per vim mentis gratissimus error,*' might reasonably have exclaimed, '*Pol, me occidistis, amici.*'

Possibly the reader may suppose, that, in this particular instance of charging his own decays upon the state of the atmosphere, Kant was actuated by the weakness of vanity, or some unwillingness to face the real fact that his powers were decaying. But this was not the case. He was perfectly aware of his own condition, and, as early as 1799, he said, in my presence, to a party of his friends—'Gentlemen, I am old, and weak, and childish, and you must treat me as a child.' Or perhaps it may be thought that he shrank from the contemplation of death, which, as apoplexy seemed to be threatened by the pains in his head, might have happened any day. But neither was this the case. He now lived in a continual state of resignation, and prepared to meet any dispensation of Providence. 'Gentlemen,' said he one day to his guests, 'I do not fear to die. I assure you, as in the presence of God, that if I were this night to be made suddenly aware that I was on the point of being summoned, I would raise my hands to heaven, fold them, and say, Blessed be God! If indeed it were possible that a whisper such as this could reach my ear—Fourscore years thou hast lived, in which time thou hast inflicted much evil upon thy fellow-men, the case would be otherwise.' Whosoever has heard Kant speak of his own death, will bear witness to the tone of earnest sincerity which, on such occasions, marked his manner and utterance.

A third sign of his decaying faculties was, that he now lost all accurate measure of time. One minute, nay, without exaggeration, a much less space of time, stretched out in his apprehension of things to a wearisome duration. Of this I can give one rather amusing instance, which was of constant recurrence. At the beginning of the last year of his life, he fell into a custom of taking immediately after dinner a cup of coffee, especially on those days when it happened that I was of his party. And such was the importance he attached to this little pleasure, that he would even make a memorandum beforehand, in the blank-paper book I had given him, that on the next day I was to dine with him, and consequently that there was to be coffee. Sometimes it would happen, that the interest of conversation carried him past the time at which he felt the craving for it; and this I was not sorry to observe, as I feared that coffee, which he had never been accustomed to, [Footnote: How this happened to be the case in Germany, Mr. Wasianski has not explained. Perhaps the English merchants at Königsberg, being amongst Kant's oldest and most intimate friends, had early familiarized him to the practice of drinking tea, and to other English tastes. However, Jachmann tells us, that Kant was extravagantly fond of coffee, but forced himself to abstain from it under a notion that it was very unwholesome.] might disturb his rest at night. But, if this did not happen, then commenced a scene of some interest. Coffee must be brought 'upon the spot,' (a word he had constantly in his mouth during his latter days,) 'in a moment.' And the expressions of his impatience, though from old habit still gentle, were so lively, and had so much of infantine naïveté about them, that none of us could forbear smiling. Knowing what would happen, I had taken care that all the preparations should be made beforehand; the coffee was ground; the water was boiling; and the very moment the word was given, his servant shot in like an arrow, and plunged the coffee into the water. All that remained, therefore, was to give it time to boil up. But this trifling delay seemed unendurable to Kant. All consolations were thrown away upon him: vary the formula as we might, he was never at a loss for a reply. If it was said—'Dear Professor, the coffee will be brought up in a moment.'—'*Will* be!' he would say, 'but there's the rub, that it only *will* be:

> Man never is, but always to be blest.'

If another cried out—'The coffee is coming immediately.'—'Yes,' he would retort, 'and so is the next hour: and, by the way, it's about that length of time that I have waited for it.' Then he would collect himself with a stoical air, and say—'Well, one can die after all: it is but dying; and in the next world, thank God! there is no drinking of coffee, and consequently no—waiting for it.' Sometimes he would rise from his chair, open the door, and cry out with a feeble querulousness—'Coffee! coffee!' And when at length he heard the servant's step upon the stairs, he would turn round to us, and, as joyfully as ever sailor from the mast-head, he would call out—'Land, land! my dear friends, I see land.'

This general decline in Kant's powers, active and passive, gradually brought about a revolution in his habits of life. Heretofore, as I have already mentioned, he went to bed at ten, and rose a little before five. The latter practice he still observed, but not the other. In 1802 he retired as early as nine, and afterwards still earlier. He found himself so much refreshed by this addition to his rest, that at first he was disposed to utter a *Euraeka*, as over some great discovery in the art of restoring exhausted nature: but afterwards, on pushing it still farther, he did not find the success answer his expectations. His walks he now limited to a few turns in the King's gardens, which were at no great distance from his own house. In order to walk more firmly, he adopted a peculiar method of stepping; he carried his foot to the ground, not forward, and obliquely, but perpendicularly, and with a kind of stamp, so as to secure a larger basis, by setting down the entire sole at once. Notwithstanding this precaution, upon one occasion he fell in the street. He was quite unable to raise himself; and two young ladies, who saw the accident, ran to his assistance. With his usual graciousness of manner he thanked them fervently for their assistance, and presented one of them with a rose which he happened to have in his hand. This lady was not personally known to Kant; but she was greatly delighted with his little present, and still keeps the rose as a frail memorial of her transitory interview with the great philosopher.

This accident, as I have reason to think, was the cause of his henceforth renouncing exercise altogether. All labors, even that of reading, were now performed slowly, and with manifest effort; and those which cost him any bodily exertion became very exhausting to him. His feet refused to do their office more and more; he fell continually, both when moving across the room, and even when standing still: yet he seldom suffered from these falls; and he constantly laughed at them, maintaining that it was impossible he could hurt himself, from the extreme lightness of his person, which was indeed by this time the merest skeleton. Very often, especially in the morning, he dropped asleep in his chair from pure weariness: on these occasions he fell forward upon the floor, and lay there unable to raise himself up, until accident brought one of his servants or his friends into the room. Afterwards these falls were prevented, by substituting a chair with circular supports, that met and clasped in front.

These unseasonable dozings exposed him to another danger. He fell repeatedly, whilst reading, with his head into the candles; a cotton nightcap which he wore was instantly in a blaze, and flaming about his head. Whenever this happened, Kant behaved with great presence of mind.

Disregarding the pain, he seized the blazing cap, drew it from his head, laid it quietly on the floor, and trod out the flames with his feet. Yet, as this last act brought his dressing-gown into a dangerous neighborhood to the flames, I changed the form of his cap, persuaded him to arrange the candles differently, and had a decanter of water placed constantly by his side; and in this way I applied a remedy to a danger, which would else probably have been fatal to him.

From the sallies of impatience, which I have described in the case of the coffee, there was reason to fear that, with the increasing infirmities of Kant, would grow up a general waywardness and obstinacy of temper. For my own sake, therefore, and not less for his, I now laid down one rule for my future conduct in his house; which was, that I would, on no occasion, allow my reverence for him to interfere with the firmest expression of my opinion on subjects relating to his own health; and in cases of great importance, that I would make no compromise with his particular humors, but insist, not only on my view of the case, but also on the practical adoption of my views; or, if this were refused me, that I would take my departure at once, and not be made responsible for the comfort of a person whom I had no power to influence. And this behavior on my part it was that won Kant's confidence; for there was nothing which disgusted him so much as any approach to fawning or sycophancy. As his imbecility increased, he became daily more liable to mental delusions; and, in particular, he fell into many fantastic notions about the conduct of his servants, and, in consequence, into a peevish mode of treating them. Upon these occasions I generally observed a deep silence. But sometimes he would ask me for my opinion; and when this happened, I did not scruple to say, 'Ingenuously, then, Mr. Professor, I think that you are in the wrong.'—'You think so?' he would reply calmly, at the same time asking for my reasons, which he would listen to with great patience, and openness to conviction. Indeed, it was evident that the firmest opposition, so long as it rested upon assignable grounds and principles, won upon his regard; whilst his own nobleness of character still moved him to habitual contempt for timorous and partial acquiescence in his opinions, even when his infirmities made him most anxious for such acquiescence.

Earlier in life Kant had been little used to contradiction. His superb understanding, his brilliancy in conversation, founded in part upon his ready and sometimes rather caustic wit, and in part upon his prodigious command of knowledge—the air of noble self-confidence which the consciousness of these advantages impressed upon his manners—and the general knowledge of the severe innocence of his life—all combined to give him a station of superiority to others, which generally secured him from open contradiction. And if it sometimes happened that he met a noisy and intemperate opposition, supported by any pretences to wit, he usually withdrew himself from that sort of unprofitable altercation with dignity, by contriving to give such a turn to the conversation as won the general favor of the company to himself, and impressed, silence, or modesty at least, upon the boldest disputant. From a person so little familiar with opposition, it could scarcely have been anticipated that he should daily surrender his wishes to mine—if not without discussion, yet always without displeasure. So, however, it was. No habit, of whatever long standing, could be objected to as injurious to his health, but he would generally renounce it. And he had this excellent custom in such cases, that either he would resolutely and at once decide for his own opinion, or, if he professed to follow his friend's, he would follow it sincerely, and not try it unfairly by trying it imperfectly. Any plan, however trifling, which he had once consented to adopt on the suggestion of another, was never afterwards defeated or embarrassed by unseasonable interposition from his own humors. And thus, the very period of his decay drew forth so many fresh expressions of his character, in its amiable or noble features, as daily increased my affection and reverence for his person.

Having mentioned his servants, I shall here take occasion to give some account of his man-servant Lampe. It was a great misfortune for Kant, in his old age and infirmities, that this man also became old, and subject to a different sort of infirmities. This Lampe had originally served in the Prussian army; on quitting which he entered the service of Kant. In this situation he had lived about forty years; and, though always dull and stupid, had, in the early part of this period, discharged his duties with tolerable fidelity. But latterly, presuming upon his own indispensableness, from his perfect knowledge of all the domestic arrangements, and upon his master's weakness, he had fallen into great irregularities and neglect of his duties. Kant had been obliged, therefore, of late, to threaten repeatedly that he would discharge him. I, who knew that Kant, though one of the kindest-hearted men, was also one of the firmest, foresaw that this discharge, once given, would be irrevocable: for the word of Kant was as sacred as other men's oaths. Consequently, upon every opportunity, I remonstrated with Lampe on the folly of his conduct, and his wife joined me on these occasions. Indeed, it was high time that a change should be made in some quarter; for it now became dangerous to leave Kant, who was constantly falling from weakness, to the care of an old ruffian, who was himself apt to fall from intoxication. The fact was, that from the moment I undertook the management of Kant's affairs, Lampe saw there was an end to his old system of abusing his master's confidence in pecuniary affairs, and the other advantages which he took of his helpless situation. This made him desperate, and he behaved worse and worse; until one morning, in January, 1802, Kant told me, that, humiliating as he felt such a confession, the fact was, that Lampe had just treated him in a way which he was ashamed to repeat. I was too much shocked to distress him by inquiring into the particulars. But the result was, that Kant now insisted, temperately but firmly, on Lampe's dismissal. Accordingly, a new servant, of the name of Kaufmann, was immediately engaged; and on the next day Lampe was discharged with a handsome pension for life.

Here I must mention a little circumstance which does honor to Kant's benevolence. In his last will, on the assumption that Lampe would continue with him to his death, he had made a very liberal provision for him; but upon this new arrangement of the pension, which was to take effect immediately, it became necessary to revoke that part of his will, which he did in a separate codicil, that began thus:—'In consequence of the ill behavior of my servant Lampe, I think fit,' &c. But soon after, considering that such a record of Lampe's misconduct might be seriously injurious to his interests, he cancelled the passage, and expressed it in such a way, that no trace remained behind of his just displeasure. And his benign nature was gratified with knowing, that, this one sentence blotted out, there remained no other in all his numerous writings, published or confidential, which spoke the language of anger, or could leave any ground for doubting that he died in charity with all the world. Upon Lampe's calling to demand a written character, he was, however, a good deal embarrassed; his stern reverence for truth being, in this instance, armed against the first impulses of his kindness. Long and anxiously he sat, with the certificate lying before him, debating how he should fill up the blanks. I was present, but in such a matter I did not take the liberty of suggesting any advice. At last, he took his pen, and filled up the blank as follows:—'—has served me long and faithfully,'—(for Kant was not aware that he had robbed him,)—'but did not display those particular qualifications which fitted him for waiting on an old and infirm man like myself.'

This scene of disturbance over, which to Kant, a lover of peace and tranquillity, caused a shock that he would gladly have been spared; it was fortunate that no other of that nature occurred during the rest of his life. Kaufmann, the successor of Lampe, turned out to be a respectable and upright man, and soon conceived a great attachment to his master's person. Things now put on a new face in Kant's family: by the removal of one of the belligerents, peace was once more restored amongst his servants; for hitherto there had been eternal wars between Lampe and the cook. Sometimes it was Lampe that carried a war of aggression into the cook's territory of the kitchen; sometimes it was the cook that revenged these insults, by sallying out upon Lampe in the neutral ground of the hall, or invaded him even in his own sanctuary of the butler's pantry. The uproars were everlasting; and thus far it was fortunate for the peace of the philosopher, that his hearing had begun to fail; by which means he was spared many an exhibition of hateful passions and ruffian violence, which annoyed his guests and friends. But now all things had changed: deep silence reigned in the pantry; the kitchen rang no more with martial alarums; and the hall was unvexed with skirmish or pursuit. Yet it may be readily supposed that to Kant, at the age of seventy-eight, changes, even for the better, were not welcome: so intense had been the uniformity of his life and habits, that the least innovation in the arrangement of articles as trifling as a penknife, or a pair of scissors, disturbed him; and not merely if they were pushed two or three inches out of their customary position, but even if they were laid a little awry; and as to larger objects, such as chairs, &c., any dislocation of their usual arrangement, any trans position, or addition to their number, perfectly confounded him; and his eye appeared restlessly to haunt the seat of the mal-arrangement, until the ancient order was restored. With such habits the reader may conceive how distressing it must have been to him, at this period of decaying powers, to adapt himself to a new servant, a new voice, a new step, &c.

Aware of this, I had on the day before he entered upon his duties, written down for the new servant upon a sheet of paper the entire routine of Kant's daily life, down to the minutest and most trivial circumstances; all which he mastered with the greatest rapidity. To make sure, however, we went through a rehearsal of the whole ritual; he performing the manoeuvres, I looking on and giving the word. Still I felt uneasy at the idea of his being left entirely to his own discretion on his first *debut* in good earnest, and therefore I made a point of attending on this important day; and in the few instances where the new recruit missed the accurate manoeuvre, a glance or a nod from me easily made him comprehend his failure.

One part only there was of the daily ceremonial, where all of us were at a loss, as it was a part which no mortal eyes had ever witnessed but those of Lampe: this was breakfast. However, that we might do all in our power, I myself attended at four o'clock in the morning. The day happened, as I remember, to be the 1st of February, 1802. Precisely at five, Kant made his appearance; and nothing could equal his astonishment on finding me in the room. Fresh from the confusion of dreaming, and bewildered alike by the sight of his new servant, by Lampe's absence, and by my presence, he could with difficulty be made to comprehend the purpose of my visit. A friend in need is a friend indeed; and we would now have given any money to that learned person who could have instructed us in the arrangement of the breakfast table. But this was a mystery revealed to none but Lampe. At length Kant took this task upon himself; and apparently all was now settled to his satisfaction. Yet still it struck me that he was under some embarrassment or constraint. Upon this I said—that, with his permission, I would take a cup of tea, and afterwards smoke a pipe with him. He accepted my offer with his usual courteous demeanor; but seemed unable to familiarize himself with the novelty of his situation. I was at this time sitting directly opposite to him; and at last he frankly told me, but with the kindest and most apologetic air, that he was really under the necessity of begging that I would sit out of his sight; for that, having sat alone at the breakfast table for considerably more than half a century, he could not abruptly adapt his mind to a change in this respect; and he found his thoughts very sensibly disturbed. I did as he desired; the servant retired into an antiroom, where he waited within call; and Kant recovered his wonted composure. Just the same scene passed over again, when I called at the same hour on a fine summer morning some months after.

Henceforth all went right: or, if occasionally some little mistake occurred, Kant showed himself very considerate and indulgent, and would remark of his own accord, that a new servant could not be expected to know all his peculiar ways and humors. In one respect, indeed, this man adapted himself to Kant's scholarlike taste, in a way which Lampe was incapable of doing. Kant was somewhat fastidious in matters of pronunciation; and this man had a great facility in catching the true sound of Latin words, the titles of books, and the names or designations of Kant's friends: not one of which accomplishments could Lampe, the most insufferable of blockheads, ever attain to. In particular, I have been told by Kant's old friends, that for the space of more than thirty years, during which he had been in the habit of reading the newspaper published by Hartung, Lampe delivered it with the same identical blunder on every day of publication.—'Mr. Professor, here is Hart*mann's* journal.' Upon which Kant would reply—'Eh! what?—What's that you say? Hartmann's journal? I tell you, it is not Hartmann, but Hartung: now, repeat it after me—not Hartmann, but Hartung.' Then Lampe, looking sulky, and drawing himself up with the stiff air of a soldier on guard, and in the very same monotonous tone with which he had been used to sing out his challenge of—*Who goes there?* would roar—'not Hartmann, but Hartung.' 'Now again!' Kant would say: on which again Lampe roared—'not Hartmann, but Hartung.' 'Now a third time,' cried Kant: on which for a third time the unhappy Lampe would howl out—'not Hartmann, but Hartung.' And this whimsical scene of parade duty was continually repeated: duly as the day of publication came, the irreclaimable old dunce was put through the same manoeuvres, which were as invariably followed by the same blunder on the next. In spite, however, of this advantage, in the new servant, and his general superiority to his predecessor, Kant's nature was too kind and good, and too indulgent to all people's infirmities but his own, not to miss the voice and the 'old familiar face' that he had been accustomed to for forty years. And I met with what struck me as an affecting instance of Kant's yearning after his old good-for-nothing servant in his memorandum-book: other people record what they wish to remember; but Kant had here recorded what he was to forget. 'Mem.: February, 1802, the name of Lampe must now be remembered no more.'

In the spring of this year, 1802, I advised Kant to take the air. It was very long since he had been out of doors, [Footnote: Wasianski here returns thanks to some unknown person, who, having observed that Kant in his latter walks took pleasure in leaning against a particular wall to view the prospect, had caused a seat to be fixed at that point for his use.] and walking was now out of the question. But I thought the motion of a carriage and the air would be likely to revive him. On the power of vernal sights and sounds I did not much rely; for these had long ceased to affect him. Of all the changes that spring brings with it, there was one only that now interested Kant; and he longed for it with an eagerness and intensity of expectation, that it was almost painful to witness: this was the return of a hedge sparrow that sang in his garden, and before his window. This bird, either the same, or one of the next generation, had sung for years in the same situation; and Kant grew uneasy when the cold weather, lasting longer than usual, retarded its return. Like Lord Bacon, indeed, he had a childlike love for birds in general, and in particular, took pains to encourage the sparrows to build above the windows of his study; and when this happened, (as it often did, from the silence which prevailed in his study,) he watched their proceedings with the delight and the tenderness which others give to a human interest. To return to the point I was speaking of, Kant was at first very unwilling to accede to my proposal of going abroad. 'I shall sink down in the carriage,' said he, 'and fall together like a heap of old rags.' But I persisted with a gentle importunity in urging him to the attempt, assuring him that we would return immediately if he found the effort too much for him. Accordingly, upon a tolerably warm day of early [Footnote: Mr. Wasianski says—*late* in summer: but, as he elsewhere describes by the same expression of 'late in summer,' a day which was confessedly *before* the longest day, and as the multitude of birds which continued to sing will not allow us to suppose that the summer could be very far advanced, I have translated accordingly.] summer, I, and an old friend of Kant's, accompanied him to a little place which I rented in the country. As we drove through the streets, Kant was delighted to find that he could sit upright, and bear the motion of the carriage, and seemed to draw youthful pleasure from the sight of the towers and other public buildings, which he had not seen for years. We reached the place of our destination in high spirits. Kant drank a cup of coffee, and attempted to smoke a little. After this, he sat and sunned himself, listening with delight to the warbling of birds, which congregated in great numbers about this spot. He distinguished every bird by its song, and called it by its right name. After staying about half an hour, we set off on our homeward journey, Kant still cheerful, but apparently satiated with his day's enjoyment.

I had on this occasion purposely avoided taking him to any public gardens, that I might not disturb his pleasure by exposing him to the distressing gaze of public curiosity. However, it was known in Königsberg that Kant had gone out; and accordingly, as the carriage moved through the streets which led to his residence, there was a general rush from all quarters in that direction, and, when we turned into the street where the house stood, we found it already choked up with people. As we slowly drew up to the door, a lane was formed in the crowd, through which Kant was led, I and my friend supporting him on our arms. Looking at the crowd, I observed the faces of many persons of rank, and distinguished strangers, some of whom now saw Kant for the first time, and many of them for the last.

As the winter of 1802-3 approached, he complained more than ever of an affection of the stomach, which no medical man had been able to mitigate, or even to explain. The winter passed over in a complaining way; he was weary of life, and longed for the hour of dismission. 'I can be of service to the world no more,' said he, 'and am a burden to myself.' Often I endeavored to cheer him by the anticipation of excursions that we would make together when summer came again. On these he calculated with so much earnestness, that he had made a regular scale or classification of them—1. Airings; 2. Journeys; 3. Travels. And nothing could equal the yearning impatience expressed for the coming of spring and summer, not so much for their own peculiar attractions, as because they were the seasons for travelling. In his memorandum-book, he made this note:—'The three summer months are June, July, and August'—meaning that they were the three months for travelling. And in conversation he expressed the feverish strength of his wishes so plaintively and affectingly, that everybody was drawn into powerful sympathy with him, and wished for some magical means of ante-dating the course of the seasons.

In this winter his bed-room was often warmed. This was the room in which he kept his little collection of books, of about four hundred and fifty volumes, chiefly presentation-copies from the authors. It may seem singular that Kant, who read so extensively, should have no larger library; but he had less need of one than most scholars, having in his earlier years been librarian at the Royal Library of the Castle; and since then having enjoyed from the liberality of Hartknoch, his publisher, (who, in his turn, had profited by the liberal terms on which Kant had made over to him the copyright of his own works,) the first sight of every new book that appeared.

At the close of this winter, that is in 1803, Kant first began to complain of unpleasant dreams, sometimes of very terrific ones, which awakened him in great agitation. Oftentimes melodies, which he had heard in earliest youth sung in the streets of Königsberg, resounded painfully in his ears, and dwelt upon them in a way from which no efforts of abstraction could release him. These kept him awake to unseasonable hours; and often when, after long watching, he had fallen asleep, however deep his sleep might be, it was suddenly broken up by terrific dreams, which alarmed him beyond description. Almost every night, the bell-rope, which communicated with a bell in the room above his own, where his servant slept, was pulled violently, and with the utmost agitation. No matter how fast the servant might hurry down, he was almost always too late, and was pretty sure to find his master out of bed, and often making his way in terror to some other part of the house. The weakness of his feet exposed him to such dreadful falls on these occasions, that at length (but with much difficulty) I persuaded him to let his servant sleep in the same room with himself.

The morbid affection of the stomach began now to be more and more distressing; and he tried various applications, which he had formerly been loud in condemning, such as a few drops of rum upon a piece of sugar, naphtha, [Footnote: For Kant's particular complaint, as described by other biographers, a quarter of a grain of opium, every twelve hours, would have been the best remedy, perhaps a perfect remedy.] &c. But all these were only palliatives; for his advanced age precluded the hope of a radical cure. His dreadful dreams became continually more appalling: single scenes, or passages in these dreams, were sufficient to compose the whole course of mighty tragedies, the impression from which was so profound as to stretch far into his waking hours. Amongst other phantasmata more shocking and indescribable, his dreams constantly represented to him the forms of murderers advancing to his bedside; and so agitated was he by the awful trains of phantoms that swept past him nightly, that in the first confusion of awaking he generally mistook his servant, who was hastening to his assistance, for a murderer. In the day-time we often conversed upon these shadowy illusions; and Kant, with his usual spirit of stoical contempt for nervous weakness of every sort, laughed at them; and, to fortify his own resolution to contend against them, he wrote down in his memorandum-book, 'There must be no yielding to panics of darkness.' At my suggestion, however, he now burned a light in his chamber, so placed as that the rays might be shaded from his face. At first he was very averse to this, though gradually he became reconciled to it. But that he could bear it at all, was to me an expression of the great revolution accomplished by the terrific agency of his dreams. Heretofore, darkness and utter silence were the two pillars on which his sleep rested: no step must approach his room; and as to light, if he saw but a moonbeam penetrating a crevice of the shutters, it made him unhappy; and, in fact, the windows of his bed-chamber were barricadoed night and day. But now darkness was a terror to him, and silence an oppression. In addition to his lamp, therefore, he had now a repeater in his room; the sound was at first too loud, but, after muffling the hammer with cloth, both the ticking and the striking became companionable sounds to him.

At this time (spring of 1803) his appetite began to fail, which I thought no good sign. Many persons insist that Kant was in the habit of eating too much for health. [Footnote: Who these worthy people were that criticised Kant's eating, is not mentioned. They could have had no opportunity of exercising their abilities on this question, except as hosts, guests, or fellow-guests; and in any of those characters, a gentleman, one would suppose, must feel himself degraded by directing his attention to a point of that nature. However, the merits of the case stand thus between the parlies: Kant, it is agreed by all his biographers, ate only once a day; for as to his breakfast, it was nothing more than a very weak infusion of tea, (vide Jachmann's Letters, p. 163,) with no bread, or eatable of any kind. Now, his critics, by general confession, ate their way, from 'morn to dewy eve,' through the following course of meals: 1. Breakfast early in the morning; 2. Breakfast à la fourchette about ten, A.M.; 3. Dinner at one or two; 4. Vesper Brod; 5. Abend Brod; all which does really seem a very fair allowance for a man who means to lecture upon abstinence at night. But I shall cut this matter short by stating one plain fact; there were two things, and no more, for which Kant had an inordinate craving during his whole life; these were tobacco and coffee; and from both these he abstained almost altogether, merely under a sense of duty, resting probably upon erroneous grounds. Of the first he allowed himself a very small quantity, (and everybody knows that temperance is a more difficult virtue than abstinence;) of the other none at all, until the labors of his life were accomplished.] I, however, cannot assent to this opinion; for he ate but once a day, and drank no beer. Of this liquor, (I mean the strong black beer,) he was, indeed, the most determined enemy. If ever a man died prematurely, Kant would say—'He has been drinking beer, I presume.' Or, if another were indisposed, you might be sure he would ask, 'But does he drink beer?' And, according to the answer on this point, he regulated his anticipations for the patient. Strong beer, in short, he uniformly maintained to be a slow poison. Voltaire, by the way, had said to a young physician who denounced coffee under the same bad name of a 'slow poison,' 'You're right there, my friend, however; slow it is, and horribly slow; for I have been drinking it these seventy years, and it has not killed me yet;' but this was an answer which, in the case of beer, Kant would not allow of.

On the 22d of April, 1803, his birth-day, the last which he lived to see, was celebrated in a full assembly of his friends. This festival he had long looked forward to with great expectation, and delighted even to hear the progress made in the preparations for it. But when the day came, the over-excitement and tension of expectation seemed to have defeated itself. He tried to appear happy; but the bustle of a numerous company confounded and distressed him; and his spirits were manifestly forced. He seemed first to revive to any real sense of pleasure at night, when the company had departed, and he was undressing in his study. He then talked with much pleasure about the presents which, as usual, would be made to his servants on this occasion; for Kant was never happy himself, unless he saw all around him happy. He was a great maker of presents; but at the same time he had no toleration for the studied theatrical effect, the accompaniment of formal congratulations, and the sentimental pathos with which birth-day presents are made in Germany. [Footnote: In this, as in many other things, the taste of Kant was entirely English and Roman; as, on the other hand, some eminent Englishmen, I am sorry to say, have, on this very point, shown the effeminacy and *falsetto* taste of the Germans. In particular, Mr. Coleridge, describing, in The Friend, the custom amongst German children of making presents to their parents on Christmas Eve, (a custom which he unaccountably supposes to be peculiar to Ratzeburg,) represents the mother as 'weeping aloud for joy'—the old idiot of a father with 'tears running down his face,' &c. &c., and all for what? For a snuff-box, a pencil-case, or some article of jewellery. Now, we English agree with Kant on such maudlin display of stage sentimentality, and are prone to suspect that papa's tears are the product of rum-punch. Tenderness let us have by all means, and the deepest you can imagine, but upon proportionate occasions, and with causes fitted to justify it and sustain its dignity.] In all this, his masculine taste gave him a sense of something fade and ludicrous.

The summer of 1803 was now come, and, visiting Kant one day, I was thunderstruck to hear him direct me, in the most serious tone, to provide the funds necessary for an extensive foreign tour. I made no opposition, but asked his reasons for such a plan; he alleged the miserable sensations he had in his stomach, which were no longer endurable. Knowing what power over Kant a quotation from a Roman poet had always had, I simply replied—'Post equitem sedet atra cura,' and for the present he said no more. But the touching and pathetic earnestness with which he was continually ejaculating prayers for warmer weather, made it doubtful to me whether his wishes on this point ought not, partially at least, to be gratified; and I therefore proposed to him a little excursion to the cottage we had visited the year before. 'Anywhere,' said he, 'no matter whither, provided it be far enough.' Towards the latter end of June, therefore, we executed this scheme; on getting into the carriage, the order of the day with Kant was, 'Distance, distance. Only let us go far enough,' said he: but scarcely had we reached the city-gates before the journey seemed already to have lasted too long. On reaching the cottage we found coffee waiting for us; but he would scarcely allow himself time for drinking it, before he ordered the carriage to the door; and the journey back seemed insupportably long to him, though it was performed in something less than twenty minutes. 'Is this never to have an end?' was his continual exclamation; and great was his joy when he found himself once more in his study, undressed, and in bed. And for this night he slept in peace, and once again was liberated from the persecution of dreams.

Soon after he began again to talk of journeys, of travels in remote countries, &c., and, in consequence, we repeated our former excursion several times; and though the circumstances were pretty nearly the same on every occasion, and always terminating in disappointment as to the immediate pleasure anticipated, yet, undoubtedly, they were, on the whole, salutary to his spirits. In particular, the cottage itself, standing under the shelter of tall alders, with a valley stretched beneath it, through which a little brook meandered, broken by a water-fall, whose pealing sound dwelt pleasantly on the ear, sometimes, on a quiet sunny day, gave a lively delight to Kant: and once, under accidental circumstances of summer clouds and sun-lights, the little pastoral landscape suddenly awakened a lively remembrance which had been long laid asleep, of a heavenly summer morning in youth, which he had passed in a bower upon the banks of a rivulet that ran through the grounds of a dear and early friend, Gen. Von Lossow. The strength of the impression was such, that he seemed actually to be living over that morning again, thinking as he then thought, and conversing with those that were no more.

His very last excursion was in August of this year, (1803,) not to my cottage, but to the garden of a friend. But on this day he manifested great impatience. It had been arranged that he was to meet an old friend at the gardens; and I, with two other gentlemen, attended him. It happened that *out* party arrived first; and such was Kant's weakness, and total loss of power to estimate the duration of time, that, after waiting a few moments, he insisted that some hours had elapsed—that his friend could not be expected—and went away in great discomposure of mind. And so ended Kant's travelling in this world.

In the beginning of autumn the sight of his right eye began to fail him; the left he had long lost the use of. This earliest of his losses, by the way, he discovered by mere accident, and without any previous warning. Sitting down one day to rest himself in the course of a walk, it occurred to him that he would try the comparative strength of his eyes; but on taking out a newspaper which he had in his pocket, he was surprised to find that with his left eye he could not distinguish a letter. In earlier life he had two remarkable affections of the eyes: once, on returning from a walk, he saw objects double for a long space of time; and twice he became stone-blind. Whether these accidents are to be considered as uncommon, I leave to the decision of oculists. Certain it is, they gave very little disturbance to Kant; who, until old age had reduced his powers, lived in a constant state of stoical preparation for the worst that could befall him. I was now shocked to think of the degree in which his burthensome sense of dependence would be aggravated, if he should totally lose the power of sight. As it was, he read and wrote with great difficulty: in fact, his writing was little better than that which most people can produce as a trial of skill with their eyes shut. From old habits of solitary study, he had no pleasure in hearing others read to him; and he daily distressed me by the pathetic earnestness of his entreaties that I would have a reading-glass devised for him. Whatever my own optical skill could suggest, I tried; and the best opticians were sent for to bring their glasses, and take his directions for altering them; but all was to no purpose.

In this last year of his life Kant very unwillingly received the visits of strangers; and, unless under particular circumstances, wholly declined them. Yet, when travellers had come a very great way out of their road to see him, I confess that I was at a loss how to conduct myself. To have refused too pertinaciously, could not but give me the air of wishing to make myself of importance. And I must acknowledge, that, amongst some instances of importunity and coarse expressions of low-bred curiosity, I witnessed, on the part of many people of rank, a most delicate sensibility to the condition of the aged recluse. On sending in their cards, they would generally accompany them by some message, expressive of their unwillingness to gratify their wish to see him at any risk of distressing him. The fact was, that such visits *did* distress him much; for he felt it a degradation to be exhibited in his helpless state, when he was aware of his own incapacity to meet properly the attention that was paid to him. Some, however, were admitted, [Footnote: To whom it appears that Kant would generally reply, upon their expressing the pleasure it gave them to see him, 'In me you behold a poor superannuated, weak, old man.'] according to the circumstances of the case, and the state of Kant's spirits at the moment. Amongst these, I remember that we were particularly pleased with M. Otto, the same who signed the treaty of peace between France and England with the present Lord Liverpool, (then Lord Hawkesbury.) A young Russian also rises to my recollection at this moment, from the excessive (and I think unaffected) enthusiasm which he displayed. On being introduced to Kant, he advanced hastily, took both his hands, and kissed them. Kant, who, from living so much amongst his English friends, had a good deal of the English dignified reserve about him, and hated anything like *scenes*, appeared to shrink a little from this mode of salutation, and was rather embarrassed. However, the young man's manner, I believe, was not at all beyond his genuine feelings; for next day he called again, made some inquiries about Kant's health, was very anxious to know whether his old age were burthensome to him, and above all things entreated for some little memorial of the great man to carry away with him. By accident the servant had found a small cancelled fragment of the original MS. of Kant's 'Anthropologie:' this, with my sanction, he gave to the Russian; who received it with rapture, kissed it, and then gave him in return the only dollar he had about him; and, thinking that not enough, actually pulled off his coat and waistcoat and forced them upon the man. Kant, whose native simplicity of character very much indisposed him to sympathy with any extravagances of feeling, could not, however, forbear smiling good-humoredly on being made acquainted with this instance of *naïveté* and enthusiasm in his young admirer.

I now come to an event in Kant's life, which ushered in its closing stage. On the 8th of October, 1803, for the first time since his youth, he was seriously ill. When a student at the University, he had once suffered from an ague, which, however, gave way to pedestrian exercise; and in later years, he had endured some pain from a contusion on his head; but, with these two exceptions, (if they can be considered such,) he had never (properly speaking) been ill. The cause of his illness was this: his appetite had latterly been irregular, or rather I should say depraved; and he no longer took pleasure in anything but bread and butter, and English cheese.[Footnote: Mr. W. here falls into the ordinary mistake of confounding the cause and the occasion, and would leave the impression, that Kant (who from his youth up had been a model of temperance) died of sensual indulgence. The cause of Kant's death was clearly the general decay of the vital powers, and in particular the atony of the digestive organs, which must soon have destroyed him under any care or abstinence whatever. This was the cause. The accidental occasion, which made that cause operative on the 7th of

October, might or might not be what Mr. W. says. But in Kant's burthensome state of existence, it could not be a question of much importance whether his illness were to commence in an October or a November.] On the 7th of October, at dinner, he ate little else, in spite of everything that I and another friend then dining with him, could urge to dissuade him. And for the first time I fancied that he seemed displeased with my importunity, as though I were overstepping the just line of my duties. He insisted that the cheese never had done him any harm, nor would now. I had no course left me but to hold my tongue; and he did as he pleased. The consequence was what might have been anticipated—a restless night, succeeded by a day of memorable illness. The next morning all went on as usual, till nine o'clock, when Kant, who was then leaning on his sister's arm, suddenly fell senseless to the ground. A messenger was immediately despatched for me; and I hurried down to his house, where I found him lying in his bed, which had now been removed into his study, speechless and insensible. I had already summoned his physician; but, before he arrived, nature put forth efforts which brought Kant a little to himself. In about an hour he opened his eyes, and continued to mutter unintelligibly till towards the evening, when he rallied a little, and began to talk rationally. For the first time in his life, he was now, for a few days, confined to his bed, and ate nothing. On the 12th October, he again took some refreshment, and would have had his favorite food; but I was now resolved, at any risk of his displeasure, to oppose him firmly. I therefore stated to him the whole consequences of his last indulgence, of all which he manifestly had no recollection. He listened to what I said very attentively, and calmly expressed his conviction that I was perfectly in the wrong; but for the present he submitted. However, some days after, I found that he had offered a florin for a little bread and cheese, and then a dollar, and even more. Being again refused, he complained heavily; but gradually he weaned himself from asking for it, though at times he betrayed involuntarily how much he desired it.

On the 13th of October, his usual dinner parties were resumed, and he was considered convalescent; but it was seldom indeed that he recovered the tone of tranquil spirits which he had preserved until his late attack. Hitherto he had always loved to prolong this meal, the only one he took—or, as he expressed it in classical phrase, 'coenam *ducere*;' but now it was difficult to hurry it over fast enough for his wishes. From dinner, which terminated about two o'clock, he went straight to bed, and at intervals fell into slumbers; from which, however, he was regularly awoke by phantasmata or terrific dreams. At seven in the evening came on duly a period of great agitation, which lasted till five or six in the morning—sometimes later; and he continued through the night alternately to walk about and lie down, occasionally tranquil, but more often in great distress. It now became necessary that somebody should sit up with him, his man-servant being wearied out with the toils of the day. No person seemed to be so proper for this office as his sister, both as having long received a very liberal pension from him, and also as his nearest relative, who would be the best witness to the fact that her illustrious brother had wanted no comforts or attention in his last hours, which his situation admitted of. Accordingly she was applied to, and undertook to watch him alternately with his footman—a separate table being kept for her, and a very handsome addition made to her allowance. She turned out to be a quiet gentle-minded woman, who raised no disturbances amongst the servants, and soon won her brother's regard by the modest and retiring style of her manners; I may add, also, by the truly sisterly affection which she displayed towards him to the last.

The 8th of October had grievously affected Kant's faculties, but had not wholly destroyed them. For short intervals the clouds seemed to roll away that had settled upon his majestic intellect, and it shone forth as heretofore. During these moments of brief self-possession, his wonted benignity returned to him; and he expressed his gratitude for the exertions of those about him, and his sense of the trouble they underwent, in a very affecting way. With regard to his man-servant in particular, he was very anxious that he should be rewarded by liberal presents; and he pressed me earnestly on no account to be parsimonious. Indeed Kant was nothing less than princely in his use of money; and there was no occasion on which he was known to express the passion of scorn very powerfully, but when he was commenting on mean and penurious acts or habits. Those who knew him only in the streets, fancied that he was not liberal; for he steadily refused, upon principle, to relieve all common beggars. But, on the other hand, he was liberal to the public charitable institutions; he secretly assisted his own poor relations in a much ampler way than could reasonably have been expected of him; and it now appeared that he had many other deserving pensioners upon his bounty; a fact that was utterly unknown to any of us, until his increasing blindness and other infirmities devolved the duty of paying these pensions upon myself. It must be recollected, also, that Kant's whole fortune, which amounted to about twenty thousand dollars, was the product of his own honorable toils for nearly threescore years; and that he had himself suffered all the hardships of poverty in his youth, though he never once ran into any man's debt,—circumstances in his history, which, as they express how fully he must have been acquainted with the value of money, greatly enhance the merit of his munificence.

In December, 1803, he became incapable of signing his name. His sight, indeed, had for some time failed him so much, that at dinner he could not find his spoon without assistance; and, when I happened to dine with him, I first cut in pieces whatever was on his plate, next put it into a spoon, and then guided his hand to find the spoon. But his inability to sign his name did not arise merely from blindness: the fact was, that, from irretention of memory, he could not recollect the letters which composed his name; and, when they were repeated to him, he could not represent the figure of the letters in his imagination. At the latter end of November, I had remarked that these incapacities were rapidly growing upon him, and in consequence I prevailed on him to sign beforehand all the receipts, &c., which would be wanted at the end of the year; and, afterwards, on my representation, to prevent all disputes, he gave me a regular legal power to sign on his behalf.

Much as Kant was now reduced, yet he had occasionally moods of social hilarity. His birth-day was always an agreeable subject to him: some weeks before his death, I was calculating the time which it still wanted of that anniversary, and cheering him with the prospect of the rejoicings which would then take place: 'All your old friends,' said I, 'will meet together, and drink a glass of champagne to your health.' 'That,' said he, 'must be done upon the spot:' and he was not satisfied till the party was actually assembled. He drank a glass of wine with them, and with great elevation of spirits celebrated this birth-day which he was destined never to see.

In the latter weeks of his life, however, a great change took place in the tone of his spirits. At his dinner-table, where heretofore such a cloudless spirit of joviality had reigned, there was now a melancholy silence. It disturbed him to see his two dinner companions conversing privately together, whilst he himself sat like a mute on the stage with no part to perform. Yet to have engaged him in the conversation would have been still more distressing; for his hearing was now very imperfect; the effort to hear was itself painful to him; and his expressions, even when his thoughts were accurate enough, became nearly unintelligible. It is remarkable, however, that at the very lowest point of his depression, when he became perfectly incapable of conversing with any rational meaning on the ordinary affairs of life, he was still able to answer correctly and distinctly, in a degree that was perfectly astonishing, upon any question of philosophy or of science, especially of physical geography, [Footnote: *Physical* Geography, in opposition to *Political*.] chemistry, or natural history. He talked satisfactorily, in his very worst state, of the gases, and stated very accurately different propositions of Kepler's, especially the law of the planetary motions. And I remember in particular, that upon the very last Monday of his life, when the extremity of his weakness moved a circle of his friends to tears, and he sat amongst us insensible to all we could say to him, cowering down, or rather I might say collapsing into a shapeless heap upon his chair, deaf, blind, torpid, motionless,—even then I whispered to the others that I would engage that Kant should take his part in conversation with propriety and animation. This they found it difficult to believe. Upon which I drew close to his ear, and put a question to him about the Moors of Barbary. To the surprise of everybody but myself, he immediately gave us a summary account of their habits and customs; and told us by the way, that in the word *Algiers,* the *g* ought to be pronounced hard (as in the English word *gear*).

During the last fortnight of Kant's life, he busied himself unceasingly in a way that seemed not merely purposeless but self-contradictory. Twenty times in a minute he would unloose and tie his neck handkerchief—so also with a sort of belt which he wore about his dressing-gown, the moment it was clasped, he unclasped it with impatience, and was then equally impatient to have it clasped again. But no description can convey an adequate impression of the weary restlessness with which from morning to night he pursued these labors of Sisyphus—doing and undoing—fretting that he could not do it, fretting that he had done it.

By this time he seldom knew any of us who were about him, but took us all for strangers. This happened first with his sister, then with me, and finally with his servant. Such an alienation distressed me more than any other instance of his decay: though I knew that he had not really withdrawn his affection from me, yet his air and mode of addressing me gave me constantly that feeling. So much the more affecting was it, when the sanity of his perceptions and his remembrances returned; but these intervals were of slower and slower occurrence. In this condition, silent or babbling childishly, self-involved and torpidly abstracted, or else busy with self-created phantoms and delusions, what a contrast did he offer to *that* Kant who had once been the brilliant centre of the most brilliant circles for rank, wit, or knowledge, that Prussia afforded! A distinguished person from Berlin, who had called upon him during the preceding summer, was greatly shocked at his appearance, and said, 'This is not Kant that I have seen, but the shell of Kant!' How much more would he have said this, if he had seen him now!

Now came February, 1804, which was the last month that Kant was destined to see. It is remarkable that, in the memorandum book which I have before mentioned, I found a fragment of an old song, (inserted by Kant, and dated in the summer about six months before the time of his death,) which expressed that February was the month in which people had the least weight to carry, for the obvious reason that it was shorter by two and by three days than the others; and the concluding sentiment was in a tone of fanciful pathos to this effect—'Oh, happy February! in which man has least to bear—least pain, least sorrow, least self-reproach!' Even of this short month, however, Kant had not twelve entire days to bear; for it was on the 12th that he died; and in fact he may be said to have been dying from the 1st. He now barely vegetated; though there were still transitory gleams flashing by fits from the embers of his ancient intellect.

On the 3d of February the springs of life seemed to be ceasing from their play, for, from this day, strictly speaking, he ate nothing more. His existence henceforward seemed to be the mere prolongation of an impetus derived from an eighty years' life, after the moving power of the mechanism was withdrawn. His physician visited him every day at a particular hour; and it was settled that I should always be there to meet him. Nine days before his death, on paying his usual visit, the following little circumstance occurred, which affected us both, by recalling forcibly to our minds the ineradicable courtesy and goodness of Kant's nature. When the physician was announced, I went up to Kant and said to him, 'Here is Dr. A——.' Kant rose from his chair, and, offering his hand to the Doctor, murmured something in which the word 'posts' was frequently repeated, but with an air as though he wished to be helped out with the rest of the sentence. Dr. A——, who thought that, by *posts*, he meant the stations for relays of post-horses, and therefore that his mind was wandering, replied that all the horses were engaged, and begged him to compose himself. But Kant went on, with great effort to himself, and added—'Many posts, heavy posts—then much goodness—then much gratitude.' All this he said with apparent incoherence, but with great warmth, and increasing self-possession. I meantime perfectly divined what it was that Kant, under his cloud of imbecility, wished to say, and I interpreted accordingly. 'What the Professor wishes to say, Dr. A——, is this, that, considering the many and weighty offices which you fill in the city and in the university, it argues great goodness on your part to give up so much of your time to him,' (for Dr. A—— would never take any fees from Kant;) 'and that he has the deepest sense of this goodness.' 'Right,' said Kant, earnestly, 'right!' But he still continued to stand, and was nearly sinking to the ground. Upon which I remarked to the physician, that I was so well acquainted with Kant, that I was satisfied he would not sit down, however much he suffered from standing, until he knew that his visitors were seated. The Doctor seemed to doubt this—but Kant, who heard what I said, by a prodigious effort confirmed my construction of his conduct, and spoke distinctly these words—'God forbid I should be sunk so low as to forget the offices of humanity.'

When dinner was announced, Dr. A—— took his leave. Another guest had now arrived, and I was in hopes, from the animation which Kant had so recently displayed, that we should to-day have a pleasant party, but my hopes were vain—Kant was more than usually exhausted, and though he raised a spoon to his mouth, he swallowed nothing. For some time everything had been tasteless to him; and I had endeavored, but with little success, to stimulate the organs of taste by nutmeg, cinnamon, &c. To-day all failed, and I could not even prevail upon him to taste a biscuit, rusk, or anything of that sort. I had once heard him say that several of his friends, who had died of *marasmus*, had closed their illness by four or five days of entire freedom from pain, but totally without appetite, and then slumbered tranquilly away. Through this state I apprehended that he was himself now passing.

Saturday, the 4th of February, I heard his guests loudly expressing their fears that they should never meet him again; and I could not but share these fears myself. However, on

Sunday, the 5th, I dined at his table in company with his particular friend Mr. R. R. V. Kant was still present, but so weak that his head drooped upon his knees, and he sank down against the right side of the chair. I went and arranged his pillows so as to raise and support his head; and, having done this, I said—'Now, my dear Sir, you are again in right order.' Great was our astonishment when he answered clearly and audibly in the Roman military phrase—'Yes, *testudine et facie;*' and immediately after added, 'Ready for the enemy, and in battle array.' His powers of mind were (if I may be allowed that expression) smouldering away in their ashes; but every now and then some lambent flame, or grand emanation of light, shot forth to make it evident that the ancient fire still slumbered below.

Monday, the 6th, he was much weaker and more torpid: he spoke not a word, except on the occasion of my question about the Moors, as previously stated, and sate with sightless eyes, lost in himself, and manifesting no sense of our presence, so that we had the feeling of some mighty shade or phantom from some forgotten century being seated amongst us.

About this time, Kant had become much more tranquil and composed. In the earlier periods of his illness, when his yet unbroken strength was brought into active contest with the first attacks of decay, he was apt to be peevish, and sometimes spoke roughly or even harshly to his servants. This, though very opposite to his natural disposition, was altogether excusable under the circumstances. He could not make himself understood: things were therefore brought to him continually which he had not asked for; and often it happened that what he really wanted he could not obtain, because all his efforts to name it were unintelligible. A violent nervous irritation, besides, affected him from the unsettling of the equilibrium in the different functions of his nature; weakness in one organ being made more palpable to him by disproportionate strength in another. But now the strife was over;

the whole system was at length undermined, and in rapid and harmonious progress to dissolution. And from this time forward, no movement of impatience, or expression of fretfulness, ever escaped him.

I now visited him three times a-day; and on

Tuesday, Feb. 7th, going about dinner-time, I found the usual party of friends sitting down alone; for Kant was in bed. This was a new scene in his house, and increased our fears that his end was now at hand. However, having seen him rally so often, I would not run the risk of leaving him without a dinner-party for the next day; and accordingly, at the customary hour of one, we assembled in his house on

Wednesday, Feb. 8th. I paid my respects to him as cheerfully as possible, and ordered dinner to be served up. Kant sat at the table with us; and, taking a spoon with a little soup in it, put it to his lips; but immediately put it down again, and retired to bed, from which he never rose again, except during the few minutes when it was re-arranged.

Thursday, the 9th, he had sunk into the weakness of a dying person, and the corpse-like appearance had already taken possession of him. I visited him frequently through the day; and, going at ten o'clock at night, I found him in a state of insensibility. I could not draw any sign from him that he knew me, and I left him to the care of his sister and his servant.

Friday, the 10th, I went to see him at six o'clock in the morning. It was very stormy, and a deep snow had fallen in the night-time. And, by the way, I remember that a gang of house-breakers had forced their way through the premises in order to reach Kant's next neighbor, who was a goldsmith. As I drew near to his bed-side, I said, 'Good morning.' He returned my salutation by saying, 'Good morning,' but in so feeble and faltering a voice that it was hardly articulate. I was rejoiced to find him sensible, and I asked him if he knew me:—'Yes,' he replied; and, stretching out his hand, touched me gently upon the cheek. Through the rest of the day, whenever I visited him, he seemed to have relapsed into a state of insensibility.

Saturday, the 11th, he lay with fixed and rayless eyes; but to all appearance in perfect peace. I asked him again, on this day, if he knew me. He was speechless, but he turned his face towards me and made signs that I should kiss him. Deep emotion thrilled me, as I stooped down to kiss his pallid lips; for I knew that in this solemn act of tenderness he meant to express his thankfulness for our long friendship, and to signify his affection and his last farewell. I had never seen him confer this mark of his love upon anybody, except once, and that was a few weeks before his death, when he drew his sister to him and kissed her. The kiss which he now gave to me was the last memorial that he knew me.

Whatever fluid was now offered to him passed the oesophagus with a rattling sound, as often happens with dying people; and there were all the signs of death being close at hand.

I wished to stay with him till all was over; and as I had been witness of his life, to be witness also of his departure; and therefore I never quitted him except when I was called off for a few minutes to attend some private business. The whole of this night I spent at his bed-side. Though he had passed the day in a state of insensibility, yet in the evening he made intelligible signs that he wished to have his bed put in order; he was therefore lifted out in our arms, and the bed-clothes and pillows being hastily arranged, he was carried back again. He did not sleep; and a spoonful of liquid, which was sometimes put to his lips, he usually pushed aside; but about one o'clock in the night he himself made a motion towards the spoon, from which I collected that he was thirsty; and I gave him a small quantity of wine and water sweetened; but the muscles of his mouth had not strength enough to retain it, so that to prevent its flowing back he raised his hand to his lips, until with a rattling sound it was swallowed. He seemed to wish for more; and I continued to give him more, until he said, in a way that I was just able to understand,—'It is enough.' And these were his last words. At intervals he pushed away the bed-clothes, and exposed his person; I constantly restored the clothes to their situation, and on one of these occasions I found that the whole body and extremities were already growing cold, and the pulse intermitting.

At a quarter after three o'clock on Sunday morning, February 12, Kant stretched himself out as if taking a position for his final act, and settled into the precise posture which he preserved to the moment of death. The pulse was now no longer perceptible to the touch in his hands, feet or neck. I tried every part where a pulse beats, and found none anywhere but in the left hip, where it beat with violence, but often intermitted.

About ten o'clock in the forenoon he suffered a remarkable change; his eye was rigid and his face and lips became discolored by a cadaverous pallor. Still, such was the effect of his previous habits, that no trace appeared of the cold sweat which naturally accompanies the last mortal agony.

It was near eleven o'clock when the moment of dissolution approached. His sister was standing at the foot of the bed, his sister's son at the head. I, for the purpose of still observing the fluctuations of the pulse in his hip, was kneeling at the bed-side; and I called his servant to come and witness the death of his good master. Now began the last agony, if to him it could be called an agony, where there seemed to be no struggle. And precisely at this moment, his distinguished friend, Mr. R. R. V., whom I had summoned by a messenger, entered the room. First of all, the breath grew feebler; then it missed its regularity of return; then it wholly intermitted, and the upper lip was slightly convulsed; after this there followed one slight respiration or sigh; and after that no more; but the pulse still beat for a few seconds—slower and fainter, till it ceased altogether; the mechanism stopped; the last motion was at an end; and exactly at that moment the clock struck eleven.

Soon after his death the head of Kant was shaved; and, under the direction of Professor Knorr, a plaster cast was taken, not a masque merely, but a cast of the whole bead, designed (I believe) to enrich the craniological collection of Dr. Gall.

The corpse being laid out and properly attired, immense numbers of people of every rank, from the highest to the lowest, flocked to see it. Everybody was anxious to make use of the last opportunity he would have for entitling himself to say—'I too have seen Kant.' This went on for many days—during which, from morning to night, the house was thronged with the public. Great was the astonishment of all people at the meagreness of Kant's appearance; and it was universally agreed that a corpse so wasted and fleshless had never been beheld. His head rested upon the same cushion on which once the gentlemen of the university had presented an address to him; and I thought that I could not apply it to a more honorable purpose than by placing it in the coffin, as the final pillow of that immortal head.

Upon the style and mode of his funeral, Kant had expressed his wishes in earlier years in a separate memorandum. He there desired that it should take place early in the morning, with as little noise and disturbance as possible, and attended only by a few of his most intimate friends. Happening to meet with this memorandum, whilst I was engaged at his request in arranging his papers, I very frankly gave him my opinion, that such an injunction would lay me, as the executor of his will, under great embarrassments; for that circumstances might very probably arise under which it would be next to impossible to carry it into effect. Upon this Kant tore the paper, and left the whole to my own discretion. The fact was, I foresaw that the students of the University would never allow themselves to be robbed of this occasion for expressing their veneration by a public funeral. The event showed that I was right; for a funeral such as Kant's, one so solemn and so magnificent, the city of Königsberg has never witnessed before or since. The public journals, and separate accounts in pamphlets, etc., have given so minute an account of its details, that I shall here notice only the heads of the ceremony.

On the 28th of February, at two o'clock in the afternoon, all the dignitaries of church and state, not only those resident in Königsberg, but from the remotest parts of Prussia, assembled in the church of the Castle. Hence they were escorted by the whole body of the University, splendidly dressed for the occasion, and by many military officers of rank, with whom Kant had always been a great favorite, to the house of the deceased Professor; from which the corpse was carried by torch-light, the bells of every church in Königsberg tolling, to the Cathedral which was lit up by innumerable wax-lights. A never-ending train of many thousand persons followed it on foot. In the Cathedral, after the usual burial rites, accompanied with every possible expression of national veneration to the deceased, there was a grand musical service, most admirably performed, at the close of which Kant's mortal remains were lowered into the academic vault, where he now rests among the ancient patriarchs of the University. PEACE BE TO HIS DUST, AND EVERLASTING HONOR!